See more, do

GW01086603

First-time ba

Shaun Rafferty

SE Asia ◊ Central America ◊ New Zealand ◊ East Coast Oz ◊ Fiji

AuthorHouse™ UK Ltd.
500 Avebury Boulevard
Central Milton Keynes, MK9 2BE
www.authorhouse.co.uk
Phone: 08001974150

First published by AuthorHouse   08/02/2010

ISBN: 978-1-4520-6572-4

This book is printed on acid-free paper.

See more, do more, travel further

CONTENTS

MEET YOUR TRAVEL BUDDIES

Shaun Rafferty (Me!)

Like so many, looking back, I only really went to university to prolong my entrance into the real world and even after finishing uni at 22 years old, I still didn't want to get a 'proper job' and settle down – sound familiar?! I was bored with my mundane job and 'routine' lifestyle. I got my real freedom when my best mate *(Simon Cantwell)* and I split up with our long term girlfriends – we decided that a 6 month voyage around Southeast Asia was just the thing we needed. Completely unprepared and fairly naive, we embarked on an epic adventure and had the time of our lives roaming carefree throughout the cultural extremes of Asia. Although usually fuelled by a cocktail of cheap beer and buckets of local rum, it was a real eye opener and since that trip I've been completely addicted to travelling – many trips later I still find myself working in dead-end jobs just so that I can save up enough money and escape another cold European winter!

Inspired by many friends *(Emlyn, Nick...)*, work colleagues *(Simon Hill...)* and complete 'randomers' who've had similar aspirations but are either too afraid to actually do it, or just don't know where to begin and can't grasp the concept of the whole idea, I decided to put together this book. I want to show people that travelling isn't difficult and that anyone can do it! I want to share with as many people as I can the way I backpack and trek the globe on a shoe-string. Honestly, you don't need much cash, just some curiosity, enthusiasm and a sense of adventure! I don't know everything and I'm still learning new things with every trip, I just want to share with you how I skimp my way around the globe – anyone can do it! Travelling gives you an itch that you just can't satisfy!

Frida Engberg

Leaving college at 18, I left the Swedish countryside after a just a year for the bright lights of Oslo in search of a change and a bit of money. During my time in Norway, I embarked on a brief road-trip around Eastern Europe. This inspired me and kick-started my interest in travel and new cultures. Getting a bit tired of city-life and speaking to a fair share of people who'd just arrived fresh from backpacking, my best friend and I decided to head to for the delights of Southeast Asia. For two young blue-eyed Swedish girls it was an unforgettable experience! From the fantastic food and drink to the beautiful beaches and varied activities, and despite all the ups and downs, it was an enjoyable life-changing adventure. As soon as I arrived home it wasn't long till I developed the classic 'itchy feet' syndrome and many part-time jobs ensured that I managed to save up just enough cash and head off every winter since. Now at university in England, I envy those who can just drop everything, grab their backpack and head to destinations more exotic. Trying to plan trips around semesters, I hope to see many more places and the list is ever growing! Happy travels.

We hope we can inspire you to have an unforgettable trip... happy travels!

Be inspired... *Discover the world through backpacking*

Whether you're planning on taking a gap year, have just finished university, organising a career break or simply want to embark on the adventure of a lifetime, backpacking offers an opportunity for everyone to travel on any budget. It's all about striping away the constraints of the 'typical package-holiday' giving you freedom and independence to 'Do-It-Yourself'. It allows you to have a more authentic experience away from the tourist gaze and the artificial culture that exists in package-resorts. Largely unplanned, backpacking is spontaneous and gives you a unique opportunity to explore off-the-beaten track at your own pace where you can immerse yourself in genuine culture and interact with the local folk. Life outside of the tourist resorts isn't just more exciting and authentic – it's a lot cheaper too! By utilising local transport, eating local specialities, snaking from street kitchens and staying in

> ### Think you're too old...? *Think again!*
>
> You really can discover the world on a shoestring and whether you're 25 or 75, you're never too old travel – I met an 84 year old chap in Nicaragua who was drinking rum and roughing it at the same hostel as us lot – he said he was travelling on his own because all of his friends were dead! I've also met a cheery 72 year old woman on a jungle trek in Chiang Mai *(North Thailand)* who, to my disbelief, 'out-hiked' the majority of us!

backpacker orientated accommodation away from the tourist complexes, you'll get a lot more for your money than just two weeks in Spain or Turkey and you'll do a lot more than just laze by the pool! Backpacking is a collection of unique experiences, not tacky souvenirs and manufactured fun!

Whatever your passion... Backpacking is jam-packed with possibilities

Whether you want to party all night long on a tropical island, take time out to reflect and discover yourself, brush up on your linguistic skills or play an active part in volunteer projects, the opportunities and rewards that backpacking offers are as endless:

o **Embrace adventure...** Indulge in an ever expanding array of extreme activities from hiking and white-water rafting to bungy jumping and skydiving, for the ultimate adrenaline rush

o **Discover the outdoors...** Trek in magnificent tropical rainforests, peer into smouldering volcanoes, hike the majestic wilderness of immense glaciers, stew in hot springs and explore the ancient ruins of New World temples

o **Worship the sun** on palm fringe shores, bathe in crystal-clear turquoise lagoons and conquer the most challenging surf breaks

o **Tantalise your taste buds...** Sample the freshest BBQ fish, brave the spiciest authentic curries and experiment with the finest exotic street food and indulge in a array of mesmerizing cuisine from around the world

o **Take the plunge...** Discover a fascinating world of delicate reefs, intriguing shipwrecks and diverse tropical marine life and immerse yourself in some of the most desirable *(and affordable)* diving locations around the world

o **Give something back...** Get involved in a volunteer project and make a difference to those less fortunate or help giant sea turtles hatch under the cover of darkness on remote white sand beaches in pristine national parks

o **Interact with culture and its many faces...** Pick up the local lingo and enrol onto a language programme or learn to whip-up favourite regional dishes on a cooking course

o **Swing your hips** to the local beat in top nightclubs, party on the beach till sunrise and nurse your hangover in a hammock under the shade of a palm tree

Don't be shy... *Get more from your time away*

Embrace everything that's different and immerse yourself in unfamiliar cultures, intriguing local traditions and the rustic backpacking lifestyle – the more you put into your trip, and the more open-minded you are, the more you'll get out of your trip and the more authentic experience you'll have. By all means flop on the beach and drink 'till you pass-out, but actively seek to get involved with stuff and push the boundaries. Use local modes of transport, sleep in hostels and guesthouses and sample the traditional grub at local food shacks, street kitchens and restaurants – it's cheaper and you'll experience the 'real' country first-hand. Steer clear of the over-packaged commercialised towns and resorts where any genuine culture will have been eroded by foreign investment and large scale luxury hotels – if you're after a stress-free luxury break in the sun with swimming pools and familiar foods complemented by all of the comforts and mod-cons of western-style living, take a two week holiday in Spain or Turkey!

Backpacking is exhilarating and demanding but at the same time it's extremely rewarding and satisfying. Whatever your age, profession or background, you'll develop new skills; budgeting, independence, linguistic skills, social skills and you'll grow as a person as you broaden your horizons beyond your imagination. Get taught to play the guitar by a complete stranger on a bus journey, learn how to prepare freshly caught fish by a local on the beach or pick up a bit of local dialect on a volunteer programme! Backpacking is an educational and life changing experience for everyone and you don't need much cash to do it! It really does allow you to see more, do more and travel further than a restrictive conventional package-holiday.

The people you meet... *From every corner of the globe*

Travel is not just where you go and what you do though, it's also the people you meet. So be confident, open up and talk to people – it's amazing how far a simple 'Hi' will get you! On your journey you'll meet some of the most inspiring, weird, captivating and unforgettable people, both local folk and fellow likeminded travellers – and don't be surprised if some of these will become friends for life as you develop an international network of friends! I met my girlfriend *(Frida)* in the middle of the Thai jungle on a trek in Chiang Mai during 2006, and after bumping into her through the remainder of my trip in Vietnam, Cambodia and Malaysia, we've been together ever since – you never know what can happen and who you'll meet on your adventures!

You're an individual... *Travel the way that suits you!*

At the end of the day it doesn't matter how you travel, the main thing is that you enjoy yourself and do what you want to do – not travel how other people think you should travel. Guidebooks are what they say – a guide – backpacking is very subjective, you're an individual and everyone's got different ideas, opinions, interests and aspirations. People naturally want different things out of their trip. This book has been written and structured as a guideline for the 'average backpacker'. As you become a more accomplished traveller you'll develop your own travelling techniques, discover your own way of travelling and know the things that 'float-your-boat'! Travelling is only as good as you make it –

> **Be warned...** *Travelling is highly ADDICITIVE!*
>
> After your first trip, I guarantee that you'll have itchy feet – you'll be dreaming of new adventures in new destinations and you'll be sketching out your next trip on napkins and notebooks before you know it! After a few hot winters, you're first cold one back home is a hard and long one!

so don't be shy, get amongst it, get involved, embrace the unknown, have fun and enjoy! What's the worst that could happen...!?

This book isn't intended solely as a guide while you're travelling. It has been designed as a tool to help you prepare for every aspect of your travels, from planning your itinerary and packing your bag to visa applications and budgeting. It has been written and structured to:

a) Answer those inevitable first-time questions and combat your anxieties

b) Build up your confidence, ignite your creativity and broaden your imagination

c) Make travelling for the first time *SIMPLE* and *EXCITING*

It has been organised into 6 independent sections...

1. Where to go... *Planning your itinerary*   *(Page... 11)*

How do you know where to go and how do you build an itinerary for your first backpacking experience? With a seemingly endless list of possible destinations, it can be a tricky decision. This brief chapter will make this decision a little easier and will show you how to go about creating an exciting and manageable itinerary that's tailored to you. If you're a seasoned traveller, skip this chapter.

2. The Guide... *Region by region*   *(Page... 21)*

This is the heart of the book... It's been subdivided to guide you through **three** of the most popular regions that are ideal first-time backpacking destinations. Use this section to examine each region in-depth and make use of the ***suggested itineraries***, the ***budget directory*** and the ***country guides*** to draw up an exciting tailored itinerary of countries to explore. Whether you want to dabble with culture, party in paradise or simply get away, this section will help you create an exciting itinerary that is tailored to your travel experience, interests and most of all, your budget. But this section hasn't just been designed merely as a tool for planning, it's also intend for use on the road – that's why it's crammed with mini-itineraries, off-the-beaten track suggestions and heaps of advice of what to do, and where to stay in the popular destinations. It's been carefully structured for ease of use so that you can spend more time checking out what's going on out of the bus window and engaging in chat with locals and fellow shoe-stringers, than hopelessly flicking through its pages!

3. Budgeting... *See more, do more, travel further!*   *(Page... 193)*

Often overlooked and neglected, budgeting is a boring but essential element of any backpacking trip. Trying to create a realistic budget for a first trip can be a daunting and an extremely difficult task, and of course, how could you possibly know what to budget for if you've not been travelling before! This section will make budgeting a breeze and get you travelling on a shoestring! It's jam-packed with expert advice on how to manage your money, from thinking in terms of daily budgets and budgeting on the road to choosing the right bank account and organising your money before you go. Backpackers tend to be **'time-rich'** and **'cash-poor'** so being efficient with your often limited funds is the name of the game – this section is dedicated to making your money go further so you can make the most of your time away by seeing more, doing more and travelling further.

4. Equipment... *What to (and what not to) cram in your backpack!*   *(Page... 215)*

Restricted by the size and dimensions of your backpack, coupled with the tough weight limits imposed by airlines, it can be difficult to know what to pack, what to sacrifice and what you can stock up on when you arrive. This section covers everything you need to know from choosing the right backpack to comprehensive lists on essential inventory and suitable clothing. It even offers tips on how to pack your bag to make your life on the road a little easier and more comfortable.

5. Health... *Staying healthy*

Staying healthy while you're away is important. You don't want to spend the majority of your time hidden in your room with shitty sheets or confined to a gloomy hospital room, when you could be soaking up the sun on tranquil beaches. Prevention is better than cure! Use the advice in this chapter to find out what precautions you should take to get in shape for your trip. Find out what diseases could lead to a slow horrible death and what arm full of jabs you'll need to need to stay alive! It'll examine how to put together a basic first-aid kit and provide valuable tips on how to stay healthy while you're away, offering guidance on issues such as, anti-malarial drugs, traveller's diarrhoea and protecting yourself from the punishing sun. Establish a basic knowledge of the potential diseases and take advantage of the *A-Z Diseases & Definitions* directory.

6. Booking your trip... *The big adventure!*

After all of your research and planning it's time to finalise some dates and book your adventure! This section strips away the pre-departure complications and guides you through booking your trip step by step... Don't spend over the odds getting away – make sure you get the best airfare deals around so that you've got more money to spend when you're away! The idea of visas, official red tape and travel insurance can be intimidating, confusing and time consuming. It needn't be. Loaded with expert tips, this section will help you get to grips with the concept of visas and all the pre-departure 'nitty gritty'. Make sure you're fully covered for any unfortunate and unforeseen events during your time away and use the advice in this section to suss out the ins-and-outs of travel insurance, reduce your insurance premiums and avoid any nasty hidden surprises.

1) WHERE TO GO...

... Planning your itinerary

CONTENTS

Most guidebooks are written with the assumption that you already know where you want to go! For a first-time traveller, the question **'where to go'** is fundamental. It's the biggest question you should ask yourself and it's the most important decision that you'll make – each region, and each individual country, have different things to offer. It **can** be an overwhelming, confusing and frustrating task. All of the other questions that relate to your budget, itinerary and the length of your trip, all stem from this first question... Where to go?

Don't worry you're not alone, it's a dilemma for every first-time traveller, and it needn't be a daunting task. Planning where to go and drawing up an itinerary should be **fun** and **exciting** – it's part of the whole travel experience. The following section will illustrate how you could go about planning where to go and developing an interesting itinerary...

PLANNING YOUR ITINERARY... *Thinking in terms of 'Regions'*

This is where the fun begins! You'll hear time and time again that it's a complete waste of time planning what countries to visit and the activities to pursue. To some extent that's right, backpacking is spontaneous and your planned itinerary will inevitably change but it's definitely not a waste of time either – it's half the fun. It's like window shopping, whetting your appetite! Planning gives you an insight into a region as a whole and gives you the knowledge, and more importantly the confidence, to change your planned itinerary – it makes you aware of what's out there. It gives you an idea of what you want to do and see and it gets your creative juices flowing!

You'll not regret the time and energy you put into this initial question and there's no rigid model to creating an itinerary – they're very subjective since people like different things, want different things out of their trip and have very different budgets! Ideally, to create an exciting, manageable and realistic itinerary that's tailored to your interests, aspirations and financial position, you should start by selecting a region and then identify what countries and activities you should try and cram in. It's a very practical and logical way to build a tailored itinerary. You <u>can</u> piece together an itinerary around a particular country that you've wanted to go to for ages, say Thailand, and many people do. However, by using this broad 'narrowing down' regional approach, you'll have a more rewarding trip and be able to build a great manageable itinerary that's completely tailored to you. It'll also mean that you'll be less inclined to plan your route in too much detail allowing you to be a lot more flexible and spontaneous. Here's the basic 'regional approach' to build an itinerary:

1) Select an appropriate region

2) Identify a list of exciting countries

3) Draw up a list of appealing activities & popular towns

Your plans will naturally evolve... *Be open-minded!*

Don't think of your itinerary as a strict schedule! Your itinerary will almost certainly change when you're out on the road, so think of it as a rough guideline. After you've decided on an ideal region, your best bet is to select an entry point and a departure destination *(major regional gateways are a good choice)* and just sketch out a rough route between them following a loose 'time-table'.

You'll meet plenty of seasoned backpackers who'll offer heaps of advice of the places you 'must visit' and hear lots of intriguing stories of the places *(and guesthouses)* to avoid! Consequently, you'll probably deviate from your planned route a little to visit recommendations, avoid places you had previously planned to go to and stay longer in others – some places may not match your expectations while others may exceed them. You'll also meet lots of other travellers who you become friendly with and you'll no doubt alter you plans at some point to coincide with their route and time-frame. Just be open-minded and flexible – it's what backpacking is all about, having the freedom go where you want and do what you want, when you want to! Whether you want to have the best tan ever, release that party animal in you or become a cultural connoisseur, do as little or as much as you like, just enjoy yourself!

SELECTING A REGION... *What do you want to get out of your trip?*

As I've said, to begin with, you should be thinking in 'general terms' of regions rather than specific countries as you're probably not going to spend your entire time in one particular country *(Oz / NZ are perhaps the exceptions here)*. Each region offers something different so when selecting a region to explore, think of what you want to get out of your trip. It may be the case that you just want to go Thailand or Mexico, but once you realise how cheap and easy it is to just 'pop across the border' into the neighbouring countries, and see what their neighbours have to offer, you'll soon want to roam around! Your biggest expense is your airfare out there, so justify that expense and make sure you make the most of your time away and do everything you can! When you're thinking about what region to explore you should be considering a number of things:

a) **How long you've got** – you'll require more time in some regions

b) **How much money you have** – some regions are significantly more expensive than others. For example, your money will last twice as long in SE than it will in Oz

c) **What you want to get out of your trip** – some regions are more diverse, challenging and culturally rewarding than others. Do you want a comfy trip or do you fancy a bit of roughing it? Would you be contempt just to sit on a beach all day or do you want some cultural awaking and maybe the chance of some volunteer opportunities?

d) **How much culture shock you want** – some parts of the world are very different, but just how different do you want? If squat toilets and street food horrify you, maybe consider the familiar comforts of Oz or NZ as opposed to Latin America or SE Asia!

e) **Whether you plan to work** – countries such as Australia are brimming with worthwhile job opportunities, while others like Cambodia offer few realistic and practical employment options!

Certain regions, and even different countries, offer something slightly different and are more suitable depending on your aspirations, expectations, current circumstances and confidence. The scenarios below highlight the three most common predicaments:

o **Scenario A:** If you've got a fair bit of money saved up and want a 'comfy' and kind of 'prolonged holiday' type trip with lots of sun and perhaps the possibility of work and no real culture shock, Australia or New Zealand would be a fitting choice

o **Scenario B:** On the other hand, if you've got limited funds but a lot of spare time and want to immerse yourself in different cultures and don't mind a fair bit of roughing it, then SE Asia or Central America would be a more rewarding and practical destination

o **Scenario C:** If you really want an adventure, have plenty of cash saved up and a lot of spare time, you could consider a 'Round-the-World trip'. In this case you should still compare regions so that you can decide which ones to include on your RTW ticket and what order to do them in

To help you compare and select a suitable region and piece together an exciting itinerary for your first big adventure, this chapter has been sub-divided to reveal three of the most popular backpacking regions. If you're feeling a bit more adventurous and want to see many places that are scattered across the globe, jump in at the deep end with the **Round-the-World** section that gives you the low down on RTW tickets and suggested global-itineraries...

COMPARING REGIONS... *The 'Why go to...' sections*

Each 'Regional Guide' kicks off with a **'Why go to...'** section that's been divided up into a number of subsections to help you get to grips with and compare each region:

a) **Introduction** – each 'Why go to...' section begins proceedings with a map and a brief introduction to help you familiarise yourself with each region

b) **'Why is.... good for backpacking'** – these sections are perhaps the best way of comparing the regions. They indicate why a particular region is good for backpacking so that you can select the ideal region that relates to your situation and will satisfy what you want to get out of your trip

c) **Highlights** – this is a brief list of the region's 'best-bits' to get you excited! You can compare what each region has to offer, and see if anything really takes your fancy. The highlights vary dramatically from region to region. You'll find a concentration of adrenaline fuelled activities in Australasia while other regions like Central America boast a wealth of cultural based highlights

d) **Costs, Money & What to Expect** – this is an important section that deals with the practicalities of your trip. Most importantly it compares the cost of specific things, from transport and accommodation to food and activities, between the regions to help you create and prepare an affordable trip

The countries in each regional section are in a specific order so that they follow the main suggested itinerary. They have not been ordered alphabetically or by personal preference.

Additional info... *A helping hand*

Your transport options: These sections have been slipped in to help prepare you for your adventure – the various modes of transport in regions like SE Asia and Latin America are very different to what you're used to at home and to what you'll find in Australia and New Zealand. It contains useful advice on the various types of wacky transport that you'll come across, the cost of them and where and when to utilise them. In the Australasia 'regional section', you'll find a beefed up 'Your Transport Options' sub-section just before the Mini Guides of each country.

Extras: You'll also find a range of additional information, and this varies slightly from region to region. You'll find a useful and exciting 'food & drink' piece in the SE Asia section, and a 'mini-itineraries' sub-section to help you plan an adventure through some of the more challenging and less-travelled countries of Indonesia and the Philippines.

The three regional sections have been designed to help you create an exciting and manageable regional itinerary. After you've selected a suitable region, not only do you need to select a list of countries to cram into your itinerary, you'll need to plan a logical route, decide how long you're going to be away for, when to go and find the best *(and cheapest)* way to get there. Consequently, you'll find a number of helpful subsections before the individual country guides and mini guides:

a) **Suggested itineraries** – these itineraries indicate the well-trodden routes through the regions highlighting the most popular towns and backpacker hotspots

b) **When to go** – coincide your trip with the best of the weather! These small sections help you plan the timing of your trip and pinpoint the best time(s) to go. These are general 'regional' guidelines but slight regional differences do exist so look in the 'At a Glance' sections in each country guide for accurate seasons

c) **Getting there & away** – this is a very useful section indicating the major regional gateways where you'll get the cheapest airfares. The majority of regional itineraries will begin and end at these major gateways

d) **How long...?** – there isn't a specific subsection dedicated to this but you'll find that the suggested itineraries have recommended time-scales. In addition, you'll find suggested times for each individual country in the 'At a Glance' sections. As a general rule, **4-days** is more than enough time in each town

Which countries & what to do...? *Pick 'n' Mix using the 'Mini Guides'*

Ok, so once you've selected your region and dealt with when and how to get there, you'll have to decide what countries to include in your trip. The easiest way is to take advantage of the **'suggested itineraries'** for guidance, the regions **highlights** section for a wee bit of inspiration & the **'Budget Directory'** to draw up a list of affordable countries. You can get more in depth by delving into the **'MINI GUIDE'** sections where you can **pick 'n' mix** the countries, towns and activities to create an exciting itinerary that's tailored not only to your budget but also your interests. Whether you're at home planning your trip, or you're out and about, use these sections to decided where to go and what to do. You'll find the main backpacker destinations with lists of the main highlights plus the main backpacker area in each place.

The 'Budget Directory'... *Compare countries*

Ideally, I really wanted to insert a regional map with the countries coloured coded in terms of price – red being the most expensive down to yellow being the cheapest countries in the region – but because of the print costs involved, I've had to modify that idea and create this 'Budget Directory'. You'll find this section just before the individual country guides. It's been designed to help you compare the countries from that particular region in terms of **price** and **ease of travel**.

'Price' relates to the average daily living expenses for the 'standard first-time backpacker', taking into consideration the costs associated with accommodation, transport, activities and food and drink. This will enable you to work out the most expensive countries in the region and indicate the countries where you can linger for longer because your money will go further! 'Ease of travel' not only relates to how challenging it is to get around a particular country, it also takes into consideration cultural extremes, linguistic barriers and the level of experience needed to explore it. A country with a high grading indicates that it's relatively easy to get around, with good tourist infrastructure and few cultural barriers. I hope you'll find this a helpful quick reference tool.

USING THE 'MINI GUIDE(S)'... *Simple!*

You'll find a Mini Guide for each country after the 'At a Glance' section, map and brief introduction. Apart from simplicity and ease of use, it's been designed for **two** main purposes:

1) **At home** – it can be used to whet your appetite, plan your itinerary and sketch out a rough route when you're at home. It'll give you an idea of what each country has to offer

2) **On-the-road** – this is its principal intention. It can be utilised as a tool when you're actually on the road providing you with useful information of where to go, how to get there, where to stay and what to do. They also provide details of common routes...

Mini itineraries... Generally each Mini Guide kicks off with a mini itinerary outlining any well-trodden-paths through that particular country and general suggestions. Where countries are split into regions, you may also find regional itineraries. Mini and regional itineraries will look like this:

Luang Prabang ➔ Vang Vieng ➔ Vientiane

Destinations... Any destination that's included in the mini-itineraries will be explored in the Mini Guide. Each destination in the 'Mini Guide' will have the following features and information that's highlighted in the example below:

Text boxes... You'll find useful text boxes to highlight the most popular activities, any essential info and tips

PHI PHI... *The beach from 'The Beach'!*

Koh Phi Phi Don is one of Thailand well discovered beauties where stunning limestone cliffs, crystal clear water and powder sand beaches will leave you speechless. To top it off, this compact stunner boasts an energetic nightlife that's complemented by a wealth of worthwhile activities including; world-class **diving** *(comparable to that found on Koh Toa)*, great **snorkelling**, relaxing **sea-kayaking**. You can even step into the ring and have **Muay Thai** – the **Reggae Bar** offers you the chance to test out your moves with other drunken fun with your mates! As well as the you'll be rewarded with a free bucket of rum!

Maya Beach daytrips...

This is what's caused Phi Phi's recent boom in tourism. Everyone's seen the film 'The Beach', now here's your chance to make your own foot prints next to Leonardo De Caprio's on **Maya Beach**! Tours can be

Main bodies of text... A description of the destination briefly highlighting the reasons to go, what to do, where to stay and, if necessary, how to get there

Main backpacker area... If there's a certain *(cheap)* area where backpackers congregate, or there's a popular hostel or guesthouse, it'll be listed here to save you roaming around strange cities & missing out!

en astronomical and there's no denying that the mall scale resorts and hotels are beginning to at put you off, there's still a strong backpacker of cheap accommodation in the form of beach n dorms if you look around. Most bars offer 2-4-ed) buckets and free BBQ food. Even the 7-r prices *(probably to finance the air-con!)* so buy at cheaper rates from the numerous local shops. Many travellers buy a couple of bottles of Chang from local shops and wander around the narrow streets and linger on the beach before hitting the 'clubs' later on – it's sociable and cheap!

Main backpacker area – Anywhere! Most of is located just before the main beach

Highlights – Maya Beach daytrip, snorkelli Muay Thai in the Reggae Bar, m ng on the b

Highlights... Every destination will have a list of the 'best-bits'. These can be activities, landmarks, or sights and give you an idea of what each place has to offer and what you should try and 'tick-off' when you get there!

Along with the 'Main backpacker area' and 'Highlights', some destinations also have additional information such as 'Getting there & away', 'Transfers' or 'Useful websites' – for ease of use and quick reference purposes, they'll be set out the same way as the 'Highlights' and 'Main backpacker area' bits are.

Off-the-beaten track... *Spice things up a bit*

Travelling isn't just the destination, it's the journey – it's all about the unexpected places and unique experiences along the way and the wacky transport you'll utilise. While I've listed the most popular destinations in each country, I've also briefly touched on some less-travelled places to explore and you'll find this section at the end of many Mini Guides. It's been designed to give you the inspiration and knowhow to get 'off-the-beaten track'. If you really want to get off-the-beaten track then you shouldn't have any guidebook, recommendations or directions – it's raw backpacking – if 'off-the-beaten track' was listed in a 'typical guidebook style', with detailed recommendations and suggestions, it would quickly become the 'normal route' swamped with the 'package-backpacker' and those little hidden gems would lose their charm – there has to be some places where it's still fun to travel on your own wit and intuition and challenge yourself!

Consequently, this section will give you a **rough idea** of where to go if you want to deviate from the well-trodden route   information will be vague and sketchy at best to ensure that you 'DIY it' as much as possible and enjoy your own unique and authentic adventure!

2) THE GUIDE...

... *Region by region*

MAP CONTENTS... *Quick reference*

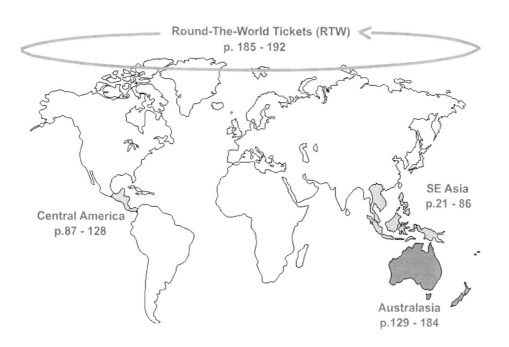

Round-The-World Tickets (RTW)
p. 185 - 192

SE Asia
p.21 - 86

Central America
p.87 - 128

Australasia
p.129 - 184

www.backpackerguides.co.uk

A DETAILED REGIONAL CONTENTS...

Southeast Asia

Beaches ◊ Culture ◊ Nightlife

WHY GO TO... *SE ASIA?*

Use this themed section to help you decide what region to go to. Compare this section to the Central American and Australasian equivalents to find your perfect tailored destination.

SE ASIA... *An introduction*

It's far too easy to refer to Southeast Asia as a single entity but this region's about as diverse as it gets. From the mainland tip of the continent, SE Asia's a region that's scattered across the equator forming a broken chain from Australasia to China. Backpackers have long been lured here by the regions sun-kissed beaches, tropical climate and boozy ambience but, as most quickly discover, that's only the tip of the iceberg. Dreamy landscapes provide plenty of inland adventure while a wealth of history and culture, from saffron-cloaked monks to the wondrous relics of Angkor, enchant even the most culture-phobic types. Language, cuisine and tradition constantly shift from one country to the next ensuring that you never get bored. From the hustle and bustle of chaotic urban sprawls to authentic rural villages and idyllic tropical isles, the individual countries are as diverse as the region itself. The fairly compact mainland lends itself to exciting well-trodden looping circuits while the two extensive archipelagos of the Philippines and Indonesia provide the setting for some grand island hopping and off-the-beaten track adventures. SE Asia is a unique region that balances the 21st Century conveniences with ancient beliefs, Buddhism and a colourful blend of intriguing traditions.

For both first-time and seasoned travellers, SE Asia has been the **number one** backpacker destination for a while now, and for good reason. Backpackers tend to be 'time-rich' and 'cash-poor' and Asia is arguably the cheapest place in the world to travel – overall it's cheaper than Central America, most of South America and a hell of a lot cheaper than Oz, New Zealand and the Pacific. On top of this you've got a well established tourist industry with great infrastructure and a fantastic range of accommodation that's tailored to the needs of budget travellers. Consequently, SE Asia has a very strong traveller's scene and is regarded by many as one of the most backpacker friendly regions in the world – it caters for all travellers regardless of your experience, ability or confidence. In Thailand, you've got a well polished travellers gem while the lesser-travelled countries of Indonesia and the Philippines offer off-the-beaten track opportunities for the more adventurous and time-rich backpacker.

In terms of activities, scenery and memorable experiences, Asia offers everything from spectacular diving, scrumptious beaches and ancient ruins to mouth-watering food, intriguing culture and a wealth of rewarding volunteer opportunities. Cultural differences are enjoyable and welcoming as opposed to daunting and problematic. They also become gradually more extreme as you head out of Thailand so you're not dumped straight in at the deep end and you'll have some control over your exposure to culture shock! Despite a mix of baffling tonal languages around the region, you'll be pleased to hear that SE Asia has a high English literacy rate. Southeast Asia sets the scene for one of the grandest yet softest introductions into the intriguing world of backpacking – if you're an anxious first-time traveller, there truly isn't a better region to test the water than SE Asia.

SE Asia is an ideal destination...

o If you're a **first-time traveller**, a bit **apprehensive** but still want to experience something a bit different – SE Asia, and Thailand in particular, is probably the most backpacker friendly region in the world

o If you want to interact with **different cultures** – Southeast Asia offers a kaleidoscope of approachable and intriguing cultures and traditions

o If you want to indulge in **mouth-watering cuisine** and add a string to your culinary bow – from simple Pad Thai to quirky regional delicacies, this region serves up a gastronomic extravaganza that won't disappoint

o If you've got **limited funds & a lot of spare time** – your money **can** go *(very)* far here and there's lots to keep you entertained!

o If you're a **party animal** and want to dance the night away on paradise islands and recover on sun-kissed beaches – plenty of surprisingly pleasant hangovers await!

o If you want to give something back and take advantage of a wide variety of **volunteer opportunities**

HIGHLIGHTS... *Don't miss the best bits!*

You won't be able to see and do everything that Asia has to offer in just one trip, and you'd be mad to try! What follows is a selection of Asia's 'best bits' to whet your appetite and give you an idea of what to include in your itinerary. Compare Asia's 'best bits' to Central America's and Australasia's 'best bits' to help you choose a region.

TUBING *(Laos)*   Embark on the ultimate aquatic bar crawl on giant inner tubes through picturesque limestone karsts, munch on mushroom pizzas and laze about in chilled-out TV-restaurants watching endless repeats of Friends and the Simpsons in Laos' premier traveller's town. Vang Vieng is one of Asia's most talked about destinations and its reputation is well founded – it really doesn't get much better than this!

ANGKOR WOT *(Cambodia)*   Marvel at the world's mother-of-all temples and the heart and soul of the Khmer Nation. Angkor is a true cultural awakening and the entire site, comprising of hundreds of temples, is outstanding, inspiring and unforgettable. Base yourself in the nearby lively town of Siem Reap to continue your cultural education

S21 MUSEUM & THE KILLING FIELDS *(Cambodia)*   Explore Cambodia's brutal past and embark on a sobering visit through these two extraordinary sites. S-21, a former school, was a huge detention centre where 1000,s of people were tortured before being brutally executed at the Killing fields of Choeung Ek. This hard-hitting preservation of S-21 and the erection of a 'skull-tower' in Choeung Ek stand as a testament to all those who were unnecessarily murdered

KOH CHANG *(Thailand)*   This is the ultimate backpacker island – it's a place to stop travelling and start relaxing. Rustic bars, sandy beaches, friendly locals and a laidback traveller's crowd make this island stand out from the 'overdeveloped' rest.

JUNGLE TREKS *(Thailand)*   Chiang Mai is home of the legendary jungle trek where not only will you hike through well-preserved rainforest, you'll also ride elephant through dense foliage, navigate fast-flowing rapids on homemade bamboo rafts and get your head down in authentic rural villages. Chiang Mai is also the cultural heart of Thailand

PHI PHI *(Thailand)*   One of Thailand's well-discovered gems, this little beauty will not let you down. While its nightlife is booming, it's the island's spectacular natural setting and Maya Beach – the beach from The Beach – that draws in the crowds. Sometimes overcrowded and a little overpriced, it's a must do for any credible itinerary

FULL MOON PARTY *(Koh Pha-Ngan)*   The ultimate beach party and, over the last decade or so, it's become a cult pilgrimage for hard-core party animals and merry drinkers alike. Every full-moon, 10,000+ travellers flock to this beautiful Thai island to dance the night away on a cocktail of rum, beer and mushrooms. Koh Pha-Ngan is Thailand's answer to Spain's Ibiza!

HA LONG BAY *(Vietnam)*   This is a popular UNESCO world heritage site where visitors come to cruise the clear emerald waters and explore the misty picturesque patchwork of rugged limestone islands. Two and three day boat trips are extremely popular

HOI AN *(Vietnam))*   This picturesque riverside town is a great place to linger for countless days boasting plenty of fresh beer, good food, quaint architecture and expanse empty beaches that are a stone's throw away. Moreover, Hoi An is famous for its hoards of Tailors where you can get decent quality tailored made suits whipped up in a matter of days

TRACK THE WAR *(Vietnam)*   From the battle scared DMZ and the lesser-known Vinh Moch tunnels to the popular Cu Chi Tunnels and the hard hitting War Remnants Museum, relics of this brutal war lay scattered throughout this country giving you the opportunity to explore it first-hand without the bias of Hollywood's multi-millions!

NATIONAL PARKS   From the Kinabalu and Taman Negara National Parks in Malaysia to Indonesian National parks of Komodo and Gunung Leuser, vast pockets of this region are protected havens for nature buffs and avid hikers boasting pristine forests, ancient volcanic peaks and an abundance of wildlife. The sheer biodiversity is staggering where you'll be able to see anything from exotic birdlife and cheeky monkeys to fierce Komodo Dragons and shy big-cats!

SWIM WITH WHALE SHARKS *(Donsol)*   This once sleepy Filipino fishing village has been rejuvenated by the discovery of whale sharks just off its coast. Handfuls of travellers venture here for a unique chance to snorkel and swim beside the world's biggest fish

NORTH PANDAN ISLAND *(Philippines)*   This is the Philippines' ultimate island experience where you can swim with giant Turtles quite literally meters off the beach and chow down an exquisite banquette before relaxing with a few beers in the islands beachfront bar. The nearby Apo Reef also provides some fantastic diving. Only a few backpackers venture here and you'll find few footprints on the beach

THE GILL ISLANDS *(Indonesia)*   Do as much or as little as you like on these speckles of pure tropical bliss where only well-informed travellers venture and discover true paradise. Fantastic diving, lashing of golden sun and postcard-perfect beaches wait for you on this trio of isolated isles

BALI *(Indonesia)*   This is Indonesia's cult surfing destination, where you can ride excellent breaks, chat to fellow boarders and progress your surfing 'career'. But it's not all about the waves and this famous destination draws in plenty of beach-floppers and enthusiastic drinkers from around the world. It's a great play to party, play, relax and shop. Probably one of the best introductions to Indonesia, it's a good base to head off and explore the rest of the archipelago

DIVING!   Explore live beneath the waves and take advantage of some of the world's best diving at rock bottom prices. From fun dives to PADI courses, it's the perfect region to get your diving licence or fill you log book up with some incredible dives. While Koh Tao steals the show and is undoubtedly SE Asia's premier diving hotspot, there are heaps of world-class diving sites dotted around the region's varied coastline

BEACHES!   Lap up the tropical rays on sun-kissed beaches or nurse your hangover under the shade of a palm tree, SE Asia boasts some of the world's most idyllic beaches and secluded bays where you can slip in a beach coma for weeks on end

ISLAND HOPPING *(Indonesia & Philippines)*   The Filipino Visayas are a kaleidoscope of magical tropical islands offering the perfect opportunity for some grand island-hopping adventures while the entire Indonesian archipelago lends itself to endless island hopping. Endure unreliable ferry connections, tedious delays and rustic transport and reward yourself with unspoilt islands and empty beaches where only a handful dare venture!

OFF-THE-BEATEN TRACK   While the popular countries of Thailand, Malaysia, Cambodia and even Vietnam have become well-trodden, hope of off-the-beaten track adventures come in the form of the Philippines and Indonesia. Since they cannot be reached by land, vast parts of these two countries remain unexplored where barren beaches, dense tropical rainforest, exotic and wired wildlife and traditional villages eagerly await your arrival. They won't disappoint

GASTRONOMIC DELIGHTS!   One of the best ways to experience a country and explore its culture and traditions is through its food... South SE Asia is perhaps one of the best examples of this where there's a tantalising range of delicious dishes that aptly reflects the sheer diversity of this fascinating region. From kick-arse curries to authentic Pad Thai, it's one of the regions great appeals so check out the next section and explore the weird and wonder delicacies of these captivating cultures.

ASIAN FOOD & DRINK... *A gastronomic extravaganza*

One of the delights of visiting Asia is the cuisine. Eating is an integral part of Asian culture and there are literally thousands of traditional dishes – you'll be spoilt by the sheer variety of weird and wonderful dishes. From simple rice dishes and kick-arse curries to intriguing local specialities that include duck embryos and dog meat, whatever tickles your taste buds you're sure to find it in Asia! If you want the 'real-deal' and sample some 'proper' authentic dishes at local prices, keep away from the tourist traps and head off in search of local cafés and street kitchens. Street food is an important part of everyday life throughout SE Asia so drop into the markets and snack from food stalls, it's cheap, cheerful and it's a cool way to get up close and personal with the locals and their cuisine – you'll find some of the best grub in the most random places and get the best surprises by using the trusted pointing method to overcome the language barrier and select unfamiliar dishes!

Not to be missed... *The best dishes & beers!*

Below is a brief rundown of the traditional and most popular dishes that you should try and sample when you're roaming around Asia. These dishes are only the tip of a gastronomic iceberg limited only by your culinary inhibitions so go beyond these lists and try something new every day! Street food is found everywhere throughout Asia and while it's more accessible for travellers in Thailand, most of the dishes mentioned in the other countries can also be found in markets and on street stalls.

> ### Bia Hoi... *fresh beer!*
> Memorise these words – BIA HOI. If Carlsberg done Asian beer... *It's probably the cheapest beer in the world* and you can get smashed for just a few dollars – even tight arses can get a round in! Often served in plastic litre-jugs, keep an eye out for little plastic chairs outside local style cafés with a silver keg in the corner, away from the main tourist areas!

THAILAND

When it comes to food, Thailand is arguably the daddy with a mouth-watering selection of irresistible and exotic dishes. You'll more than likely be familiar with a lot of these but nothing compares to the real thing! You'll also find some equally satisfying and well-known beverages to wash it down with as well!

- o **Food:** Pad Thai, Papaya Salad, Yellow/Green/Red Curry, Penang Curry, Massamam Curry, Jungle Curry, Tom Yam, chicken-cashew-nut. Fresh barbecued seafood; red snapper, barracuda, swordfish, mussels & many more
- o **Street food:** Pad Thai, spring rolls, corn-on-the-cob, fried rice & noodles dishes, meat sticks, curried rice, sticky rice, chocolate pancakes, fried insects
- o **Drink:** Chang *(nice and strong@6.4% & cheap too!)*, Shinga, Tiger, Heineken, Sangsum Rum – served in buckets of course, often with coke & M-151 *(Red Bull)*!

CAMBODIA

- o **Food:** Lok Lak, Fish Amok, Khmer Curry, traditional Khmer BBQ *(choose between a combination of Kangaroo, snake, ostrich, alligator)*, Cambodian spring rolls, sticky rice
- o **Drink:** Angkor – the national beer, Beer Laos, Tiger

INDONESIA

- o **Food:** Jajanan *(sweet & savoury snacks)*. Lots of simple fish, rice and noodle dishes, sticky rice, nasi goring *(fried rice)*, Gado-gado *(vegetables & peanut sauce)*, Sate *(skewered meat)*, Maniki *(bat!)* & dog meat!
- o **Drink:** Although predominantly Islamic, you'll still find a number of decent beers including Bintang & Anker

- o   **Food:** Kway teow *(noodles)*, rending tok *(beef cooked in coconut)*, epok-epok *(pastries filled with fried fish & coconut)* rustic Indian dishes & Chinese food
- o   **Drink:** Tiger

THE PHILIPPINES

- o   **Food:** Adobo *(pork/chicken cooked in vinegar, soy sauce and garlic)*, sinigáng *(pork fish or prawns in sour soup)* and various forms of bangus *(milkfish)*. There are so many dishes, your best bet is to go to Turu-turó *(basic roadside canteen)* and point at whatever takes your fancy!
- o   **Drink:** Colt 45, San Miguel, Red Horse & Tanduay Rum

VIETNAM

- o   **Food:** Noodle soup *(pho)*, Cao Loa, Nuoc Mam *(a quintessential Vietnamese dish – often a sauce. The strong mam tom version is often severed with dog meat!)*, Vietnamese spring rolls *(Nem)*, dog meat, duck embryo
- o   **Drink:** Saigon, 333, BGI, fresh beer, draught beer *(the cheapest beer in the world known as **bia hoi** – see text box on previous page)*

I dare you... *Go on, be a culinary daredevil!*

If you travel around Asia for long enough you're guaranteed to encounter some regional delicacies that you'll find unusual and equally challenging! Fiercely omnivorous Asians find nothing weird with eating your canine friend or munching their way through an aborted duck embryo. It's also somewhat reassuring to know that there's somewhere in the world where you can eat the things that can kill you from mighty sharks to slithering serpents! Here's a sample of what you might encounter, so don't be shy, be a daredevil and compete with your mates and try as many of them as you can:

Fried crickets, cockroaches & maggots – found all over Asia from street carts in Bangkok to rural villages in Vietnam you can feast on a bag of crunchy fried insects for a quick snack! In all honesty, they're no worse than a bag of Pork Scratching! Sizeable crispy cockroaches with a chewy centre are probably the most challenging!

BBQ giant spiders – you'll find barbequed spiders in the most random of places, usually sold on stalls next to the side of the road. They're as fresh as it gets – you can usually select which crawling eight-legged monster you want to pop on the BBQ. Chew on the crispy legs before indulging on the chewy body – Enjoy!

Grilled snake – you can sample snake as part of a traditional Khmer BBQs in Cambodia along with other animals that should be eating you such as shark and crocodile! In some parts of Vietnam – usually the more rural areas and Hoi An – they'll kill a venomous snake before your eyes, cut out its beating heart and offer it to you it with a shot of the serpent's blood... Bottoms up!

Duck embryo – a delicacy I've yet to grown the balls to try! These can be ordered with a down of feathers and a soft beak according to the carnivores taste!

Dog meat – found all over Vietnam this delicacy can be found on basic street stalls to upmarket restaurant menus. You'll also find it throughout Indonesia where it's served in a kind of thick stew!

Bat *(Maniki)* – complete with head, wings and feet you can wrap your laughing-gear around a whole stewed bat from street kitchens throughout Indonesia!

Thirsty?   Why not up the ante and wash it all down with some warm **snake blood vodka** – available from all respectable bars throughout Vietnam, bottoms up!

Believe it or not the Asian climate isn't all long hot summer days! It's characterised by two distinct seasons;

- o **THE WET SEASON:**   May - Oct   Characterised by; *downpours, cloud, high humidity*
- o **THE DRY SEASON:**   Nov - April   Characterised by; *dry, hot weather, lower humidity*

If you've got no constraints on the timing of your trip, make good predictable weather your priority! Although there are some regional variations, early **November** to late **March** is generally the best time to go to Asia where the weather's not only hot and dry but bearable and not too sticky! Bear in mind that this period is also the busiest season where the prices are inflated. Peak periods, such as Christmas, are even pricier as package-holidaymakers flock to destinations such as Thailand. The **shoulder months** of October/early November and April/May are significantly cheaper although the weather can be a little unpredictable albeit still hot. It's also worth remembering that some seaside towns will be in semi-hibernation during the shoulder months – although this is not necessarily a bad thing if you want some peace and quiet and would like to take advantage of lower off-peak rates and empty beaches!

All-year-round: All of Southeast Asia lies within the tropics. Consequently, regardless of when you visit, the weather is more than likely going to be warm! During the dry season, temperatures are usually cooler, but it's less humid, not so sticky and a lot more bearable making it the typical 'peak season'. If you visit during the 'wet season', don't despair. Temperatures will often be hotter but it'll be more humid and cloudier with typical rainfalls in afternoon or night-time downpours. However, these typically last for no longer than an hour. Some of the regions destinations, such as northern Vietnam, run on opposite seasons to the rest of the region. Don't worry, the majority of people still venture around these parts during the 'wet season' because it's convenient to do so as the rest of the region's blessed with the best of the weather. Nothing's ever simple!

GETTING THERE & AWAY... *Regional hubs & suitable airline tickets*

Where to fly into/out of... *The regional hub(s)*

Bangkok *(Thailand)* is the regional hub and where most backpackers enter and exit the region. You'll find the cheapest airfares to and from Bangkok although cheap tickets can also be found in and out of **Kuala Lumpur** *(Malaysia)* and occasionally from the city-state of **Singapore**.

Type of airline ticket... *Your options*

This will depend on what type of itinerary you're pursing. See section 6, Booking your trip... for additional information on airlines, tickets and how to reduce the price of your airline ticket:

- o **Looping itinerary:** SE Asia allows for fantastic looping itineraries so a **standard return ticket** from Bangkok *(Thailand)* is the most common choice

- o **Linear itinerary:** If you want to pursue a more linear itinerary consider flying into Kuala Lumpur *(Malaysia)* and out of Hanoi *(North Vietnam)* with **two single tickets** or consider an **open-jaw ticket** if you're not sure what date you want to fly back on or you're feel that you may venture up to Hong Kong and want to fly out from there

- o **RTW ticket:** If you're lucky enough to be on a RTW ticket and want to include a realistic and manageable surface sector across Asia, consider flying into Singapore or Kuala Lumpur *(Malaysia)* and out of Hanoi *(North Vietnam)* or Hong Kong *(China)* to get the most out of your RTW ticket without being over ambitious!

THE CLASSIC LOOPING ITINERARY...

Essentially two loops, this well-trodden-route ensures that you'll experience nearly everything that SE Asia has to offer in one mammoth sitting.

THAILAND ➔ LAOS ➔ VIETNAM ➔ CAMBODIA ➔ THAILAND ➔ MALAYSIA ➔ THAILAND

Suggested time:	3-5 months
Entry / exit points:	Bangkok *(Thailand)*
The countries/route:	**Thailand** – Bangkok, Chiang Mai

Thailand – Bangkok, Chiang Mai
Laos – Luang Prabang, Vang Vieng, Vientiane
Vietnam – Hanoi, Dong Ha, Hué, Hoi An, Nha Trang, Dalat,HCMC
Cambodia – Phnom Penh, Sihanoukville, Siem Reap
Thailand – Koh Chang, Bangkok, Koh Toa, Koh Pha-Ngan, Koh Samui, Krabi, Phi Phi
Malaysia – Langkawi *(Penang, Pangkor & KL optional)*

After a few days in Thailand's hectic capital, hop on the night train to the trekking and cultural capital of **Chiang Mai**. Once you're 'cultured-out' get on the slow boat to the photogenic town of **Luang Prabang**. From here bus it to the ultimate traveller's town of **Vang Vieng** where you can tube down the river and drink copious amounts of beer in rustic bars and TV-restaurants. Next stop **Vientiane,** where you can hop on a bus for a long journey to Vietnam's capital, **Hanoi**. Slide down

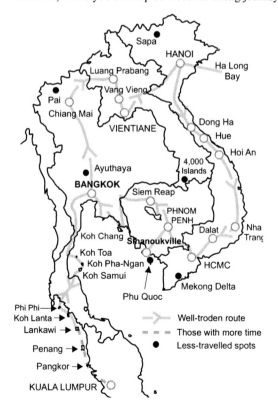

Nam's slim shape stopping-off at the battle scared **DMZ** *(Dong Ha)*, the food capital **Hué**, picturesque **Hoi An** and the beaches of **Nha Trang**. After enjoying the cooler climate of **Dalat**, finish-off in **HCMC** before popping across the border to **Phnom Penh**. Flop on the beaches in Sihanoukville, before dosing up on some culture in **Siem Reap** and exploring the ancient ruins of **Angkor**. Head back into Thailand to relax and recharge on **Koh Chang** before hitting the beautiful party islands of **Koh Tao, Koh Pha-Ngan** and **Koh Samui** for a spot of diving and some heavy nights. Try and coincide your trip with the epic *Full-Moon Party* on Koh Pha-Ngan. From here, you've got a few options further south, including **Phi Phi, Koh Lanta, Langkawi, Penang, Pangkor** and **Kuala Lumpur**. As you'll have to backtrack to get up to Bangkok to fly home, ration some of the southern highlights so that you can and do a few of them on your way back up. Depending on time, consider this route: **Phi Phi, Langkawi, Pangkor, KL, Penang, Koh Lanta, Bangkok.**

THE LINEAR ALTERNATIVE...

Sometimes it's more practical to pursue a linear surface sector across SE Asia and it means that you'll be doing no backtracking whatsoever – you'll probably even get to see more of Malaysia. The route is generally quicker while you'll still visit most of SE Asia's highlights.

MALAYSIA ➔ THAILAND ➔ CAMBODIA ➔ VIETNAM

Suggested time: 10+ weeks

Entry / exit points: Kuala Lumpur *(Malaysia)* / Hanoi *(Vietnam)*

The countries/route: **Malaysia** – KL, Pangkor, Penang, Langkawi
Thailand – Koh Lanta, Phi Phi, Krabi, Koh Samui, Koh Pha-Ngan, Koh Tao, Bangkok, Koh Chang
Cambodia – Siem Reap, Phnom Penh, Sihanoukville
Vietnam – HCMC, Nha Trang, Hoi An, Hué, Dong Ha, Hanoi *(Ha Long Bay)*

Spend a few days in **KL**, then bus it up the west coast and take some time out on a few tropical retreats. From the beautiful tax-free haven of **Langkawi**, hop across the border into Thailand to kick back and relax on **Koh Lanta** before drinking the night away and visiting Maya Beach *(The Beach)* on **Phi Phi**. If you want some outdoor adventure, stop off at **Krabi** before you hit the ever-popular southern islands to enjoy the beaches of **Koh Samui**, the energetic nightlife of **Koh Pha-Ngan** and the top-notch diving on **Koh Tao**. Next stop is the bustling capital of Bangkok before spending a few lethargic days on the backpacker island of **Koh Chang**. Scurry across the border into Cambodia to spend a few days of cultural awakening in **Siem Reap** and the ancient **Temples of Angkor**. From here, head to **Phnom Pehn** for a sobering peek into Pol Pots' brutal reign before heading south to tan it up in Cambodia's beach capital, **Sihanoukville**. Vietnam's slender figure endures a logical and simple route. Start your Nam adventure in **Saigon**, before hitting the cooler climate of **Dalat** and getting some beach time in **Nha Trang** and kitting yourself out in a snug tailored suit in **Hoi An.** Stuff your face in the cultural heart of Vietnam, aka **Hue**, before exploring the **DMZ** and hitting Vietnam's crazy capital, **Hanoi,** and cruising through the picturesque **Ha Long Bay**.

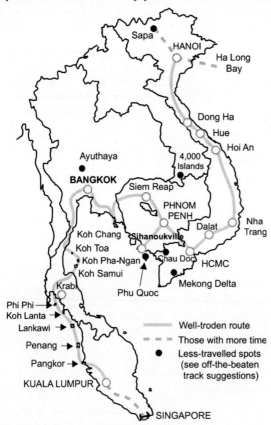

Map labels: Sapa, HANOI, Ha Long Bay, Dong Ha, Hue, Hoi An, Ayuthaya, 4,000 Islands, BANGKOK, Siem Reap, PHNOM PENH, Dalat, Nha Trang, Koh Chang, Sihanoukville, Koh Toa, Chau Doc, Koh Pha-Ngan, HCMC, Koh Samui, Mekong Delta, Krabi, Phu Quoc, Phi Phi, Koh Lanta, Lankawi, Penang, Pangkor, KUALA LUMPUR, SINGAPORE

Legend: Well-troden route / Those with more time / Less-travelled spots (see off-the-beaten track suggestions)

Why not add the Philippines or Indonesia to your adventure? Despite their obvious attractions, it's common for Indonesia and the Philippines to be left off a backpacker's itinerary. Since they cannot be reached by land, they really do represent the last frontier of SE Asia and they're largely undeveloped for western backpackers. They warrant as much time as you can give them and make a worthwhile and refreshing side-trip from the well-beaten track. The longer you dedicate to these countries the more you'll get from your experience there. Because they're largely unscathed by the mass tourism that engulfs the vast majority of SE Asia, you'll have a more authentic experience and your money **can** go a little further here.

> ### Get a guidebook...!
>
> Now these two island nations can be very challenging to explore. I know I've said that this makes it fun, exciting and rewarding allowing you to get off-the-beaten track, but these are two countries that I'd strongly advise that you get an individual guidebook for. They really are invaluable once you're there and you'll still be able to have a unique adventure, albeit a less frustrating one! Even if it's for detailed maps, get one!

However, bear in mind that the number of islands and scale of the two countries means that you're likely to spend considerably more on transport once you're there. Basically, be prepared to reach deep into your pockets if you intend to do some serious exploring and island hopping! Unlike the rest of SE Asia, TATs *(Tourist Information Offices)* are sparse and this can make getting around a little tricky at times. On the flip side, this means that there are fewer middle men taking a cut and the challenge of getting around is potentially more rewarding and memorable! Some of my most enjoyable journeys have been on the roof of a jeepney hugging the east coast of Mindoro *(Philippines)* soaking up spectacular coastal views and basking under the tropical sun. You can get reasonably priced flights to both countries from Bangkok, Kuala Lumpur, Saigon and Singapore.

INDONESIA... *Endless island hopping*

Arguably, it's impossible to see all of Indonesia and experience everything this vast island nation has to offer in a single lifetime. The sheer number of islands makes it incredibly difficult to create suggested itineraries – however, this very problem represents a great opportunity for you to have a truly unique and authentic experience off-the-beaten track. Seasoned shoe-stringers come back to Indonesia time after time for this very reason – you'll always be able to have a different, varied and unique island hopping adventure in Indonesia no matter how many times you visit!

A recommended & popular linear route... *Easterly does it*

As I've mentioned, it's hard to create a realistic and manageable route through Indonesia but the most common route that's ideal for first-time travelers is a linear itinerary as follows:

Suggested time: 4+ weeks *(the longer the better)*

Entry point: Belawan – comfortable high-speed ferry from Penang *(Malaysia)*

Exit Point: Bali – regional & international flights

Belawan ➔ Bukit Lawang ➔ Jakarta ➔ Gunung Bromo ➔ Bali ➔ Lombok ➔ Gili Islands ➔ Bali

This route ensures that you get off-the-beaten track as well as hitting the most popular tourist hotspots. Again this is only a guideline so be adventurous and stray off this route – there are many interesting places in between each town so have your own unique and rewarding adventure.

THE PHILIPPINES... *Island hopping*

The number of islands and the undeveloped infrastructure is a big draw for travellers who want rustic adventures away from the crowds, but this also means that it's hard to create manageable itineraries, especially for first-time travellers. Below are two fairly simple routes that'll ensure you have an interesting and varied trip. These are only a rough guideline so if you're confident feel free to modify them and deviate – you're guaranteed to find plenty of interesting places along the way.

The linear itinerary... *Swathe through the majestic Visayas*

Suggested time: 6+ weeks *(the longer the better)*
Entry / exit points: Manila / Cebu

Manila ➔ Puerto Galera ➔ **VISAYAS** *(Boracay, Sipalay, Guimaras, Dumaguete& Bohol are popular spots for a start)* ➔ Cebu

Start your trip in the Philippines' bustling capital city before heading a few hours south for some sun, relaxation, and perhaps a spot of diving, in the low-key beach resorts of **Puerto Galera**. Above all, this linear itinerary ensures that you cut right through the beautiful, lethargic and sun-soaked **Visayas**. Linked by an armada of ferries and catamarans, after a few days in the popular tourist resort of **Boracay**, you can blissfully hopscotch between these palm-fringed islands to find your own secluded beaches, hidden lagoons and picturesque bays before hitting bustling **Cebu** to fly out. There are simply thousands of islands, some unmarked on most maps – get to know the locals and discover the well hidden gems! The more time you have the better!

The looping itinerary... *Northern exposure*

Suggested time: 4+ weeks *(the longer the better)*
Entry / exit points: Manila

Manila ➔ Sagada/Banaue ➔ Manila ➔ Daet ➔ Donsol ➔ Boracay ➔ North Pandan Island ➔ Puerto Galera ➔ Tagaytay ➔ Manila

This exciting looping itinerary offers everything from snorkelling with turtles *(North Pandan Island)* and swimming alongside whale sharks *(Donsol)* to sunbathing on pristine beaches *(White Beach in Boracay)* and chilling-out in idyllic mountaintop retreats *(Sagada & Banaue)* with much more in between. Getting between some places can be a bit challenging – Donsol to Boracay for example – but you're guaranteed to find some intriguing places en-route that'll make your Filipino adventure different from everybody else's!

Off-the-beaten track travel tips... *Domestic flights*

You'll find that transport in the Philippines and Indonesia is even more undeveloped, testing and time consuming than elsewhere in Asia. The key is to be **patient** and **flexible** coupled with **good planning** and **a laidback attitude**! Transport between some islands is not only irregular but also extremely unreliable and slow – it's common for weekly ferries to be cancelled at the last minute leaving you frustratingly stranded for another week! Journeys that would be a simple bus trip in Thailand will often be a complicated and time consuming adventure involving multiple trikes, busses and ferries! You really do need to conduct some serious research and planning to get around – before you get there and while you're there. Ask around at local markets and in shops to find out how to get to places. As a *(wealthy)* foreigner expect to pay a little more, but while you're finding out about getting from A to B also enquire in shops how much the locals pay to get there so you don't unknowingly pay <u>way over</u> the top!

Flying: If you haven't got much time or your patience is wearing thin, **flying** is a realistic option. Flying is not only quicker, more convenient and comfortable, it's surprisingly economical – local carriers offer fantastic domestic flights that only cost a few pennies more than a long uncomfortable bus ride. It's that economical even the locals use aviation as a major mode of transport.

The Filipino archipelago is huge and extensive while the world's largest archipelago – Indonesia – stretches

> ### Time flies...
>
> This can't be stressed enough – **the more time you have the better**. It's easy to get over ambitious in these countries by pursuing an imaginative itinerary! The less time you have, the more you'll need to use domestic carriers and the more you'll benefit from flying.

across 3 time-zones so flying is often the only realistic way to cover a lot of their expansive highlights. Having said that, local transport is a great way to get about – ok you're not going to get anywhere quickly but you'll be able to absorb the breathtaking scenery and have some memorable encounters with the locals and their lifestyle. Essentially, fly to the main 'hubs' and then explore the surrounding regions/islands via local transport. By **using a mix** of flying and local transport you'll be able to hit all of the highlights while having an authentic experience.

COSTS, MONEY & WHAT TO EXPECT... *How cheap is cheap!?*

You'll hear the generalisation 'Asia is so cheap' time and time again, and for the majority of westerners that's true – it's cheaper than Central America and Australasia but some areas may not be as cheap as you'd expect. Generally speaking Thailand, Malaysia and Singapore are the more expensive countries in SE Asia. Thailand's other neighbouring countries, Laos and Cambodia, are noticeably cheaper but are slightly more expensive than Vietnam. Elsewhere, off-the-beaten track, Indonesia and the Philippines are as cheap, if not cheaper, than Vietnam once you get there – they only become more expensive when you do some serious island hopping because of the amount of transport you'll use!

Daily budgets for first-time travellers range from **800BHT in Thailand** *(about £14)* to **US$15 in Vietnam** *(about £9)*

Below is a broad overview of your main expenses in SE Asia:

ACCOMMODATION... *Cheap sleeps as low as £4!*

By western standards accommodation across SE Asia is very affordable and it's cheaper than Central America and Down Under. Primarily, backpackers stay in **guesthouses** and **beach huts** but you'll also find a small scattering of **hostels** as well. Most accommodation offer single, double and triple rooms. Prices are usually **per room, not per person**. Dorm accommodation is rare and doesn't really work out cheaper if you're travelling with someone.

In some of the cheaper countries, such as Cambodia and Vietnam, you'll be able to find bargains in the form of 'budget hotels' at hostel prices. Prices vary a little across the region with Thailand's southern islands amongst the more expensive. Here you can expect to pay up to **1,000BHT** a night for a double room *(nearly £20)* during peak season and don't expect the quality to be better because it's more expensive! Fortunately it's better news elsewhere in Thailand where you can pick up a double room

> ### Toilets... *Ready, steady, squat!*
> Ok, so the toilets across SE Asia can come as quite a shock. A fair amount of them are squat toilets where you'll have to hover and aim into a hole in the ground – as well as pissing down your leg, on your feet and on the floor, they can be quite confusing to use! There'll usually be a scoop and bucket of water next to the toilet – this is for 'flushing' the toilet after you've done your business and not for washing your hands, feet or face! You won't find any toilet paper either – it blocks up the pipes anyway – but you'll usually find a 'bum-gun' to wash your behind. Again this isn't to wash yourself and don't try to 'flush' the toilet with it – you'll just spray the contents of the toilet all over yourself! You'll miss the bum-gun when you get home! Baby wipes are a good idea, especially for emergencies!

for around **300BHT** – around a fiver (*£5*). You'll find the cheaper accommodation in Vietnam and Cambodia where you'll be forking out around **US$5-US$10** for a double room *(roughly £3-£6)*. Perhaps, obviously, prices are inflated during peak times and bargains can be found during low seasons. You'll find internet and travel services on offer at the majority of guesthouses as well as visa services. Make sure you see the room before you hand over any money as the standard of accommodation varies greatly across the region. By western standards rooms can be fairly dirty, facilities very basic and beds uncomfortable – think of them as rustic! Showers are usually cold and air-con's a luxury that'll usually bump up the price of a room considerably.

FOOD & DRINK... *Budget bites from 50p!*

You'll be able to eat out in **cafés** and **restaurants** every night which is good because there's little accommodation with cooking facilities and communal kitchens! You won't need much more than a couple of quid to eat out and you'll be able to eat at local **food shacks** and **street kitchens** even cheaper. Don't be shy and don't believe all of the horror stories you hear about street food – you're more likely to get ill from eating at a more western-style Asian restaurant where the ingredients could have been sat out the back in the soaring heat for hours and where you can't see your meal being cooked! **Street food** from carts all over SE Asia is unbelievably cheap and you'll be able to pick from a range of interesting dishes from **25BHT** *(50p)* Pad Thai in Thailand to steaming hot noodle soup for less than a **US-dollar** in Vietnam. You can see all of the ingredients and it's cooked before your eyes so you can see that it's safe to eat! Cheap and cheerful turu-turos *(literally point-point)* are the basic Filipino eatery where you order by pointing at whatever precooked food behind the glass counter takes your fancy!

Don't expect the same sort of kitchen crockery that you'd use at home though – most meals are served on plastic dishes and wooden bowls while street food is often served on paper plates and polystyrene trays. While knife and forks are used in tourist oriented restaurants, chopsticks are used throughout the region. If you're not confident and get confronted by a pair of sticks, just ask for a knife and fork – Asians are used to us fumbling westerners and will usually come to the rescue with a fork if they see you struggling! Drinking tap water isn't advised throughout the region so buy bottled water from shops.

ALCOHOL... *Bargain beer from as little as 40p a litre!*

You'll be pleased to hear that getting drunk in Asia is very cheap by western standards – alcohol's a lot cheaper than Europe, North America and Down Under but a little more expensive than most of Central America. Beers in local shops will set you back around **60BHT** – less than a pound – for a large bottle of Chang in Thailand and a **US-dollar** or two for a big beer Laos in Cambodia and Laos – roughly double these prices for beers in bars and 'restaurants'. You'll find the **world's cheapest beer** in Vietnam which is simply known as draught beer *(Bia Hoi)* – served in litre jugs you'll get wrecked for just a few US-dollars and it doesn't taste bad either! If you're more of a spirits connoisseur you'll be pleased to hear that you can get 'buckets of rum' from around **200BHT** – that's less four quid *(£4)*! If you can stomach it, the local 'rice-spirits' are even cheaper! If you venture over to the Philippines you can get hold of bottles of rum for around **70Peso** – that's less than a pound!

Of course you'll find variations across the region and it's the same pattern with Thailand, Malaysia and Singapore being a little pricier than the rest. Malaysia is notably more expensive for alcohol, but if you head to Langkawi – the tax-free island – you'll find alcohol nearer Thai prices. Be careful though, despite alcohol being ridiculously cheap, you'll find that it can easily become your biggest expense and can more than double your daily budget in Asia! Bucket-monsters be warned!

ACTIVITIES... *Snorkelling trips from 300BHT – that's about £6!*

There's a range of decent activities on offer across SE Asia from snorkelling in turquoise waters to trekking in lush tropical jungles. You'll find that most of these are generally cheaper than they would be in Central America and much cheaper than the equivalent activities in New Zealand or Oz. Some of the world's cheapest diving courses can be found on Thailand's ever growing popular southern islands where fun dives cost around **1,000BHT** and 4-day open water PADI & SSI courses are a bargain with prices starting from **9,000BHT** – accommodation is usually included. You can swim with whale sharks in Donsol *(Philippines)* for **1,100 pesos** – roughly **£15** – while fantastic value 3-day/2-night jungle treks can be found for **1,500BHT** in Thailand's northern city of Chiang Mai. Entrance to the ancient Angkor Wat Temples in Cambodia will only set you back around **US$25** for a day-pass and the Maya Bay – aka 'The Beach' – daytrip in Thailand shouldn't cost you more than **800BHT**. Sobering visits to the S-21 Museum and the Killing Fields in Phnom Phen *(Cambodia)* are a snip at around **US$2** entrance fee to each site – optional guided tours are only an extra few US-dollars. Daytrips to explore Vietnam's war torn past are good value for money with a visit to the Chu Chi Tunnels setting you back around **US$5** and excellent personalised DMZ tours come in at about **US$15**. Snorkelling trips will usually set you back around **300BHT** while the ever-popular tubing in Vang Vieng *(Laos)* costs no more than **US$10** – you'll just need more for drink along the way!

TRANSPORT... *US$8 for a 12hr bus journey in Vietnam!*

Transport in Asia is as cheap as it is varied *(see next section to check out the diversity!)*. Transport costs throughout the region don't vary that much. Thailand, Malaysia and Singapore are slightly more expensive although it tends to be better organised and of better quality. Wherever you are in SE Asia be prepared to have your patience tested! From Thailand to the Philippines, busses and ferries are often late, overcrowded and prices are often inconsistent – especially outside of Malaysia and Thailand. In comparison, transport in SE Asia is slightly more expensive than in Central America but a lot cheaper than getting around down under.

Although slower, local busses are always cheaper than tourist 'VIP' busses or private shuttle busses and give you a unique opportunity to interact with the locals. Night busses, sleeper trains and overnight ferries are generally cheaper and will save you a nights' accommodation! You'll pay around **US$8** *(£5)* for an overnight bus between towns along the coast in Vietnam and about **400BHT** *(about £7)* for a combined night bus and ferry ticket to the southern islands from Bangkok in Thailand. **Air Asia** is the region's main budget airline and offers extensive routes around SE Asia at Ryan Air prices – www.airasia.com. Obviously the more travelling around you do, the bigger your transport expense will be! The Philippines and Indonesia are cheaper in terms of food, alcohol and accommodation but because of the sheer number of islands and undeveloped infrastructure, the cost of transport really adds up if you do some serious island hopping.

YOUR MAIN TRANSPORT OPTIONS... *Innovative, fun & exciting!*

Transport in SE Asia is as strange and it is diverse! It's not just a case of getting from A to B, the transport is fun, exciting and memorable – it's just so different from 'conventional western' forms of transport! On the other hand, transport in SE Asia is notoriously slow, inefficient, uncomfortable and unpunctual. Patience is the key, and believe it or not, these classic characteristics will be the making of your trip. It'll make it not only authentic and original but exciting and memorable! It can also be a hair raising and exhilarating experience – you'll find yourself swaying in the wind on the roof of Jeepneys, clinging on for dear life on the back of nippy motorbikes and cramped up in the foetal position with livestock, locals and other weary travellers on overcrowded chicken busses and ferries. Approach transport in Asia with an open mind and release your thoughts from the perils of what could be – you're going to have some memorable trips, especially outside of Malaysia and Thailand! Remember travelling is about the journey!

Asians are very practical and resourceful and you'll see this reflected time and time again in their innovative modes of transport. The sheer variety of transport you'll encounter is half the appeal of Asia itself! With the exception of Indonesia and the Philippines, getting form town to town is an easy affair – most of the time you just have to pop into a travel agency or guesthouse and they'll arrange it all for you and there's a range of preset routes and tickets to popular destinations. In Indonesia and the Philippines there are fewer agencies and backpacker orientated travel desks in guesthouses to do this for you meaning that you'll have to go direct to the bus depots, ferry terminals and train stations to enquire about getting from A to B and book your tickets direct.

What follows is a little taster of the various modes of transport that you'll come across and use during your time in Asia. You can't really plan or book what types of transport you'll be using – this is just to make you aware of the options available to you. While some follow a loose timetable, most you can just flag down like regular taxis:

Busses & Minivans

Where: Everywhere

When: Between towns & cities and over border crossings

How Much: Fairly cheap – although 'private' minibuses are expensive

Busses and minivans form the main mode of transport betweens towns throughout Asia. The quality and comfort of busses varies dramatically from cosy VIP tourist busses in Thailand to loud and rickety buses with no windows *(or apparent MOT)* in the Philippines and Indonesia! You'll also come across night busses, particularly in Thailand and Vietnam – these are very cost effective and save precious time. Bus journeys can be a long and tedious affair often blighted by delays and late departures so take your own supply of food and drink so you're not forced to buy meals during stops at inflated prices. Expect busses, and particularly economy busses and minivans outside of Thailand, to be overcrowded and uncomfortable. VIP busses and the more tourist orientated busses tend to have set prices and routes where you buy tickets in advance – you can usually haggle a little bit if you buy your tickets from a travel desk where they'll sacrifice some of their commission! You usually pay, and haggle, with minivan drivers before you get in.

Minivans tend to be quicker *(and pricier!)* than busses although they can be very cramped – don't be surprised to asked to fit two people on a seat! A common trick is to get you and your friends to hire or go by another minibus that can leave straightaway – in reality it's a private mini-bus and while it'll be a lot more comfortable and less cramped, you'll be paying through the roof for it if you compare it to the local mini bus! Luggage is usually placed under the seats and on top of your laps! Occasionally, it will be strapped to the roof.

Tuk-tuks *(Bajaj in Indonesia)*

Where: Cambodia, Indonesia, Laos & Thailand

When: Around town

How Much: Cheap but be aware of scams!

A great Asian experience! These three wheeled carts are the chief transport around town in many parts of Asia! Although varying slightly from country to country, the humble Tuk-Tuk *(Bajaj in Indonesia)* is a true Asian icon offering affordable, fun and exciting transport around town *(above, a Cambodian version)*. A ride on one of these brightly coloured bumbling carts is a 'must-do' during your time in Asia – the ride will be noisy, smelly, bumpy, harrowing and a grand adventure – if you egg them on, the drivers *(in Bangkok)* will race, pull wheelies and screech around corners on two wheels! After the novelty wears off though, you'll realise that metered taxis are actually cheaper and safer! When the price sounds too good to be true, it often is as you'll being taken to and hassled at jewellers, TATs *(Tourist Information Offices)* and tailor shops before you eventually arrive at your destination. Remember this – 10 Baht, 10 stops! Luggage is carried in the cart with you.

Motorbike taxis *(Ojeks in Indonesia)*

Where: Cambodia, Indonesia, Malaysia, Thailand & Vietnam

When: Around town

How Much: Very cheap especially if you're on your lonesome!

These are fun! Fairly high risk but a big thrill, motorbike taxis *(Ojeks in Indonesia)* are abundant in major towns and cities across Asia. They offer a quick, convenient and economical mode of transport through the chocked up cities of Asia and they're especially useful in busy cities, such as Bangkok and Saigon *(HCMC)*, where they can nip in-and-out of the notorious Asian traffic jam!

Metered taxis are cheaper and safer if you're not on your lonesome. Always haggle and agree on a price **before** you hop on and don't forget to get off on the left-hand side to avoid burning your leg on the exhaust – I speak from experience! Luggage is either balanced in the foot well between the driver and the handle bars or on your back. If helmets are provided, whatever its condition, wear it – you may be stopped by police and fined in some cities.

Ferries, catamarans & longboats

Where: Everywhere *(yes even in land locked Laos!)*

When: Between islands & river side-towns

How Much: Usually very affordable, especially in the less commercialised regions

Whether it's a relaxing slow boat down the Mekong, a commercial ferry to Thailand's southern party islands or a local catamaran to an isolated Indonesian atoll, boats will more than likely form a major part of your transport around SE Asia – you'll have some spectacular and memorable boat journeys and they should be seen as a more than just a form of transport. Some of the best boat trips include the 2-day longboat down the Mekong from Houayxai to Luang Probang in Laos and cruises through the towering limestone outcrops of Ha Long Bay in Vietnam. Longboats *(picture above)* are extremely common through Thailand's southern islands.

Small boats and catamarans are a lifeline forming the principle mode of transport in the island nations of Indonesia and the Philippines, although you'll find that they're severely overcrowded, highly irregular and painfully slow – you'll grow to love it! Bear in mind that long distance trips in these countries can last several days, so make sure that you do some preparation;

- o Take some form of entertainment e.g. playing cards, an i-Pod or a bottle of rum!
- o Take a supply of food and water – you don't know the quality or the cost of what's on board if there's anything at all. Breakdowns and delays are common so be prepared for your journey to take longer than anticipated
- o Bring some warm *(preferably waterproof)* clothing – lower decks can be drafty and damp while higher decks get battered by waves in stormy weather!
- o Travel sickness tablets – ferries set off despite some hair-raising weather conditions so if you're prone to travel sickness make sure you have some close to hand!

Use your daypack – keep warm clothes at the top of your day-sack and make sure all of your valuables are in your daypack so that you can keep an eye on them

Taxis

Where: Everywhere

When: Around town

How Much: Economical if there's more than one of you

The bog standard taxi can be found in all major cities around SE Asia. Generally speaking, taxis are so cheap – even in Thailand – that if there are two or more of you with luggage, it's hardly worth bothering with an uncomfortable overcrowded bus that's a few pennies cheaper! You'll also appreciate the added comfort of air-con. The situation varies from place to place but you have to be cautious over the price of taxis – you'll either have to make sure the cheeky buggers put the meter on or agree on a reasonable price before you get in!

Occasionally, you'll encounter drivers that refuse to put the meter on or claim that it's broken to try and get a higher fare from unsuspecting tourists. Be firm and persistent until you find a fair one that's willing to put the meter on – and make sure they put it on once your inside, otherwise ask and if they refuse get out! Sometimes, it's common practice for taxis not to use their meters *(especially for tourists)* so you'll have to negotiate the price before you get in – make sure you ask a few to get an idea of what fare you should be looking at paying. It's a great chance to hone your haggling skills – just remember that the price is per cab, not per person.

Jeepneys & Tricycles

Where: Philippines

When: Around town *(Tricycles)* & between towns *(Jeepneys)*

How Much: Very cheap although trike drivers will try and rip you off so be firm!

Tricycles... Vibrant tricycles are the tuk-tuks of the Philippines providing a whacky and fun form of transport around town. Essentially they're Philippines answer to a budget-taxi. While they're very cheap, drivers will try their best to get more from you so agree on a price before you get in and cram as many people on and in the trike as you can! You can usually find the fare pricing on the inside window of the side car – it's normally based on x-amount for the first 2km plus so much for each km thereafter. If in doubt pop in a shop and ask a local for a rough idea. Luggage is put on the roof or taken into the side car with you.

Jeepneys... Pimped up flamboyant Jeepneys – originally made from left over US military jeeps – are the most popular means of public transportation between towns. Jeepneys run regularly and are very cheap – cheaper than a tricycle over significant distances *(say 5km or more)*. They get fairly packed but don't despair, there's always room on the roof where you'll get some exhilarating views under the basking sun! Luggage is usually just thrown onto the roof where it slides around between the outer railings – don't panic lost luggage is surprisingly rare but make sure that you take your daypack inside with you!

Cyclos *(Becaks in Indonesia)*

Where: Vietnam/Cambodia/Indonesia & parts of Thailand

When: Around town

How Much: Very cheap

Sometimes referred to as *(cycle)* Rickshaws in the rest of Asia, they're essentially a hybrid-bike sporting a comfy 'bucket-seat' on the front and are a unique transport option that's particularly common in Vietnam and Indonesia. They provide an economical way to explore the towns at a slow, relaxing and sedate pace. Try and engaged in some chit-chat with the drivers and explore these intriguing towns from a unique local perspective – many of the drivers know every inch of their territory. Despite being banned in some cities, you'll still find the becaks all over Indonesia.

Be warned though, it's not uncommon for cyclo drivers to exploit inexperienced tourists! Bargain **before** you jump in and don't expect the drivers to have change for large bills! Make sure you're clear whether the price is for the vehicle or per person. You can negotiate hourly and even daily rates if you plan to visit several locations.

Bemos

Where: Indonesia

When: Around town & between towns *(especially in rural regions)*

How Much: Very cheap

Bemo – an abbreviation of becak motor – form the backbone of urban transport throughout the Indonesian archipelago. You'll find a phenomenon of exuberantly decorated bemos that are pimped up with huge spoilers, shiny alloys and decorated with wild and wacky paint jobs – the top-volume music and thumping bass also makes riding the bemo an ear-shattering and memorable experience! They're a true expression of their owner's imagination and an element of competition that pushes the bemo drivers to wilder and wackier heights! Following a complex web of interlocking and loosely fixed routes, bemos operate in virtually every city and town in the country. They're often the main transport in remote rural areas where timetabled buses do not run. With a couple of thousand rupiah and a fair degree of time and patience you can get just about anywhere by bemo.

Flights

Where: Everywhere, particularly useful in Indonesia & the Philippines

When: Between countries *(International)*, towns & islands *(Domestic)*!

How Much: Varies although a good selection of budget airlines can make it very economical

Air Asia is the main budget airline with a number other local carriers also offering budget airfares. Flying is a great option if you're short on time and regional flights can save you any tedious backtracking. If you're planning to venture over to Indonesia and the Philippines you should seriously consider domestic flights once you're there to save you heaps of time and inconvenience as you navigate your way around the thousands of remote islands.

Trains

Where: Malaysia, Singapore, Thailand & Vietnam

When: Between towns & cities

How Much: Can be fairly expensive – opt for night 'sleeper' trains just because they're cheaper!

Perhaps unfairly, the mighty train is often overlooked by most backpackers travelling around Asia. Granted they're not a viable widespread option but trains can provide a useful, interesting and economic form of transport in a few countries – hop on the sleeper train from Bangkok and wake up refreshed in cultural north or travel up and down the length of Vietnam on the Reunification Express. Kuala Lumpur boasts a good underground system, while Bangkok has an extensive and punctual monorail system that covers most of this sprawling city. Remember that if you use sleeper trains you'll be saving on accommodation costs!

$ THE BUDGET DIRECTORY $

This section covers and 'ranks' countries from Southeast Asia. The budget directory should be used as a tool for planning your itinerary *(for more accurate daily budgets see 'At a glance' section for each country)*. The countries have been graded by **cheapness** and **ease of travel** to help you create an affordable and realistic itinerary that is tailored to your budget, travel experience and confidence:

- o **Cheapness** refers to how affordable each country is for the 'average backpacker' in comparison to a theoretical ***'Asian average' (5)***. For example, a country with a grading of 9 means the country is very cheap for backpackers compared to other countries in Asia. Generally speaking, Asia is very affordable for the westerners but regional variations do exist and you'll find that countries such as Thailand, although cheap by western standards, are still significantly more expensive than Vietnam or Indonesia. The scale factors in the 'average' cost of food, accommodation, transport, communication and daily activities *(daytrips and sightseeing etc...)*

- o **Ease of Travel** relates to how challenging it is to travel around a given country reflecting the general level of *(tourist)* infrastructure and also taking into consideration obstacles such as language barriers and culture differences. A grading of 10 could indicate that a country has good transport options, limited culture shock and it's easy to communicate *(i.e. the country could have a high English literacy rate)*. Countries with a high grade are more suitable for 'first-time backpackers' who are a bit apprehensive, would like to build up some confidence and don't won't to jump straight in at the deep end! A low grading is by no means detrimental. While it may mean that the country could have limited tourist infrastructure, a greater language barrier and more extreme cultural differences, these challenges are both potential rewarding and an appeal in themselves

The countries are graded from 1 to 10; 1 being very expensive and more challenging to travel and 10 being very cheap and easy to travel.

	Cheapness	Ease of Travel	Page
Thailand...	3	10	...42
Laos...	7	7	...49
Vietnam...	8	8	...53
Cambodia...	7	9	...59
Malaysia...	2	7	...63
Singapore...	1	9	...70

OFF-THE-BEATEN TRACK...

	Cheapness	Ease of Travel	Page
Philippines...	7	3	...72
Indonesia...	8	1	...79

THAILAND

A GRAND INTRODUCTION!

AT A GLANCE

Capital – Bangkok

Population – 63 million

Language(s) – Thai *(English widely spoken)*

Currency – Baht *(BHT)*

ATMs – Plentiful, even on the islands

Climate – Tropical

Best time to go – Nov - early March *(high season)*

Mar - Sept for peninsular east coast

Time zone – GMT +7hours

Suggested daily budget – 800BHT

More on the southern islands

Suggested time – 3+ weeks

Visas – Free 30-day visa for most nationalities at airports *(14-day visa at overland borders)*

Thailand is the number one destination in SE Asia, and arguably *the* travelling hotspot in the world. Boasting an unrivalled travel industry that's completely tailored to budget travel, it has the perfect blend for first-time backpackers and hardcore shoestringers alike – the charm of this enchanting country draws back hoards of travellers trip after trip. For first-timers, Thailand has the perfect balance between East and West. It's the ideal place to ease yourself into the backpacking lifestyle and immerse yourself in a fascinating culture that's so very foreign yet comfortably familiar. While it's beginning to get more expense as the package-holidaymakers catch on to this well-discovered backpacker's paradise, vast pockets of the country are still dominated by carefree long-haired travellers. Top-notch curries, street food, cheap beer, stunning beaches, bumbling tuk-tuks, and friendly monks are just the start. Whether you want to trek to minority villages, haggle in bustling markets, clamber over ancient ruins, explore life beneath the waves or sun yourself and get blind drunk on tropical islands, this long-standing favourite has got something for everyone. It's not the regions cheapest country by far, but it's the country that nearly everyone begins their SE Asia experience and rightly so. All roads lead to Bangkok and it's the transport hub of SE Asia. Consequently, once you've built up some confidence and drank one bucket of rum to many, Thailand's the perfect jumping-off point to the more culturally extreme and diverse countries of SE Asia...

There are just sooOOO many popular destinations in Thailand! Ideally you need to dedicate at least a month to cram most of them into your trip, but you can do a good selection of them briefly in a two to three week stint using. Here are the most popular backpacker spots to make your itinerary a credible one:

BANGKOK... *The regions buzzing crossroads*

Welcome to Thailand! Thailand's bustling capital city is a Mecca for all travellers and the transport hub of SE Asia. Bangkok's a great introduction to Thailand and backpacking in general – think of it as your initiation! Quarantine yourself here for a couple of days, shake off your jetlag and plan your exotic adventures. You'll find yourself here on a number of occasions as you explore SE Asia – you only need to look around to spot the cheery sunburnt faces of seasoned travellers amongst the bewildered look of pasty skinned new arrivals! Bangkok has fantastic transport links to practically everywhere so most people utilise it as a base-camp.

Getting from the airport...

Make sure you head straight outside of the airport and get a ticket for a **metered taxi** from the taxi desk next to the taxi-rank. Fares between the Airport and Khao San Road should cost around 250BHT plus the toll *(50BHT)*. Make sure the driver puts the meter as you set off – scams are common where drivers will try and charge you to the tune of 1,000BHT! If you're on your own, you can catch the shuttle-bus for 150BHT, but it's a long, tedious and cramped affair!

Bangkok is loved by most and loathed by some. Sure, it's hot, humid, dirty and smelly – you need only to step out of the airport and inhale to realise the scale of the city's huge pollution problem. However, despite its urban ills Bangkok has a distinct charm about it and even if you hate it at first, you'll grow to love it! Despite being the capital, you'll also realise how cheap Bangkok is after you've ventured to other parts of Thailand – especially the popular southern islands. Home to the legendary street food, you can snack your way through a gauntlet of gourmet street kitchens and food stalls. A mix of decent markets and ultra modern shopping centres offers you a chance to indulge in some retail therapy – head to the colossal **MBK shopping centre** by metered taxi! Bangkok also boasts a few worthwhile sights to soak up and kick-start your cultural education.

Khao San Road: Perhaps the most famous backpacker area in the world. This is the traveller's city within the city – every backpacker heads straight from the airport to this flamboyant street! It caters for every traveller's need with affordable accommodation, great shopping, comprehensive budget travel services and an energetic nightlife. It's also just a few minute's walk from major sights including the **Grand Palace**. The area buzzes with an international crowd of budget travellers, hoards of market vendors, a gauntlet of exotic street food and dozens of bumbling tuk-tuks. Admittedly there's not much to do during the day once you've seen the major landmarks except soak up the incredible atmosphere, haggle with market traders, snack on the street food and socialise in a wealth of drinking holes! Khao San Road is a unique experience in itself.

The buzz isn't just contained to Khao San – it emphatically spills out into the surrounding **Banglamphu area** where you'll find slightly cheaper eateries, night spots and better value guesthouses. If you want to immerse yourself in some culture and expel that murky hangover from your thumping head, travel a little north to **Ayutthaya** and check out some historic temples after your Khao San experience.

Main backpacker area – Khao San Road & the surrounding Banglamphu area

Highlights – Khao San Road. Cheap accommodation. Shopping; markets & MBK centre. Bargain street food, restaurants, pubs & clubs. Numerous daytrips including; the floating market, the Grand Palace, Tiger Temple & others further afield such as the Kwai River Bridge

CHIANG MAI... *The trekking capital*

Thailand's second largest city is arguably Thailand's cheapest city boasting delicious Burmese-style cuisine, plenty of cheap accommodation and charming traditional temples. Chiang Mai is a true cultural experience where most visitors prolong their stay to take a short course in **Thai cookery** or **traditional massage**. A rummage around Chiang Mai's bustling **Night Bazaar** is a must while you're here. There's also some top quality **Muay Thai** not to be missed where you can cheer on Thai and fellow westerners in an electric filled atmosphere – knockouts are common! While Chiang Mai makes culture bearable and almost enjoyable, it's perhaps best known as the hub of the trekking industry – you'll hear travellers talking about these famous **jungle treks** all over Asia. You can give your adrenaline glands a workout at the **jungle bungy jump** which dangles you over a refreshing cool lake – www.junglebungy.com. Popular daytrips include **Chiang Rai** and the **Golden Triangle**.

Jungle Treks...

This is Chiang Mai's most popular activity. Two and three-day treks are great value offering a fantastic opportunity to visit remote minority villages and explore pristine forests. As well as trekking, you'll ride elephants through the jungle and navigate fast flowing rivers on home-made bamboo rafts! Opt for the 3-day/2-night trek to get the best value for money.

Guesthouse accommodation is spread all over the city and touts usually wait at the bus and train stations. The **Royal Guest House** offers the cheapest accommodation with double rooms from an unbelievable 150BHT – that's about three quid! You can book everything from treks to bungy jumps in this welcoming guesthouse. The cheapest way to get to Chiang Mai is aboard the overnight train from Bangkok – the overhead sleeping compartments are the cheapest *(and hottest!)* and tickets can be purchased practically anywhere along Khao San Road!

Chiang Mai ➔ Laos: From Chiang Mai, most make their way to Luang Probang *(Laos)* via a scenic **slow-boat trip** down the Mekong River – it takes two days so stock up on beer/rum to pass the time and avoid over inflated prices on the boat! You'll also stopover in a very weird riverside town called **Pak Beng** – a truly memorable experience and not for all the right reasons! If you've got some spare time, make full use of your free visa entitlements and head northwest to the less-travelled adventure hippie town of **Pai** before heading back east to cross over the border into Laos.

Recommended guesthouse – Royal Guest House

Highlights – Trekking, jungle bungy jump, Thai cookery & traditional massage classes, Mekong slow boat *(to Laos)*, Muay Thai, Night Bazaar, daytrips, fantastic cuisine & budget lodgings

KOH CHANG... *The traveller's island*

This is the ultimate traveller's island and my favourite place in Thailand and it's only half-a-day's journey east of Bangkok. Despite being earmarked for luxury developed, for now Koh Chang still retains all the hallmarks of a true backpacker's retreat; its laidback, low-key and friendly but most importantly it's rustic and cheap where you'll find some of Thailand's cheapest beachfront sleeps and local top-notch grub – it's what Samui used to be like in the 1980s! Upmarket developments are starting to spring up but these are concentrated along the west coast close to the main piers. On the whole it remains largely undeveloped – especially compared to Thailand's southern hotspots.

Lonely Beach: this is the traveller's hub and one of the least developed 'beachside-towns' that attracts a young, less-groomed crowd and you won't need a diving-licence to hold a conversation! The town's relaxed and friendly atmosphere rubs-off on everyone and it's a great place to get chatting to locals and travellers over a chang or two. Retro wooden-style bars and rustic restaurants are scattered around the beach and along unpaved roads – the **Tree House**, stretching over the water, is a popular restaurant/drinking hole. If you managed to peel yourself away from the beach and out of the laidback bars, trek inland through virgin jungle to discover mountainous waterfalls and absorb spectacular coastal views or hire a motorbike and explore the road that loops the island.

Another popular destination is **Long Beach** on the east coast – it's a bit of a mission to get here but it's more undeveloped and isolated than Lonely Beach. Check out the **New Tree House** and become part of 'the tribe'! Heading back towards Bangkok? Why not check out the charming and less-travelled tropical island of **Koh Samet** on the way. Otherwise, head over the border to Siem Reap in Cambodia and check out the majestic Angkor Wat for a cultural awakening.

Main backpacker area – Lonely Beach. Lost Beach is a very quiet backpacker alternative

Highlights – Lazy days, the chilled-out atmosphere, retro-bars, cheap food, beer & beach huts!

THE SOUTHERN ISLANDS... *Thailand's premier hotspot!*

Travellers flock here in search of paradise and these renowned tropical islands won't disappoint. The Gulf Coast Islands – Koh Toa, Koh Pha-Ngan & Koh Samui – are extremely popular with sun-worshippers, beach lovers, divers and party-goers alike. On the Andaman Coast, energetic Phi Phi & laidback Koh Lanta are the backpacker's choice. They're all easily accessible from Bangkok – the most popular way to reach them is via the combined 'overnight bus & morning ferry ticket'. This can be bought virtually anywhere along Khao San. Any respectable itinerary will feature these dreamy islands, sun drenched beaches and world-class dive sites – dedicate at <u>least</u> 2 weeks:

KOH SAMUI... *The resort island!*

Koh Samui is a well established and extremely popular tropical beauty boasting gorgeous beaches, a happening nightlife, great shops and fantastic restaurants. While it's hard to spot other backpackers through the hoards of package-holidaymakers and despite all of those footprints in the sand, Samui still has some magic of its own. It's true to say that cheap backpacker-orientated digs are becoming increasingly hard to find, especially next to the main beaches, and

> **The airport...** *Fly or 'bus it'?*
>
> Samui's busy little airport offers reasonable and convenient links to Bangkok & Phuket. However, even if you're short on time, the popular 'overnight VIP bus & ferry' remains the shoestringers choice – at around 600BHT it's a lot cheaper and you'll save on a night's accommodation!

budget travellers are slowly being priced-out. That said, Koh Samui is an ideal first destination after Bangkok and a chance to flop on the beach before raving the night away on Koh Pha-Ngan!

Chewang Beach is the place to be on Koh Samui – it's the most developed area where you can eat, drink and beach it up with the crowds – check out the **Green Mango, ICE bar** and the **Reggae Bar** for the late night drunken antics! Above all, Koh Samui is a unique dining experience where you can sample some of the tastiest seafood in attractive yet rustic beachfront restaurants. **Hat Lamai,** a few clicks south of Chewang, is a good alternative if you can't find any cheap lodgings.

Main backpacker area – Chewang Beach & Lamai

Highlights – Seafood on the beach, Muay Thai, jungle trekking, kayaking, Ice-Bar & nightlife!

KOH PHA-NGAN... <u>*THE*</u> *party island*

Three words: **Full - Moon - Party**! Drink copious amounts of rum from buckets, experiment with body paint, stagger around shitfaced and dance the night away on Thailand's premier tropical party island. **Haad Rin** is home to the original **Full Moon Party** where 10,000+ travellers flock to the island and embark on the ultimate party pilgrimage. It's definitely not a great place for recovering alcoholics but a great opportunity for all you hardcore party-goers to bang out a few shapes on the beach – stock up on headaches tablets if you intend to sober up at any point! Get there a few days in advance as accommodation fills up pretty quick and the prices reflect the size of the moon! While the fun happens on the beautiful *(although littered after full-moon)* **Sunrise Beach**, try and stay in **Sunset Beach.** It's only a 5min walk and the accommodation's not only cheaper but quieter!

If it's all too much for you, hop on a taxi-boat and go around to **Haad Yuan** where you'll discover a beautiful secluded bay and great accommodation that's cheaper than Sunrise and Sunset Beaches – check out **Barcelona, Big Blue** and **Bamboo Huts.** If you stay in Haad Yuan make sure you check out **Eden Bar** – it's a relaxed chilled-out bar tucked away on the hilltop overlooking the bay *(it's got twister on the floor that I helped to paint!).* If you can't make it for the monthly Full Moon Party don't despair, every night's a party night and there are half-moon parties and black-moon parties to keep you in the party mood throughout the month. You'll find plenty of TV-restaurants showing films to 'lounge around in' during the day to soothe your throbbing head!

All partied out...? There's more than just drinking and despite its party image, this is an island of two faces. If you're party shy or just too hung over for more indulgence, Koh Pha-Ngan is a beautiful island to explore. So don't be put off by the drunken madness that engulfs the south of the island, head up the east coast by **'taxi-boat'** and check out the many gorgeous secluded bays – head towards **Thong Nai Pan Noi** *(northeast coast)* where you can stay at a great low-key backpacker resort called **Star Huts**. It's possible to spend an entire day kayaking from bay-to-bay enjoying the island's northern isolated beaches away from the mainstream party-goers!

Main backpacker area – Haad Rin: Sunset beach is quieter and slightly cheaper than Sunrise Beach! Star huts is a low-key backpackers resort along the northeast of the island

Highlights – Full-Moon-Party, buckets, nightlife & hangovers! TV-restaurants, kayaking, beaches & secluded-bays

KOH TOA... *The diver's island*

Arguably one of Thailand's most beautiful islands, Koh Toa boasts postcard perfect white-sand beaches and translucent tropical waters. Travellers flock here to explore life beneath the waves and take advantage of the bargain **top-notch diving**. Most travellers tend to stay on the west side of the island predominantly in **Sairre Beach** where you'll find a good selection of beachfront restaurants and cheap lodgings. Bear in mind that Koh Toa is a diver's island, so don't expect the same banging nightlife here as you'll find on its lively neighbouring islands! The eastside is less developed and makes a great retreat if you want to 'get away from it all' – **Tanote Bay,** accessible by 'taxi-truck', is a well preserved and low-key secluded bay with excellent snorkelling.

Diving: This is SE Asia's premier diving spot and it's brimming with decent and affordable diving complexes – if diving's on your itinerary you simply cannot afford to miss out on Koh Toa. You'll get a lot for your pound here – it's amongst the cheapest place to dive in the world, which is surprising when you consider its spectacular setting. You'll find a concentration of diving resorts on the southwest and west side of the island offering the full range courses from fun-dives and discovery-dives to 4-day open-water and dive master courses *(PADI & SSI)*. Accommodation is usually free or at least discounted if you're diving – some even throw in free breakfast and meals!

If you're not taking the plunge: If you're not interested in diving, Koh Toa should still be high on your 'to-do-list'. It can be a little tricky to find accommodation if you're not diving but there are a number of reasonably priced beach huts that aren't linked with any diving resorts such as **SB Cabanas** *(Sairre Beach)*. While the others are out on the boats exploring the underwater world, hop on a ridiculously cheap motorbike and explore the rugged centre of the island, take a daytrip to the spectacular **Nang Yuan Island** – the only tri-beach in the world – or get '**tan**tastic' and relax on idyllic beaches with a refreshing beer or ten. Be warned though, motorbike accidents are common, especially when you see the mountainous road conditions, so be careful – it can be very harmful to you and your budget! Accommodation fills up very quickly before and after the Full-Moon-Party on Koh Pha-Ngan.

Main backpacker area – Backpackers & divers swarm around Sairre Beach *(the west side)*

Highlights – Diving & snorkelling, beaches, Nang Yang Island, beachside restaurants & BBQs

PHI PHI... *The beach from 'The Beach'!*

Koh Phi Phi Don is one of Thailand's well discovered beauties where stunning limestone cliffs, crystal clear water and powder sand beaches will leave you speechless. To top it off, this compact stunner boasts an energetic nightlife that's complemented by a wealth of worthwhile activities including; world-class **diving** *(comparable to that found on Koh Toa)*, great **snorkelling**, dare-devil **cliff jumping** and relaxing **sea kayaking**. You can even step into the ring and have a go at some **Muay Thai** – the **Reggae Bar** offers you the chance to test out your moves with other westerners – a great bit of drunken fun with

Maya Beach daytrips...

This is what's caused Phi Phi's recent boom in tourism. Everyone's seen the film 'The Beach', now here's your chance to make your own foot prints next to Leonardo De Caprio's on **Maya Beach**! Tours can be booked from virtually every Thai on the island so hunt around for a good deal and haggle! The Sunset Longboat Tour is your best bet and should set you back around 600BHT.

your mates! As well as the bruises, win, lose or draw, you'll be rewarded with a free bucket of rum!

Development here has been astronomical and there's no denying that the island is overpriced – small scale resorts and hotels are beginning to dominate but don't let that put you off, there's still a strong backpacker scene and a fair amount of cheap accommodation in the form of beach huts, guesthouses and even dorms if you look around. Most bars offer 2-4-1 *(although still overpriced)* buckets and free BBQ food. Even the 7-Elevens have inflated their prices *(probably to finance the air-con!)* so buy water, alcohol and snacks at cheaper rates from the numerous <u>local</u> shops. Many travellers buy a couple of bottles of Chang from local shops and wander around the narrow streets and linger on the beach before hitting the 'clubs' later on – it's sociable and cheap!

Main backpacker area – Anywhere! Most of the cheaper accommodation is located just before the main beach *(the furthest point from the pier where they drop you off!)*

Highlights – Maya Beach daytrip, snorkelling & diving, cliff jumping, Muay Thai in the Reggae Bar, melting on the beach & the nightlife

KRABI... *The climbing Mecca*

Ok, so it's not one of the Southern Islands but it's a popular southern destination. Backpackers flock here in pursuit of the many sweaty outdoor activities so bring a lot of excess energy and a sense of adventure! Primarily, Krabi is a **climbing Mecca** where rock climbers from every corner of the globe congregate to test their nerve and endurance on some of the world's most picturesque limestone climbs. Extreme novices and hardcore cliff hangers are both equally welcome – there are simply hundreds of climbs, catering for all abilities. Guides and equipment can be hired out, usually on a half-day basis. If you're a complete novice don't worry, there are a number of climbing schools with patient and friendly guides. Rewarding climbs are complemented by stunning views over dense jungle, postcard-perfect beaches and majestic cliffs at the summit. Exploring the rugged bays by sea kayak is another popular past time. Krabi is often used as a jumping-off point to **Malaysia**, **Phi Phi** and **Koh Lanta**.

Krabi town itself isn't worth lingering around in for any amount of time – most people head straight to Krabi's popular mainland beaches of **Ao Nang**, **Hat Ton Sai** and **Hat Rai Leh**. **Hat Ton Sai** is surrounded by dramatic picturesque karst formations and has emerged as the prominent climber's hangout – it's also the cheapest and least developed beach on Krabi's mainland. Here you'll find a young laidback crowd and an energetic nightlife. Hat Rai Leh also boasts some decent climbing and a better beach but it's a very pricey destination – East Rai Leh is more affordable where you'll find shoe-string lodgings next to a muddy mangrove beach!

Main backpacker area – Shoe-string climbers congregate in Hat Ton Sai & East Rai Leh

Highlights – Rock climbing, sea kayaking, beaches & decent transport links

While most of Thailand is equally affordable and enjoyable, catering for a range of budgets and interests, there are a few places that as a budget backpacker you should steer clear of. By all means they're popular in their own right but for travellers there are far better places to spend your precious time and small budget! Try and avoid these two classic offenders:

PHUKET... *The package-holiday resort*

A very popular and well established resort but you'll find it very hard to spot other backpackers through the hoards of package-holidaymakers. A lot of commercial holidays fly direct from Europe to Phuket so there's a mass of sun-deprived families on the typical 'two week package-holiday' in the sun. **This is not Thailand** – it's dominated by large scale 'Spanish resort-style hotels' and the beaches are overrun with deckchairs and pestering beach touts. Genuine culture's long been eroded by mass tourism and the menus have been altered to western tastes. As far as backpackers are concerned, it's not a great place and because it's tailored to fatter wallets it's more expensive than elsewhere. Most travellers avoid it.

Phuket can, however, be the perfect cure for a spot of homesickness where you'll find an array of familiar homely foods and better quality accommodation – Swedish and Norwegians will feel particularly at home as some parts of Phuket are literally like a 'little Scandinavia' with a host of Nordic restaurants and menus. You can utilise this place as a jumping-off point to Phi Phi although it's easy to get to from pretty much anywhere in Southern Thailand! If you were just looking for somewhere in Southern Thailand to stay before hopping across the border into Malaysia, check out **Krabi** *(and Rai Leh)* where you can indulge in some great outdoor activities or chill out in laidback **Koh Lanta**. Essentially, this place is OK for a short luxury break in the sun. As far as backpackers are concerned – **Phuket...** *Fuck it!*

PATTAYA... *The sleazy run-down resort*

A very tacky and sleazy resort which really springs into life after sundown. Any genuine culture and traditional has been eclipsed by large-scale hotels and foreign investment. If you're a bit of a sex-pest or fancy yourself as a hardcore womaniser, like my good friend Kyle 'Maverick' Merryweather, look no further... Pattaya has more than its fair share of whorehouses and cringe worthy Go Go bars attracting an older, seedier and more affluent clientele! It's sad fact that the average foreigner here – besides those on the typical package-holiday – is essentially, a self-exiled, twice divorced, alcohol dependent, middle-aged, chunky balding man with a very young Asian girl hanging off his arm – I'll see you there in a few years then lads! If it was a short Thai holiday you were after, I'd suggest more desirable islands like Phuket and Koh Samui!

If you can turn a blind eye to the after-dark sleaze, there's a half-decent beach and some tasty tourist-orientated restaurants although it's fair to say that Thailand offers sooooo much more. If you were thinking of coming here to break up the trip from Bangkok to Koh Chang, you needn't bother – the journey lasts less than half-a-day. If it's the case that you've just got some time leftover, and you want to escape Bangkok for a few days before you fly elsewhere, consider better options that are equally close to the bustling capital such as the beautiful and quaint island of **Koh Samet** or go on a daytrip to the **Kanchanaburi** and the **River Kwai** *(the Death Railway Bridge)*.

LAOS

UP & COMING

Kick back and relax. Welcome to SE Asia's most laidback country. As you slip across the border from its neighbours, you leave behind the smog of the chaotic urban sprawls and intense commercialisation to embrace quaint towns, dramatic landscapes and rustic charm. The rugged terrain of emerald mountains and immense limestone peaks dominate the North of the country. This is where you'll find the picturesque riverside-town of Luang Prabang and, more importantly, the exciting traveller's town of Vang Vieng – relax in TV-restaurants, socialise in cheap bars and

embark on the most epic aquatic bar crawl, you simply won't want to leave! In the South, where the terrain levels out, off-the-beaten track adventures can be found. Few make it as far as Si Phan Don, but for those who do, 100's of undeveloped inland-islands and pods of freshwater dolphins await. Getting around the country can be a slow and painstaking affair – busses are irregular, boats are slow and infrastructure is generally poorer than elsewhere. However, this just adds to the charm of this 'up and coming' country, providing a welcoming escape from the rest of 'main-stream' SE Asia'. Get there quick though. While Laos' a relatively new kid on the block, it's playing a rapid game of catch-up with Thailand so it's getting more expensive by the day.

MINI GUIDE

Essentially there are three main places where backpackers tend to go in Laos, and you can follow a nice simple linear route through this 'up and coming' country. While you don't need more than 2 weeks to see the majority of Laos' 'best bits', more and more people find themselves staying here a lot longer – you only need to visit Vang Vieng to see why:

(Thailand➔) Luang Prabang ➔ Vang Vieng ➔ Vientiane *(➔ Vietnam)*

LUANG PRABANG... *The cultural capital*

Dose up on some culture in this enchanting photogenic town – Luang Prabang has an incredible collection of French colonial architecture framed by emerald-green mountains. In 1995, the 'city' was placed on the UNESCO World Heritage List and this once sleepy riverside town has been sensitively restored. Despite a boom in tourism, development has been strictly regulated and the town has retained its welcoming charm and distinct historic character. There's a host of pleasant cafés where you can relax, sample the local delicacies and soak up the laidback atmosphere. If you're feeling more active, **cycling** is one of the most popular ways to take in the sights of Luang Prabang – bikes can be rented from numerous guesthouses and shops. Despite its beauty, there's a lot more to do in Luang Probang than just take pictures and admire the architecture! For a start you've got **Phousy Market** *(a few kms south of the town centre)* and the **Hmong Night Market** *(along the main street – Sisavangvong)* to browse around. A few restaurants run half-day **cooking courses** where you can learn to rustle up some local dishes and add to your culinary portfolio and make this town the complete playground for culture vultures.

If you're fed up with culture jump on a tuk-tuk and check out the nearby **lagoons** and **waterfalls** – **Tat Kuang Si**. This is a beautiful spot featuring a multi-tiered waterfall cascading over limestone formations to form a series of turquoise-green pools – you can swim in most of them and you'll find a couple of rope-swings and jumps. Trips are advertised on tuk-tuks and by touts, just make sure you haggle – the bigger your group the more bargaining power you'll have! Another popular excursion, although slightly culture orientated, is 25km up the river to the caves at **Pak Ou** – the **Buddha Cave** is perhaps the most famous boasting an eerie collection of 'unwanted' Buddha images. Trips by boat can be arranged through most guesthouses. The only downside to this town is the above average cost of accommodation – you can still find a number of budget orientated guesthouses that offer basic rooms but you'll have to hunt around a bit.

Highlights – Waterfall daytrips, cycling, cooking courses, markets & the colonial architecture

VANG VIENG... *The laidback traveller's town*

Nestled on the Nam Song River and tucked away amid stunning limestone peaks, this is the adventure capital and there's plenty to keep you here in Laos' outdoor playground for a very, very long time – this is why you come to Laos! Most importantly, it's home of the legendary **tubing** *(see text box opposite)* where you can embark on a unique aquatic bar crawl! Accidents are common – health & safety standards either don't exist or not enforced, which is good because you'd never see anything this crazy or fun back at home – just exercise a little care when you're swinging legless from the riverbanks! It takes two hours to float non-stop down the river but

> ### Tubing... *the ultimate bar-crawl!*
> This is the number one reason to go to Laos and you'll hear travellers talking about it all over Asia! Grab yourself an inner-tube, hop on a tuk-tuk to get upstream and float down the river for the ultimate 'wet' bar-crawl – let the river take you between numerous riverside-bars and make a drunken splash in the river from elevate bamboo platforms, rope-swings and zip-lines in between guzzling bottles of beer Laos! No beer, no swing!

allow at least four hours – it all depends how many bars you stop off at and how wasted you get en-route!

Kayaking is another popular pursuit in Vang Vieng. While bog standard daytrips will take you down a few rapids and include visits to villages and caves, undoubtedly the best option is the kayak trip down to Vientiane! Prices hover around US$20 but have been steadily increasing. Another popular and worthwhile activity is **caving** in the numerous caves around Vang Vieng. **Tham Jang** and **Tham Phu Kham** are two popular caves but you'll get clued up on them when you get to Vang Vieng. A few of the caves have refreshing lagoons to cool off in as well. Most caves can be easily reached by bicycle or motorbike. Set off early to make the most of the daylight but you'll need to pack a torch as little light penetrates deep inside these extensive caves. There always touts trying to make a few quid and many caves now have an 'admission-fee' – so bring a wedge of low denomination notes, you're haggling head and a sense of humour!

When you're not getting wet down the river risking life, limb and a whooping great hangover, you can laze in the 'TV-restaurants' and watch endless showings of Friends and the Simpsons while you eat and drink to your heart's content! A lot of travellers come here in search of the **'happy menu'** – a compilation of drugs, food and drink! Depending on the attitude of local authorities – they go through phases of being ultra strict and clamp down on this – you can choose anything from weed or mushroom pizzas and shroom-shakes to regular joints and standard boxes of magic mushrooms, just ask for the 'happy menu'! As well as the bars that line the main dusty street, there's a network of bamboo bridges linking numerous laidback riverside bars. Travellers either love or loathe this incredible place and it's fair to say that most love it – you'll come across plenty of 'monged-out' travellers who've been here for weeks and have no real intention of leaving!

Main backpacker area – Anywhere. Due to its small size you're never far from the action packed river and the main strip of bars and cafés

Highlights – Tubing! Kayaking, caving and cycling. The chilled-out atmosphere, retro bars, back-to-back showings of Friends and The Simpsons & the famous 'Happy Menu'!

VIENTIANE... *The capital*

In truth there's not a lot to do in Laos' capital! Most people tend to stay a day or so on their way to and from Thailand. There are a few worthwhile sights including the golden **Pha That Luang** *(the 'Great Sacred Stupa' aka a 45m, 24ct Buddha)*, **Wat Si Saket** *(a Buddhist Temple)*, and **Patuxaim** *(the 'Victory Gate' monument)*. **Massages** and **public swimming pools** ease the boredom should you find yourself here for any prolonged period of time! There's also the **National Museum** here and the peaceful **Buddha Park** *(Xieng Khuan)* if you want to dabble in some history and culture. Foreigners can even meditate at **Wat Sok Pa Luang** in sessions that run from 16:00 until 17:30!

You'll find a small scattering of ATMs here so stock up on funds and cash in any traveller's cheques if you're heading north into the country where cashpoints and services are scarce. Something that might tempt you to stay around longer is the **Beer Laos factory tour**. Not so much of a tour, this is basically a quick whip around the distillery followed by an afternoon of *(practically free)* drinking! Budget accommodation is scarce and spread across the city so hunt around. **Cooking classes** can be arranged at the popular **Thongbay Guesthouse** – although the sleeping facilities here have mixed reviews and it's located a fair distance from the centre of town!

Moving on: You'll find good links to Vietnam and popular direct busses to Hanoi – don't expect any kind of luxury though, busses are typically rattling old bangers packed to the limit with anything from chickens to sacks of coal! Journeys are long and tedious but are cheap and rustic – don't be fooled by the touts who offer to pre-book you accommodation at inflated prices! Thailand's within touching distance across the **Thai-Lao Friendship Bridge** 20km southeast of Vientiane – regular busses and tuk-tuks will take you there. The border's open between 06:00 and 22:00 and visas are issued on arrival in both countries. Vang Vieng is a short bus journey north.

Highlights – Beer Laos factory tour, the ATM, meditation, transport links & the road out!

Off-the-beaten track... *Spice things up a bit!*

There's a great deal of less-travelled places scattered throughout this rustic country and while breakdowns, delays, cramped conditions and unexpected detours are a prominent feature of transport in Laos, this is also its great appeal! The country's tourist infrastructure is slowly catching up with Thailand's but for now these features help keep the less-travelled places off of the-well-trodden route and reward those who exert that extra energy with some enjoyable memories. There's a tonne of well-hidden treasures but to help you along the way, check out these:

MUANG SING... *Rustic treks & ethnic minorities*

Head to the ethnically diverse town of **Muang Sing** for some low-key visits to authentic **Akha villages** or treks in the lush **Nam Ha National Protected Area**. It's your best opportunity to visit ethnic minorities on a socially and environmentally low-impact tour. One to three/day guided treks can be organised through the **Guide Services Office** – located in a wooden building just off the main street – and are good value at around US$15 per day *(this includes food, water, accommodation and guide!)*.

SI PHAN DON... *Four thousand islands & rare dolphins!*

This is where the Mekong River fans out to form a picturesque and idyllic network of channels, islands, and sandbars. Here you'll witness true riverside living – water buffalo wade in the shallows next to traditional fishermen, women wash clothes just-off the riverbank while their children splash around and longtail-boats regularly trundle back and forth from the mainland. The thought of 4,000 or so islands 'inland' is intriguing enough but when it's associated with the resident and **rare Irrawaddy dolphins**, a trip here can turn into a mini-pilgrimage! Apparently you have a better chance to see the dolphins during the dry season, either early or late in the day – half-daytrips to the **sandbar viewing area** can be organised from the 'main islands'...

Don Khong & Don Det: most people stay on these popular islands – they're largest and most populous of the islands and have experienced a recent boom in tourism – and although they lack the magical ambience, peaceful silence and calming scenery of the smaller islands, they're a good base to begin your unique 'inland-island-hopping adventure'! Make sure you cycle around these 'main-islands' – you'll go through scenic rice fields and authentic local villages and past some historic sites and old temples. Only a handful of the

> ### Border crossing...
> You can head south into Cambodia from here – although this in not an official border crossing it's popular and you'll probably have to haggle over an imaginative 'entrance-fee' with guards – just be calm and patient!

islands have electricity, although this 'basic-utility' is spreading throughout the isles and is *slowly* eroding the peaceful charm and tranquillity – hopefully development will be slow!

Other less-travelled places you may want to check out include:

o **Wat Phu Champasak:** If you're heading to Si Phan Don, you may as well spend a day here for some impressive archaeological sites and decent views overlooking the Mekong Valley

o **Vieng Xai:** Spend a few quiet days in this peaceful town and explore the *(Pathet Lao)* caves that are dotted throughout this narrow valley of limestone peaks. Head to the **Kaysone Phom Vihan Memorial Tour Cave Office** to arrange tours of these historically significant caves – they served as innovative homes and shelters for the Pathet Lao leaders during a brutal war. Check out the **Plain of Jars** on your way here.

VIETNAM

UNDERRATED

AT A GLANCE

Capital – Hanoi

Population – 83 million

Language(s) – Vietnamese

Currency – Dong (VND) & US$

ATMs – In all medium sized towns

Climate – Tropical

Best time to go – December - April for the South

May - October for the North

Time zone – GMT +7hours

Suggested daily budget – 300K VND / US$15–20

Slightly more in HCMC

Suggested time – 2-3 weeks

Visas – must be arranged in advanced for most nationalities. A few countries get a 15-day visa waiver on arrival *(e.g. Scandinavia)*

Underrated barren beaches, the world's cheapest beer, bowls of steaming noodle-soup and lashings of historic war remnants are just a few reasons to explore this fascinating and equally diverse country. Sometimes neglected, Vietnam should feature strongly on any credible itinerary. The

friendly South draws in curious travellers where the hustle and bustle of Saigon makes a great base to explore the lush waterways of the Mekong Delta. The towns south of the DMZ will certainly tempt you to stay a lot longer than you had expected – feast on some of Asia's best dishes in the food capital of Hué, get tantastic on the golden sands of China Beach and get 'suited & booted' and enjoy fresh beer in the quaint riverside towns. While the bustling North, especially chaotic Hanoi, can be a little overwhelming and raw in places, embrace it and you'll be richly rewarded. While the northern folk may appear a bit fiery, even the most stern faced marker vendor will crack a smile if you're friendly, joke and laugh with them. From the stunning karst formations of Ha Long Bay to the cool trekking capital of Sapa there's plenty to make a trip up north well-worthwhile. Essentially, Vietnam's got **a lot** to offer, and for some reason, it doesn't get enough recognition. Even your money goes far here and there's plenty of scope to get off-the-beaten track where you'll meet few westerners and have some memorable experiences from chatting with locals over 12p jugs of beer in 'roadside-bars' to sampling regional delicacies with enthusiastic vendors in markets. To make the most of this incredible country, expect the unexpected and dedicate at least 2 weeks... you won't be disappointed!

Follow the war... *Must see 'highlights'*

The American War *(the Vietnam War to most of us)* had a dramatic impact on the lives of millions and it shaped the Vietnam we know today. It's been the subject of countless films and books – most financed, directed and written by US companies – and now you can follow the footsteps of the soldiers, journalists, politicians and civilians and explore the stories of a war torn generation first-hand. Anyone who's interested in this war should check these out:

Cu Chi Tunnels – explore and admire a feat of infrastructural ingenuity and try to grasp what it would have been like to live underground for countless days. Built to evade US forces, this incredible and elaborate tunnel network, located just 30km from Saigon, represents the sheer determination and innovation of the northern army

War Remnants Museum – rarely do you get the opportunity to hear the victims of US military action tell their own story. This museum documents the US atrocities during the war through photos and innovative displays. US armoured vehicles, artillery, bombs and infantry weapons are on display outside. This museum doesn't beat around the bush and it's hard hitting

China Beach – laze away the day on this beautiful beach and try to imagine the scores of American soldiers that used this beach for some much needed R&R

DMZ – The Demilitarised Zone was the no-man's land dividing the North and South. Ironically from 1954, it quickly became the one of the most heavily militarised zones in the world! Your best bet is to get a motorbike tour *(from Dong Ha)* so you can get stuck in off-the-beaten-track. Keep your eyes peeled for US tanks, bunkers and bomb craters

Ho Chi Minh Trail – this was the supply route for the Northern Army and was used to move men and munitions undetected

Vinh Moc Tunnels – these are the real deal. These tunnels have remained largely unchanged and haven't been enlarged for tourists like the Cu Chi Tunnels down south

My Lai – the small sub-districts around Quang Ngai were the site of the most horrific war crimes committed by US forces. Hundreds of villagers, who were believed to be helping the VC, were mowed down by machine gun fire from helicopter gunships, blown-up by hand grenades and rounded up to be raped and executed. Fleeing villagers, women and children included, were shot and bayoneted, livestock was slaughtered and buildings were burnt to the ground to 'teach the villagers a lesson' and set an example. The Son My Memorial stands as a testament to those who were brutally murdered.

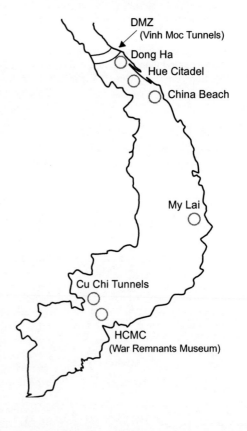

Vietnam's slender figure ensures that most travellers pursue a logical linear route from North to South i.e. Hanoi to Saigon *(or vice-versa)*. This is a fascinating and varied trail where you'll notice distinct cultural shifts as you head south from Hanoi. There's a lot to do, see and experience in Vietnam – here's a selection of the 'best bits':

(Laos ➔) Hanoi ➔ Hué ➔ Hoi An ➔ Nha Trang ➔ Dalat ➔ Saigon *(➔ Cambodia)*

HANOI... *The capital*

Vietnams bustling capital is swarming with more motorbikes than you can shake a stick at – the traffic's absolutely **mental**! Compared to most cities throughout Vietnam, Hanoi's a new kid on the block in terms of tourism but the **Old Quarter** caters exceptionally well for budget backpackers. While visitors flood here to soak up the atmosphere, browse the museums, chill-out in the cafés and sample the nightlife, most come here for **Ha Long Bay**.

Ha Long Bay: This picturesque bay is the natural wonder of Vietnam – picture 3,000 plus rugged limestone crops rising from the emerald waters of the Gulf of Tonkin. Breath taking views are combined with dozens of idyllic beaches to be worshipped and intriguing caves to be explored. Tours can be booked from guesthouses and cafés in Hanoi and are very reasonably priced starting from as little as US$15-US$25 per person for a daytrip. Ideally though, you want to buy onto a small-group tour on which you can sleep out on a boat in the bay – these will cost anywhere up to US$75 but are highly recommended. Most tours include transfers from Hanoi, decent meals, onboard accommodation and activities such as fishing, island hikes and kayaking. In the evening you can get merry, jump off the boat and swim amongst the glowing phytoplankton. The weather here can be unpredictable and it's common for fog to reduce visibility.

If the pace of life is too fast and the traffic too much, and you want to explore more of Northern Vietnam, take a few days off and head to **Sapa** on the overnight train. Unofficially the capital of the northwest hill-tribe region, Sapa is a great base for **hiking** and **biking** but it's also a lot cooler so be prepared and invest in a jacket. Before you leave Hanoi, make sure you check out the ancient art of water puppetry and watch a show for some light entertainment over a few cold beers at the **Municipal Water Puppet Theatre**!

Main backpacker area – The Old Quarter

Highlights – Ha Long Bay overnight tours, water puppet shows, Sapa, the bustling atmosphere & colonial architecture

DONG HA... *Explore the DMZ*

There's only one reason why this otherwise dreary town get's a mention in this book and that's the **DMZ Café** and its fantastic **personalised tours** of the DMZ – the hostel itself isn't fantastic but it's cheap and cheerful in true backpacker fashion. The owner, **Mr Tinh**, is a fantastic guy and he'll give you all the information and contacts that you'll need.

Most guidebooks advise you to stay in Hué and hop on an organised tour from there, but I

The DMZ tour... *Highlights*

Make sure you include these on your personalised tour, although I'm sure your driver will be keen to show you them all anyway:

o   **Vinh Moc Tunnels**
o   **Doc Mieu Base**
o   **Truong Son National Cemetery**
o   **Con Thien Firebase**
o   **Ho Chi Minh Trail**

recommend staying in Dong Ha for one night and arranging a personalised motorbike tour – you'll see a lot more. While the tourists from Hué are confined to a cramped bus, a rambling commentator with a microphone, an early start and a long trip, the DMZ café's personalised tours take you off-the-beaten track and right into the heart of the DMZ on the back of a nippy motorbike – you get your own driver 'aka tour-guide' for the best local knowledge about the sites. The highlight of the tour is undoubtedly the **Vinh Moc Tunnels** – these are more genuine than their counterparts down south, the Cu Chi tunnels – but there's a lot more to see *(see box for highlights)*. Most tours end with an hour or so on **Cua Tung Beach**. Tours can be booked through the DMZ Café with the guidance of the ever helpful Mr Tinh. They're great value for money and worth a night in Dong Ha. Prices are negotiable but usually cost around **US$15 per person** – the larger your group, the more bargaining power you'll have!

Main backpacker hostel – DMZ Café

Highlights – Personalised DMZ tours & Mr Tinh!

HUÉ... *The food capital*

Hué has long been the cultural heartbeat of Vietnam and this culinary city is affectionately known as Vietnam's **food capital** – it's set many trends in Vietnamese cooking and you'll find a fantastic array of top-notch grub at rock bottom prices. Other worthwhile attractions include the splendid **Royal Tombs** of past emperors and the remains of the **ancient Citadel**. If you want some beach-time hire a motorbike and head to the undeveloped **Thuan An Beach** – it's only 15km north of the city.

Hué lies along either side of the Perfume River. While the north-side boasts the ancient Citadel, it's the south-side where you'll find most of the backpacker orientated facilities, budget accommodation and lively bars. Most can be found in the narrow alley off **Đ Le Loi** – point it out to a motor-bike taxi and they'll know where the backpackers go! The **DMZ Bar & Café** and **Bar Why Not** are popular backpacker Watering holes.

Main backpacker area – Budget hotels can be found in the East Đ Le Loi Area

Highlights – Citadel, divine cuisine, architecture, Royal Tombs & Thuan An Beach

HOI AN... *Get suited & booted on a budget!*

This enchanting riverside town is the highlight for many travellers during their time in Vietnam. Hoi An, characterised by cobbled streets and quaint historic buildings, effortlessly oozes charm and culture from every orifice – it's a dream for any snap-happy travel photographer. It's one spot definitely worth lingering in! Famous for the hoards of **tailors**, in terms of price, Hoi An is probably the best place in the world to kit yourself out with a snug fitting top quality tailored suit. You can get anything from standard suits and tailored silk shirts to handmade shoes and humorous Dumb & Dumber-style suits! The quality ranges from poor to excellent so hunt around and get recommendations from other travellers. Haggling is the name of the game here so hone your bargaining skills and trash out some good deals! After browsing the tailors' shops settle down in one of the many riverside cafés and enjoy as much cheap **fresh beer** as you can handle – you'll find a number of lively late-night bars and clubs both sides of the river if you last that long!

You'll also find some good food in Hoi An in a selection of decent restaurants. By far the cheapest place to eat is the 'food-market' that's located by the riverside, not far from the old market – it's a collection of busy, semi-permanent rival street-kitchens and wooden benches under tarpaulin – you'll find a host of great cheap dishes and some equally cheap fresh-beer to wash it down with. You can learn how to rustle up some of these Vietnamese dishes in a **cooking class** – many of the most popular cafés offer classes where you're taught how to cook a selection of traditional dishes. **Red Bridge** – www.visithoian.com – offers some of the best, although the most expensive, courses staring at US$25. If you fancy a daytrip check out the nearby **MySon Temples, Marble Mountains** or sandy expanse of **China Beach** – all are easily accessible by a hired motorbike. There are more hotels than guesthouses but cheap sleeps can be found if you hunt around and haggle a bit!

Main backpacker area – A few conveniently located budget hotels can be found around the old market. Alternatively, cheap accommodation can be found on the outskirts of town

Highlights – Tailors, nightlife, cooking classes, food & fresh beer, beautiful architecture, China Beach, Marble Mountains & MySon Temples

NHA TRANG... *The beach capital*

This resort town is rapidly developing and is a popular destination to stop and break up the long trip down Vietnam's coastline for some fun in the sun. Nha Trang boasts fantastic sandy beaches and the clear turquoise water ensures top quality **diving**. You'll find a mouth-watering selection of restaurants and cafés and there's plenty to keep you here for a good few days. The nightlife's not too shabby either with a concentration of lively bars hugging the roads immediately behind the main beachfront. It's a place to party, eat and relax – make sure you take advantage of the fantastic service on the main beach where you can enjoy massages, manicures, cold beers, lunches and much more under the sun! If you're feeling a bit adventurous there are **daytrips, fishing expeditions** and islands to explore. You may even run into the **Easy Rider Crew**, they'll organise personalised daytrips around Nha Trang and beyond on the back of classic motorcycles – although they're usually found roaming around in Dalat.

Main backpacker area – Cheaper accommodation can be found away from the beachfront along the main through road *(D Nguyen Thien Thuat)*

Highlights – Local seafood, diving & snorkelling, fishing, Easy Rider tours, island hopping daytrips, floating bar & nightlife

DALAT... *Highland retreat*

Only a handful of travellers venture to this refreshing hill-top retreat but it's a good side trip that'll break up the journey from Nha Trang to Saigon *(HCMC)*. Dalat's the perfect base to explore the mountains, waterfalls, villages and traditional industries of the temperate central highlands. While the sights of Dalat are fairly spread out and the terrain is hilly, don't despair, you'll probably bump into the **Easy Rider Crew** during your time here...

Easy Riders: This friendly, informal crew of freelance motorbike-guides are becoming famous among travellers who are looking for a unique alternative to the traditional daytrip. Travelling with the Easy Riders is a great way to explore this mountainous region – they'll create a personal itinerary for you and ensure that you see everything that Dalat has to offer – all on the back of vintage motorcycles. You'll find them hanging around in the most popular guesthouses but you won't have to go looking for them – they'll almost certainly find you! They all speak English, some can speak French and German, and daily tours shouldn't set you back no more than US$20 – be aware of a number of people that try to imitate this crew, their tours are not as good!

Accommodation is spread throughout the town but you can find a number of decent budget options along **Truong Cong Dinh** and **Nguyen Chi Thanh.** The bus driver will usually drop you off at your desired guesthouse if you ask nicely and point to them in your guidebook!

Main backpacker guesthouses – Peace Hotel & Dreams Hotel *(both on Truong Cong Dinh)*

Highlights – Easy Rider Tours & hiking

HO CHI MINH CITY... *Formerly Saigon, capital of the South*

Saigon is a fantastic bustling city, although it's slightly more expensive than elsewhere in Vietnam. The highlight is the remarkable **Chu Chi Tunnels**, a feat that illustrates the sheer determination of the northern army. You'll also get the chance to fire off a magazine or two at the **shooting range** where you can select your weapon of choice from AK-47s and M-16s to rifles and handguns! Daytrips can be arranged through most guesthouses and travel agencies. Another very worthwhile *(and very cheap)* attraction is the hard hitting **War Remnants Museum** that puts a unique Vietnamese angle on the war preserving and exposing the crimes and aftermaths of foreign aggressive forces against the Vietnamese people – admission will only set you back a few US-dollars. If you've had enough of the war, book yourself onto one of the many relaxing **Mekong Delta daytrips** or sniff around the numerous local markets and linger in the sidewalk cafés. There's plenty to keep you here for few days.

There's a strong backpacker scene in the **Pham Ngu Lao** area *(in District 1)* with budget hotels, guesthouses and travel agents concentrated on 4 streets – **Đ De Tham**, **Đ Bui Vien**, **Đ Pham Ngu Lao** and **Mini Hotel Alley** – just point to **Pham Ngu Lao** on a map and the taxi drivers will know where you want to go! This area's packed with bars from the fancy GoGo bar on the corner to local watering holes just 200m away down the street where you can drink Bia Hoi from plastic jugs and sit on small plastic chairs and get smashed for less than US$5!

Main backpacker area – Pham Ngu Lao area

Highlights – Chu Chi Tunnels, War Remnants Museum, markets, bars & Mekong Delta daytrips

Off-the-beaten track... *Spice things up a bit!*

You can find some quieter backpacker destinations in North Vietnam such as the hilltop town of **Sapa**. Vietnam's backpacker scene has exploded in recent years but if you want to explore where few travellers go, there are still a few places that are largely untouched and the locals are still fascinated by blue eyes, blonde hair and pasty skin!

THE MEKONG DELTA... *'D.I.Y' it through this network of waterways!*

The Mekong Delta is gradually being opened up to tourism but there are still plenty of great places where very few travellers go. Most people cross the Cambodian-Vietnamese border at **Moc Bar** along the well-trodden road that links Phnom Penh and HCMC. An interesting alternative from HCMC is to get the scenic slow-boat down the Mekong River, crossing the border at **Vinh Xuong** and ending up at **Chau Doc**. Here are some ideas:

Chau Doc – This is an intriguing place to spend a night or two and stroll through its food markets and sample a few local dishes. There's also a lot of Bia Hoi if you're up for a few drinks and chit-chat with the locals! It's the perfect launching point for your Mekong Delta adventure and other nearby spots of interest here include; **Sam Mountain** and the **Ba Chau killing fields**.

Phu Quoc Island – This is a great tropical retreat just off the Vietnamese coast close to the Cambodian-Vietnamese border where you'll find perfect powdery-sand beaches, a fantastic laidback ambience and only a handful of tourists. You can easily make your way here from Chau Doc or Ba Chau.

Mekong Delta – Make your way towards Saigon *(HCMC)* and navigate an amazing water-world through the dazzling green 'rice-bowl' of the country. Many 'package-trips' from Saigon explore the main waterways but the low-key DIY options are far more rewarding where you can really take advantage of relaxing slow-boats, floating markets, fresh fish and quaint riverside market towns.

CAMBODIA

THE ANCIENT KHMER EMPIRE

AT A GLANCE

Capital – Phnom Penh

Population – 14 million

Language(s) – Khmer, English & French

Currency – Riel & unofficially US$

ATMs – In all major towns and cities

Climate – Tropical

Best time to go – Nov - mid March

Time zone – GMT +7hours

Suggested daily budget – 60-80k riel / US$15-20

Suggested time – 2 weeks

Visas – 1-month visas issued at most borders and airports for around US$20

You've undoubtedly heard of the ancient Angkor Wat, but that's just the beginning, scratch a little below the surface and there's a whole lot more... Cambodia's an intriguing and contrasting country. The WOW factor and the sense of wonder from the mighty Angkor Temples is promptly halted as you're faced with some of humanity's darkest periods. Since the end of the cruel Khmer Rouge reign, this tough spirited country has pulled together and focused on a prosperous and peaceful future. Numerous sites, especially those in Phnom Penh, now commemorate and expose these previously hidden atrocities for a chilling and soul-tugging experience where you'll develop a unique affection for the Cambodian people – despite what's gone on, they're welcoming, friendly and remarkably upbeat. Elsewhere in the country hospitable cultural cities and great traditional grub are pleasantly complement by sun-soaked low-key beach resorts. Significant investment in infrastructure over the years now makes travelling between the major sights a breeze – long gone are the days of long, cramped and spine pounding bus journeys to the Thai border – while those

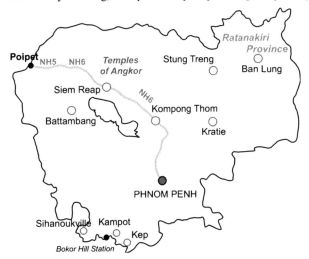

who have an adventurous streak can still find less-travelled adventures in a number of undeveloped regions. The remote jungles of the Ratanakiri Province are a stark contrast to the bustling capital and golden sands to the south providing the perfect mix of experiences to satisfy all types of travellers. All this is easily accessible and only a few hours from major cities in Thailand and Vietnam – direct busses link Bangkok to Siem Reap and Saigon to Phnom Penh. So, enlighten your mind, travel your taste buds, have a shot of culture and sun your skin...

MINI GUIDE

Essentially there are three main destinations in Cambodia that attract the backpackers – they're all within a bus journey away from each other and offer everything from gruesome history and awe-inspiring culture to banging nightlife and plenty of beach-time. Make sure you pay a visit to these:

SIEM REAP... *Gateway to the majestic Angkor Temples*

The awe-inspiring Angkor Wat is clearly the magnet for travellers here but Siem Reap has a whole lot more to offer. As well as the country's spiritual heart, it's also the food capital of Cambodia. Make sure you get stuck into the diverse and interesting restaurant menus where you can experiment with Traditional Khmer BBQs and cook you own snake, crocodile and ostrich meat or sample traditional curries served in banana leaves! There's also a great, and very cheap, **food market** *(next to the night-market)* where you can get top-notch rustic curries for less than US$2. If you've got enough time you can even learn to cook some of these authentic Khmer dishes at a number of cooking schools. **Le Tigre de Papier Cooking School** comes highly recommended – www.tigredepapier.com. Seam Reap also boasts a great **night market** where you can pick up some decent souvenirs. Don't worry it's not all culture, culture, culture though! From humble beginnings Siem Reap's nightlife has exploded in recent years and you'll find an energetic night scene and a wealth of drinking holes. You know that a town with a street named **Pub Street** would have something to shout about! **Temple Bar** and **The Angkor What? Bar** are popular with backpackers although most travellers do their best to try out every bar along this aptly named street – a pub crawl along this lively road is a must!

Angkor Temples: These temples were once the capital of Cambodia's ancient Khmer empire. Today, they're the spiritual heart of Cambodia and a source of national pride to all Khmers as they rebuild their country after years of human suffering and atrocities. Whether you find them magical and inspirational or not, they're a must-see when you're in Cambodia and even the least passionate temple enthusiast will be captivated by the sheer size and intricacy of these ancient temples.

The must-see Angkor Temples...

The temples of Angkor are numerous and spread over a large plot. You won't be able to see them all so here are the main temples you shouldn't miss out:

1) **Angkor Wat** – the daddy of temples
2) **Bayon** – the temple of many faces
3) **Ta Prohm** – Tomb Raider temple
4) **Bantreay Srei** – woman's temple

Tours can be booked through most guesthouses where a Tuk-tuk will take you to the Angkor site and you can negotiate your day's itinerary with your clued-up driver – they'll drive you around the site and ensure that you see all of the highlights and major temples. You usually have to pay for your driver and entrance fee separately. 'Early risers' and 'late-stayers' are rewarded with some spectacular sun-rises and sunsets over these impressive temples. Passes can be bought at the sites main entrance – one-day *(US$25)* and three-day passes *(around US$50)* are popular but opt for the one-day pass – it's cheaper, and providing you make an early start, gives you more than enough time to explore the main temples. The three-day pass is good if you want to explore the temples at a leisurely pace but even the most enthusiastic temple buff will be 'ruined-out' after three days! If you're feeling a bit flush you can even get an amazing aerial view of Angkor Wat and the surrounding site in a static **hot-air balloon** that's situated near the site entrance! On the way to the temples there's also the **Landmine Museum** – it's free so check it out of you've got the time on the way back!

Main backpacker area – There's a concentration of guesthouses/budget hotels around the lively **Bar Street**

Highlights – Angkor Temples, the Land-Mine Museum, Pub/Bar Street & nightlife. The night-market *(& cheap food market)*, old market, food & cooking classes

Polluted, smelly and congested this great bustling capital has something for everyone. It's fun, sobering and exciting. You'll grow to love the hustle and bustle of this intoxicating city. **Lakeside** is the bustling traveller's ghetto – although the lake was filled in during 2009/2010 – hopefully this area will still be here for you to enjoy! Here you'll find a concentration of back-to-basic budget guesthouses, cheap restaurants and a host of travel agencies and internet services. If it's been bulldozed head to the long-running **Capitol Guesthouse** just west of Monivong Blvd where there's also a backpacker scene, albeit smaller then Lakeside, where you'll find similar services and tour options.

One of the biggest attractions here is undoubtedly the **S-21 museum** *(Tuol Sleng)* and the **Killing Fields** where you can delve into Cambodia's very recent and brutal past and uncover the horrendous atrocities of Pol Pot's reign. You can visit both for a very sobering day – tuk-tuks and motorbike taxis in the Lakeside area will take you to both sites for a couple of US-dollars per person. These aren't your usual 'stiff' & boring museums – guided tours around the both sites are optional but are highly recommended and will only set you back a few US-dollars. You can 'do-your-bit' when you're in Phnom Penh as well by arranging a visit to the **orphanage** – if you want to make a difference and put a smile on a child's face, you can buy a number of basic things such as sacks of rice and stationary to hand out. A visit to the **city rubbish tip** is another shocker as you visit the families that live amongst the rats and filth trying to earn a living and combat extreme poverty. You can arrange visits to the city tip and the orphanage through a number of guesthouses and restaurants in Lakeside. If you're up for it, you can let rip in the **shooting range.** Long gone are the days where you can lob a hand grenade or fire a rocket launcher but you can still get trigger happy with a choice of weapons including, AK-47s, Shotguns, rifles and handguns!

Other more fun and uplifting spots of interest include the **Russian** and **Central Markets** where you can pick up decent quality clothes at rock bottom prices – many companies such as H&M and GAP have their clothing lines made here so you'll find some of their stock on stalls in the Russian Market. As with any backpacker area, you'll find a healthy night scene in Lakeside with plenty of bars and guesthouses boasting well stocked chillers. You'll also find a decent number of cheap restaurants offering a healthy hit-list of international food and traditional Khmer dishes in the Lakeside area – the budget highlight has to be the rustic **US$2 all-you-can-eat Indian restaurant**! More upmarket bars and restaurants are concentrated along the riverfront.

Main backpacker area – Lakeside. Riverside is also a popular but pricier 'upmarket' flashpacker area

Highlights – S-21 Museum & Killing Fields, city tip, Russian Market, Central Market, the orphanage & the $2 all-you-can-eat Indian restaurant

SIHANOUKVILLE... *Cambodia's beach capital*

Sihanoukville boasts plenty of palm-fringed, white-sand beaches and an energetic backpacker scene. This is Costa-del-Cambodia without all of the ugly white hotels. While development is inevitable and visitor numbers increase year by year, it's years behind the already over-commercialised Thai resorts of Koh Samui and Phuket! Although it claims the crown of the original backpacker beach, stay well away from **Victory Beach** – it's suffered from extensive development and oozes a somewhat sleazy atmosphere similar to that of Pattaya in Thailand. The beach is also the areas least desirable. Nowadays, backpackers tend favour the area around **Serendipity Beach** where they're well catered for and have a choice of decent, affordable guesthouses and a happening night scene – Monkey Republic is popular and has become the social hub but cheaper guesthouses can be found close by.

Sihanoukville's nightlife rivals that of Siem Reap and you're spoilt for choice when it comes to bars – the entire Serendipity beachfront in dominated by lively bars and 'clubs' where you can guzzle lots of cheap beer with like minded travellers! You can do as little as you want during the day and most tend to laze the days away getting **tan**tastic on the beach. Serendipity and Occheuteal Beach are getting fairly crowded these days with a congestion of sun loungers although you can take advantage of massages, fresh fruit and mini-lobsters offered by the local entrepreneurs. However, the beach touts – a mix of very clued-up children and persistent old women – will become tiresome after a while so if you fancy more isolated beaches and some quiet beachfront restaurants, head down towards **Otres Beach** and further beyond where you may even get a stretch of beach to yourself. Hire a motorbike out and see what you discover! If you get bored of nursing your hang-overs on the beach, there are some half decent **boat trips** and **island hopping adventures** that can be booked through most guesthouses.

Main backpacker area – Serendipity Beach *(near the golden lion roundabout)*

Highlights – Secluded beaches, island hopping daytrips & nightlife

Off-the-beaten track... *Spice things up a bit!*

If you've grown bored of the sun, sand and beer in Sihanoukville, head to the less-travelled town of **Kampot** – a relaxed riverside town amid a stunning setting and a great base to explore caves and pagodas beyond. Other nearby and quieter attractions include the **Bokor Hill Station.** A pleasant boat service, often dubbed the most scenic river trips, connects Siem Reap with the less-visited town of **Battambang** – a charming riverside town that boasts a rich legacy of colonial architecture. It makes a good base to explore nearby temples and scenic villages.

Mini Itinerary: If you visit Battambang it can eliminate the backtracking of the conventional route through Cambodia and create a more linear itinerary through Cambodia – you'll also see more of this fascinating country! These routes are based on the popular looping route through SE Asia – entering Cambodia from Vietnam and leaving across the border into Thailand:

Phnom Penh ➔ Sihanoukville ➔ Battambang ➔ Siem Reap

Rather than...

Phnom Penh ➔ Sihanoukville ➔ Phnom Penh ➔ Siem Reap

There's a fair bit off-the-beaten track to explore and it's far to say that anything northeast of National Highway 6 *(NH6)* is fairly unexplored. If you've got the time to spare and want to get well off-the-beaten track, start your exploration into the country's northeast Province of **Rakanakiri**:

RAKANAKIRI PROVINCE... *Rugged jungle & tribal villages*

Although one of the most popular provinces in the area, it still remains off-the-beaten track for the average backpacker – probably because it's an awkward detour from the conventional route through Cambodia. Ethnic minorities, elephant treks, refreshing waterfalls, picturesque lagoons and dense jungle are just some of the natural wonders that this region offers.

Ban Lung is the provincial capital of Rakanakiri Province and the most popular base from which to explore the natural attractions, trek through tribal villages, cool-off under waterfalls and soak up some spectacular scenery. The awful roads in the region will have throw dust in your mouth and eyes during the dry season and have you sloshing about in sticky mud during the wet season but this adds to the rustic isolated experience and keeps the less-adventurous at bay!

MALAYSIA

DISCOVER THE OUTDOORS

AT A GLANCE

Capital – Kuala Lumpur

Population – 23 million

Language(s) – Malay

Currency – Ringgit (RM)

ATMs – In all major towns & cities

Climate – Tropical

Best time to go – June-Sept although peak-times are generally Nov-Feb. Rains heavily during Oct/Nov and April/May

Time zone - GMT +8hrs

Suggested daily budget – 80-100RM

Suggested time – 2-3 weeks

Visas – 1-month visas at most land borders for US$20

Compared to the chaos of other Southeast Asian countries, the hassles here are fewer and the streets are noticeably tidier. Promoting itself as 'Truly Asia', whether you're after some relaxing beach time, a satisfying dose of culture or a rewarding adventure in less-travelled destinations, there's something for everyone in Malaysia. The harmonious blend of modern shopping halls, futuristic cityscapes and state-of-the-art technology with undeveloped tropical islands, pristine national parks and spectacular natural landscapes has the ability to both stimulate and soothe your senses. It's quite literally a country of two halves...

Bordering Thailand, **_Peninsular Malaysia_** is the well-trodden half which, despite the droves of tourists, it boasts plenty of tropical island retreats, well-preserved national parks, charming colonial towns and the excitement of the sleek capital city. Those in search of off-the-beaten track opportunities quickly adopt the adventurous spirit of the Borneo Jungle where you can negotiate fast flowing rivers, interact with semi-wild Orang-Utans, hike high-altitude peaks and meet tribes in traditional villages. If you skip **_Malaysian Borneo_**, you'll miss something very special. The views from Mt. Kinabalu alone are well worth the effort. While it's one of the more expensive countries in the region, it's both time and money well spent. Go there and get involved. At the very least, give Peninsular Malaysia a chance, you won't regret it!

MINI GUIDE

Malaysia's geographical make-up, being physically divided into two regions – Peninsular Malaysia and Borneo Malaysia – ensures a few well-trodden routes and plenty of less-travelled ones. Make sure you do the usual east coast itinerary listed below but make an effort to explore the 'off-the-beaten track' spots that this section touches on to create a unique and individual itinerary:

(Thailand ➔*)* Langkawi ➔ Penang ➔ Pangkor ➔ Kuala Lumpur

LANGKAWI... *Beautiful & tax free!*

Located close to the Thai-Malaysian border and easily accessible, idyllic Langkawi is a long standing backpacker favourite – for many travellers Langkawi is their Malaysian highlight. Blessed with stunning beaches and a rugged jungle interior there's something for everyone. Most come here looking for sun, sea and relaxation but it gets better... Langkawi was declared a **duty-free zone** in 1986. Since then backpackers have enjoyed cheap beer and more wallet friendly nights!

Apart from going a deeper shade of brown on white sand beaches, there's a fair bit to keep you entertained if you want to get active. **Water-sports** options are plentiful if your budget's healthy, with everything available from banana boats to parasailing, while for those who like to keep two feet firmly on the

---

Zakrys Guesthouse...

This family run guesthouse is about as good as backpacker digs get! Regular communal BBQs are complemented by a trust beer fridge that's always well stocked – just don't take the piss and own-up to what you've actually drunk! You also get a communal kitchen and separate lounge area with a TV and a wedge of DVDs to make this a very sociable and laidback guesthouse. Other benefits include; internet, free Wi-Fi, free tea & coffee and cheap motorbike rental. It's conveniently located in Pantai Tengah – a few hundred meters away from a great sandy beach. Local shops, restaurants and food stalls are all a 'stone's throw away'. Check it out and make sure you stay there!

www.zackryguesthouse.langkawinetworks.com

---

ground and want something a bit cheaper, **trekking** in the mountains is a popular past time. Other outdoor options include **diving**, **snorkelling** and **boat trips**. While there's a host of other *(often quite tacky)* attractions and sights including; **Underwater World**, **Pulau Paya Marine Park** and **Langkaiw Wildlife Park**, the **Langkawi Cable Car** tops them all – it's the steepest cable car in the world offering fantastic coastal views from a dizzy 600+ metres. Proposed future developments even include a bungee jump at the site!

Budget backpacker accommodation is generally found on the islands southwest coast at **Pantai Cenang** and **Panati Tengah** – although, because of the islands popularity, prices are on the up. **Zakrys Guesthouse** is the backpacker's choice *(see text box)*. While luxury resorts have sprung up, away from the built-up areas Langkawi is still a rural Malay island of small villages, rice paddies and natural beauty so make sure that you spend some time exploring it. A hired motorbike is a great way to get about and experience this great island – make sure you check out **Seven Wells**, **Durian Perangin Waterfall** and **The Lake of the Pregnant Maiden**.

Main backpacker area – Pantai Cenang & Pantai Tengah. Stay @ **Zakrys Guesthouse!**

Highlights – Langkawi Cable Car, pristine beaches, jungle treks, motorbike adventures, water-sports, cheaper beer & Zakrys Guesthouse!

PENANG *(Georgetown)... Discover colonial heritage*

Penang is the oldest British settlement in Malaysia and the city has plenty reminders of colonial rule dotted throughout its winding streets – a wander around the **Colonial District** is fascinating for all those interested in history and architecture. The island also boasts some ok beaches, and above all, top-notch grub in **Chinatown** and **Little India**. It's not quite the island retreat of Pangkor, but if you're coming from Thailand, this island offers you some sought after modern comforts and a bit of retail therapy – you'll find a glitzy shopping mall in Georgetown and an air-conditioned multi-screen cinema! A 24-hour ferry links operates between Penang and the mainland town of **Butterworth**.

Georgetown, often referred to simply as Penang, it's the islands capital and where most backpackers head to – you'll find the usual array of backpacker services and guesthouses. This place is a real Chinatown where you'll find those great oriental flavours. There's also a large number of Indian restaurants where you can brave yourself through some kick-arse curries – you'll notice dozens of Tandoori-ovens dotted along the streets!

Avoid **Batu Ferringhi**. While a few backpacker options remain here, the town is dominated by large scale luxury developments and caters for package–holidaymakers – the main tourist drag is lined with tacky shops, up-market restaurants and posh hotels. Batu Ferringhi does have a half-decent beach with a variety of water-sports on offer if your budget allows it. If you want some beach time hop on the local bus from Georgetown – this coastal road is a picturesque stretch of small coves and secluded beaches, some are worth checking out. The beaches along the north coast are the most accessible *(and crowded)*, while the beaches closer to the city suffer from pollution. The beaches down south are generally inaccessible but are deserted if you manage to get to one!

Main backpacker area – Georgetown *(on the north eastern corner of the island)*

Highlights – Chinatown, Little India, Colonial District, half-decent beaches

PANGKOR... *Tropical island retreat*

A short ferry ride from the mainland town of **Lumut**, Pangkor is the perfect island retreat. This beautiful island is a low-key resort island noted for its fine beaches – you'll find them a lot cleaner and emptier than most of Thailand's beaches. The jungle-clad hills of the interior are virtually untouched and are home to an abundance of wildlife. Armed with its very distinct fleet of pink taxis, getting around the island is very simple but if you want to burn off some of those beer calories hire a bike and **cycle** around it for some great coastal views – it only takes a few hours and you'll hear and see some spectacular wildlife – Frida had monkeys jump out in front of her and one even stole my lunch! Pangkor also offers some interesting jungle **walks** with popular trails including: Teluk Nipah to Foo Lin Kong and Pasir Bogak to Bukit Pangkor – be warned though, trails are often overgrown! Out of the jungle and off-shore, **snorkelling gear**, **boats** and **jet skis** can be hired at hotels and on the beach in Teluk Nipah and Pasir Bogak. Boats can be hired to go to **Pulau Sembilan** – a group of nine islands where you'll find deserted white sand beaches and a chance for some **sports fishing**.

Teluk Nipah: This is the main backpacker area with a host of cheap accommodation, restaurants, street vendors and internet services as well as the islands best beach. More expensive digs are appearing around the backpacker hostels so get here before it becomes another Koh Samui! South of Teluk Nipah you'll find the most developed and busiest beach, **Pasir Bogak** which has the up-market hotels.

Main backpacker area – Teluk Nipah *(west side of the island)*

Highlights – Wildlife, great beaches, snorkelling, walking & tranquillity! Pulau Sembilan

KUALA LUMPUR... *The capital*

KL's capital city infuses modern aspirations and economic achievements with a pleasing blend of history and culture. The 21st century skyline of ultra-modern skyscrapers, dominated by the jaw-dropping Petronas Towers, stands tall alongside old colonial buildings and modern Islamic architecture. Underneath the modern exterior of this prosperous city you'll uncover a wealth of culture, tradition and multiculturalism. You only need to traipse around vibrant **Chinatown**, charming **Little India** and the historic **Colonial District** to experience the city's cultural melting pot *(a popular cultural highlight that's free!)*. While it's probably the most expensive place in Malaysia, KL can be done on a budget and a lot of its attractions are free! KL is also one of the region's major transport hubs where you can get very competitive international flights.

The city's two biggest attractions dominate its skyline: The **Petronas Towers** are an impressive symbol of KL's economic achievements. If you get up early, you'll be rewarded with some superb – and free – panoramic views of this bustling urban jungle from the **Skybridge**. KL's skyline also boasts the 4th highest telecommunications tower 'Menara Kuala Lumpur' or just the **KL Tower** to you and me! You can get to the observation deck of this 421m tower for some excellent views and a spot of grub *(and of course a tonnes of tacky souvenirs)*. Other spots of interest include: strolling around the relaxing

> **The PETRONAS Towers... *Free!!!***
>
> At 451m, these 88-storey twin-towers are one of the tallest buildings in the world. Unique in design the towers are instantly recognisable. You can up as far as the 41st floor and walk along the **Skybridge** that connects the two towers – while it's only a fairly disappointing 146m above the ground, less than a third of its overall height, **admission is free**! Get there early as queues are long and they only issue a certain number of tickets a day.

Lake Gardens *(free!)*, browsing around the famous **JL Petaling Market** deep in Chinatown or haggling in the bustling **Chow Kit Market** just north of the city centre and pretending to be interested in history in the **National Museum**. A number of worthwhile attractions such as the **Batu Caves**, **Zoo Negra**, **Orang Museum** and **Templer Park** are an easy daytrip away – most can be arrange at Pudu Hostel.

You'll find the usual array of entertainment and activities that you'll find in any modern city from shopping malls and markets to restaurants and cinemas – if you want to 'shop 'til you drop' then visit the impressive **Suria KLCC shopping complex**. You need a lot of spare cash if you want a few big nights out – alcohol is expensive but KL boasts an abundance of lively bars and energetic nightclubs, particularly in the popular **Golden Triangle** and **Bangsar** districts if your budget allows. If you're skint, cheaper late night alternatives include stuffing your face with popcorn at one of the many multi-screen cinema complexes or trying to get a strike at the bowling alley! You'll find some fantastic cuisine in KL – Malay, Indian and Chinese cooking dominate the menus but you can also find an array of international dishes. The cheaper food can be found in local-owned restaurants and from food stalls in the outer-districts such as Chinatown and Little India.

Pudu Hostel: The majority of budget backpacker accommodation is found in Chinatown. **Pudu Hostel** is my recommendation here and it's conveniently located opposite Puduraya Bus Station. Although appearing slightly dodgy on the third floor, it's well equipped boasting a large and speedy internet café *(1st floor)*, lounge area, DVDs and Sky, a beer fridge, pool table and a useful notice board bristling with travel tips and advice – they also run regular shuttle busses to **Taman Negra National Park**. This Hostel offers small and clean dorms with breakfast thrown in for free!

Main backpacker hostel – Pudu Hostel

HIGHlights – The PETRONAS Towers, KL Tower, Chinatown, Little India, the Colonial District, Lake Gardens *(& Bird Park)*, shopping *(Suria KLCC shopping complex),* daytrips & nightlife

TAMAN NEGARA... *Malaysia's premier National Park*

If it's the great Malaysian jungle you want to see, then top of your list should be Taman Negara National Park. Dedicate a few days here to get to most out of the park and make sure you spend a night or two in a **jungle hide** for wildlife spotting *(see text box)* and get on a **longboat trip** up one of the park's rivers. The more you put into your visit here, the more you'll get out of it. While in theory you could spot endangered species such as elephants, rhinos and big cats, numbers are very low – they're endangered after all – and because the jungle's very dense, you could be metres away from these shy animals and you'd never know it! To increase your chances of spotting these species, make sure you do an extended overnight trek away from the busy park headquarters – remember sightings, even of monkeys, can never be guaranteed! At an estimated 130 million years old it's claimed that this is the oldest jungle in the world, so if you don't see much other than the usual monkeys, snakes, birds and insects, don't go away disappointed – you've just roughed it in and explored one of the most pristine primary rainforests on the planet!

Trekking: There are a number of decent short *(day)* walks around **Nusa Camp** – the refreshing **Abai Falls** is only an hour's walk from the site, while **Gunung Warisan**, a popular sunny clearing, is a couple of hours from the camp. For longer treks, like the popular **Rentis Tenor** and **Kuala Keniam** trails, that take a few days, you'll need a guide – daily and overnight rates apply and work out very affordable if you're a sizable group. Other popular activities include **fishing** and **boat trips**.

Sleeping: There are a few places to sleep in this National park including the park HQ. While camping here is fairly cheap, **Kuala Tahan** across the river is a cheaper alternative popular with backpackers. **Nusa Camp**, 15 minutes upstream from **Kuala Tahan**, is a more rustic 'jungle camp' for those with an adventurous streak and it's easily accessible via the **riverbus service.** The best time to visit the park is during the dry season *(Feb - Sept)* although try and visit before the busy period during April to August.

Hides *(bumbuns)*...

Increase your chances of spotting tapir, wild boar or deer and, if you're very lucky, some of the endangered list by spending a night in a hide – book at the Wildlife Dep. at least a day before. Even if you don't see much you'll hear some fantastic sounds. All hides are built over looking salt licks and grassy clearings. As well and being very affordable, they're very rustic sleeping 6-8 people and boast pit toilets creating an unforgettable experience! Bring a sleeping bag, torch and supplies.

Popular hides, that are easily accessible from Kuala Tahan, include **Tabing** and **Kumbang**, although Hides further afield will give you a greater chance of that 'rare sighting'.

Getting there: Many guesthouses in KL will get you here on a number of pre-set trips. If you want to DIY it and experience the fantastic river trip here's the route:

Get to Jerantut *(bus or train)* ➔ Kuala Tembeling *(bus)* ➔ Park HQ at Kuala Tahan *(via boat)*

Getting around: The **riverbus service** is the cheapest & easiest way to get around the park

Cheapest sleeps – The village of Kuala Tahan, Nusa Camp & camping at HQ

Highlights – Trekking, fishing, tours, boat trips, hides & wildlife spotting

Off-the-beaten track... Spice things up a bit!

EASTERN PENINSULAR MALAYSIA... *Mildly off-the-beaten track*

Most travellers follow a convenient and logical linear route down through Malaysia, often hugging the western coast starting from Langkawi – probably due to its proximity and good transport links to Phi Phi in neighbouring Thailand. However, if you've got the time get off your backside and head over to the stunning eastern coast of Peninsular Malaysia. Essentially, you can create a looping-itinerary through Malaysia with a stopover in Singapore and avoid any backtracking should you be heading back up into Thailand. Just bear in mind that the coastlines monsoon season coincides with the west coast's peak season. So if you're planning to head here after the west coast you will have to accept that the weather can be a tad unpredictable and some resorts shut-up shop – although you'll enjoy cheaper rates and empty beaches! Here are two fantastic, and fairly popular spots just off the eastern coast – you're bound to find a many interesting places in between:

PULAU PERHENTIAN... Snorkel, dive or just soak up some rays on these two beautiful white-sand fringed islands. Located 20km off the north east coastline, they're just a short boat trip from **Kuala Besut** and are becoming increasingly popular. With its abundance of cheap chalets, lively bars and budget restaurants, **Kecil** is the backpacker's favourite. **Besar** offers higher standard accommodation and a quieter atmosphere. Activities on both islands include; snorkelling, diving, jungle walks and beach time. If you're undecided you can hop from island to island in under 10 minutes via regular boats.

PULAU TIOMAN... Relax on the islands pristine beaches, snorkel and dive in the surrounding crystal-clear waters or get active and hike its mountainous interior – this is a truly beautiful island. Unfortunately, while it's fairly off-the-beaten track for backpackers, it's has become increasingly popular with package-holidaymakers who fly direct to the island. Budget accommodation can still be found in **Air Batang** *(ABC)* and **Salang** on the northwest side of the island. **Juara**, on the east coast, also has some good budget options. Backpackers tend to get here via ferries from the mainland town of **Mersing**. During the off-peak season and low monsoon season *(Jan-Feb)* Tioman can be practically deserted. While rainy days are common, they're interspersed with decent periods of sunshine and calm seas – if you're not rushed for time, as ferry timetables can be interrupted during bad monsoon weather, it can be an ideal time to visit where you'll enjoy cheaper rates, fewer footprints on the stunning beaches and next to no package holidaymakers!

Mini-itinerary: By venturing over to the Eastern Peninsular, you could create a kind of horseshoe-looping itinerary through Malaysia to/from Thailand. It could look something like this:

Thailand *(e.g. Phi Phi)* ➔ Langkaiw ➔ Pangkor ➔ Kuala Lumpur ➔ Melaka ➔ Singapore ➔ Palau Tioman ➔ Tarman Negra ➔ Palau Perhentian ➔ **Thailand** *(e.g. Krabi)*

Fewer people venture over the eastern half of Malaysia – probably because it cannot be reached by land and inevitably involves extra flights – but there's so much to do here and the extra effort and expense is well justified. Your best bet is to follow a linear itinerary, so you'll usually need **two** single airline tickets – **Air Asia** do some great deals.

Entry / exit points:

○ **Kuching** – the main entry point into **SARAWAK**

○ **Kota Kinabalu** – the main gateway for **SABAH**

If your budget permits and you've got plenty of time to spare head over to Malaysian Borneo and make your way between these highlights:

KINABALU NATIONAL PARK... While Mt Kinabalu is the biggest tourist attraction in Sabah, few backpackers venture here and the vast 754-sq-km of the park ensures that'll you'll see very few people! Just shy of 4,100m it's a beastly mountain even compared to the mighty Himalayas, although this is actually one of the easiest mountains to climb in the world. All ages and fitness levels have reached the summit and enjoyed spectacular views – on a very clear day you can even spot the Philippines nestling on the horizon, although such days are fairly rare! Make sure you bring some warm waterproof clothing and decent footwear. Along with your permit *(available from the National Park HQ)* you'll need some stamina and determination! Guides are available but not essential – they're for the weak package-holidaymakers! Relax and soak your aching muscles in the **Poring Hot Srings**.

SUNGAI KINABATANGAN... Any nature lover will relish navigating Sabah's longest river – it's probably the best place in SE Asia to observe wildlife. You'll have the chance to spot marbled cats, the flat-headed cat *(at night)*, giant squirrels, deer, elephants and rhinos *(very shy)* and an incredible variety of bird-life including hornbills. Luck and your guides knowledge will be the key factors influencing what you'll see! Backpackers are catered for in jungle camps.

SEPILOK ORANG-UTAN REHAB-CENTRE... Get up close with one of our unique primates at one of only four orang-utan centres in the world! Not so much off-the-beaten track anymore, this rehab-centre is a victim of its own success as hoards of package-holidaymakers flood the centre to get snap happy. Still, it's a very worthwhile place to visit while you're venturing around rural Sabah.

To give yourself a more linear itinerary check out...

○ **KUCHING...** *The region's most historic & busy town*

○ **THE BATANG REJANG...** *The heart of the Borneo Jungle!*

SINGAPORE
THE CITY-STATE!

AT A GLANCE

Capital – Singapore!

Population – 5 million

Language(s) – English, Malay, Mandarin & Tamil

Currency – Singapore dollar (S$)

ATMs – Abundant

Climate – Tropical

Best time to go – Anytime but Nov - Jan is cooler

Time zone – GMT +8hours

Suggested daily budget – S$50

Suggested time – 4 days

Visas – Most nationalities receive a free 30-day tourist visa on arrival

Located on the tip of Peninsular Malaysia, Singapore is by far Southeast Asia's smallest country. This squeaky-clean city-state is a complete contrast compare to Thailand and even Malaysia – as soon as you cross the border you'll notice it's cleaner, more prosperous, ultra-modern and, unfortunately, more expensive! One of the richest countries in Southeast Asia, it's what most countries in the region aspire to be. Famous for its smooth efficiency, you'll find superior and punctual transport infrastructure coupled with cleaner and higher quality accommodation. While these characteristics *can* take away some of the fun and adventure of the 'typical' chaotic Asian city, they won't render your experience here a sterile one. It's an enjoyable city where generous open spaces and lush tree-shaded streets provide a welcome retreat. Man-made beaches give lethargic travellers a healthy dose of sun while modern shopping malls and busy markets are an irresistible magnet for shopaholics. Singapore also boasts a mouth-watering and diverse menu where a visit to a bustling hawker-centre will introduce you to a tantalising selection of authentic Asian dishes. Perhaps, surprisingly, Singapore offers a good range of outdoor activities from hikes and mountain biking to golf and off-shore activities. Singapore's modern harbour is the city's biggest draw boasting cityscape-views and a host of popular tourist attractions. While it's undoubtedly harder on the wallet and often a major time consuming detour, this tiny city state crams in more than you'd ever think offering a truly unique Asian experience.

HIGHLIGHTS... *Singapore's best bits!*

For just a small city state, Singapore crams in a fair but to do in its bustling city centre, vibrant ethnic districts and ultra-modern waterfront. Here's a little sample of what's on offer:

- o **Sentosa Island...** *The tourist magnet*

  Tourists flock here to visit numerous attractions including **Underwater World** *(where you can swim with sharks)*, **Fort Siloso**, **Carlsberg Sky Tower** and the Magical Sentosa laser-light-and-music show. The artificial beach is pleasant enough with an array of water-sports to keep you occupied. The coolest way to arrive is by cable car, but ferries, busses and the MRT are cheaper!

Ethnic districts... *Chinatown, Little India & Kampung Glam*

Amid a waft of spice and hustle and bustle, these vibrant districts are crammed with stalls, eateries and bags of tradition. Check out **Chinatown Heritage Centre** for some history and culture or stroll around the character filled alleyways and soak up the colourful vibe of **Little India**. In the **Muslim Quarter** *(Kampung Glam)* you'll find the biggest mosque in Singapore.

o **Museums...** *A (cheap) slice of culture*

You'll find a wealth of decent museums for a sizeable slice of culture including the **Changi Prision Museum & Chapel, Asian Civilisation Museum and Singapore Art Museum** – the latter two are popular with shoe-stingers as they're **free** on Friday nights!

Other highlights – Food, relaxing Botanic Gardens, Colonial District, adventure packed Bukit Timah Nature Reserve, Night Safari, beaches *(Sentosa & Pulau Ubin)* & harbour cruises

Drinking... *Get your wallet out!*

Fashionable **Clarke Quay** is where you'll find the classy bars and energetic nightlife. However, knocking back a few and staying up late in Singapore will set you back a fair bit – especially when compared to its Asian counterparts – but it'd be rude not to go out a least once while you're here. Pricewise it's almost not worth bothering with, but fortunately you'll come across some attractive promotions that'll make your night on the tiles a little less painful – although the phrases can be somewhat confusing. For example, you can clearly see the ambiguous use of 'Sin-glish' here:

o **One-for-one**: If you pay for a drink you'd expect to get one, but this seemingly obvious statement actually means buy one-get-one-free!

o **Housepour:** These are essentially house-spirits. You'll often see 'free housepour' where house-spirits are free once you've paid the cover charge

Then you've got the usual **ladies nights** where girls annoyingly drink for free – unfortunately cross dressing doesn't entitle you to any freebies. Thankfully, as they usually do in the UK, happy hours often extend for good few hours! You also get crazy-hour where drinks can be ¼ of the usual price!

Main backpacker area – Convenient and cheap hostels can be found in the **Colonial District** while equally cheap hostels in **Chinatown & Little India** will give you insights into other cultures

Across to Indonesia... *Ferry connections*

While the majority of travellers head back up through Malaysia, get connections back up to Thailand or fly elsewhere from Singapore's international airport, the more adventurous backpackers and those blessed with more time, hop on the ferry and head over to Sumatra for an Indonesian island hopping adventure *(page 79)*. Ferries and busses make up the well-trodden route connections between Singapore and Pekanbaru *(via Palua Batam)* on the Indonesian mainland. Visas are granted at the border on arrival and cost around US$25. If you've got a bit of spare time, break up the trip and head-off to the quiet retreat of **Pulau Bintan** to find a cluster of quiet sandy beaches and a string of small secluded islands – boat connections are from Pulau Batam.

PHILIPPINES

ISLAND HOPPING ADVENTURES

AT A GLANCE

Capital – Manila

Number of Islands – 7,107ish!

Population – 88 million

Language(s) – Filipino, English & Spanish

Currency – Filipino Peso

ATMs – In most major towns

(scarce on smaller islands)

Climate – Tropical

Best time to go – Nov - April

Avoid east islands Nov - Jan

Time zone – GMT +8hours

Suggested time – 4+ weeks

Suggested daily budget – 750-1,000peso

(More if you intend to do some serious island hopping)

Visas – Most nationalities receive a free 21-day visa on arrival

This vast and diverse archipelago has long been overlooked by the majority of travellers. Located on the far side of the South China Sea, it's this isolation and the extra financial expense to get here that has kept the Philippines such a well kept secret. While there are a few popular tourist hotspots, such as Boracay, this is one of the best places to lose yourself off-the-beaten track and embark on some truly memorable island hopping adventures. From ancient rice terraces and stunning landscapes to pristine beaches and friendly local folk, this kaleidoscope of coral fringed isles will WOW even the most weary and seasoned backpacker. The extra flights really are money well spent. It can be tough and testing but if you're willing to embrace the challenge of unreliable travel and adopt the lethargic pace of simple island life, you can look forward to many long sundrenched days on secluded beaches and pleasant rum-induced hangovers! With so many islands and so few tourists, you'll always have the sense that there's plenty more 'to be discovered' and with over 7,000 islands, the possibilities are endless... so go ahead maroon yourself! Dedicate as much time as you can spare!

In terms of the number of islands, the Philippines is a **huge** country and you could spend months exploring just a few of them. In general, to get around use local busses to make your way from town to town while ferries and catamarans link the thousands of islands. Use Domestic flights for longer stints and if you're short on time. Getting between the islands takes time, patience and a bit of planning but here are a few worthwhile places to explore that can be realistically reached to make a variety of interesting, affordable and manageable itineraries that won't give you too much of a headache – consider a looping itinerary starting and finishing in **Manila** or a linear route from the capital to **Cebu** *(see also mini-itineraries p.31)*...

MANILA... *The hustling great capital*

Not really a highlight, more of a low-light! Although an intriguing experience, you really don't want to hang around here for too long. It essentially serves as the Philippines major entry/exit point where you'll find the majority of cheap international flights to and from the city's international airport. Consequently, backpackers find themselves here out of necessity rather than choice – much like San José in Costa Rica! Once the jewel in Spain's crown, there's no denying that Manila has decayed into a chaotic, dirty and intimidating city. The urban ills are extreme in Manila and with no distinct centre it's sprawled out. Although some actually find these characteristics the city's biggest attraction! You'll come across a handful extreme optimists and a minority of guidebooks that try and make something of Manila glossing over the obvious drawbacks. In reality, the fantastic transport links to most places in the country is Manila's major plus point – many travellers simply use Manila as a transport hub.

On a cheerier note, Manila has some fine shopping centres in nearly every neighbourhood – the grandest in **Makati**. There are few worthwhile sites to see in Manila and the best way to see them is on a **walking tour** – there are two official city tours; Carlos Celdran and Ivan Mandy. If you want to stay in Manila, most budget accommodation is found in **Malate** and **Ermita**, particularly along M Adriatico St, A Mabini St and MH del Pilar St where you'll find a small concentration of backpackers and an energetic night scene. **Ritzal Park** – some 60 hectares of open lawns, paved walks and wooded areas just north of Malate and Ermita – provides a temporary escape from the urban madness and swarming traffic. Bloodthirsty travellers will enjoy a bout of Cockfighting – **Liberstad Cockpit** has a highly charged atmosphere and is close to Malate.

In all honesty, while there are a few things to see, leave as quickly as you can – there are far better places in the Philippines, so invest your time in more rewarding and idyllic destinations! Most hop on the next convenient bus/boat shortly after landing to escape Manila's mayhem heading to more desirable locations including **Puerto Galera** and **Marinduque** or to the idyllic retreats in North Luzon *(Vigan and Sagada)*. If time doesn't permit you to venture too far, i.e. you're coming to the end of your Filipino adventure and fly in a few days, other more pleasant locations such as **Anilao** and **Tagaytay** are only a short bus journey a few hours south of Manila.

Walking tours – Carlos: www.celdrantours.blogspot.com & Ivan: www.oldmanilawalks.com

Main backpacker neighbourhoods – Ermita & Malate

Highlights – Petty crime, congestion, transport links, walking tours, Ritzal Park & shopping

PUERTO GALERA *(Mindoro Island)... Laidback beach resorts*

Located only a few hours south of Manila on the northern tip of Mindoro, the Philippines' least developed island, Puerto Galera, is a string of sandy beaches and low-key resorts. It's a great first stop to relax after the hustle and bustle of Manila or the perfect beach retreat before you head to

Manila to leave the Philippines. There's a range of diving shops and worthwhile dive sites in picturesque bays and vibrant reefs. Most backpackers head to the less-developed **Sabang Beach** where budget travellers are well catered for. While Sabang hasn't got a beach to shout about, **Small La Laguna** is an easy walk over the rocks and has a pleasant sandy beach. Sabang has its fair share of bars, including two floating bars, and a mix of local and tourist orientated eateries.

White Beach, 8kms west of Sabang, is where you'll find the more upmarket and expensive accommodation as well as one of the area's best beaches. The advice here is to stay in Sabang and if you want some 'beach-time' and indulge in some water-sports head over to White Beach by Jeepney – they run roughly every hour from Sabang and are very cheap. You can get there by trike although it <u>will</u> be more expensive despite what they say! If you've got a few days here hire a motorbike and do some exploring – it's a fantastic island to explore with breathtaking coastal scenery and some scrumptious deserted beaches hidden along the entire coast. Make sure you cool off in the **Tamaraw Falls** – 14km from Puerto Galera along some scenic mountainous roads.

Main backpacker area – Sabang Beach

Highlights – Diving & snorkelling, nightlife *(check out the floating bar)*, Tamaraw Falls & the surrounding scenery

NORTH PANDAN ISLAND... *Turtle Island*

This remote and unspoilt tropical island is one of the best island experiences you'll find in the whole of Asia. During the day you can literally just wade a few metres offshore and **snorkel with greenback turtles** as they graze on the sea grass. After the suns gone down you can relax in the islands friendly beach bar and gorge on the fantastic all-you-can-eat buffet – the food is absolutely divine and you won't find better in the rest of Asia! The accommodation is great, even the budget bungalows, but the island does have a limit supply of electricity and consequently none of the rooms have fans. Be prepared for some unbearably hot and sticky nights – I used to brave the mosquitoes and sleep outside to cool down! Some of the **world's best diving** can be found here at the nearby **Apo Reef**. Admission to the National Park is fairly pricey but it's most definitely money well spent if you're a keen diver.

Unfortunately, this experience does come at a price and this idyllic island is a fairly pricey destination for any budget backpacker but it's highly recommended and well worth the extra pesos. Unless you fly to **San José** *(southwest Mindoro)* it's a bit of a mission to get here but the long, varied and intriguing journey – usually involving a combination of trikes, jeepneys, catamarans and local busses – will reward you with some breathtaking views and memorable encounters with the local folk. Getting here is half the fun! If you're not diving, three or four days will be plenty of time as lethargic island life can get a bit too slow. The island is very popular and can only cater for a limited number of guests at a time, which only preserves and enhances the isolated island experience, so book your stay in advance. For more information and bookings check out www.pandan.com or visit their Facebook page www.facebook.com/PandanIsland

Main backpacker area – Only one resort on the island, opt for the more affordable budget bungalows

Highlights – Turtles, Apo Reef *(diving & snorkelling)*, exquisite food & slow paced island life.

SAGADA & BANAUE... *Tranquil mountaintop retreats*

Ok, so it's a bit out of the way and quite a detour from the gorgeous tropical islands down south, but North Luzon is a popular spot for backpackers and is slightly off-the-beaten track. Temperatures in the highlands can be a bit chilly so make sure you've got a half-decent coat!

These are the two most popular spots:

Sagada: Travellers have been flocking here for years to chill-out in this refreshingly cool and tranquil town – it's the regional backpacker HQ! You can hang about out here for days, even weeks, admiring the amazing mountain scenery and mingling with laidback travellers over a couple of beers or a few joints while appreciating the absence of noise and pollution! When you're feeling active head to the Tourist Info Centre *(TIC)* and enquire about **hiking, cave exploration** and the intriguing, and equally ancient, **hanging coffins**. It's a good idea to hire a guide from the TIC – they operate on a fixed rate and know the area inside out. Accommodation fills up pretty quickly between March & May, aka, the high season.

Banaue: The town itself isn't great, and it's nowhere near the idyllic hilltop retreat of Sagada, but it sits at the foot of a truly awesome attraction – the awe inspiring ancient **rice terraces**. These impressive mudded walled terraces are North Luzon's most famous sight and were chiselled out of the hillside more than 2000 years ago by the Ifugao tribe! Along with the other rice terraces in the region, they're constantly in flux taking on a different look according to the time of year and harvesting cycle – some people feel they're most impressive a few months before harvest *(harvest usually around June)* where they're transforming from a vibrant green to a rich golden colour, while others appreciate the naked organic look around planting time *(around March)*.

There's no shortage of aggressive touts, freelance-guides and trike drivers looking to make a quick buck form the crowds of tourists so head to **Banuae TIC** for accredited and well-equipped guides. The **view-point** – which is actually 4 viewpoints dotted about 200m apart along the road to Bontoc – is a short trike ride and is one of the best places to look out over these ancient terraces. The best time to view the terraces from here is late afternoon when they're backlit by the setting sun. Budget hotels and guesthouse can be found along **Main Road**.

Further afield: If you want to spend a bit more time in North Luzon, take a step back in time in **Vigan**, check out the mummies of untouched **Kabayan** or surf the breaks in **San Fernando**

Highlights – The ancient rice terraces & the view point. Hiking, cave exploration and random ancient coffins!

DAET... *The laidback surfer's hangout*

Not many travellers venture here but it's a good place to stop and break up the long trip from Manila to Donsol. In fact, this laidback seaside town is a very popular Filipino tourist destination, and a popular surfing hotspot. The town itself is ok and characterised by a plague of tricycles – luckily, after you've had your fun riding on top and hanging off the side of them, you can escape this 3-wheeled madness 4kms north of the town at a decent sandy beach called **Bagasbas Beach...**

This is a great laidback surfer's hangout where you'll find some good breaks to surf. While the surf is biggest between August and October, anytime of the year is good and it's the perfect place to learn. You can rent boards during the day, soak up the sun on the beach or splash around in the waves before necking some monster bottles of Colt 45 'on-the-rocks' and enjoying some quirky nightlife with the locals in affordable beachside bars and cafés. If you're lucky enough you may hit the town during one of its regular surf competitions. While it's predominately a Filipino hotspot there are a few backpacker orientated digs just behind **Bagasbas Beach** although you'll find more abundant and cheap 'budget hotels' in the town centre as well as a good night market with lots of cheap eats and tasty street kitchens.

Main backpacker area – No particular area although the cheaper accommodation can be found in the centre of Daet. **Wiltan Hotel** offers cheap and basic rooms smack bang in the centre of town – it's even got a pool!

Highlights – Surfing, Bagasbas Beach & quirky nightlife

DONSOL... *Swim with whale sharks*

There's only one reason to venture to this sleeping fishing town and that's the rare opportunity to snorkel with the world's biggest fish – **whale sharks** – and don't worry they're gentle plankton eating giants! To book your encounter just turn up at the visitor centre by 6am and you'll be allocated a boat and 'whale spotter' – the centre's 1.5km north of the **Donsol River Bridge** but ask any trike driver and they'll take you there. **Rates in 2010 were;** F$500 for the boat & guide, F$300 registration fee and F$300 mask & fin hire. It's run on a 'first come first served' basis, so get there early or book it the night before to avoid a prolonged stay in this otherwise dreary town! The early start is rewarded with breathtaking encounters of these gentle giants and it's not just a case of if you'll see one, it's more how many you'll have the pleasure of swimming with. It's an exhilarating experience jumping off a moving catamaran and frantically looking around to see these giants suddenly emerge from the cloudy plankton rich water – you need to be a fairly good swimmer to keep up but you'll be able to get very close! Take an underwater camera. Diving is not permitted.

While some choose to make a flying visit by arriving in Donsol *(very)* early, swim with these big fish and leave the town straight after, this makes a very rushed day. While there's not a lot to do in Donsol it's worth getting here the day before to book your tour, have some chit-chat with other travellers and leave the next afternoon after your swim. This way you can relax and enjoy your exhilarating encounter with one of nature's magnificent beasts! There are a number of tour guides offering boat trips up the river to witness the resident **fire-fly display** – the tours come with mixed reviews but are fairly cheap none the less! If you've enjoyed your encounter, consider heading south to dive and mingle with manta rays in the **'Manta Bowl'** in **Ticao Pass**.

Peak season: February – May, although whales have appeared as early as November and have stayed as late as June.

Main backpacker area – No particular area although the cheaper accommodation can be found in the town centre – **Hernandez Guesthouse** is a good option – while the beachfront can be very pricey

Highlights – Snorkelling with whale sharks & the dubious fire-fly tour

BORACAY... *The Philippines premier tourist hotspot & gateway to the Visayas*

Comparable to Thailand's Koh Samui or Phuket, Boracay is the Philippines' premier tourist hotspot and is a magnetic for planeloads of holidaymakers who flock here in search of sun, sea and sex. While it's part of the Visayas *(covered later on)* I thought I'd give this energetic resort a special mention as this is where most backpackers begin *(or end)* their island hopping adventure through the palm-fringed shores of the majestic **Visayas.** You'll find the usually array of tacky souvenir shops, tourist-orientated restaurants, a vast array of expensive water-sports and a happening nightlife in Boracay. **White Beach**, the centre of Boracay's tourist area, is undoubtedly the area's best beach although you have to navigate your way between all the beach towels! Touts pester you like flies around shit and yet despite this overwhelming concentration of 'mass-tourism' and all those footprints in the sand, Boracay is still a fantastic place to spend a few days and go crazy out before you succumb to the lethargic island pace of the more isolated atolls further afield.

Backpacker orientated digs are scarce and while most of the accommodation isn't great value compared to options elsewhere in the country, you're paying for the spectacular location. Having said that, bargains can be found during the low-season *(June-Nov)* where prices can be slashed by up to 50%! Be aware that rates are inflated beyond peak rates over Christmas, New Year and Easter. If the tourists get too much head over to **Romblon**- an island only a 'stone's throw away' but light years away in terms of development – and begin your majestic island hopping.

Highlights – Nightlife, restaurants, cafés, ZORBing, beaches, water-sports, snorkelling & diving

THE VISAYAS... *Blissful island hopping*

Slip effortlessly into a beach coma – these are the true paradise islands of the Philippines and are the highlight of most traveller's Filipino adventure. These islands are also sheltered from the monsoon rains and have a less-pronounced rainy season. I could write a whole detailed section on these stunning islands, and it's not that I can't be arsed, but I think that half the appeal of these isles is to blissfully hopscotch between them to find your own secluded bays, deserted beaches and crystal clear lagoons on less-travelled islands. I'd suggest making your own way between the energetic and popular beach-resort of **Boracay** to the hustle and bustle of **Cebu** and lose yourself amongst an idyllic patchwork of lethargic sun-soaked islands with a bottle of rum or two! Do as little as you like sizzling on the beaches or do as much island hopping as you can handle!

Away from these popular spots is where you're real adventure begins – get friendly with the islanders who have intricate local knowledge and may be willing to take you to some subdued islands that aren't on most maps where you can maroon yourself on pristine white-sand beaches and tiny palm-fringed islands! Those who brave the perils of irregular boat connections will be rewarded with isolation, tranquillity and the urged never to these captivating tropical islands. As well as succumbing to the laidback rhythm of simple island life, you can explore life beneath the waves and engage in some of the country's best diving, fish in pristine tropical waters, surf decent breaks and trek in rugged jungles. Your best bet is to sketch out a rough route between the popular spots and make an effort to stray off in between:

Entry / exit points: Boracay / Cebu, aka the gateways!

Popular spots – Boracay *(White Beach)*, Romblon, Padre Burgos, Bohol, Guimaras, Sipalay, Siquijor, Malapascua, Bantayan & Cebu

CEBU... *Philippines' second city*

This is the Philippines' cosmopolitan second city and the hub of the Visayas. It's also home to the nation's second busiest airport. I felt that I should touch on this bustling city separately in a bit more detail as this is where most backpackers end *(or start)* their island hopping and Filipino adventure. Cebu is far more bearable than Manila and you don't have to endure such an intoxicating concentration of urban ills. That said Cebu is still a bustling metropolis in a developing country so you don't want to spend too long here – most backpackers utilise it as a **transport hub.** You'll find cheap international connections from here coupled with a comprehensive network of affordable domestic flights to most airports in the Filipino archipelago.

Above all, Cebu is another **gateway to the Visayas** – use it as a base camp to navigate your way around the beautiful outer lying islands much like you'd use Bangkok to explore Thailand or Nadi to explore the Mamanucas and Yasawa islands in Fiji. Most travellers hop on the first convenient bus and head to idyllic off-shore islands of **Bantayan** and **Malapascua** *(North of Cebu)* or **Moalboal** *(South of Cebu)* where you can organise a number of activities and drink copious amounts of alcohol with like-minded travellers! Otherwise, head straight to **Bohol** to kick start your island hopping adventure.

If you do find yourself stuck here for any prolonged period of time – anything more than two consecutive days is far too long really – there are a few sights to check out including **Basilica Minore del Santo Niño, Fort San Pedro** and **Megellan's Cross.** Cebuanos love **shopping** and this passion for retail therapy is symbolised by two huge, glitzy and arm-guarded shopping malls – **Ayala Centre** and **SM City.** A number of other malls will also keep you distracted from the poorer demographic slice of society! If you fancy a spot of **diving** head to over to **Mactan Island** – the glorified mudflat where you landed – where you'll find a number of dive resorts. As for sleeping, budget accommodation is spread throughout town, but is concentrated in the scruffier **Downtown!** Safer and better quality hotels can be found uptown particularly around **Ayala Centre.**

Highlights – Shopping, transport links & its position as the gateway to the Visayas

Off-the-beaten track... *Spice things up a bit!*

It's hard enough to create a realistic and manageable itinerary and not be too over-ambitious, but if you're 'time-rich' and fancy wandering even further off-the-beaten track dedicate more time exploring and marooning yourself on the 1,000's of islands in the **Visayas**. Otherwise, after you've gazed in awe at the ancient rice terraces in **Banaue** and spent a bit of time in the refreshing mountaintop town of **Sagada,** invest a chunk of time roaming around North Luzon – take a step back in time in **Vigan**, check out the mummies of untouched **Kabayan** or surf the breaks in **San Fernando** *(La Union)*.

If time **and money** permit – as it'll probably involve a few domestic flights or some good planning using local ferries – head over to **Palawan** and follow a linear route through this less-travelled and rugged island.

PALAWAN... Stretching from the Mindoro Straight down to the tip of Borneo, this coral fringed stretch of pristine islands is one of the real treasures of the Philippines – and thankfully due to its distance and location away from the rest of the Filipino archipelago, it remains largely off-the-beaten track. For that reason I'm not going to go into much detail, just whet your appetite! Palawan offers everything from world class wreck diving, top-notch snorkelling, intriguing subterranean rivers and rugged jungle trekking to make it the ultimate destination for nature lovers and adventure-sport fanatics! The stunning seascapes of the **Bacuit Archipelago**, the magical turquoise lakes of **Coron Island** and the endless string of beautiful and isolated beaches also provide as much respite as you could ever want!

Ferry connections from Luzon and convenient flights make Palawan a fairly easy destination to get to, but the rugged interior topography coupled a lack of paved roads makes it time consuming to travel around – however the views and places you'll discover along the way are well worth the effort and time. It's a very rewarding island that offers something a bit different.

Some 'tip-bits' – Consider making your way to some of the following places, you're guaranteed to find some hidden gems along the way as well:

o   **Puerto Princesa** – Stock up on your cash reserves and take a quick peek at Palawan museum

o   **Sabang** – Flop on the beaches for some rest and recuperation before heading off and exploring the 8kms of Subterranean River in the National Park – a true Palawan highlight

o   **Port Barton** – Laze the days away in a hammock, snorkel in the crystal-clear waters of secluded bays or do some exploring on the nearby islands in this tranquil town that's well and truly off-the-tourist radar

o   **Coron & the Calamian Group** – Explore sunken WWII ships wrecks on exhilarating dive trips, experience the heat of Barracuda Lake and its swirling volcanic thermals or simply chill-out in hidden lagoons on these stunning less-travelled islands

INDONESIA

OFF-THE-BEATEN TRACK

AT A GLANCE

Capital – Jakarta

Number of Islands – Over 17,000!

Population – 200+ million

Language(s) – Bahasa *(Indonesia)*

Currency – Rupiah & US-dollar

ATMs – In most major towns, scarce on less-developed islands

Climate – Tropical

Best time to go – May - Sept

Time zone(s) – Hours ahead of GMT

Sumatra, Java, W&C Kalimantan: +7

Bali, Nusa Tenggara, S&E Kalimantan: +8

Papua & Maluku: +9

Suggested daily budget – US$15-20 *(more if you want to do some serious island hopping)*

Suggested time – 4-6 weeks *(1-2 weeks Bali)*

Visas – A one-month tourist visa costs US$20 and is issued on arrival

Indonesia is one of the last great frontiers in Asian travel. Anyone who's looking for some back-to-basic backpacking, rustic adventure and a challenge, look no further – travelling doesn't get rawer than this! Stretching nearly 5,000kms, this vast patchwork of undeveloped islands has the potential for endless adventures that's only limited by your timeframe and stamina. Where else can you stalk ancient dragons, observe primitive tribes, hike active volcanoes, surf world-class breaks, maroon yourself on 'Robinson Crusoe' style islands and dance the night away in lively clubs. The experiences are as diverse as they are memorable and the breathtaking scenery provides the perfect backdrop. Given the sheer number of islands and the irregular and sporadic ferry connections, it's best not to be too selective about your Indonesian itinerary – just go with the flow and embrace the unknown. The best thing about travelling here is that your experience will always be a unique one. A voyage through this archipelago is never just an ordinary trip – it's a grand adventure. Pack some humour, patience and a true sense of adventure... you'll be truly rewarded.

MINI GUIDE

If you thought the islands of the Philippines were numerous and challenging, you've seen nothing yet – Indonesia's archipelago completely eclipses that! Creating a realistic and manageable itinerary through this patchwork of isles can seem an impossible task requiring plenty of research and planning... Your best bet, however, is to sketch out a <u>very rough route</u> between these popular highlights, relish the unknown and endure unreliable boat connections to find many fascinating and secluded places in between – there's simply far too many places to write about! Just use your wit, intuition and curiosity – you'll meet plenty of travellers who can offer you advice on the little gems they've found and tales of the places you should avoid! If you're planning a trip to Indonesia you clearly want some off-the-beaten track action! This is raw travelling at its best! Here's a very general 'regional route' *(detailed regional itineraries are in relevant later sub-sections)*:

(Regional flight ➔) Bali & Lombok ➔ Java ➔ Sumatra *(➔ Malaysia)*

These are the most popular 'standard' backpacker destinations – consider entering **Bali**, heading west through Java and Sumatra and leaving for Malaysia via **Belawan** *(or vice-versa)*. If you're short on time you could just get a return flight to Bali and explore a bit of Nusa Tenggara:

BALI... *Indonesia's veteran resort-island*

This is Indonesia's premier tourist destination and the principle gateway into Indonesia. Hoards of package-holidaymakers flock here for the endless sunshine, sandy beaches, big surf and parties aplenty but you'll also find a pleasing mix of untouched wilderness and exciting activities all wrapped up in a vibrant Hindu dressing. Despite its popularity, Bali is surprisingly cheap compared to other parts of SE Asia, albeit more expensive than elsewhere in Indonesia. With good transport links and a busy international airport, Bali's favourite 'first-stop' and will ease you into Indonesia's enchanting but equally challenging archipelago. Bali's **dry season** runs from April-September so you can time this with the start or end of your SE Asian adventure. While most head straight to the beach and surf capital of Kuta, Bali has got something for everyone:

Southern Bali is where you'll find the main tanning beaches, the epic nightlife, late night shenanigans and the inevitable hangovers. **Kuta Beach** is the backpacker's hotspot where seasoned pros, surfing wannabes, party-goers and sun-worshippers congregate. There's no denying that there is extensive development here but it's not on the same scale as Thailand's Phuket or Mexico's Cancún – development has been fairly low-rise and almost sympathetic retaining a degree of dignity, although its innocence has long gone! **Poppies Gang I and II** is where you'll find the no-frills budget accommodation – it's ideally sandwiched between the main beach and the lively clubs around the Bali-bomb memorial. A bustling collection of cafés, lively

> ### Bali-Bungy...
> Give your adrenaline glands a workout while absorbing some stunning views on top of this 45m beachfront bungy jump. If you need some Dutch-courage, head over to the jump when you're leaving the clubs – set within the grounds of the Double Six night club, it's open in the early hours for nervous intoxicated travellers to clear their murky heads!

restaurants and affordable pool-bars are scattered through a maze of streets where you'll also find hoards of street vendors selling cheap surf-wear and souvenirs, and locals playing checkers with bottle tops! **Seminyak** – just north of the bungy jump – is a popular alternative to Kuta where fantastic nightlife is complemented by a stack of cheap accommodation.

Away from the crowds: Generally, the further north you venture the fewer tourists you'll bump into. There's plenty of tranquil fishing villages dotted along the northern coast and dozens of refreshing inland retreats, so after you've expelled your excess energy partying in the hotspots, take some time out and explore the rest of this fascinating island. To begin with, check these out: **Denpasar** boats a wealth of Hindu Temples and the islands largest market *(Pasar Badung)* but if

you're looking for a cultural overload, head to **Ubud** – the cultural-capital of Bali –
where you'll find an array of museums & galleries, numerous temples, ancient sites and
a range of courses in languages, traditional arts, Balinese cooking and dancing. While Ubud is still
a relaxed place, development and tourist numerous have been dramatically increasing – but you
can still find plenty of budget accommodation! Head further north and you can base yourself in
Tampaksiring to explore the tranquil valley of **Gunung Kawi** to see one of Bali's most ancient
and charming monuments. From here you could continue north to reach the coast...

North Bali: This is a relaxing contrast to the 'chaos' of the Kuta region – some travellers prefer
this stretch of coastline to the south coast road. **Lovina** is popular with shoe-stringers boasting
great beaches and plenty of cheap digs. Many travellers, who are heading to Java, continue west
along the coast ending up in **Gilimanuk**.

Mini itinerary: Kuta ➔ Denpasar ➔ Ubud ➔ Tampaksiring ➔ Lovina ➔ Gilimanuk

Main backpacker area – Kuta, budget accommodation is found around Poppies Gang I & II

Highlights – Surfing, beaches, Bali-Bungy, cheap shopping, restaurants & nightlife. Cultural
highlights include; Ubud & Gunung Kawi.

NUSA TENGGARA...

When travellers are content that they can't go a deeper shade of brown, endure another drop of
alcohol or conquer any more surf breaks in Bali, they head east over to the islands of Nusa
Tenggara in search of fewer tourists and a slower pace of life. Here you'll find stunning beaches,
prolific surf, the tropical **Gili Islands**, rugged **Komodo** and the brilliantly coloured lakes of
Kelimutu *(Flores)*. Although improving, transport is sporadic here adding to the rustic charm that
Bali has long lost and that hard-core travellers are itching for. Here are the most popular spots but
if you keep heading east towards **Flores** you're guaranteed some great off-the-beaten track action:

LOMBOK... *Gateway to Nusa Tenggara*

This is the most popular destination in Nusa Tenggara and the principle first-stop after Bali. From
inland to coast, there's plenty to do. The Sacred mountain of **Grunung Rinjani** – one of
Indonesia's tallest peaks – looms over Lombok and entices trekkers to conquer its peak, while the
big breaks of the south are a magnet for surfers. **Kuta** and **Selong Blanak** are the two most
popular and accessible surf towns.

While **Mataram** is the main town in Lombok and is the base for some organised trips, most
travellers head straight to **Senggiri** – a series of sweeping bays and decent beaches just north.
Rapid development followed by a slump in tourism means that Senggiri is one of the best-value
destinations in Indonesia and an ideal spot for shoe-stringers – the **Gili Islands** are only a boat ride
away, so it's the perfect beachfront retreat to save a few pennies! Most backpackers avoid **Bangsal.**

North Lombok is sparsely populated, with limited public transport and only a handful of
travellers. The picturesque village of **Senaru** is the base camp for a climb up Gunung Rinjani –
you can book small-group treks here through the **Rinjani Trek Centre**. All-inclusive large-scale
treks can be arranged in Mataram and Senggiri but these tend to be filled with package-
holidaymakers from Bali! **Sapit** – reachable by Bemo – is another popular town where you can
chill-out admiring some fantastic views and stew in hot springs!

Main backpacker area(s) – **Surfers:** Kuta   **Trekkers:** Senaru   **Beach-bums:** Senggiri

Highlights – Trekking, hot springs, surfing, beaches, peaceful inland-retreats & diving

GILI ISLANDS... *Sun-soaked paradise islands*

Set in the turquoise waters northwest of Lombok, these three beautiful coral-fringed islands are the ultimate tropical get-away. They draw a steady stream of laidback travellers who seek nothing more than sun, sea and carefree drinking. You'll find few pestering touts and no motorised transport where you can do as little as you like in peace and quiet. If you're feeling a bit active and aren't too hungover, these sun-drenched islands offer some fantastic diving & snorkelling – turtles and seasonal manta rays amid an abundance of marine life can be seen at most dive sites.

Gili Air is the closest to the mainland and popular with families and budget backpackers looking for home-stays. Laidback **Gili Meno**, the 'middle-island', is the smallest and quietest out of the trio where you can maroon yourself for days, weeks and even months to enjoy near isolation on pristine beaches under the sizzling tropical sun. Wannabe alcoholics can rejoice on the fantastic party island of **Gili Trawangan** – despite being the farthest out, it's the largest and loudest with the most visitors, best infrastructure and a healthy night scene that encompasses a mix of soft drugs and alcohol! These speckles of paradise have it all where well-informed travellers have been chilling-out for years! Prices yo-yo throughout the year and are higher than elsewhere in Indo.

Getting there & Away – Boats leave from **Senggigi** *(with fewer touts)* & **Bangsal** on Lombok

Main backpacker island(s) – Depends on want you want, see above paragraph!

Highlights – Stunning beaches, isolation & a happening nightlife

KOMODO... *Discover a prehistoric world!*

This rugged and desolate island is sandwiched between Sumbawa and Flores. Komodo is a largely untouched World Heritage Site and provides a unique stepping stone back into a prehistoric world – it's home to the world's largest monitor lizard – the **Komodo dragon**. At 3m long, weighing in at over 100kg and boasting powerful septic jaws, they feed on wild boar, deer and buffalo – they're an awesome sight to be seen! See text box for info.

The only village on Komodo is **Kampung** on the east side although most visitors stay in **Loh Liang** where you'll find huts, an information centre and a cafeteria. Many come here just to see the dragons but Komodo offers a number of other activities, such as walks to **Poreng Valley & Loh Sabita**, treks up **Gunung Ara** and good snorkelling at **Red Beach**.

Dragon spotting...

On Komodo, **Banu Nggulung**, a dry riverbed a half-hour walk from Loh Liang is the most accessible place to see the dragons – they're fed periodically but long gone are the days where live goats are thrown in for tourist to witness nature at its cruellest!

There are no feeding spots on Rinca, but guides will take you to the dragon's favourite locations. They're most common around the **PHKA post**. While the dragons are a docile bunch, attacks have occurred so hire a guide – available at both PHKA camps. Sightings aren't guaranteed!

Rinca: Komodo's neighbouring island, **Rinca**, is less-travelled where you'll also find these prehistoric beasts roaming around and more abundant wildlife. You'll find a PHKA camp at **Loh Buaya** although it's possible to camp at some of the villages. There are no regular boats, so you'll have to get a charter boat from **Labuanbajo** on Komodo. There's a park entrance fee on arrival in Loh Linag *(Komodo)* – it's valid for 7-days and keep hold of your ticket because Rinca is part of the same national park should you decide to go.

Useful websites – www.komodonationalpark.org

Main backpacker area – Loh Liang *(Komodo)* & Loh Buaya *(Rinca)*

Highlights – Dragon spotting, walking & snorkelling

This vast archipelago is the most densely populated region of Indonesia. It's the heart of the country's political and economic power and where the contrasts are stark. Amongst all of this modernisation, prosperity and growth you'll notice unwary levels of pollution, dire poverty and political unrest that cumulate to make this a truly intriguing region to explore. Although, it's perhaps Java's stunning natural beauty that really steals the show – ragged cliffs, deserted beaches, quaint tropical islands and smoking volcanic peaks are waiting outside of the urban jungles.

Popular backpacker entry / exit points:

- o **From Bali:**   **Gilimanuk** ←→ **Banyuwangi** *(Java)* – ferry

  Denpasar ←→ **Many major cities** in Java – bus

- o **From Sumatra:**   **Bakauheni** ←→ **Merak** *(Java)* – ferry

- o **Airports:**   **Jakarta** is Indonesia's busiest international airports and one of the best places to hunt for cheap airfares

Most backpackers follow this **well-trodden route** either flying directly into Jakarta or coming over from Sumatra *(or vice-versa from Bali)*. By all means don't stay in each place – it's just to illustrate the common path so try and deviate to find some undiscovered points of interest:

Jakarta → Bogor → Bandung → Pangandaran → Yoyakarta → Solo → Surabaya → Grunung Bromo before heading over to Bali *(via Banyuwangi)*

By far the most popular, and perhaps stunning destination, is the 'other-worldy' landscape of Gunung Bromo...

GUNUNG BROMO... *Spectacular volcanic landscape*

The **Tengger Massif** is an awesome volcanic landscape. Greedily incorporating three ancient volcanic peaks – Batok, Kursi and Bromo – and flanked by Java's highest and most active peak, Gunung Semeru, it's one if the most impressive sights in Indonesia. The immense **Tengger crater** stretches 10km across and its steep walls plummet into an expanse of sea of laver-sand. Emerging from the crater floor, the puffing peak of Grunung Bromo pierces into the sky. However, compared to other major peaks, Bromo's grey cone isn't the most spectacular in itself, but the beauty is in its setting – location, location, location! The breathtaking views down into the smoking crater extend over the whole desolate landscape making Bromo stand out from the crowd. The ideal time to visit is dry season – April-October – but because of the altitude it's cold at any time of year so bring appropriate clothing!

Cemoro Lawang: This is the most popular place to stay right at the lip of the crater, high on the **Tengger crater** and right at the start of the walk to Bromo. Prices are inflated but you're paying for the stunning views and it's a great place to chill-out with the back drop of these immense peaks. The town of **Probolinggo,** along the well-trodden 'Surabaya – Banyuwangi route', is a good jumping-off point to reach Cemoro Lawang – you'll have to pay a National Park Entrance fee just before the town. You can hike on your lonesome or as part of a group – there's heaps of tracks and info in Cemoro Lawang. Try and set off early so you can see the lava glowing in the night sky and witness a breathtaking sunrise over this incredible landscape.

Main backpacker area – Cemoro Lawang

Highlights – Volcano hikes & just gazing into the guts of this desolate landscape

SUMATRA...

Sumatra is a vast beautiful island boasting blankets of primary forest, lofty mountains, diverse species, barren beaches and plenty of outdoor activities. Nature's wonders are complemented by sparsely populated and remote villages, a rich tribal heritage and a melting pot of ethnic minorities. **Belawan**, Medan's seaport, is a popular entry / exit point into Indonesia from Malaysia. Consequently, many travellers – particularly those pursing a linear itinerary – begin or end the Indonesian adventure in ever popular North Sumatra:

Popular backpacker entry / exit points:

- o **From Malaysia:** **Penang** ⬅➔ **Belawan** *(Sumatra)* – ferry

  Melaka ⬅➔ **Dumai** *(Sumatra)* – ferry, is becoming increasingly popular

- o **From Java:** **Merak** ⬅➔ **Bakauheni** *(Sumatra)* – bus & ferry

  Jakarta ⬅➔ **Padang** *(Sumatra)* – weekly ferry that avoids the tedious bus journeys of the above route

- o **Airports:** **Medan** has the widest choice of destinations incl. KL, Singapore & a few domestic connections incl. Jakarta

Despite improvements in the Trans-Sumatran Hwy, bus journeys tend to be very long and tedious – especially on Sumatra's secondary roads – so stock up on supplies and bring some patience and determination! While **Medan** is the capital of North Sumatra, and the third largest city in Indonesia, most backpackers spend little time in its choked-up urban chaos immediately heading 96km northwest to the **Bukit Lawang** to begin their outdoor adventure...

BUKIT LAWANG... *Unique Orang-Utan encounters*

The town's main attraction is undoubtedly the **Bohorok Orang-Utan Viewing Centre** which has put this once quiet hamlet firmly on the tourist map. The feeding area *(twice daily 08:30 & 15:00)* offers a unique opportunity to see semi-wild orang-utans up close – get there early to watch them arrive and swing through the trees! A steady stream of backpackers arrive at the town during the week, while at the weekends, hoards of day-trippers from Medan descend on the town like a swarm of locus clogging up the narrow streets and otherwise peaceful cafés. Despite this, it's still a great place to hang-out and relax. After spending some time observing our primates, most travellers prolong their stay to explore the surrounding dense forest and have some fun on the fast-flowing rivers...

Activities: Nestled on the eastern fringe of **Gunung Leuser National Park**, Bukit Lawang is a great base for jungle treks – almost every guesthouse offers a range of tours, from 3-hour hikes to 2-day and 4-day treks. You need a licensed guide to enter the national park and rates are supposed to be fixed by the Sumatra Guide Association so check a few to compare prices! **White-water rafting** and **kayaking** trips on the scenic Wampu River and the more turbulent Asahan River can be organised through a few outfits in town. Inflated inner-tubes can be rented from many locals for a spot of tubing but don't expect anything like the drunken madness of Vang Vieng in Laos! The current accommodation options in Bukit Lawang are concentrated in two main areas – on the left bank of the River Bohorok near the village entrance, and on the right bank, near the Feeding Centre.

Useful websites – www.bukitlawang.com

Highlights – Trekking, caving, tubing, rafting & kayaking & the Bohorok Orang-utan Centre

Moving on from Bukit Lawang... *Where to next?*

Sumatra is a fascinating island to explore, and at four times the size of Java and having a quarter of the population of its neighbouring island, there are plenty of less-travelled places and back-to-basic adventures to be discovered... Most travellers follow this well-trodden route through Sumatra, entering from Malaysia *(via Belawan)* before head over to Java *(via Bakauheni)*. To a large extent it's confined to North and West Sumatra so stray-off between Padang and Bundarlampung:

Bukit Lawang ➔ Berastagi ➔ Danau Toba ➔ Nias ➔ Bukittinggi ➔ Padang ➔ Bandarlampung

Here are a few places to give you a few ideas and help you sketch out a rough route:

- o Explore life beneath the waves at some of the country's top dive sites around blissful **Pulau Weh** – the tropical island paradise isolated just off Sumatra's northern tip

- o Cool-off and chill-out in the clear waters of SE Asia's largest lake, **Danau Toba.** Set in mist-clad mountains, it's a spectacular and refreshing retreat a few clicks south of **Bakit Lawang.** Many stay in the popular town of **TukTuk** but if you're after genuine culture stay in one of the villages on the other side of this inland-island

- o Discover the cultural heartland of Sumatra in **Bukittinggi** before hopping across to the isolated and quaint **Mentawi Islands** for some soothing beach-time and lashings of tropical sun

Off-the-beaten track... *Spice things up a bit!*

Most people follow a popular and logical linear route through Sumatra, Java, Bali and Nusa Tenggara. Those short on time often just explore Bali and Lombok with a return ticket from Bali. Of course these typical itineraries are very practical and cost efficient but, if time and patience permit, try and explore the less-travelled regions of **Kalimantan**, **Sulawesi**, **Maluku**, **Papua** and the blissful **Banda Islands**.

Away from the few main towns, minority groups and off-the-beaten track adventures await. Rugged terrain and dense jungle coupled with sparse populations and adverse tropical weather ensures that communication and travel through them is slow and difficult at the best of times! If you want a challenge away from crowds, it doesn't get much better than this. If you really want to get into the guts of these remote regions without feeling rushed, you'll need to invest a lot of time and a longer visa – especially considering that a lot of the local rural transport runs sporadically and can be extremely weather dependant! In other areas, some villages can only be reached on foot!

Some 'tip-bits':

Here are a few better-known places a bit out of the way to help you plan a route and get your bearings – you're guaranteed to find plenty of intriguing places and hidden gems trying to get to them:

- o **Tanjung Puting National Park** *(Kalimantan)* – Roam around this 4,150sq km of tropical rainforest, mangrove forest and wetlands to discover a mind-boggling variety of fauna including crocs, exotic bird-life, orang-utans, gibbons, deadly snakes, dolphins and mudskippers *(a weird fish that can breathe air and 'walk' on land)*. A number of research camps, **Camp Leakey** being the primary site, offer regular glimpses of wild orang-utans foraging in their natural habitats

- Baliem Valley *(Papua)* – Take a trip into this isolated landscape of dense jungle, towering peaks, ethnic minorities and ancient traditions. This is a truly unique and 'lost world' where recently discovered tribes continue to thrive and evade any form of modern progression – these guys haven't even had the industrial revolution yet! This is a rare pocket of the planet that has remained hidden from view! Base yourself in **Wamena** for trekking trips – the town is pricey mind as everything's flown in from Jayapura!

- Bunaken Marine National Park *(Sulawesi)* – This park encompasses the most northern tip of Sulawesi where you can sizzle on pristine beaches and go the darkest shade of brown or get wet exploring the vibrant reefs and experience some of Indonesia's best diving and snorkelling. The colonial town of **Manado**, on the mainland, is a popular jump-off point while the beautiful island **Pulau Bunaken** of is where most prolong their stay in seductive tropical style

- Banda Islands – This picturesque cluster of 10 tropical islands is brimming with colonial forts, beautiful barren beaches and studded with rugged volcanoes. Being perched on some impressive undersea drops-offs and boasting some vibrant coral reefs and crystal-clear waters, these islands have become a cult destination for diving fanatics and beach-floppers alike

  The two main islands – **Pulau Neira** and **Pulau Banda Besar** – curl in crescents around **Pulau Gunung Api** in typical picturesque fashion. While these islands remain off the radar for the meantime, visitor numbers are increasing, so head to the outlying islands of **Hatta**, **Ai** and **Neilaka** where the tropical bliss is further intensified and you can still get an island to yourself – well almost!

A more detailed map...

Here's a more detailed map with most of the towns and destinations mentioned in the mini-itineraries marked on so you can visualise the well trodden routes.

Central America

Action ◊ Off-the-beaten track adventure ◊ Culture

WHY GO TO... *C.AMERICA?*

GET OFF-THE-BEATEN TRACK

Use this themed section to help you decide what region to go to. Compare this section to the Asian and Australasian equivalents to find your perfect tailored destination.

CENTRAL AMERICA... *An introduction*

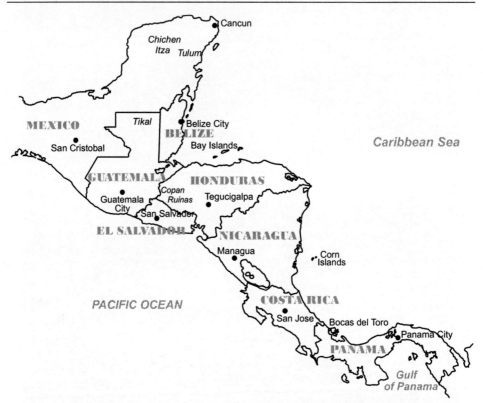

A region that's just waking up from a bad dream of war, dictatorships and corruption, Central America is now open for business. Tiny on a map, and bridging the gap between North and South America, this compact region is crammed with untold adventure. Blessed with an extensive coastline, this slender region is flanked by the colourful Caribbean Sea on one side and the crashing waves of the Pacific Ocean on the other. Its rugged mountainous interior is studded with volcanic peaks, blanketed by dense jungle and peppered with scatterings of crumbling Mayan ruins and 16th Century colonial towns. This backdrop provides the perfect setting for any number of activities, from peering into active volcanoes to stewing in hot springs the possibilities are only limited by your imagination. Despite their turbulent past, it's perhaps the region's friendly and upbeat folk that's most captivating. Central America is a true cultural treat blending a distinct Latino spirit and a vibrant colonial past with a mellow Caribbean vibe and Garifuna influences. The dominant Spanish language is briefly interrupted by the gentle patter of Creole and several Mayan dialects. Family stays, volunteer opportunities and traveller-orientated language schools truly open up this fascinating region for a rewarding cultural awakening. Intriguing for first-time backpackers and affordable for hardcore shoe-stringers, this region has something for everyone...

Central America is a great alternative to or the perfect follow on trip to SE Asia. Although it's slightly more expensive than SE Asia, it's still a lot cheaper than Oz, New Zealand, USA and the Pacific. The tourist infrastructure is not as developed as that in SE Asia but backpackers are still well catered for with reasonable transport options and a range of accommodation to suit all budgets. With the exception of Costa Rica and Mexico, the region is less commercialised than SE Asia so you'll find fewer crowds of package-holidaymakers, less flash-packers, a more rustic backpacker scene and fewer footprints on the beaches! Despite its compact size, this region gives you a rare opportunity to tramp on roads less-travelled and have some authentic encounters with the locals and their lifestyle. Its turbulent war-torn past and high-profile political corruption has helped to preserve the authenticity of this region and in countries where few go, folks are friendly and countless off-the-beaten track adventures await.

If you're a bit more adventurous, itching for a bit different and want get away from the development that's softened the challenge of SE Asia you'll relish a trip around Central America. Spanish is the dominant language in the region with English only spoken in Belize and along the Caribbean Coast – this represents not only a challenge but a fantastic opportunity brush up on your linguistic skills where you'll find dozens of wallet-friendly language schools dotted throughout the region and plenty of rewarding opportunities to dabble with a dose of culture. Whatever your passion though, this diverse region is bursting with everything; scale crumbling ruins, hike smouldering volcanoes, worship the sun on deserted beaches, conquer big waves, swing your hips in salsa classes, learn the local lingo, look forward to rum induced hangovers and indulge yourself in the Latino spirit!

Central America is an ideal destination...

- o   If you want to immerse yourself and interact with **different cultures & languages**

- o   If you've got **limited funds** but a **lot of spare time** – like in Southeast Asia, you money **can** go *(very)* far!

- o   Alternatively, if you've got a **limited amount of time**, the regions slender figure means that it's neatly compact so you can whip through the highlights quicker than you can trek through SE Asia or roam around Australasia

- o   If you want a bit of a **challenge** – infrastructure is less-developed and regions are more remote. Backpacking here is still in its infancy. Here children are still dazed by your towering height, intrigued by your blinding skin colour and stare curiously into blue eyes.

- o   If you want to waggle your multi-lingual tongue and **learn another language** *(Spanish)* – the region's blessed with dozens of top-notch language schools although numerous volunteer opportunities will also get you dabbling with a few Mayan dialects

- o   If you want to get **off-the-beaten track** – encounters here are usually more authentic than in over-packaged Thailand and you'll bump into fewer travellers. With the exception of the Philippines & Indonesia, there are a greater proportion of towns that aren't geared towards tourism and there are plenty of less-travelled roads

- o   If you're a **couple** – although there's an energetic alcohol fuelled party scene, travelling in Central America is a more relaxed, 'chilled-out' and low-key affair making it more ideal for couples than SE Asia

HIGHLIGHTS... *Don't miss the best bits!*

Despite her slender figure, you won't be able to see and do everything that Central America has to offer on your first trip, and you'd be mad to try! Above all, Central America oozes culture in abundance and offers an array of ways to interact with it and really get stuck in. You'll also find a pleasing amount of adventure activities to get your heart racing and, of course, a fair share of lively booze-fuelled party towns. Here are a few things you should try and cram into your itinerary:

ANCIENT MAYAN RUINS   Feel small and insignificant as you gaze up at some magnificent Mayan ruins. Being the biggest, set deep in the jungle, and laying half unexcavated, popular Tikal in Guatemala, grabs the headlines and gets the biggest 'wows'. However, while mighty Tikal dwarfs the other Mayan ruins, other equally intriguing Mayan sites can be found scattered throughout Central America – from the cliff-top ruins at Chichén Itza in Mexico to the hilly inland setting of Copán in Honduras, each has site had its own distinctive and enchanting appeal

CAYE CAULKER *(Belize)*   Do as little as you like on this laidback Caribbean island of sand streets, airy beachfront shacks and friendly islanders. Watersports are the name of the game here where, if you can snap out of relaxation mode and stagger away from the chilled-out bars, you can find some world-class diving and snorkelling in Belize's awesome Blue Hole or cruise the perfect turquoise waters on a peaceful sailboat

CENOTÉ EXPLORATION *(Mexico)*   Take diving to a different level – there's simply very few places in the world where you can find a series of pitch black and flooded underground caverns to explore. It's even rarer to find Cenotés that are so accessible to the 'average backpacker'. You'll find a range of snorkelling & diving options in Mexico's hippie town of Tulum

VOLCANO HIKING & BOARDING *(Guatemala, Nica & Costa Rica)*   Navigate foggy asteroid-like terrain, toast marsh mellows and sizzle steaks over flowing lava and red hot crevices – thankfully, it appears that in Antigua health & safety rules appear very relaxed so you can get up close and personal with one of nature's most powerful beasts! If you want to take it to the extreme, why not surf down the side of a conical peak on a 'volcano board' in León *(Nicaragua)*

HOT SPRINGS   Soothe your aching muscles, get wrinkly and stew in hot springs with a beer or two in the geothermal active countries of Guatemala and Costa Rica. Steer clear of the over-developed concrete ones that are targeted at package-holidaymakers, ask around and seek out the real-deal. It's pure relaxation

TOP NOTCH SPANISH SCHOOLS *(Guatemala)*   Get to grips with the local lingo and interact with the Latino folk and enrol on a top-notch course for next to nothing. While the well-renowned and charming town of Antigua is the most popular place to train your tongue, other less-travelled towns like Quetzaltenango also offer good wallet-friendly Spanish schools – and without the distracting nightlife and outdoor activities of lively Antigua!

SALSA CLASSES   Learn to swing your hips and impress the opposite sex in true Latino style! If you look hard enough and ask the locals, you can find quality little dancing outfits that offer one-to-one tuition

COLONIAL TOWNS   Central America boasts some of the best well-preserved colonial towns in the world. From 16th century Granada and its colonial rival León in Nicaragua to the slightly less-travelled examples of Quetzaltenango in Guatemala and San Cristóbal de Las Casa in Mexico, they're as interesting as they are varied. These enchanting towns will engage with even the most hardened cultural sceptic and slow down the fast paced 'rushing travellers'

NATIONAL PARKS   This compact region is blessed with an abundance of biodiversity and dense tropical forest and thankfully a lot of this is now protected. From Belize's Crooked Tree Wildlife Sanctuary to Costa Rica's isolated Parque Nacional Totuguero, wherever you are in Central America you'll have a unique opportunity to explore some stunning pockets of pristine natural beauty. Jungle walks reward you with the 'symphony of the forest', sightings of monkey, birds, crocs and turtles and even rare glimpses of elusive big-cats

CANOPY ZIP LINING *(Costa Rica)*   Attach yourself to over a kilometre of wire suspended high in the rainforest canopy, left you legs and eagerly wait for a gentle push that'll send you whizzing through the treetops at high speed only to emerging from of the canopy to find yourself hundreds of feet in the air over deep gorges, fast flowing rivers and magnificent waterfalls – welcome to Zip Lining! You'll find these heart racing 'zip-line' tours in La Fortuna *(Costa Rica)*

BUDGET DIVING *(Honduras)*   Get stalked by gangs of friendly sharks, swim with graceful manta rays, glide through schools of tropical fish and feast your eyes on vibrant coral reef – Central America offers some fantastic diving sites. From Belize's impressive Caribbean Blue Hole to the prime pacific dives sites just off Playa Tamarindo, you've got two coastlines and two mighty oceans to scuba dive in! Moreover, you'll find the worlds cheapest diving at the legendary shoe-stringers island of Utila – it doesn't get cheaper than this

SURFING   From the little known and laidback surf retreats along El Salvador's coast to the crowded waves of San Juan del Sur, this region boasts some awesome breaks to ride. Whether you're an eager beginner or a seasoned pro, the majority of beaches are awash with friendly surf culture where it would just be rude not to get involved!

BOCAS DEL TORO *(Panama)*   Panamas premier hotspot is home to laidback locals and an upbeat traveller's scene. Cracking nightlife is complemented by a fair share of activities on and off the shore and some funky backpacker digs – check out the innovative wooden 'Aqua Lounge' that extends over the sea and is reachable by boat from the 'mainland'. In fact, Bocas del Toro is actually a small six-island archipelago, so if the hangovers get to much boat-it to the next island in search of seclusion! You'd be crazy to miss out

OFF-THE-BEATEN TRACK   Despites it's compact size, this region offers some superb opportunities to venture where fewer travellers go and reward yourself with authentic encounters with minority groups, untouched landscapes, wild and remote rainforest and secluded beaches. The La Mosquitia region, stretching across the eastern parts of Honduras and Nica, offers prime-time isolation and appealing challenges while pretty much the whole of El Salvador offers more manageable off-the-beaten track adventures

BEERS + SPIRITS   Knock back the famous tipples of Mexico that include Sol, Corona and Tequila and discover some local treats such as Flor de Caña in Nicaragua as you get delve deep into this fascinating and varied region. Forget buckets, they're so Asia, drink your rum and coke from a see-through bags with a straw – handy for 'on-the-bus' drinking! After many rum induced hangovers, you'll become quite the rum connoisseur!

FOOD   Forget your American style Tex-Mex, drop into the local markets and snack at the food shacks to discover the real taste of Central America. There's more than just 'rice and beans' or deep fried plantain! So travel your taste buds and stay away from the boring tourist orientated eateries and embark on a grand flavour trail

BEACHES   From the golden-sand beaches of Costa Rica and the popular strips in Mexico to El Salvador's underrated black-sand beauties and the empty sands of the Corn Islands, you'll be spoilt for choice when it comes to beaches in Central America. You'll come back the deepest shade of brown, no worries

As with Asian the climate, Central America is characterised by two distinct seasons:

- THE WET SEASON: May – Oct   Characterised by; *downpours, cloud, high humidity*

- THE DRY SEASON: Nov – April   Characterised by; *dry, hot weather, lower humidity*

If you've got no constraints on the timing of your trip, make good predictable weather your priority! Although there are some regional variations, early **November** to late **March** is generally the best time to go to Central America where the weather is not only hot and dry but bearable and not too sticky! Bear in mind that this period is also the busiest season and prices are inflated. Peak periods, such as Christmas, are even pricier as package-holidaymakers flock to destinations such as Mexico and Costa Rica. You may want to avoid or time your trip with events such as Spring Break where college and university students swell the population and increase the decibels of towns like Cancún *(Mexico)*.

The **shoulder months** of October/early November and April/May are noticeably cheaper although the weather can be a little unpredictable albeit still hot. It's also worth remembering that some seaside towns will be in semi-hibernation during the shoulder months – although this is not necessarily a bad thing if you want some peace and quiet and would like to take advantage of lower off-peak rates.

North to South: If you intend to pursue the popular linear itinerary, in terms of weather, it's better to travel from the north of the region to the south. The dry seasons of Costa Rica and Panama start and end a few months after their northern counterparts. By starting your trip in the north of the region you'll hit the south later on towards the end of your trip when their dry seasons are beginning, so effectively you'll be optimising the dry seasons and giving yourself a longer stretch of better weather.

THE LOGICAL LINEAR ROUTE...

Ok so there's a tiny bit of backtracking at the end, but this practical linear route takes in most of the regions highlights and gets you all the exotic ink marks from all of the countries in the region!

MEXICO ➔ BELIZE ➔ GUATEMALA ➔ HONDURAS *(Optional)* **➔ EL SALVADOR ➔ NICARAGUA ➔ COSTA RICA ➔ PANAMA ➔ COSTA RICA**

Suggested time:　　　3-5 months *(longer if you want to study Spanish)*

Entry/exit points:　　Cancún *(Mexico)* / San José *(Costa Rice)*

The countries/route:　**Mexico** – Cancún, Isla Mujeres, Tulum

Belize – Caye Caulker,

Guatemala – Flores, Cobán & Lanquín, Antigua

Honduras *(if you want to dive)* – Copán Ruinas, Utila, Tela

El Salvador – San Salvador, Costa del Bálsamo, Perquín *(optional)*

Nicaragua – León, Isla de Ometepe, San Juan del Sur

Costa Rica – Playa Tamarindo, La Fortuna, San José, Puerto Viejo

Panama - Bocas del Toro

Begin your Latino adventure in alcoholic style in loud and proud **Cancún** and then drag your hung-over self to the backpacker friendly island of **Isla Mujeres**. From here, head south to the chilled-out hippie town of **Tulum**. Next up, is Belize's enchanting Caribbean island, **Caye Caulker,** for some sun, sea and rum. **Flores** is the first stop in Guatemala where you can explore the mighty **Tikal** ruins. Continuing through Guatemala, hit the chilled-out retreat of **Lanquin** before enrolling on a language course in **Antigua**. Keen divers should take a detour to the **Bay Islands** *(Utila)* where you'll be rewarded with the world's cheapest diving – to break-up the detour, stop-off at **Tela** for some beach-time and Copan for a dose of culture. Beach devotes should dedicate endless days to El Salvador's sands along its **Costa Balsamo – Playa El Zonte** is a popular low-key beach-town. Skip through Honduras for a spot of culture in **León** before getting back to nature on **Isla de Ometepe**. Do as little as you like in the beach towns of **San Juan** and **Tamarindo** before signing up for a host of exciting activities in the region's premier adventure town, **La Fortuna**. Finish off your trip in the surf spot of **Puerto Viejo** and lively **Bocas** before backtracking to **San José** to fly home.

The well-trodden route
Off-the-beaten track
For keen divers
● Less travelled destinations

THE MINI LOOPING ALTERNATIVES...

While linear routes are more practical, there are **two** action packed mini-looping itineraries that you could pursue. These are slightly shorter routes and could be more suitable if you're a bit tight on time or money. Just because they're shorter, by no means are they less challenging. In fact, these imaginative routes get you off-the-beaten track far more that the conventional linear route:

1) THE NORTHERN LOOP:

This northern circuit can be completed in slightly less time than the popular linear route but it's still jam-packed with adventure, culture and alcohol-fuelled late nights! This route incorporates all of the northern region's best bits but it also gets you off-the-beaten track and into the guts of Belize, Honduras and underrated El Salvador.

GUATEMALA → BELIZE → HONDURAS → NICARAGUA → EL SALVADOR → GUATEMALA

Suggested time:	7-10 weeks
Entry/exit points:	Guatemala City *(Guatemala)*
The countries/route:	**Guatemala** – Guatemala City, Cobán *(& Lanquin)*, Flores *(& Tikal)*
	Belize – Caye Caulker, Dangriga, Hopkins, Placencia
	Honduras – Bay Islands *(Utila)*, Copán Ruinas, Tegucigalpa
	Nicaragua – León, Managua, Isla de Ometepe, San Juan del Sur, Granada
	El Salvador – Perquín, Costa del Bálsamo, San Salvador
	Guatemala – Antigua, Guatemala City

Start you adventure in **Guatemala City** and head over to explore **Cobán,** chill-out in **Lanquin** and cool-off in the turquoise pools of **Semuc Champey.** Next, venture up to **Flores** to check out the mother of all Mayan Ruins, **Tikal.** Nip across the border to Belize and chill-out on the Caribbean island of **Caye Caulker.** When you slip out of lethargic island life, hug the Caribbean coast and drop in the less-visited towns of **Dangriga, Hoptkins** and **Placenia** before boating-it over to **Utila** for some of the world's cheapest diving *(via Puerto Cortés and La Ceiba)*. Continue through Honduras visiting the Ruins in **Copán** and the country's capital before dropping into the Colonial town of **León.** After a taste of culture head over to **Isla de Ometepe** for some hiking before flopping on the beaches at the top surf spot of **San Juan del Sur**. Pop into **Granada** for a second serving of culture before visiting sobering **Perquin** before exploring El Salvador's underrated **Costa del Balsamo**. Finally, head back into Guatemala to train your tongue and hike an active volcano in picturesque **Antigua** before flying from the capital.

- The northern loop(s)
- Off-the-beaten track detour
- Less-travelled destinations

2) THE SOUTHERN 'LOOP':

The southern loop is actually two mini looping itineraries that'll get you exploring every inch of Costa Rica from the popular adventure town of La Fortuna to remote off-the-beaten track spots like Corcovado National Park. This route will also ensure that you see most of Nica and a good selection of Panama. From adrenaline fuelled activities in La Fortuna and up-all-nighters in Bocas del Toro to the biodiversity of Tortuguero and the remoteness of the Corn Islands, this trail has got something for everyone.

COSTA RICA ➜ PANAMA ➜ COSTA RICA ➜ NICARAGUA ➜ COSTA RICA

Suggested time:	7-10 weeks
Entry/exit points:	San José *(Costa Rica)*
The countries/route:	**Costa Rica** – San José, Puerto Viejo de Talamanca
	Panama – Bocas del Toro, Boquete
	Costa Rica – Parque Nacional Corovado, San José, La Fortuna, Playa Tamarindo
	Nicaragua – San Juan del Sur, Isla de Ometepe, Granada, Managua, (Bluefields) Corn Islands, El Castillo
	Costa Rica – Tortuguero, San José

Escape **San José** as quick as you can and head towards the Caribbean Coast to chill-out in a hammock in the surfing retreat of **Puerto Viejo.** Hop across the border to **Bocas del Toro** for some energetic nightlife and mellow Caribbean charm. When you're finally sober, head to the less-travelled mountain-top retreat of **Boquete**. Continue the off-the-beaten track adventure and slip across the border to explore the unspoilt **Parque Nacional Corcovado**. From here, head north towards the adventure town of **La Fortuna** for some exciting outdoor activities and volcano hiking. The beach towns of **Playa Tamarindo** and **San Juan del Sur** are next up where you can conquer some of the region's best breaks and soak up the sun before exploring the unique twin-volcano

island, **Isla de Ometepe,** for some hiking and spectacular views. Dose up on some culture in the charming colonial town of **Granada** before getting off-the-beaten track and venture over to the quirky **Corn Islands** – getting here is an adventure in itself! Stop-over in **Bluefields** if you need to break up the journey. Continue deep on roads less-travelled and check out remote **El Castillo** and untouched **Tortuguero** for some of the region's most memorable journeys before flying home from Costa Rica's Captial, **San José.** Fuel your trip with Flor de Caña – tasty local Rum!

Where to fly into/out of... *The regional hub(s)*

San José *(Costa Rica)* and **Cancún** *(Mexico)* are the regional hubs and where most backpackers enter and exit the region. You'll find the cheapest airfares to and from these although cheap tickets can also be found in and out of **Guatemala City** *(Guatemala)* and **Panama City** *(Panama)*.

Type of airline ticket... *Your options*

This will depend on what type of itinerary you're pursing. Getting to Central America is a little trickier than getting to SE Asia if you want to save a few quid – direct flights exist but are fairly pricey compared to other more imaginative options if you're prepared to do a bit of research and be a bit creative with your flights! *(See section 6, Booking your trip... for additional information on airlines, tickets and how to reduce the price of your airline ticket)*:

- o **Linear itinerary:** This is the more practical option. On a linear itinerary you want to be flying into Cancún *(Mexico)* and out of San José *(Costa Rica)* or vice versa with **two single tickets.** You can fly direct to the major cities of Central America from Europe but these tend to be expensive compared to other options. Sounds crazy but if you do some research it <u>can</u> be cheaper to get **two single tickets** and a **return ticket**. Look around for a cheap return deal to somewhere in the USA – New York is ideal – and the get two single tickets with budget airlines – **Jet Blue** for example – to link your USA location with your entry and departure points in Central America! So in this example you'd have a return ticket from Europe to New York and a single ticket from the Big Apple to Cancún and another single ticket from San José to NY before flying back to Europe on your return ticket.

  Consider an **open-jaw ticket** if you're not sure what date you want to fly back on or you feel that you may venture deeper in Mexico or Panama and reach their capital cities.

- o **Looping itinerary:** Central America's slim figure renders looping itineraries impractical but if you have to get a return ticket, your best bet is to fly in and out of San José *(Costa Rica)*. Again look at getting two return tickets, one to and from San José to New York with a budget airline and a return to and from the Big Apple to your home country.

- o **RTW ticket:** If you're lucky enough to be on a RTW ticket and want to include a realistic and manageable surface sector through Central America, consider flying into Panama City *(Panama)* or San José *(Costa Rica)* and out of Cancún *(Mexico)* or Mexico City *(Mexico)* to achieve a sizeable surface sector that gets the most out of your RTW ticket.

For the majority of westerners Central America is a fantastically cheap destination – overall it's cheaper than Australasia but it's a little more expensive than SE Asia. The costs of airline tickets to get to Central America are similar to the cost of getting to Asia and significantly cheaper than getting to Australasia *(from Europe)*. As with Asia, bear in mind that some countries may not be as cheap as you'd expect and daily budgets do vary considerably across the region. Generally speaking Belize, Costa Rica and Mexico are the more expensive countries in Central America – although these are still very cheap compared to the developed countries of Europe and North America. El Salvador, Guatemala, Honduras and Nicaragua are the least developed and cheaper countries. The following prices are all in US-dollars for easy comparison.

Daily budgets for first-time travellers range from **US$35-45** or **450 -600 pesos in Mexico** *(about £20-27)* to **US$20** or **175 quetzal in Guatemala** *(around £12)*

Below is a broad overview of your main expenses in Central America:

ACCOMMODATION... *Sleep in a hammock for US$5!*

Being a lot cheaper than Australasia, accommodation across Central America is very affordable although it's a little more expensive than Asia. Backpackers primarily stay in **hostels** although Asian style **guesthouses** and **beach huts** are common, especially in Belize, El Salvador and Guatemala. Most offer single, double and triple rooms. **Dormitories** are very common, particularly in hostels, and are great to reduce you accommodation costs if you're travelling on your lonesome or want to be sociable. If you're travelling with company dorms don't usually work out cheaper as prices are normally **per room not per person**. Unlike Asia you'll be surprised to find a lot more **camping options** spread across Central America so it's worthwhile taking a tent to reduce your accommodation costs.

Prices don't vary that much across the region with Mexico being the only exception with noticeably pricier accommodation than elsewhere. Expect to pay between **US$6** and **US$12** for a night's kip in a dorm and up to **US$20** for a double room. You can have an interesting night's sleep in a **hammock** for around **US$5** in some hostels or 'upgrade' and stay in a tent for between **US$6** and **US$10** – prices are usually per tent. Perhaps, obviously, prices are inflated during peak times and bargains can be found during low seasons. Make sure you ask around a few guesthouses to get the best deal and make sure you see the room before you hand over any money as the standard of accommodation varies greatly across the region. By western standards rooms can be fairly dirty and beds uncomfortable! Showers are usually cold and air-condition's a luxury that'll bump the price of a room up. You'll find the usual array of internet and travel services at the majority of backpacker accommodation as well as communal kitchens in hostels. It's extremely rare to find traditional laundrettes but you'll find a host local 'entrepreneurs' offering to wash, dry and fold your clothes for a few US-dollars – prices are per Kilo.

FOOD & DRINK... *Cook your own!*

You'll find that with a larger proportion of hostels there's more accommodation with cooking facilities in Central America than in Asia. This means you can cook your own food and save a few quid. Kitchens are communal so be economical and sociable by cooking in groups – it's a great way to make new friends as well as reduce your food bill! Buy your ingredients in local markets and shops – you'll find that most of the shops are run by fairly rude Chinese people and haggling is fairly difficult!

As in Asia, you can still eat out for a couple of quid in local restaurants and cafés. Street food isn't as wide spread as it is in Asia but local food shacks and street kitchens are scattered throughout the region and are as cheap as their Asian counterparts. If you can't stomach anymore rice & beans head to the local markets where you'll find an array of interesting snacks and meals. You can find delicious tacos for less than a **US-dollar** in Mexican markets and fried chicken with plantain from food stalls in Panama for no more than a **couple of US-dollars**. In local eateries, the language barrier often means that ordering your food usually involves a game of 'charades' and what you get can be a bit of a lottery! You can't drink the water from the tap so you'll need to buy bottled water from shops. It's a bit of a shock but some cities are fast-food centrals boasting the full portfolio of greasy joints from Maccy-D's and Burger King to KFC and Dunkin' Donuts – San Salvador is a prime example where you're never far from a taste of home! The bad news is prices aren't that much cheaper than at home making it expensive for the region.

ALCOHOL... *Local rum from US$5 a bottle!*

Alcohol is very affordable by western standards and you don't need to be a lightweight to have a very cheap night – it's a lot cheaper than Europe, North America and Down Under. Getting drunk is a popular past time in Central America and you can get monster 1.25litre bottles of Sol and Corona for around **US$2-3** in local bars/restaurants and even cheaper in shops. Obviously prices are heavily inflated in popular tourist resorts like Cancún – get drunk at your hostel and buy beer from local shops is the tight-arse advice here. You can find bottles of local rum, such as Flor de Caña in Nicaragua, and Smirnoff Vodka for around **US$5**. On the whole you'll find that alcohol in Central America is generally cheaper than most parts of SE Asia! When you buy beers from shops make sure you take your empties back to get your 'deposit' back. Scavenge around and collect enough bottles that other people have left behind to get enough money for a free beer!

ACTIVITIES... *The world's cheapest diving*

You'll find a fair few more adrenaline fuelled activities in Central America than in SE Asia and you won't need deep pockets to pursue them. You won't see much difference in price compared to SE Asia but activities are a lot cheaper than Fiji, Oz and NZ. A lot of the more extreme activities are found in Costa Rica but you'll be pleasantly surprised to still find them good value for money. The more expensive activities include – white-water rafting that'll cost you about **US$60**, towering bungy jumps from **US$40** and fast paced canopy tours that'll set you back around **US$45**. You can give your adrenaline glands a workout elsewhere – **US$49** will get you exploring mysterious cenotés in Tulum *(Mexico)* while **US$23** will get you a day's extreme volcano boarding in León *(Nicaragua)*. Throughout the region you can hike active volcanoes, stew in hot springs and hire kayaks or bikes and still get change from **US$15**. Entrance to ancient Mayan temples across Central America range from a couple of **US-dollars** to **US$10** – tours around the towering pyramids of Tikal cost around **US$40**.

The world's cheapest scuba diving courses can be found on the famous Bay Islands *(Honduras)* – it's hard to believe but they're even cheaper than the ever popular courses on Koh Toa *(Thailand)* and elsewhere in SE Asia, albeit a little less organised! Fun dives come in at around **US$30** and you can find 4-day open-water PADI courses from as little as **US$225**! If you're not keen on diving, fantastic snorkelling is an equally cheap activity. Surfing is another popular past-time that doesn't cost a fortune – half-a-day's rental will only set you back around **US$10** even in surfing hotspots such as Playa Tamarindo *(Costa Rica)*. If you're really into your surfing you can negotiate cheaper weekly rates or buy a second-hand board – sell it when you're finished with it.

TRANSPORT... *Pimped up US School busses with fares from 25cents!*

Transport across the region is great value for money and prices varies moderately throughout the region - transport is slightly more expensive in Costa Rica and Mexico and is a little cheaper in El Salvador and Honduras. In general, transport in Central America is cheaper than in Asia. The compact geographical nature of the region certainly helps to further reduce your transport costs.

On the whole you won't find the transport as varied or as interesting as the wacky modes of transportation in Asia but transport is on the whole slightly cheaper. Punctuality and overcrowding are common problems that'll constantly cause you a headache. There are fewer backpacker orientated options compared to SE Asia and Australasia. Consequently, it's slightly more challenging to get around Central America and you'll find that **public transport** will form the bulk of your transport and this can be **more rewarding** and **cheaper**.

Mini / Shuttle Busses

Where: Everywhere

When: Between towns & over border crossings

How Much: Cheap

Land transport in Central America and Mexico is all about the shuttle *(micro)* bus. They form transport links between most towns and are reasonably priced albeit often overcrowded. In theory there should be a fixed price to each destination but in reality they'll charge you whatever they like – so take note of what the locals are paying and bearing in mind you'll probably have to pay a little more than them, negotiate a fair price before you get in and hand them your luggage. Luggage is crammed in with you, under the seats or on your lap and occasionally it's strapped to the roof – just take a quick peek and check it's strapped on securely! Expect busses to be overcrowded, unpunctual and uncomfortable at times!

Old U.S. School Busses

Where: El Salvador

When: Between towns

How Much: Very cheap

Pimped up, brightly coloured old US-school busses pumping out Latino music form one of the main public transport options in El Salvador – especially along Costa del Bálsamo. A ride on one of these is a must do when you're venturing around off-the-beaten track in El Salvador. They follow a loose timetable along set routes and bus stops are dotted along the roads otherwise wave your arm to flag them down. Fares are very cheap and it's more than just a ride – it's a unique experience! Luggage is taken on board with you and crammed under your seat or on your lap.

Chicken Busses

Where: Everywhere

When: Around town & between towns

How Much: Very cheap

The beloved chicken bus really is a **local** form of transport! They're the most common form of local transport in the region, although it's not "bus del pollo" *(as it would be in Spanish)* it's still "chicken bus"! The back door is used as much as the front door and sometimes people bring their livestock on the bus – hence the name. In Panama, the buses are giant canvases, painted in vivid colours by local artists. The best place to find out about the local "Chicken Bus" is to ask around in shops and markets. Baggage is crammed in wherever there's space – inside and on the roof – so make use of your day pack to keep your valuables safe! Pictured above, Nick and I on the back of a chicken buss in Guatemala!

Taxis

Where: Everywhere

When: Around town

How Much: Can be economical for two or more people

The bog standard taxi can be found in most urban areas across Central America, providing safe door to door transport around town. As in Asia, many of the drivers will refuse to use their meters, so negotiate a fair price before you get in and make sure that the price is per cab and not per person! Some of the independent and dodgier taxis will take you betweens towns but make sure you agree on a set price before you get in – it's not uncommon for travellers to be left in the middle of nowhere because they haven't clearly agreed on a fare and refuse to pay the drivers usually overinflated price.

Tuk-tuks

Where: Guatemala & a few random places

When: Around town

How Much: Cheap

Tuk-tuks bumble their way through the streets of Guatemala's *(pictured right)* towns offering a fun and fairly cheap form of transport around town. Haggle and agree on a price before you get in and make sure you are clear whether the price is per person or per vehicle – scams are common! Luggage in carried inside the cart with you. Pay with small denomination coins and notes or ideally have the correct fare to avoid unnecessary confrontation.

Cyclos

Where: In random areas, usually at border crossings!

When: Around town

How Much: Very cheap but be aware of scams *(particularly at border crossings)*

These are quite rare and usually operate at border crossing to exploit unaware tourists! They'll offer to take you and your bag across the border insisting it's a long way but in reality you can nearly always walk it no problem! Where they operate around towns, apply the same caution as in Asia – haggle and agree on a price **before** you hop in and make sure you have the right change!

Car hire

Where: Everywhere

When: Explore off-the-beaten track

How Much: Very cheap

You'll benefit most from car hire in Mexico where you'll find the usual array of hire companies such as Europcar and Hertz. As usual, if you're travelling as part of a group it'll work out fairly economical and a lot more convenient compared to public transport. Vehicle hire also gives you the freedom to get even further off-the-beaten track where even public busses are scarce and irregular.

Boats

Where: Primarily Belize & Honduras

When: Between islands & a link to the main-land

How Much: Very cheap

You'll only really need to use motorboats to get to a few Caribbean islands such as the Bay Islands in Honduras. In Belize however, the motorboat plays a larger role providing Public transport between the Cayes – you'll more than likely head to Caye Caulker. Most routes have set fares so usually there's no room to haggle or be ripped off!

Flights

Where: Everywhere

When: Between cities *(domestic flights)* & between countries *(regional-flights)*

How Much: The most expensive form of transport

There's no great urgency or practical benefit to fly when you're exploring Central America, although the occasional flight to remote off-the-beaten track areas can reduce tedious backtracking. The Corn Islands is the perfect example here – the plane pictured above was our very small aircraft from Big Corn to Managua, it landed in a field halfway through the flight to drop-off and pick up passengers like a regular bus! Otherwise, short regional flights can prevent backtracking through the region if you're pursuing a linear itinerary and you've got a return ticket home from either Cancún *(Mexico)* or San José *(Costa Rica)*.

Flying can be a big advantage in Mexico where distances are great. **Mexicana Airlines** offer a good value air-pass called the **Mayapass**. The big advantage of an airpass – besides the sale price – is that you can string together a series of one-way flights, instead of wasting a lot of time backtracking or travelling cast distances across the vast expanse of Mexico. Check it out on: www.mexicana.com.mx

$ THE BUDGET DIRECTORY $

This section compares and 'organises' countries from Central America. The budget directory should be used as a tool for planning your itinerary *(for more accurate daily budgets see 'At a Glance' section for each country)*. The countries have been graded by **cheapness** and **ease of travel** to help you create an affordable and realistic itinerary that is tailored to your budget, travel experience and confidence;

- o **Cheapness** refers to how affordable each country is for the 'average backpacker' in comparison to a theoretical 'Central American average' *(5)*. For example, a country with a grading of 9 means the country is very cheap for backpackers compared to other countries in Central America. Generally speaking, Central America is very affordable for the average westerner but regional variations do exist and you'll find that countries such as Costa Rica, although cheap by western standards, are still significantly more expensive than Nicaragua or Guatemala. The scale factors in the 'average' cost of food, accommodation, transport, communication and daily activities *(daytrips and sightseeing etc...)*

- o **Ease of Travel** relates to how challenging it is to travel in a given country reflecting the general level of *(tourist)* infrastructure and also taking into consideration obstacles such as language barriers and culture differences. A grading of 10 could indicate that a country has good transport options, limited culture shock and it's easy to communicate *(i.e. the country could have a high English literacy rate)*. Countries with a high grade are more suitable for 'first-time backpackers' who are a bit apprehensive, would like to build up some confidence and don't won't to jump straight in at the deep end! A low grading is by no means detrimental. While it may mean that the country could have limited tourist infrastructure, a greater language barrier and more extreme cultural differences, these challenges are both potential more rewarding and an appeal in themselves

The countries are graded from 1 to 10; 1 being very expensive and more challenging to travel and 10 being very cheap and easy to travel.

	Cheapness	Ease of Travel	Page
Mexico...	2	8	...103
Belize...	3	7	...106
Guatemala...	9	7	...109
Honduras...	6	2	...112
El Salvador...	8	3	...115
Nicaragua...	9	7	...118
Costa Rica...	3	7	...122
Panama...	5	5	...126

MEXICO *(The Yucatán)*

GATEWAY TO C. AMERICA

AT A GLANCE

Capital – Mexico City

Population – 108 million *(6.1m in this region)*

Language(s) – Spanish

Currency – Peso

ATMs – Plentiful

Climate – Varies from tropical to desert

Best time to go – Late Nov - April aka 'summer'

Time zone – GMT minus 6hours

Suggested daily budget – 450-600 pesos

Suggested time – 2+ weeks

Visas – Not required for residents of the EU & USA, Oz, Canada & New Zealand

The Yucatán is a popular gateway to Central America providing the perfect location to shake-off your jetlag and acclimatise – think of it as your decompression chamber, softening your landing in a strange new world, familiar enough to feel like a hot and sunny version of home, but exotic enough to give you an idea of the adventures that lay ahead. From the region's main entry point, the infamous beach-resort of Cancún, the familiarities of home are slowly eroded and replaced by more authentic Latino culture to casually ease first-time travellers into an epic adventure. Corona, Sol and Tequila will also facilitate your introduction in true Mexican style! For the majority of backpackers, the vast Yucatán region that extends between the Gulf of Mexico and the Caribbean Sea, *is* Mexico. Away from the bright lights and booze-fuelled antics of Cancún, better strips of

sand, vibrant coral reef, superb diving, mellow hippie towns and chilled out islands await. These popular spots are complemented by a scattering of ancient Mayan Ruins and a decent number of less-travelled towns. If you fall in love with the region, swap your flip-flops and boardies for some warmer attire and embark on the cooler and less-trodden *'Chiapas-Loop'*. There's more to this region than most people think and if you've got the time don't regard this region merely as gateway to Central America...

MINI GUIDE

Package-holidays aside, travellers fly into Mexico to begin their exotic Latino adventure. The coast of the Yucatán provides the perfect mix of authentic culture and alcohol fuelled socialising that's complemented with lashings of beach time and exciting activities. The most popular destinations form a nice simple linear itinerary that takes you south towards the borders of Belize & Guatemala:

Cancún ➜ Isla Mujeres ➜ Tulum (➜ Belize)

CANCÚN... *The resort town*

The American's equivalent of Spain, it's a prime destination for package tourists from the US and the number one spot for horny university students on drunken rampages during spring break! Very touristy, the 20km beachfront is dominated by fancy restaurants and expensive hotel complexes. The beach is open to the public, although the hotels will have you believe otherwise and the problem is getting to them – you'll need to sneak through the hotels undetected to gain beach access! Buzzing bars and loud clubs can be found on nearly every corner and it's got to be said that the nightlife is fantastic: All-you-can-drink offers and other promotions are common and ensure that the clubs are filled until the early hours of the morning.

Cancún's a bit of a mixed bag, and in truth, it's not great for budget backpackers and most shoe-stringers head straight from Cancún airport to **Isla Mujeres** by bus. Having said that, you can enjoy Cancún – it's a good place to start your trip and shake off your jetlag or a great way to end your trip in booze-oriented style – that's if you've got any cash left over! Backpackers tend to stay **in town** away from '**Zona Holtelera**' *(the beaches and resorts)* where you can enjoy a quieter more authentic Mexican lifestyle. Here you can interact with the residents and seek out the local markets, watering holes and cafés. If you want some beach time grab some lunch and hop on the local bus to Zona Holtelera and return to town as the evening draws in for cheaper grub and drinks.

Main backpacker area – Backpacker hostels can be found in town away from the beaches and resorts. **The Weary Traveller** is a popular hostel

Highlights – Beaches, nightlife & more nightlife

ISLA MUJERES... *The backpacker's island retreat*

A small island 6kms away from the mainland port of Punta Sam, Isla Mujeres is the perfect backpacker's retreat that feels a million miles away from the bright lights of overdeveloped Cancún. Day-trippers do pour onto the island, but thankfully most bypass the main town and head straight to the overpriced nature park located at the south of the island. The island's laidback atmosphere is complemented by numerous **tranquil beaches** where sun worshippers melt away on hot golden sand with crystal-clear turquoise water lapping at their feet.

The best beach is **Playa Norte** – located on the northwest of the island and conveniently away from the day trippers! **Divers** and **snorkelers** are drawn to the island by the offshore reefs that are rich with marine life and offer good reef and cave dives as well as a decent wreck dive. Bars and restaurants can be found all over town where travellers and friendly locals chat over a quiet beer or cocktail in true Caribbean fashion. It's easy to stay here for a long time! The best way to get to the Island is from Puerto Juárez where the earliest latest and more frequent services operate from.

Main backpacker area – Backpackers stay in the main town on the north of the island. The streets of López Mateos, Guererro and Hidalgo are packed with cheap accommodation and are ideally located next to islands best beach – Playa Norte.

Highlights – Beaches, diving, snorkelling & chilled-out nightlife

TULUM... *The laidback hippie town*

Indie travellers flock to this sleepy seaside town seeking the chilled-out atmosphere that Tulum effortlessly exudes. You'll find weed smoking wannabe-hippies gathered around beach bonfires chatting with merry drinkers. Boasting cheap accommodation, novel sand-floor cabañas, a beautiful beach, reasonable nightlife and a sociable crowd, Tulum is a big-time backpacker destination. Those who seek a bit of solitude and tranquillity with some culture and history thrown in will adore Tulum. There's also a fair few activities to keep the more adventurous entertained making Tulum an all-round travellers favourite. Despite its obvious draw, don't be tempted to stay by the beach – you can find some cheapish accommodation but everything else is in town and you'll be forced to eat and pay over the odds in beachfront restaurants. Most hostels in town run regular courtesy *(aka free)* busses to and from the beach anyway!

As well as the beach there are a number of activities and daytrips to keep you occupied. Explore some ancient Mayan history and wander to the cliff top **Tulum Ruins**, situated near the north end of the beach, entry will only set you back around 50 Pesos. If you want to do something a bit different, experience a new realm of diving and pursue some cave and tavern exploration in an ancient underwater river system that runs deep into the jungle. **Cenoté diving & snorkelling** trips can be arranged through a number of operators. Cavern dives cost around US$125 while snorkelling will set you back around US$50. Check out this website for more info – www.cenotedive.com. Equally good but more conventional open-water scuba diving can be found at the nearby reef with trips organised by a number of operators based in and around Tulum. If you want to dabble with culture, the nearby **Chichén Itzá Ruins** are a worthwhile daytrip and will get a 'wow' from even the most ruined-out backpacker – if you're travelling with some mates, there's no need to book onto an expensive organised tour, hire a car instead!

Main backpacker area – Hostels can be found in town on the main road away from the beach. The Weary Traveller is a popular hostel.

Highlights – The beach, good nightlife and the laidback ambience, Tulum Ruins, diving & snorkelling, cenoté exploration & the Chichén Itzá Ruins

BELIZE

CARIBBEAN DELIGHT

AT A GLANCE

Capital – Belize City

Population – 0.3million

Language(s) – English, Creole Spanish & Garifuna

Currency – Belize dollar (BZ$)

ATMs – Plentiful in main towns and the Cayes

Climate – Tropical

Best time to go – Nov - May *(dry season)*

Time zone – GMT minus 6 hours

Suggested daily budget – BZ$70-90 *(US$35-45)*

Suggested time – 1-2 weeks

Visas – Not required for residents of N. America, Oz, New Zealand & most European countries

Before I had been there, people always asked me 'Why are you going to Belize, what's there?'! And, to be honest, I struggled to answer. Yet, after experiencing it first-hand, the draws become blindingly obvious and I can safely say that it's an underrated little beauty with plenty to offer. The well-travelled northeast of the country is where you'll find the sun-baked Cayes – tropical islands where the smell of grilled lobster cold Belikin beers and the infectious reggae vibe will entice you

to spend countless lazy days. Then there's the world-class diving and snorkelling on the nearby technicolour reef and the famous Blue Hole where you'll swim with sharks, manta rays are scores of tropical fish. Armchair dwellers can even soak it all up from the 'safety' of relaxing sailboats! Unbelievably, the rest of the country remains less-travelled. The northwest is an outdoors enthusiasts dream where there are caves to explore, overgrown trails to hike, rivers to raft and wildlife to stalk. The jungle is peppered with less-visited ancient Mayan ruins so you'll be able to get decent snapshots without the tourists! To the south of the country, there's a great string of sleepy coastal towns which offer sun, sea and sand in abundance with lashings of culture and friendly locals. Compact and easy to get around, Belize offers an slice of Caribbean paradise and an alternative Central American experience that has a distinct reggae twist. It's hard to believe that there's not an emphatic hype about this place – get there before the droves of tourists do... As a local once said to me, 'Ya man, you bet-ta Beliiiize it'!

Belize isn't widely known as an established backpacker destination but it does have a few little gems and plenty of scope to go off-the-beaten track. Most travellers spend their entire time in the popular island of Caye Caulker only touching the country's capital to hop on a bus over the border to Guatemala. In truth, you don't really want to spend any prolonged period of time in the capital anyway! Below you'll find the most popular destination and a few less-travelled areas:

(Mexico e.g. Tulum →) Caye Caulker ➔ Belize City *(➔ Guatemala e.g. Flores)*

If you want to break up the trip between Tulum and Caye Caulker or night draws in a bit too quickly, as it did in our case, you can find refuge in the Quirky town of **Coral** – there's not a lot to do in this strange town and the locals are welcoming yet somewhat intimidating at the same time, but **Maya World Guesthouse** is a good overnight stop with a friendly and enthusiastic owner.

CAYE CAULKER... *The backpacker's Caribbean island*

This is the main reason to visit Belize! While nearby Ambergris Caye is the more luxurious isle, Belize's diminutive Caye Caulker is an inexpensive celebration of Caribbean life perfectly tailored for budget backpackers – it's less resort conscious and features an abundance of cheap accommodation, sand roads and budget eateries. Caye Caulker is a true authentic Caribbean experience with scrumptious seafood, chilled-out bars and friendly 'doped-up' local folk that cumulate to give a truly laidback ambience. There are no cars on the island – retro bicycles and electric golf-carts form the main transport around this tiny island emulate the easy going Caribbean vibe. Seafood features strongly on the menu here and the island is famous for its whole BBQ lobster – a must try when you here and a delicacy that you won't find cheaper anywhere else. Try and find **The Lobster King** for the freshest and cheapest BBQ Lobster! Caye Caulker is actually two islands since Hurricane Hattie split the island and a popular bar fittingly named the **'Split Bar'** is now located here! The biggest down side is a very distinct lack of a decent beach although water sports are the name of the game here:

Activities: Divers from around the world flock here eager to explore **The Blue Hole**. Situated in the middle of Lighthouse Reef it's a famous sink hole of startling blue water, approximately 120m deep and 300m wide, teaming with a variety of reef sharks and rays including; black tips, bulls, lemons and even hammerhead and tiger sharks! As well as some balls, you'll need an open-water license and dives can be arranged from more or less every dive shack on the island so look around for the best deals. Don't despair if you can't dive, **snorkelling** trips also operate in the Blue Hole *(and they're cheaper!)*.

> ### Sailboat tours...
>
> You simply can't come to Caye Caulker and hop aboard a sailboat - these tours are fantastic. Not only are you rewarded with a relaxing day sailing the pristine Caribbean waters feasting on delicious food and getting tipsy on fresh punch, you'll also enjoy some of the world's most rewarding **snorkelling** amid scores of tropical fish, reef sharks and graceful rays.

Highly recommended **sailboat tours** are also big business on the island and can be arranged from dozens of operators *(see text box above)*. **Sea kayaks, snorkelling gear** and **Lillo's** can be hired from a number of shacks on the island. Sand flies seem to be hungrier here than anywhere else, so take some decent repellent – for some reason baby oil works best!

Main backpacker area – A host of cheap guesthouses can be found the length of **Front Street**

Highlights – Scrumptious seafood *(lobsters)* at bargain prices, fishing, sailing trips, snorkelling & diving, The split-bar & The Blue Hole

Off-the-beaten track... *Spice things up a bit!*

Many backpackers stick religiously to laidback ambience of Caye Caulker and the striking draw of the mighty Blue Hole but there are a few other worthwhile places to check out in Belize if you're not a whirlwind tour of Central America.

Lamanai – This is arguably one of the most impressive sites in the north of the country. Take a nippy riverboat cruise up the New River to these famous Mayan remnants – much of the site still remains unexcavated but this only adds the authenticity and eeriness of these ancient ruins. The archaeological site is impressive enough but the trip up the river is an adventure in itself where you'll almost certainly spot a lurking croc or two and an abundance birdlife. Tours usually depart from and around **Orange Walk** – this is also a great place to dedicate some time to.

Mini itinerary: South of Belize City you can pursue an interesting coastal route of sleepy beach towns and even pop across to Honduras.

Dangriga ➔ Hopkins ➔ Seine Bight ➔ Mango Creek ➔ Placencia ➔ Puerto Cortés *(Honduras)*

Dangriga – This is the south's largest town, but it's a lot calmer and friendlier than bustling Belize City. Here you can indulge yourself in some real Garífuna culture and mingle with the locals over a few Belikin beers and the patter of Creole in true carefree fashion. One of the best times to visit this town is **Garífuna Settlement Day**, held annually on the 19th of November, when the city explodes into a frenzy of dancing, merry drinking and energetic celebration of their heritage.

Hopkins – Just south of Dangriga, this small fishing village boasts a great beach, scrumptious fresh seafood and welcoming local folk. It's true that there's not much to do, but doing nothing is the name of the game here! This town runs at a very leisurely pace and the beachside cabins ensure that you can make the most of this chill-out coastal retreat. Most shoe-stringers come here to pursue low-key pastimes such as swimming, sunbathing and drinking!

Placencia – Once upon a time, Placencia was a Caye isolated and cut-off by the sea. Today you can actually drive to it. This Caye, resembles its siblings in the north and effortlessly exudes that blissful laidback ambience. Friendly locals and palm-lined beaches keep lethargic travellers here for longer than they intended! From Placencia, it's possible to get a boat *(Gulf Cruza)* over to Puerto Cortés in Honduras – although services usually only run on a weekly basis.

GUATEMALA

A CHEAP SLICE OF CULTURE

AT A GLANCE

Capital – Guatemala City
Population – 11.2 million
Language(s) – Spanish & Mayan
Currency – Quetzal, US$ readily accepted
ATMs – Plentiful
Climate – Tropical. Cool in highlands
Best time to go – Nov - April *(dry season)*
Time zone – GMT minus 6hours
Suggested daily budget – 175quetzal / US$20
Suggested time – 2-3 weeks
Visas – North American & EU citizens require a valid passport at border

This is the land of rugged volcanoes, enchanting colonial towns and lofty temples that rise above virgin jungle full of exotic wildlife. A country that was once notoriously dangerous to venture around is now safe and easy to explore. For the hardcore shoe-stringer, this is where the Latino adventure really begins for this is a country that's very easy on the wallet! The well-trodden trail exposes even the most oblivious traveller to a sizeable hit of culture, scenic landscapes, relaxing highland retreats and captivating ancient ruins while the picturesque town of Antigua will convince the most hurried traveller to stay longer; train your tongue in a top-notch budget Spanish schools to train your tongue, peer into active volcanoes to hike and haggle in bustling markets. For the really curious, scratch below the surface and the possibilities are endless. This is a country that

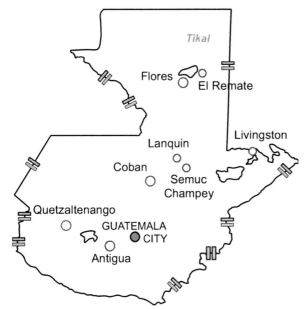

really opens up to you if you put the effort in. Plenty of volunteer opportunities will satisfy anyone looking for a bit of self-enlightenment and rural living while hideaways like Lanquin provide respite for the weary. Far too many are guilty of skipping through this country, yet away from the popular hotspots are plenty of untold adventures on roads less-travelled. Substitute air-con shuttle-busses for chicken busses, sign up for volunteer programmes and enrol on a language course. The more you put in, the more you'll get out. Mighty Tikal is just the tip of the iceberg, prepare to be overwhelmed...

MINI GUIDE

Entering via Belize, there's a great linear itinerary that'll have you clambering over the mightiest of Mayan temples, hiking active peaks, chilling-out in rural villages and dabbling with the lingo:

(Belize ➔) Flores *(Tikal)* ➔ Cobán ➔ Antigua *(➔ El Salvador / Honduras)*

FLORES... *The gateway to ancient Tikal*

Flores is the name usually given to three settlements; Flores, San Elena and San Benito. The actual settlement of Flores is built on an island in Lago de Petén Itzá – the big arse lake – connected to the town of Santa Elena by a 500m causeway. Flores is a quaint and prosperous looking town with clean narrow streets lined with charming red-roofed houses. Santa Elena and San Benito are visibly more disorganised and exhibit all the features of 'working towns'. Flores is a pleasant town with all the backpacker services that you'll require but it's an expensive destination for the average 'budget-traveller' and noticeably pricier than elsewhere in Guatemala. Most travellers only stay a couple of days to clamber over the ancient ruins of **Tikal** before moving on swiftly on with a keen eye on their cash reserves! Determined shoe-stringers head to the remote and tiny lakeside village of **El Remate** that's located halfway between Flores and Tikal.

Tikal: Tikal is the mother of all Mayan temples dwarfing other ancient sites such as Chichén Itzá. Set deep in dense tropical rainforest, its steep sided temples rise to heights of over 40m eager to break through the jungle canopy in search of sunlight. Some temples remain unexcavated half buried under rich soil and vegetation. Howler monkeys perch on the ruins and swing noisily above your head in the treetops. Tikal offers a unique experience that no other Mayan site can offer, not only because of its sheer size but because of its remoteness and rich biodiversity. You're even allowed to climb some of the temples where – if you don't fall down the very steep sides – you can look out over this vast complex and gaze into the dense jungle.

Daytrips can be arranged in Flores and El Remate. The **sunrise tour** comes with mixed views – it's more expensive and the early rise by no means guarantees a spectacular sunrise. More often than not the sun fails to pierce through the thick morning mist and most experience a 'dimmer-switch' start to the morning as opposed to the striking sunrise and morning song of the jungle that's promise! However, you are rewarded with a unique eerie feeling as you walk around these ancient temples before sunrise and clambering high above the tree tops for everything to slowly appear before your eyes. Whatever tour you go on, finish off the day with a refreshing dip in **Lago de Petén Itzá** *(the big lake!)* before putting your feet up with a few beers and some grub in a lakeside restaurant in Flores. Film buffs will recognise Tikal as the Rebel Base from Star Wars!

Main backpacker area – Flores & El Remate

Highlights – Tikal, charming streets and Lago de Petén Itzá *(the big lake!)*

COBÁN & AROUND... *The picturesque retreat(s)*

Cobán and the surrounding area is characterised by small traditional villages, caves, waterfalls and lagoons. It's becoming a popular backpacker destination. The main town of Cobán is characterised by chilly and rainy weather but it's a pleasant town providing an ideal base to head off and explore further afield – here you'll find all the backpacker services that you're likely to need and they're all conveniently concentrated within a few blocks of the plaza. If you decide to stay in Cobán, cheap accommodation can be found within a few blocks of the **Main Plaza**.

One of the best excursions from Cobán is to the caves near **Lanquín**. This network of caves is deep and extensive; while the first hundred meters or so of the cavern is illuminated by a series of electric lights, a vast proportion of this cave has yet to be explored! The cavern is home to thousands of bats who emerge at sunset from the cavern entrance as a dense ball of flapping wings – an interesting spectacle that needs to be observed. The quiet village of **Lanquín**, laying 61km along bumpy roads east of Cobán, is a lengthy daytrip so most backpackers opt to stay in Lanquín for a few days. **El Retiro** is perhaps the most popular backpacker retreat offering affordable digs. Set in lush green fields overlooking a wide river – perfect for swimming and tubing – this is the perfect place to chill out. Evening bonfires and a lively bar ensures a very laidback sociable atmosphere that'll almost certainly make you prolong your stay. El Retiro is famous for its excellent value vegetarian food – meat eaters don't despair, there's a monster Chicken BBQ every Wednesday night! While the food here is fantastic, it's worth venturing into town for some regional cuisine in local-style restaurants.

Nine kilometres south of Lanquín you'll find a worthwhile daytrip – **Semuc Champey**. It's an area famed for its natural limestone bridge where, after a long, steep and sweaty walk, you'll find a series of gorgeous turquoise lagoons to cool off in. If you want to stay around here for a bit, **Las Marías** offers decent and very affordable accommodation just 1 km short of the lagoons.

Main backpacker area – Lanquín *(El Retiro)*, Semuc Champey *(Las Marías)*

Highlights – Lanquín caves, Semuc Champey, rural villages & rustic backpacker complexes

ANTIGUA... *Waggle your multi-lingual tongue or hike an active volcano*

Experts consider Antigua one of the most well-preserved colonial cities in Latin America while backpackers consider it a budget traveller's Mecca – an equatorial Europe filled with coffee shops, bars, international restaurants, Spanish schools and hostels, yet in easy reach of Guatemala's stunning outdoor attractions. While Antigua doesn't offer true Mayan immersion like other Guatemalan villages, the town is unmistakably charming with cobbled streets, mustard coloured buildings and relics of a colonial past against a superbly stunning backdrop of three volcanic peaks. This town's got something for everyone where you'll find weary travellers practising their Spanish, nursing hangovers and discussing their daily activities in restaurants, markets and 'cinema-cafes'.

Spanish schools: Antigua's mix of affordable top-notch Spanish schools and lively bars ensures a constant stream of 'wannabe bi-lingual' travellers and enthusiastic carefree drinkers from around the world. While Antigua is renowned for its abundance of language schools, and many travellers prolong their stay to pick up some local lingo, prices and teacher quality do vary greatly so ask around hostels and talk to other travellers for recommendations. Hostels and bars regularly run themed nights and drinking competitions although most enforce a 1:00am curfew – partygoers don't despair, this doesn't make much difference as people just start drinking earlier!

Volcano hikes: Volcano Pacaya offers the best volcano tours around – health & safety clearly isn't an issue and nowhere else can you get so close. Hikes take you right up onto the lava plains, where if you're lucky enough, you'll see fresh lava oozing out of cracks. At the very least you'll come across deep red-hot crevices where the heat's so intense, and you can get so close, people take steaks and marsh mellows to cook! If you go on a late afternoon tour, darkness creeps in when you're at the summit and the lava flows and cracks illuminate all around you! It's a truly unique landscape that has a 'moon-like' ambience about it – you'd be mad to miss it. The terrain is rough and hot so take adequate footwear and a warm top – my mates shoes went very soft and actually started to melt! While the other volcanoes are dormant, they offer superb views where you'll encounter fewer tourists. Other activities here include **white-water rafting**, **horse-riding** and **cycling**. Tours can be booked all over town. The hike to the top isn't too strenuous but if you're unfit or just plain lazy you can reach the summit on horseback!

Main backpacker area – Hostels can be found along **6a Av Norte** *(the main street)*. Popular hostels are Black Cat & Jungle Party

Highlights – Spanish schools, local markets, active volcano hikes, outdoor activities & nightlife

HONDURAS

BUDGET DIVING!

Honduras is the second largest of the Central American countries with a cool, rugged interior and a sun-kissed Caribbean coastline. Most come here to take advantage of the world's cheapest diving and vibrant coral reef that can be found around the tropical Bay Islands before moving swiftly on. While other worthwhile attractions including golden mainland beaches, great seafood and intricately carved Mayan ruins entice curious travellers to stay a little longer, it's perhaps the scope to go off-the-beaten track that's most attractive for the adventurous shoe-stringer. Cloud forests, Biosphere Reserves, protected coastlands, wetlands and lagoons dominate one of Central America's largest wilderness areas where you can visit isolated villages, stalk exotic wildlife, trek through lush rainforests and meet very few travellers. Don't make the classic mistake and neglect this very affordable country. Diving aside, pack some patience and a sense of adventure...

There's pretty much only one reason why people come to Honduras – **the budget diving** – so most backpackers inevitably head straight to the Bay Islands on a return trip. However, there are a few other worthwhile attractions along the way and plenty of options to explore roads less-travelled:

(➔ *Guatemala)* Copán Ruinas ➔ Tela ➔ Utila (➔ *Guatemala)*

THE BAY ISLANDS... *The world's cheapest scuba diving!*

The remote Bay Islands nestle in the mellow waters of the Caribbean Sea 18 miles off the mainland. They've become a cult destination for wannabe divers and have long been established as the **cheapest place in the world** to get your open-water licence and explore life beneath the waves. The surrounding reefs, a continuation of the expanding Mesoamerican Reef that starts in Belize, teem with fish, corals, rays, sea turtles and reef sharks offering superb diving and snorkelling. You may even be fortunate enough to have a unique encounter with the legendary whale shark.

Utila: The Bay Islands are a trio of tropical English speaking islands – **Guanaja**, **Roatán** and **Utila.** Guanaja is the most expensive island and well out of backpacker range. While nearby Roatan is larger and more reasonable, **Utila** is the shoe-stringer's diving haven where the rock-bottom diving costs are complemented by cheaper accommodation, lively bars and carefree restaurants. Countless dive shops line the streets of this laidback isle drawing in eager backpackers from all across the globe. Most dive shops will throw in free or discounted accommodation.

Getting there: Visiting these islands can be a significant and time consuming detour. However, the extra effort is fully justified and the cost is offset by the budget diving – it you want to dive, it really doesn't get any cheaper than this. Two daily ferries service Utila – the Galaxy II and the Utila Princess – departing from the mainland town of **La Ceiba**. Flights work out around double the cost of the ferry but will get you to Utila from La Ceiba in a comfortable 15 minutes. Mosquitoes and sand flies are ravenous on these islands, particularly during rainy season *(Late Oct - Feb)*, so stock up on repellent! For more information check out www.aboututila.com. If you fancy some beach time check out the sands at **Tela** on your way to/from Utila and stop-off at **Copan Ruinas** for a hit of culture – it'll break up the detour and make the journey less tedious.

Main backpacker area – Most budget divers congregate on cheaper Utila

Highlights – Unbelievably cheap top-quality diving

COPÁN RUINAS... *Delve into local Mayan history*

If you're a bit of a culture buff and have an interest in **Mayan ruins,** you'll relish a trip to the nearby ruins of Copán that exhibit remarkably detailed stone carvings on well preserved temples. In town, **Museo de Arqueología Maya** is an excellent and worthwhile museum dedicated to local Mayan history. The town it's self is charming with cobblestone streets, cute red roofed houses and quaint colonial buildings. While Copán has become a popular tourist hotspot, it has retained its authentic charm and remains a small quiet town. Everything's within a few blocks of the central park and the ruins are a pleasant 15 minute stroll, one kilometre away from town. The town isn't raving at night but there are a few lively bars including **Tunkul Bar** and **Café Via Via's**. Aside from the ruins, there's a range of tours that can be organised from Copán including, **caving, river tubing** and **horse riding**. **Mayan village tours** and visits to **coffee plantations** can also be organised through numerous local companies.

Main backpacker hostels – Café Via Via & Hotel Gemelos

Highlights – Copán Ruins, Museo de Arqueología Maya & horse riding

Off-the-beaten track... *Spice things up a bit!*

Probably due to the country's size and underdeveloped infrastructure, much of the country, particularly regions away from its borders with neighbouring countries, is off-the-beaten track. Consequently, the country's eastern most province, where it meets with the Caribbean Sea, is an area few backpackers explore. While information is usually sketchy in these 'off-the-beaten track sections', I've given you a little more info so you don't miss out!

LA MOSQUITIA... *Truly off-the-beaten track*

This region encompasses the entire northeast portion of the country and with a very limited road network, the region is fairly inaccessible. Consequently, only a handful of intrepid travellers venture here. This is a genuinely remote area for the truly adventurous backpacker and those who make it here are thrilled by what they find. The preservation of the natural beauty is simply breathtaking and it's biodiversity unrivalled. Lurking in the dense jungle you'll spot monkeys, snakes, exotic and birdlife while crocodiles loiter in mangrove-lined rivers. If you're lucky, some visitors have even caught rare glimpses of shy jaguars. The region is sparsely populated with fascinating indigenous tribes. Unfortunately, compared to other parts to the country, it's a little more expensive and prices are often open to negotiation. Having said that, it's money well spent – rarely do you get the opportunity to explore such an isolated and undeveloped region.

Sleeping & tours: The entire region is largely undeveloped for tourism so there are few lodging options. Backpackers have several good options in the region's largest town **Puerto Lempira**. **Las Marias**, a town of around 300 people, is located in the heart of the biosphere reserve and is a good base camp for shoestring travellers. Here you'll find a couple of popular budget lodging options and cheaper tours can be arranged through local guides who'll take you deeper into the jungle. While guided tours appear fairly expensive compared to DIY options, they'll guarantee a rewarding and productive trip providing invaluable local knowledge and expertise. If you're planning to go to this region stock up supplies before you leave. Downpours are common and few places have reliable electricity!

Getting there & away – Flights connect **La Ceiba** to **Puerto Lempira** but for a truly rewarding experience try and bus it – limp along town by town and you'll discovery tonnes of interesting things along the way. If you're heading to La Mosquitia from the Bay Islands, consider stopping off at **Trujillo** along the way for some for some lethargic beach-time! If you haven't got the time or patience to explore the challenging eastern most region, **La Tigra National Park**, just a few kilometres from **Tegucigalpa**, is a very accessible could forest. If that stimulates your sense of adventure, the small interior town of **La Union** is a manageable jumping off point to roads less-travelled.

Main backpacker towns – Las Marias & Puerto Lempira

Highlights – Río Plátano Biosphere Reserve, awe-inspiring natural beauty, biodiversity & adventure off-the-beaten track

Mini-itinerary:

If you've got the time, be as adventurous as you like. Your best bet is to jot down a few destinations and just try and make your way between them... it's the journey and what you find in between that's the adventure. A long ambitious tour of the remote country could look something like this.

(Guatemala ➔*)* Copán Ruinas ➔ Tela ➔ Utila ➔ Trujillo ➔ Las Mariás ➔ Puerto Lempira ➔Tegucigalpa *(*➔ *Nicaragua/El Salvador)*

EL SALVADOR

OFF-THE-BEATEN TRACK

Visions of wars and a reputation for crime coupled with a distinct lack of well-publicised attractions cause many travellers to simply bypass El Salvador without a second thought. This is a tragic mistake. The war years are long gone, crime levels are no worse than other countries in the region and El Salvador is a largely undiscovered gem of untold off-the-beaten track adventures. Its landscape is appealingly diverse – barren black-sands that span the length of the country's Pacific Coastline and laidback beach towns will satisfy beach-lovers and carefree surfers alike while the bustling cities, dense forests and craggy inland mountains provide an outlet for the more adventurous types. Perhaps one of the country's greatest assets are the friendly local folk who practically adopt you on arrival. You'll require a better command of the Spanish language here yet this just adds to the country's 'rawness' and makes it all that more rewarding. Basic but affordable guesthouses are cropping up in all corners of the country, opening new possibilities for curious shoestringers. This is backpacking in its infancy where you'll have the place virtually to yourself. Being so accessible from all of its neighbouring countries, and exceptionally easy to travel around, you'd be crazy to miss out. El Salvador's a real traveller's playground where you can have your own unique and authentic experiences... anyone who ventures here are well rewarded.

MINI GUIDE

It's a shame to think some people simply pass through this largely undiscovered country using San Salvador merely as connection-point between Guatemala and Nicaragua. Those who loiter around for longer in El Salvador head south towards the laidback coast in search of sun, sea, sand and surf. Here's a logical linear route that'll give you plenty of lethargic beaches, big waves, friendly locals and a dose of cultural indulgence:

(Guatemala ➔) San Salvador ➔ Costa del bálsamo ➔ Perquín (➔ *Nicaragua)*

SAN SALVADOR... *The Capital*

San Salvador is the largest city in El Salvador and serves as the country's capital. You'll almost certainly find yourself here at some point during your 'El Salvador experience' as it's the country's principal crossroads. The air pollution, crowded streets, urban decay and level of crime is off-putting but San Salvador can be enjoyed and these characteristics can be as intriguing as they are intimidating. Cheap accommodation and excellent transport links also make it an appealing place to set up base camp, and a few do – you'll find some of the backpacker hostels filled with chatty Peace Corp Volunteers who make for some interesting, usually biased, discussions! Brand new shopping malls display the cities more prosperous side and act as a symbol of what the city aspires to be. Familiar fast-food chains line the streets – a surprise to most tourists – providing a welcome taste of home for weary homesick travellers. Big Macs taste the same wherever you are in the world!

Most backpackers head towards the safety and convenience of **Boulevard de Los Héroes** where you'll find a small number of traveller-orientated guesthouses in close proximity to ATMs, cinemas, shopping malls, bars and restaurants. **La Estancia** and **Ximena's Guest House** are extremely popular with budget backpackers. For most travellers, their visit to San Salvador is out of unavoidable necessity but it does have a unique charm about it, albeit hidden under layers of urban ills! A few days is more than enough to recharge, stock up on supplies and get some cash.

Main backpacker area – Boulevard de Los Héroes

Highlights – Museums, shopping & modern comforts

COSTA DEL BÁLSAMO... *Beach bliss, surfers retreat*

Slip into beach-mode and sizzle under the baking sun – a bus quick bus ride south of San Salvador, Costa del Bálsamo runs from **Playa Sihuapilapa** to **La Libertad** where you'll find a string of sleepy undiscovered seaside towns and underrated black-sand beaches. Pimped up US-school busses link the towns with frequent and ultra-cheap services. If you're into your **surfing** you'll love this laidback, secluded coastline. Surfers favour the breaks at El Punto, El Sunzal, El Tunco and El Zonte. The best sunbathing beaches are eastward, at Playa San Diego. Beach bums, surfers and shoe-stringers tend to swarm in the all-round favourite of **Playa El Zonte** where you can tuck into fresh BBQ seafood at beachfront eateries and find the bulk of budget accommodation amid a laidback ambience and friendly local folk. Cheap surfboard rental can be found at most 'hotels'.

La Libertad, to the east, is the largest town along this stretch of coast and makes for an interesting daytrip – make sure you visit the pier to witness an intriguing, and sometimes disturbing, array of locally caught seafood! This town is fairly dodgy after nightfall so head westward back to the more remote coastal villages shortly after nightfall.

Main backpacker area – Playa El Zonte & Playa El Zunzal

Highlights – Deserted unspoilt beaches, surfing, seafood & local encounters

PERQUÍN... *A sobering walk through the past*

This quiet village close to Honduran border was once a long-time stronghold of the FMLN, the guerrilla group, during the civil war that ravaged the country between 1981 and 1992. If you want to uncover some of the country's bleak history there's no better place to peer into the murky past than Perquín – it's the only place in El Salvador to have a **museum** about the civil war. It's a sobering walk through El Salvador's war-torn past with the armed struggle depicted using photos, posters, weapons and stories of those who died. If you command a good understanding of Spanish, you can even get guided tours from ex-guerrillas! This area saw some of the fiercest fighting and today leftover bunkers, weathered trenches and deep bomb craters scar the surrounding landscape and act as a clear and constant reminder of this bloody conflict. A worthwhile side-trip to **El Mozote,** 10kms away, stands as a permanent reminder of the atrocities during this dark period – a moving memorial stands as a testament to the 1,000s of victims who were massacred in December 1981.

On a cheerier note, the town is a refreshing hillside retreat that still remains relatively off-the-beaten track. Set in the mountains, Perquín is blessed with beautiful surroundings, great views, an abundance of wildlife and crisp fresh air. It's a great place to **hike** or **do nothing** for a few days. You can also swim in many of the rivers and lagoons in the area. Few people make it here but those who do are given a warm welcome by the local folk who want to raise awareness of what happened here. There are a number of decent places to get a good night's sleep but **Eco Albergue Río Sapo** offers rustic bunking in riverside cabins and a lack of electricity just adds to the charm. A trip to Perquín is a memorable and educational highlight for most backpacker's.

Main backpacker hostels – Eco Albergue Río Sapo & La Cocina de Ma'Anita

Highlights – El Mozote & Museo de la Revolución

NICARAGUA

RUN TO THE SUN IN SEARCH OF RUM!

AT A GLANCE

Capital – Managua
Population – 5.3 Million
Language(s) – Spanish & English
Currency – Córdoba, US$ widely accepted
ATMs – Located in main towns
Climate – Tropical, cooler in highlands
Best time to go – Nov - mid May *(dry season)*
Time zone – GMT minus 6hours
Suggested daily budget – US$20 / 400córdobas
Suggested time – 2-3 weeks
Visas - North American & EU citizens require a valid passport at border

Nicaragua's a favourite destination for tight arses – natural disasters, civil wars and dictatorships have left Nicaragua the poorest country Central America! Nicaragua's days of armed conflict are long gone and while it's economically poor it's rich in rustic experiences. Cultural and natural wonders come in the form of fantastically preserved colonial cities, hidden jungle hamlets and interesting local folk coupled with picturesque volcanic peaks, pristine cloud forests and plenty of wildlife. From the popular beach resorts in the Pacific coast to the barren beaches on the Caribbean coastline, Nica is also flanked by an abundance of sandy beaches. From kayaking on Central America's largest lake and boarding down the side of volcanic cones to surfing oversized waves and tanning it up on the beaches, you can soak up these riches in many ways. Off the well-trodden path travel isn't easy but the rewards of reaching the Caribbean coast will enrich any adventurous shoe-stringer who makes the extra effort. Getting to the Corn Islands is a notoriously time-consuming adventure but the rewards are equally proportionate where travellers can enjoy a rustic slice of Caribbean culture. Whatever you're after, Nicaragua will offer it in abundance and all at a discounted price!

The well-trodden-route hugs Nicaragua's western coastline where you'll find some of the regions finest colonial towns, culture galore, lively beach resorts and fascinating natural formations:

(Honduras ➜) León ➜ Managua ➜ Isla de Ometepe ➜ San Juan del Sur *(➜Costa Rica)*

If you want to get off-the-beaten track, leave the western seaboard and trek across to the Caribbean coast where you'll find empty beaches and the remote and quirky **Corn Islands**. If **León** failed to suppress your cultural appetite head to **Granda** before you pop over to **Isla de Ometepe**.

LEÓN... *A cultural feast*

If you want to immerse yourself in hustle and bustle of a traditional Latino town then look no further than León for a slice of authentic culture. Situated in the most volcanic region in Central America, León served as the countries capital for over two centuries and remains deeply connected with its past boasting some of the finest colonial buildings including Central America's largest Cathedral. Today, this photogenic city is Nicaragua's second largest city. Often overlooked and overshadowed by its colonial rival, Granada, León sees fewer tourists but there's a lot to discover in this vibrant city. Explore León's cobbled streets and discover a cultural wealth of tiny parks, quaint churches, historic buildings and welcoming local folk. By night, bar-hop along narrow colonial streets and sample some fresh Victoria beer and sip glasses of Flor de Caña before you hit the after-hour drinking holes of **Don Señor's** and **Payitas**. This town definitely merits a few days for some cultural awakening.

If you're all cultured out – let's face it culture gets tiresome after a while – and you can't bear the thought of another cold beer, drag yourself hung-over-self up a volcano for some crisp fresh air and engage in the unique sport of volcano boarding! Trips can be arranged through a number of hostels including **Big Foot Hostel** and will set you back around US$23 for a day's boarding *(+US$5 national park entrance fee)* – for more info check out www.bigfootnicaragua.com. Further afield there are some unspoiled beaches 20km west of **León**. If you've truly relished your cultural experience here, head over to **Granada** to continue your cultural education!

Main backpacker area – Backpackers accommodation is spread along **2a Av SE** and the surrounding streets. Big Foot Hostel & Via Via are the most popular hostels

Highlights – Colonial architecture, nightlife & volcano boarding!

ISLA DE OMETEPE... *The volcano island!*

Isla de Ometepe is a unique geological formation consisting of two volcanoes – Volcán Concepción and Volcán Maderas – that were united by lava flow to create a single fertile island blessed with primary forest, wildlife and natural wonders – you'll see and hear howler monkeys, green parrots and blue-tailed birds all over the island. There are also a number of half-decent black-sand beaches scattered around the whole island. Thankfully the island remains largely undeveloped for tourism – a single gravel road circles the north of the island *(Volcán Concepción)* and this deteriorates as you head over Rio Istian *(the flatter piece of land linking the volcanoes)* towards the smaller of the two cones, Volcán Maderas. The easiest way of reaching the island is via car ferry that operates between Moyogalpa and San Jorge on the mainland. The island's two main towns, Altagracia and Moyogalpa, are found on Volcán Concepción and offer cheap accommodation but most travellers head further afield to **Santo Domingo** and **Balgüe** in search of a more rustic experience amid the islands beautiful setting and rich biodiversity. **Moyogalpa** has an ATM so get some cash shortly after you get off the ferry before you go further afield.

Activities: With two cones to conquer, a host of tracks to explore and heaps of natural attractions to enjoy, the island's a hikers dream. You can embark on refreshing hikes up both cones where you'll be rewarded with some secluded lagoons, gushing waterfalls and picturesque views amid a variety of tropical wildlife. The terrain is tough and the trails are hard to follow so it's best to hire a knowledgeable and inexpensive local guide. It's also possible to tackle some of these tracks on **horseback** – available to hire through local guides. Hikes up Volcán Concepción are typically arranged in Moyogalpa through **Exploring Ometepe**. Most budget backpackers opt to stay off the beaten track in **Balgüe** to climb Maderas where they're well catered for. **Santa Domingo** is perhaps the main backpacker 'town' boasting some of the island's widest black sand beaches and a number of good tracks including the hike up to **Ojo de Agua** – a secluded lagoon where you can enjoy a few beers and cool off. Keep your eyes peeled for the interesting prehistoric 'rock art' that's dotted around the island!

Main backpacker area – Santo Domingo & Balgüe on Rio Istian *(between the two cones)* and Volcán Maderas *(the smaller Volcano)* respectively

Highlights – The unique setting, horse riding, volcano hikes & rich biodiversity

SAN JUAN DEL SUR... *Nica's surfing capital*

A laidback breezy seaside town, San Juan del Sur nestles in a picturesque horseshoe-shaped cove. Travellers flock here to burn themselves on sandy beaches and conquer the decent surf breaks that the area's blessed with. The town's own beach is convenient and nice enough but better beaches can be found up and down the coast. **Playa Majagual**, 12km north of San Juan del Sur, is a popular beach where a decent backpacker resort – **Bahia Majagual Lodge** – offers some cheap accommodation *(cabins, dorms and tents)*, surf lessons, boat trips and bike rental. **Playa Madera** is considered the **best surf beach**. Most backpackers still stay in San Juan Del Sur as several hostels, including **Casa Oro**, run reasonably priced daily busses to the best beaches around San Juan del Sur. Take some food, water and beer as restaurants and shops are sparse on some of these undeveloped beaches. Surf boards can be rented though a number of hostels in San Juan del Sur. Other activities include **boat excursions, fishing trips**, and **kayaking**. Tours can be arranged through a number of operators. **Big Blue Safaris**, next to Casa Oro, is perhaps the best known tour operator. Casa Oro is the most popular backpacker hostel offering decent rooms, a large communal kitchen and lots of sociable space, all at reasonable prices.

Seafood dominates the menus here and you can indulge in fresh fish, shrimps and lobster for decent prices. Cheap meals can be found in an abundance of restaurants in town. Street kitchens offering cheap local food can be found at San Juan's market. More upmarket restaurants line the beachfront where you'll pay slightly more for ocean breezes and romantic sunset views. The town comes to life after dark where worn out travellers expel any leftover energy dancing the night away in a number of lively bars and clubs.

Main backpacker area – In town away from the beachfront. **Casa Oro** is the most popular hostel

Highlights – Beaches, surfing, fishing & nightlife

It's no secret that most travellers Nicaraguan itineraries will have them hugging the western seaboard and this means that the vast expanse to the east of Lago de Nicaragua remains largely unexplored. The Caribbean coast of Nicaragua is a long, wide flat plain covered in thick tropical rainforest boasting an abundance of wildlife – it is part of the larger sparsely populated Mosquitia region that extends into Honduras. This region was never colonised by the Spanish, in fact the leaders of the Mosquitia requested for it be ruled by the British as a defence against Spain! Consequently, this part of Nicaragua is very different where you'll find a mix of indigenous tribal languages and English spoken amid a melting pot of ethnic minorities. **Bluefields** and the **Corn Islands** *(see below)* are pretty much the only part of the coast that's visited by international tourists, so the rest is yours for the taking! Consider challenging yourself well and truly off-the-beaten track and head between **Puerto Cabezas** and **Bluefields** or even **El Castillo.**

CORN ISLANDS... *Nica's chunk of the Caribbean*

The Corn Islands, Nicaragua's only chunk of true Caribbean culture, is a melting pot of blacks, Indigenous Miskitos, former mainlanders and the occasional backpacker. Those who venture here are rewarded with a true authentic and quirky Caribbean experience: Powder white beaches, clear turquoise waters, vibrant coral reef and scrumptious seafood ensure an unhurried pace of life. Both islands are intriguingly wired and out of the two English speaking Isles, **Big Corn Island** is the backpacker's choice. Explore around the island and discover deserted tranquil beaches where it's possible to spend an entire day sizzling in solitude. The best, although more crowded, beaches are found at **Picnic Centre** *(Southwest Bay)*. Decent **snorkelling** can be found on the north and east sides of the island – taxis constantly roam around the Island and cost the same per person regardless of distance. The majority of the country's lobster is processed here, which means backpackers can enjoy top-quality tails at rock-bottom prices – check out **Fishers Cave** *(near the pier)*. Neighbouring **Little Corn Island** is an unblemished tropical paradise where even fewer travellers venture – water taxis link Little Corn to its big brother and makes for an ideal daytrip.

Getting there & away: This is where the fun begins, brace yourself for a challenge! Getting to the Corn Islands involves a fair degree of patience, a high pain threshold and a true sense of adventure! The quickest and most painless way to reach the Corn Islands is to fly *(La Costeña)* from **Managua** to **Bluefields** where a ferry will take you to the islands. A few fearless backpackers choose the *(cheaper)* long and tedious overland route that's taunted by extensive hours of discomfort and delays, although this is the whole appeal for the hardcore, aka tight, backpacker:

Managua ➔ Rama ➔ Bluefields ➔ Corn Islands *(Big Corn)*

An early rise will reward you with a 292km trip along one of the worst and uncomfortable roads in the country from Managua to Rama before embarking on an overcrowded slow boat to Bluefields! While most guidebooks suggest that you stay in **Juigalpa** or **Rama** to break up the trip, an early start will ensure that you'll reach Bluefields the same day. It's not the most welcoming or safest town and you'll feel uneasy strolling through its shady narrow streets but one night here in a rundown guesthouse is all you need to catch the ferry first thing in the morning – you wanted an adventurous trip off-the-beaten track didn't you!? You'll definitely need to pack a sense of adventure and even the most hardcore backpackers choose to fly back from the Corn Islands, even if it's just to save on time.

Main backpacker area – Big Corn Island, most of the accommodation is on the west of the island, north and south of the pier

Highlights – Isolated island life, tranquil beaches, cheap seafood & an unhurried Caribbean ambience with quirky locals!

COSTA RICA

THRILL SEEKER!

AT A GLANCE

Capital – San José

Population – 4.1 million

Language(s) – Spanish.
English on the Caribbean Coast

Currency – Colon*(es)* (C$)

ATMs – ATMs available on the Pacific Coast
Sparse on the Caribbean Coast

Climate – Tropical. Cooler in highlands

Best time to go – Dec - April *(dry season)*

Time zone – GMT minus 6hours

Suggested daily budget – 15,000C$ *(US$30)*

Suggested time – 2-3 weeks

Visas – Not required for citizens of the EU, USA, Canada, Oz & New Zealand

Costa Rica is globally renowned for its commitment to preservation. National Parks and conservation areas have ensured a country of outstanding natural beauty that's home to a rich variety of flora and fauna. Endangered sea turtles nest on both coasts while playful primates swing noisily in lush forests, crocs lurk in rivers and elusive jungle cats attempt to evade intrepid travellers. Nature lovers and keen hikers will be in their element but this is a country that thrills everyone. Carefree surfers, beach dwellers and carefree drinkers are kept happy with generous lashings of golden sand, lively beach towns and sets of oversized waves while thrill seekers need to look no further than La Fortuna for their kicks. Adrenaline junkies fly through the forest canopy

on zip-lines, melt marsh-mellows over flowing lava, raft down white-water rapids and dangle from bungy cords – all in the course of a normal day. However you spend your day, nothing relaxes you more than stewing in a hot spring. It does lack culture, but that's not why you come here and while it's arguably the most expensive country in the region, you're buying into an experience and contributing to its future preservation so others can enjoy it. It's money well spent, this is eco-tourism at its best....

There's a great 'coast to coast' route across Costa Rica that'll ensure the perfect blend of beach-time, scenic landscapes, bustling city life and top-notch inland adventure. It's Central America's eco-tourism hotspot, boosting the region's premier activity town – La Fortuna – where even the most hardcore extreme adrenaline junkies and passionate eco-tourist will get their fix. This popular linear route cuts right through the country with entry/exit points into Nicaragua to the north and Panama to the South. San José is also one of the region's main entry / exit point:

(Nicaragua➔) Playa Tamarindo ➔ La Fortuna ➔ San José ➔ Puero Viejo *(➔Panamá)*

PLAYA TAMARINDO... *Costa Rica's surfing hot spot*

Slip into a beachy existence, Tamarindo is one of the most popular tourist destinations in Nicaragua with **surfing** high on the agenda. While flush tourists flock here and the town is brimming with expensive low-key resorts, a number of cheap guesthouses can still be found tucked away. **JC & Friends** is a friendly and quirky guesthouse with dorms and a communal kitchen that's located near the supermarket away from the main beachfront.

Surfers arrive to Playa Tamarindo in their droves eager to ride the first-rate breaks. The waves on the main beach are crowded with enthusiastic beginners from the numerous surf schools. This abundance of decent surf schools and a laidback *'everyone's in the same boat'* attitude creates the perfect environment where you won't be embarrassed to give it a go and stand up on that board! More serious surfers will become quickly agitated by the concentration of cumbersome amateurs but will appreciate the bigger and more challenging waves that can be found at nearby Playa Avellana and Playa Negra. Besides the surf, the beaches are gorgeous and there's plenty to keep you occupied. **Boat trips**, **fishing**, **ATV tours**, **snorkelling**, **diving** and a host of other **water sports** can be arranged through a number of various outfits in town. The beaches of Playa Grande and Playa Langosta, part of the Costa Rican National Park system, are major nesting sites for giant leatherback turtles – **nesting season** runs from October through till March and tours led by official guides are available to witness this incredible spectacle.

Main backpacker area – A few guesthouses can be found tucked away from the main beachfront

Highlights – Decent waves, surf schools, beaches, fishing, snorkelling & diving, boat trips & turtle nesting season

LA FORTUNA... *Adrenaline junkie!*

Visitors come to this scenic town for one reason – Costa Rica's most active volcano – **Volcán Arenal**. This magnificent volcano retains its almost perfect conical shape and is very much active! If the cloud breaks during the day you can see plumes of smoke bellowing out from its crater and at nightfall you can usually see red-hot lava flowing from its peak. The town itself is fairly quiet with a good array souvenir shops cafés and restaurants. La Fortuna has a decent scattering of budget accommodation with **Hotel Dorothy**, southeast of the bull ring, being popular with backpackers. For a little **self-indulgence**, there are a number of spas and massage parlours that use locally sourced soils and minerals from Volcán Arenal. However, a quick look around town and you'll discover the real reason why people are here – the streets are lined with a healthy spread of companies offering endless tours and white-knuckle activities. While there's not much nightlife in the town, it's become a popular destination for outdoor extremists and adrenaline junkies. You'll want a bit of disposable cash for your time in La Fortuna or you'll miss out big time! This is the regions premier adventure town and ecotourism at its best!

Activities: The volcano is excitably active and, probably because Costa Rica enforces some kind of Health & Safety regulations, you won't be able to hike anywhere near as close to the action as you can at other rumbling peaks like Pacaya in Antigua. However, **volcano tours** will take you as close as possible, where you can witness the rumbling of rocks being spat from its peak and ooze red-hot lava as they tumble down the steep sides – get on a night tour where you can watch the lava glow a ferocious red. Try and get on a small tour away from the traditional 'package-trip' as most of the larger more commercialised trips only take you to a bridge where you'll view the volcano from a disappointing distance. The smaller tours go right past this and take you as close as is possibly safe. While you're in an area blessed with so much geothermal activity you'd be crazy not to take advantage of the **natural hot springs**. There are two main 'commercialised' springs, Baldi Termae and Tabacón hot springs, but if you get on a small tour they'll take you off-the-beaten track and to the real hot springs by the side of the road where there's not an ounce of concrete in sight and you can get wrinkly without paying an entrance fee!

Another huge attraction are the **zip-lines** that slice through the forest canopy. Some of the zip-lines are up to 1km long where you'll exit the jungle canopy at speed to find yourself hanging hundreds of feet in the air over canyons and spectacular waterfalls – it's fun, exciting and exhilarating, and you'd be mad to miss out on it! There are a lot of companies offering different 'packages of zip-lines', but you should be looking to get about ten zip-lines for your money! **White-water rafting** is another popular past time here and heart racing daytrips can be found at reasonable prices. If you fancy playing with gravity, **Arenal Bungee** is situated in town offering day and night jumps against the back drop of Volcán Arenal for around US$50. Other activities include, **horse riding** and the nearby **Venado Caverns**.

Main backpacker area – Hotel Dorothy is popular with shoe-stringers

Highlights – Bungy jumping, canopy tour & zip-lining, natural hot springs, Volcán Arenal, Venado Caverns & white-water rafting

SAN JOSÉ... *The capital*

San José is one of the more modern and westernised cities in Central America. Little remains of its colonial past and it's more expensive than elsewhere in Costa Rica. It's not a favourite destination for budget backpackers but travellers come here through necessity rather than choice – it's one of the region's major transport hubs with most international flights arriving and departing from here. If you're flying into San José to begin your Latino adventure don't be put off, most travellers head straight to more desirable and rural locations where you'll find what you're looking for! If it all gets too much throw yourself off the Old Colorado River Bridge just outside of San José – **Tropical Bungee** *(www.bungee.co.cr)*!

On the plus side the nightlife is good – apparently – with lively bars and loud nightclubs. However, there's no denying that it's an intimidating and sometimes dangerous city so exercise caution and use taxis after nightfall! While there's no distinct travellers' area like Khao San Road in Thailand, there are a few decent backpacker hostels spread throughout the city. Among the best are: **Hostel Pangea** *(www.hostelpangea.com)* and **Tranquilo Backpackers** *(www.tranquilobackpackers.com)* with dorms from US$12 – although I literally got thrown out of the first one by two rather large guys, quickly followed by my backpack, because I used the internet in the morning when I apparently wasn't entitled to do so – it was a bit over the top I feel! Jump in a **metered** cab to get to them. Don't organise any tours through the hostels here – book them when you arrive at other destinations where they'll be cheaper and you won't unwittingly make San José your base camp!

Main backpacker hostels – Hostel Pangea & Tranquilo Backpackers

Highlights – Tropical Bungee jump, nightlife & airport!

PUERTO VIEJO... *The laidback Caribbean surfer's hangout*

Puerto Viejo de Talamanca nestles on the coast and casually oozes a Caribbean ambience. It's a carefree village where you'll find laidback surfers gracefully paddling out to catch the next set of waves, sun-worshippers soak up the rays on the beach trying to go a deeper shade of brown and weary travellers swinging in hammocks nursing their hangovers! This 'tame appearance' is only cosmetic and there's no rest for the hung-over in Puerto Viejo – there's always something going on somewhere! Bars and restaurants come to life at night and last night's 'ball-of-fire' come out of hiding to indulge in another night of carefree drinking! Puerto Viejo has the perfect blend of surfing, nightlife and a carefree Caribbean vibe that makes this place a fantastic place to spend many countless days in true hammock dwelling style.

The town has become a prime **surfing** destination and boasts some of the country's biggest and fastest breaks. The best surf can be found at **Salsa Brava** just northeast of the main village. If you're a bit of a surf dude you'll love Puerto Viejo. The surf is at its height between December and March. Boards can be rented through a number of guesthouses. You can snorkel but visibility isn't great until the surf shrinks from late September. Accommodation is spread around the village and unfortunately the standard varies greatly. Your best bet is to ask around for **Rocking J's** – the locals and other business owners will argue till their blue in the face that it's full or has closed down but they just want your custom so keep asking! Rocking J's is a great backpacker's retreat where you can pick up a bargain night's sleep in the hammock lined communal area. Situated close to the border of Panama, it's a good stop before popping over the border to **Bocas del Toro**.

Main backpacker hostel – Rocking J's

Highlights – Surfing, beaches, unique bars & nightlife

Off-the-beaten track... *Spice things up a bit!*

Costa Rica is no doubt the most tourist-trodden country in the region but you may be surprised to find that there are a few little gems that have yet to swamped by the package-holidaymaker. Probably due to their locations, tucked away at opposite ends of the country with limited access, these two National Parks are a haven for well-informed backpackers:

Tortuguero – Home some of the greatest biodiversity in the country, Lonely Planet describes this place as Costa Rica's 'mini-Amazon' and they couldn't be more spot on! It's a haven for countless species and a guided boat tour through here is a must do – you'll spot crocs lounging on the rivers banks, monkeys swinging from the trees and even freshwater turtles basking on logs! Turtle nesting is perhaps the most popular attraction and you can hire a local guide so that you can witness this fantastic natural spectacle. Leatherbacks lay between April and May while July to October sees large numbers of green turtles nesting. Tours and guides are fantastic value averaging around US$10 – US$15. Accommodation can be scarce during peak nesting times.

Parque Nacional Corcovado – Tucked away in the southwest corner and boasting some of the last remaining tropical rainforest of the Pacific Central America, this is one of Costa Rica's most unspoilt areas. Its vast biological diversity will satisfy the most enthusiastic and passionate nature buffs. On organised ranger hikes you can spot scarlet macaws, coatis, toucans, howler monkeys, snakes, an array of birdlife and if you're really lucky, you may catch a rare glimpse of a shy jaguar. Even whales frolic in the waters just of this region's coast! Most people who venture here base themselves at **Puerto Jiménez** which offers easy access to the National Park.

PANAMA

END OF THE LINE

AT A GLANCE

Capital – Panama City
Population – 2.9 million
Language(s) – Spanish & Kuna
Currency – US-dollar (US$)
ATMs – Available in main towns
Climate – Tropical
-Best time to go – Jan - May *(dry season)*
Time zone – GMT minus 5hours
Suggested daily budget – US$25
Suggested time – 2 weeks
Visas – Granted on arrival for most nationalities

It's not the first country that springs to mind when you're running through backpacking destinations. Isolated on the end of Central America, bridging the Americas, Panama is often neglected by hurried travellers. Compared to other countries in the region, backpacker options are limited but a small number of popular hotspots are complemented by plenty of roads less-travelled and bucket loads of potential adventures away from the crowds. If you give it the time, there's something here for everyone. Beach-bums, surfer dudes and merry drinkers will be enchanted by the popular Bocas Town and being just a jog from the Costa Rican border, this is understandably Panama's prime travellers destination. Elsewhere, away from the hot and sticky coastline, the countryside offers highland retreats, indigenous villages, coffee plantations, scenic views and remote cloud forests where you'll no doubt have your own unique adventures. Then there's the capital, which despite a host of international flights, is a relatively undiscovered gem. Yet it's an intriguing melting pot of cultures where you can explore a diverse mix of districts and travel your taste buds before viewing the engineering feat of the Panama Canal – it's the perfect start or final farewell to a Central American voyage. As a complete package Panama offers a well-balanced mix of experiences along less-travelled roads. If you're on a whirlwind tour of the region, visit the energetic Bocas at the very least!

The majority of travellers just pop across the border to 'party it up' in the lively town of Bocas del Toro for a few days hardcore drinking and beach flopping before heading back into Costa Rica, often to fly out from San José. Panama has a lot more to offer and those flying from Panama City follow a varied linear route through this narrow country hitting these popular spots:

(Costa Rica➔) Bocas del Toro ➔ Boquete ➔ Panamá City

BOCAS DEL TORO... *Panamá's backpacker hotspot*

Bocas del Toro has emerged as Panama's premier backpacker destination, yet thankfully it remains rustic and undeveloped – perfect for backpackers! Just 32km from the Costa Rican border it's also easily accessible. This is the place to be in Panama and the ideal town to inflict some serious damage to your major internal organs – queue many alcohol induced antics! The archipelago is made up of six large islands and a scattering of smaller ones. The provincial capital, **Bocas Town**, is located on Isla Colón and boasts the relaxed, beachy ambiance adored by backpackers, and is an ideal base for exploring the isles further afield should you feel the urge. Here you'll find most of the budget accommodation, restaurants and bars. This slow-paced English speaking community is a great place to hang out for a few days or even base yourself for a few weeks and it's a fantastic place to get chatting with locals and travellers over a few drinks – check out the **Wreck Deck Bar**. A quick 200m taxi-boat ride across the water from this bar you'll find **Isla Carenero**, a small island featuring one of the most popular hostels that extends over the water – **Aqua Lounge**.

There are plenty of beaches scattered around Isla Colón to soak up the Caribbean rays and they're easily accessible by taxi or bicycle. Beaches aside there's plenty to keep you occupied during your time in Bocas. Various companies offer reasonably priced **diving** and **snorkelling** trips while sea **kayaks** and **surf boards** can be rented through a number of bars, hostels and shacks. December through till March sees the best breaks around the islands and popular spots include: Playa Paunch and Playa Bluff *(Isla Colón a few km's north of Bocas Town)* and Red Frog Beach and Playa Primera on Bastimentos. Local boats will take you to these surf spots for around US$10.

Main backpacker area – Bocas del Toro Town & Isla Canenero *(Aqua Lounge)*

Highlights – Diving & snorkelling, kayaking &surfing, beaches, bars & nightlife

BOQUETE... *The refreshing highlands*

Boquete is a small settlement that sits in a mountain valley amid the misty landscape of the Chiriquí Highlands. This region is well known for its cool, refreshing climate and spectacular natural landscape – it's a welcome retreat from the hot and humid micro-climates of the more popular coastal hotspots. This region flourishes with an incredible natural environment full of native flora and fauna and cultivated by indigenous tribes – flowers, coffee, vegetables and exotic fruits thrive in the highland's rich soils and support numerous villages throughout the region.

This region still remains largely undiscovered and most travellers stop here to break up the Journey from Panama City to Bocas del Toro but there are a few things that make this village a worthwhile stop. Its idyllic setting makes it a popular region for keen **hikers** where you can enjoy picturesque walks through mist-covered valleys, pristine forests and coffee plantations before conquering the summit of nearby **Volcán Baru**. More adventurous trips and guided tours can be booked through **Chiriquí River Rafting** *(www.panama-rafting.com)*. This company offers **white-water rafting** around Boquete and a range of other exciting activities including **sea kayaking**, **fishing**, and **boating** all around the Province of Chiriquí. **Café Ruiz** offer decent tours that explore the process of coffee making from 'bean to cup' *(www.caferuiz.com)*. Nestled idyllically in the highlands, evenings are chilly and temperatures can plummet to near freezing during the night so come prepared with warm clothes!

Main backpacker area – Several budget hotels in the centre of Boquete town between **Av Central** & **Av A Este**

Highlights – Hikes, picturesque walks, outdoor activities, coffee tours & the cool climate

PANAMA CITY... *The capital*

Home of the famous and engineering wonder of the Panama Canal, Panama City is a thriving modern city where you'll find a variety of charming cafés, appetising restaurants and bustling shops. The cultural conscious will appreciate an unrivalled blend of colonial *(Casco Antiguo)*, modern and rundown Havana districts. Accommodation comprises mainly of fairly expensive hotels but hope comes in the form of **Voyager International Hostel**. This hostel offers fantastic views, decent dorms and a communal kitchen at budget rates. Here you can find info about daytrips, city tours and mingle with seasoned travellers.

Fewer travellers include Panama City on their Itinerary, but it's a good entry and exit point for Central America. **Tocumen International Airport** has regular flights most Central American countries. There are also daily departures to several locations in the USA including the Big Apple and LA as well as a number of South American countries. Domestic flights depart from **Albrook Airport** where travellers can avoid long tedious bus journeys along Panamas slender figure with decent airfares to backpacker hotspots such as Bocas del Toro before slipping across the border overland into Costa Rica.

Main backpacker hostel – Voyager International Hostel

Highlights – Panamá Viejo, Casco Antiguo, the Causeway & The Panama Canal

Australasia

Adrenaline ◊ Beach-life ◊ Natural Wonders

WHY GO TO... *AUSTRALASIA?*

ENJOY LIFE IN THE SUN

Use this themed section to help you decide what region to go to. Compare this section to the Asian and Latino equivalents to find your perfect tailored destination.

AUSTRALASIA... *An introduction*

Although geographically inaccurate, for simplicity and practicality, this book will refer to Australia, Fiji and New Zealand as **Australasia**. Use this themed section to help you decide which region to go to – compare this section to the Asian and Central American equivalents to find your perfect tailored destination.

Embrace the tyranny of distance and succumb to this diverse trio of island nations. They may be extremely disproportionate in size, but each country is jammed-packed with a fantastic blend of adventure, relaxation and natural wonders. It's no secret that visitors have been flocking here for decades to escape the cold European winters. Many find themselves prolonging their stay to pursue any type of employment so they can enjoy a slower pace of life in the sun. There's plenty to keep you isolated on this side of the world indefinitely. With natural wonders that include glacial valleys, pristine national parks, the Great Barrier Reef and Ayers Rock, the region's clearly got lots to shout about. These magical landscapes are complemented by an unrivalled portfolio of extreme activities where you can do anything from bungy jumping and skydiving to jet-boating and cage-diving. Laidback beach-towns and blissful tropical islands are pleasantly contrasted by affordable ski-resorts and sophisticated city-culture. From the laidback Aussie and the friendly Kiwi to the legendary Maori and the hospitable Fijian islander the people are also as diverse as they are enchanting. It's a fascinating melting pot of cultures living in harmony. All things are possible in this captivating region. The sun rises here first for a reason!

Boasting a host of well-publicised attractions, this diverse trio are no new kids on the block when it comes to mass-tourism and backpacking. All three countries have fantastic tourist infrastructure that caters for all budgets. It's a great region for curious but anxious backpackers with familiar style western living coupled with good standards of accommodation and transport. Nervous backpackers will also be comforted by the fact that Australia, Fiji and New Zealand are all predominantly English speaking countries. There's no denying that the airline tickets are a big expense and general living costs aren't much cheaper than those in the UK or Europe but there's a wealth of job opportunities available to soften the blow and make Australasia a financially viable destination.

Between the three you've got a mix of everything – Australia offers the usual sun, sea, sand and surf in sheer abundance while the Kiwis boasts all the adrenaline fuelled and panty-wetting activities to satisfy even the hardest of hardcore adrenaline junkies. On top of this you've got everything from an energetic nightlife that'll keep you up until the early hours of the morning to vineyards and breathtaking scenery with a drop of culture thrown in for good measure! Then there's beautiful Fiji – the isles of smiles. This patchwork of tropical islands is famous for its party vibe, lethargic island life-style, warming culture and heroic island-hopping adventures.

Australasia is an ideal destination...

- o   If you **don't want such a culture shock** – they're all English speaking countries, with New Zealand and Oz in particular, having very familiar western style living!

- o   If you **don't want to 'rough it'** in dodgy guesthouses, rundown hostels and hop on rickety old busses that characterise backpacking in SE Asia and Central America – lifestyle and travel is similar to European and North American standards and a lot more comfortable *(and perhaps safer!)*

- o   If you've got **a fair bit of money saved up** and **limited time** – it's a pricey backpacker destination by any standards!

- o   Alternatively, it's good if you want to stay for a **long time**, have **limited funds** and want to seek some **employment** – there's a wealth of **backpacker job opportunities**

- o   If you want pursue a shed load of **adrenaline fuelled activities** – blessed an endless list of outdoor pursuits, New Zealand is the unrivalled home of extreme sports and you'll find a fair share in Oz as well

- o   If you want an **island hopping adventure** where you can **party** on paradise islands and learn to enjoy your hangovers – hopscotch blissfully between Fiji's 333 tropical islands where the beer is plentiful and the sun never stops shinning

- o   If you're a **first-time traveller** and a bit **apprehensive** – the limit culture shock is coupled with a well established tourist industry and a very strong backpacker scene

HIGHLIGHTS... *Don't miss the best bits!*

Australia, the pinnacle destination for many travellers, boasts a well-developed backpacker scene with plenty to keep you occupied, beaches to bake your skin and enough bars to ensure you don't sober up. However, while Australia tends to grab the headlines, it's New Zealand where adventure and adrenaline are really found in abundance. Fiji offers the endless island hoping adventures where you'll a lethargic pace of life, an array of water-sports and some culture thrown in for good measure. Here are some of the 'nuggets' you should try and jot down on your itinerary:

BUNGY JUMPING   Engage your adrenaline glands and get to ready to experience ground rush like never before. NZ is the original home of bungy jumping and where you'll find the knee-wobbling 142m Nevis Highwire. Queenstown has the daddy jumps but pretty much where ever you go in NZ & Oz you can dangle from the end of a bungy cord!

CAVING *(New Zealand)*   Top-notch adventure cave-tours in Waitomo get you abseiling down dark holes, squeezing through small crevices, splashing around in underground rivers, leaping off waterfalls in the dark and floating through glow worm-lit caverns on inner tubes!

GLACIER HIKING *(Kiwi's West Coast)*   There are few places n the world where you can hike a glacier and NZ boasts two awesome examples that are easily accessible. Grab an ice-axe and strap on your crampons, ½ and full-day hikes will have clambering up these majestic blue beauties for the ultimate ice experience that's surprisingly very affordable

TRAMPING *(New Zealand)*   NZ has some world class trails. Walks range from gentle strolls to strenuous hikes and will reward you with some of the best landscapes you'll ever see – Tongariro Crossing regularly features in the top ten walks in the world and offers spectacular views over emerald lakes, hot springs and volcanic landscapes

SHARK CAGE-DIVING *(New Zealand)*   Get up close and personal with one of nature's most ferocious predators behind the safety of a few metal bars in Kaikoura!

SKYDIVING *(Fiji, NZ & Oz)*   Strap on a parachute, and more importantly, a pair of balls and fling yourself out of a perfectly good plane at 15,000ft to observe some of the world's most memorising landscapes and the ultimate adrenaline rush. The Taupo skydive in NZ is the daddy of all jumps offering coast to coast views against the stunning backdrop of Lake Taupo and the volcanic plateau of the Tongariro National Park. In Fiji, you can even skydive without a jump suit and land on the beach in shorts and t-shirt bare-foot!

WHITE-WATER RAFTING *(NZ & Oz)*   Pump up a little dinghy, grab your buddies, a guide and a couple of paddles and head-off over the first waterfall for some rapid-riding... You'll find some great growling rivers and panty-wetting white-water rapids throughout Oz and NZ!

DOLPHIN SWIMMING *(NZ & Oz)*   Frolic around with friendly dolphins in their natural environments for one of nature's most memorable encounters. You can meet flipper in a number of spots throughout Australia and New Zealand

SKIING *(NZ)*   Yes you can even see in Kiwi land. In fact, NZ has the best skiing in the southern hemisphere. Snow bunnies head to ski-fields on the south island during the Kiwi winter. Most are within a hop, skip and jump away from the legendary town of Queenstown

FRASER ISLAND *(Australia)*   The largest sand island is the world is home to the infamous self-drive 4x4 tours. Spend three days trashing around sandy tracks with a 4x4 full of new friends, a cool box packed with grog and a load of meat for the BBQ – it's the ultimate sociable adventure!

WHITSUNDAYS *(Oz)*   One of Australia's well discovered, but not overdeveloped, gems. The Whitsundays is a group of tropical islands boasting crystal clear waters and gorgeous white-sand beaches. Sailing tours can be arranged form the lively mainland town of Airlie Beach which boasts epic nightlife and a refreshing lagoon to soothe your hangovers!

TURTLE TOTS *(Mon Repos)*   Experience one of nature's miracles during turtle nesting & hatching season. Nothing quite prepares you for witnessing a huge turtle drag itself up the beach and painstakingly dig a perfect nesting chamber to lay a cluster of around 100 ping-pong sized eggs! The is experience is only exceed by the hatching season when you can witness hundred of turtle tots emerge from the sand and scurry between your legs as they make their way to the great open ocean

AYERS ROCK *(Oz)*   Australia's Red Centre is an icon – you can't really get any more Australian. For years it's been almost a religious pilgrimage to reach it and simply no trip to Oz would be complete without gazing your eyes on this magical spectacle. Tours always treat you to an enchanting sunset over the big red rock

ISLAND HOPPING *(Fiji)*   The stunning laidback Yasawas & Mamanucas isles are a patchwork of sun-drenched tropical islands that have become an infamous backpacker destination where you can island hop to your heart's content, top up your tan, drink till you can't stand and soothe your hangover in the crystal clear tropical waters. They're a must for sociable sun-worshippers and enthusiastic hammock dwellers!

KAVA SESSIONS *(Fiji)*   Join in one of Fiji's most sociable events and sample some genuine Fijian culture – gather round in a circle, drink kava from coconut shells and slip into a comfortable seduced state, or rather a typical islander's coma – this popular 'muddy' drink will make you go numb form the head down and get you in a state of giggles. It's essentially a legal 'high' that's a fun and an important part of Fijian culture. Welcome to the isles of smiles!

SCUBA-DIVING   The vibrant Great Barrier Reef is the obvious draw for fanatic divers but there's a whole lot more and equally stunning world class dive sites scattered all around Fiji and New Zealand. This region gives you the chance to have some unique aquatic encounters with some of nature's most elegant and mighty creatures – swim with turtles, teases sharks from the safety of a cage, glide along with graceful manta rays and feel insignificant alongside giant whale sharks!

NIGHTLIFE   From sociable beach parties and chilled-out beachfront bars to energetic city pubs and sophisticated nightclubs, the nightlife is as varied and as it is epic – part animals will not be disappointed! Get on that liver transplant list now...

ROAD TRIPS   NZ & Oz boast some of the most infamous road-trips – the epic sundrenched pilgrimage up Australia's chilled-out eastern seaboard and the action-pack adrenaline-fuelled voyage from Auckland to Christchurch in NZ are the most common road-trips but there are plenty of off-the-beaten adventures to be had

BEACHES   Beach bums unite. This trio of island nations boast some of the world's most scrumptious beaches from Sydney's famous Bondi beach and the picturesque beaches of the Whitsundays in Oz to the empty slithers of hot golden sand that frame the tropical isles of Fiji, there's always a spot for your towel!

JOB OPPORTUNITIES   NZ & Oz offer some of the best job-opportunities for travellers from working in the soaring heat of the outback picking fruit to more conventional work in air-conditioned hostels helping fellow backpackers! It's a great way to boost your travelling funds and prolonging your stay down under. Many people literally 'work their way around'

OZ & NEW ZEALAND...

Located in the Southern Hemisphere, Australia and New Zealand have the four similar seasons to Europe but at opposite times – which conveniently allows you to escape the cold European winters and soak up some sun Down Under!

- o **NZ SUMMER:**   Dec - Feb are the official summer months *(12-25°C)*

- o **OZ SUMMER:**   Dec - Feb though northern Oz has a tropical climate *(12-25°C)*

Summer is the official high season while the shoulder months of October / November and March / April are cooler, quieter and slightly cheaper. New Zealand's South Island is typically a few degrees cooler than the North Island and on both main islands it's generally wetter in the west than in the east.

Ski Season: While most head to Oz, NZ and the Pacific in search of sun, sea, sand and surf, others time their trip to coincide with snow, skiing and snowboarding. If you're a snow bunny you'll want to visit New Zealand when the white stuff is thick on the ground during the winter. A good time to visit is during the annual 10-day **Queenstown Winter Festival** which takes place at the end of June – just as the NZ ski-season is kicking off *(www.winterfestival.co.nz)*:

- o **NZ SNOW SEASON:** June - Aug aka 'winter'!

Just bear in mind that if you intend to venture outside of the ski-resorts and go further afield, some of the sea-side towns and warm-weather hotspots will be in semi-hibernation or completely shut down as far as tourists are concerned!

FIJI...

Fiji has a stable tropical climate without vast extremes of hot or cold. Fiji has average temperatures of around 25°. It has two distinct seasons instead of our familiar four seasons of spring, summer, autumn *(fall)* and winter, Fiji has wet *('summer')* and dry *('winter')* seasons:

- o **THE DRY SEASON:**   May - Oct are the cooler dry months *(22-27°C)* – *'Winter'*

- o **THE WET SEASON:**   Nov - April are hotter and more humid *(26-31°C)* – *'Summer'*

While Fiji is good at any time of the year, generally speaking, the **dry season** is considered the best time to go as temperatures are cooler and humidity is just about bearable! April to October also offers the best visibility for scuba diving. 'Summer' is hotter but significantly more humid. Downpours typically last no more than 30 minutes to an hour and provide some refreshing relief to hot, sticky and humid summer days – so just enjoy it! If you're heading to Fiji during the rainy season, your best bet is to head to the drier regions such as the Mamanuca and Yasawa Isles where the sunshine is abundant practically all year round and the weather more reliable.

THE CLASSIC 'PACIFIC-LINEAR' ROUTE...

FIJI ➔ NEW ZEALAND ➔ AUSTRALIA

Suggested time: 4+ months *(a few years if you want to work!)*

Entry / exit points: Nadi *(Fiji)* / Sydney *(Oz)*

The countries/route: **Fiji** – Nadi, Yasawa & Mamanucas Isles, & Viti Levu

            New Zealand – Auckland, Rotorua, Taupo, Waitomo, Wellington, Nelson, West Coast, Queenstown, Christchurch, Kaikoura

            East Coast Oz – Cairns *(Great Barrier Reef)*, Airlie Beach *(Whitsundays)*, Fraser Island, Brisbane, Surfers Paradise, Byron Bay, Hunter Valley, Sydney *(Blue Mountains)*, Canberra, Melbourne,

Because of its diminutive size compared to Oz, many people dedicate a disproportional amount of time to the land Down Under. Don't be fooled! You need about 6 weeks in Oz to explore the east coast at an enjoyable pace and 2-3 weeks on <u>each</u> island in New Zealand. Another classic mistake is to overlook or skip through Fiji – try and stay longer than the usual two week 'pit-stop'. While you're on the other side of the world it makes sense to check out this trio of diverse countries. Obviously this is essentially three itineraries so if you've limited time and funds, pick n mix:

Mini Itinerary: Fiji

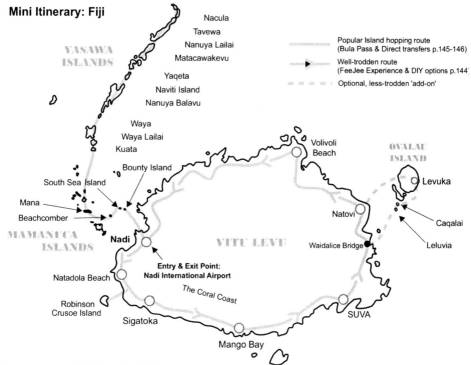

Boasting over 300 islands, Fiji is the ultimate setting for some grand island-hopping adventures. Conveniently placed **Nadi** should be utilised as a base camp. The ever popular **Yasawas** and **Mamanucas** offer an accessible slice of tropical paradise are usually the first stop where beach lovers unite for a week or two, often on the Bula Bass/direct transfers. Those with more time DIY-it pursuing looping routes around **Viti Levu** and **Ovalua** for some genuine culture and adventure.

Mini Itinerary: New Zealand

The well-trodden route
- - - Popular 'add-ons'
● Less-travelled destinations

Cape Reinga
Bay of Islands
Paihia
NORTH ISLAND
Auckland
Mercury Bay
East Cape
Waitomo
Rotorua
Taupo
Tongariro National Park
Cross the Cook Straight via ferry
WELLINGTON
SOUTH ISLAND
Nelson
Kaikoura
Franz Josef
Christchurch
Milford Sound
Queenstown
Doubtful Sound
Dunedin
STEWART ISLAND

Far flung New Zealand is bursting at the seams with adventure and this popular linear route ensures that you'll give your adrenaline glands a thorough workout and your liver a real pounding! While absorbing some of the world's most stunning glaciers, frolicking with dolphins, jumping out of planes, dangling from bungy cords and getting and battered by UV rays on sandy beaches. There are loads of DIY options but most opt for the sociable backpacker busses. Start you Kiwi adventure in the big smoke of **Auckland** and exit via chilled-out Christchurch. You can't miss what's in between!

Australia's scorched eastern seaboard is a well-trodden backpacker route – it's the ultimate beach bum pilgrimage and the scene of one the most epic road trips. Start your Aussie adventure in stylish **Sydney** and soak up the sights before heading north in your camper and a cool-box stocked with refreshing beer. Depending how time rich you are, 'pick 'n' mix' between the gems that litter the coast. Sailing the famous **Whitsundays**, trashing around a 4x4 on **Fraser Island,** watching turtles nest in **Mon Repos** and catching the perfect wave in **Byron Bays** should be on the top of your 'to-do' list. Between the popular beach towns there are many tempting detours and some of the best places will be the ones you stumble upon unexpectedly. **Cairns** is the usual finishing line although **Cooktown** and **Cape Tribulation** are popular 'add-ons' that offer some rustic and rural experiences.

Mini Itinerary: Oz

The well-trodden sundrenched route
- - - Popular 'add-ons'
For those with time!

Cooktown
Cairns
Mission Beach
Magnetic Island
Whitsunday Islands
Airlie Beach
QUEENSLAND
Bundaberg & Mon Repos
Hervey Bay
Fraser Island
Rainbow Beach
Brisbane
Surfers Paradise
SOUTH AUSTRALIA
Nimbin
Byron Bay
NEW SOUTH WALES
Port Macquarie
Hunter Valley
Blue Mountains
Newcastle
Sydney
CANBERRA
VICTORIA
Melbourne
Otway NP
Lakes District
Philip Island
Wilsons Promontory NP

For those blessed with more time...

Fiji: If you've got enough time and are fed up with the commercialisation and crowds of the Yasawas consider going off-the-beaten track and explore the **Ovalau Group** or remote **Vanua Levu** – dedicated at least a week for each as transport can be somewhat unreliable!

New Zealand: While the linear route through NZ takes in most of the highlights you can always deviate a little. The winterless **Bay of Islands** and spiritual **Cape Reinga** in the far north are very popular 'add-ons'. On the south Island, get some deep southern exposure in the less-visited Scottish-bred **Dunedin** or the remote bio-rich **Stewart Island**.

Australia: If you're a bit time-rich, get yourself over to **Melbourne** where you can follow a nice looping itinerary from Sydney to Melbourne that'll take you through **Canberra** and along Victoria's scenic coastline. No trip to Oz would be complete without a visit to that great big rock so if your budget allows it, hop on a tour and get yourself out to **Ayers Rock** and **Alice Springs**. You can also extend the classic Eastern Coast pilgrimage and head along the scenic **Ocean Road** through **Otway National Park** to **Adelaide** from **Melbourne** or head south and explore the cooler climate of **Tasmania**.

GETTING THERE & AWAY... *Regional hubs & suitable airline tickets*

Where to fly into/out of... *The regional hub(s)*

Sydney *(Australia)* is the regional hub and where most backpackers enter and exit the region. You'll find the cheapest airfares to and from Sydney although cheap tickets can also be found in and out of **Melbourne** and **Brisbane** in Oz. In New Zealand, travellers tend to fly into **Auckland** and out of **Christchurch** or vice-versa while **Nadi** is the transport hub of Fiji.

Type of airline ticket... *Your options*

This will depend on what type of itinerary you're pursing *(see section 6, Booking your trip... for additional information on airlines, tickets and how to reduce the price of your airline ticket)*:

o **Linear itinerary:** Probably your best option if you can get some good deals. If you want to pursue a practical linear itinerary consider flying into Nadi *(Fiji)* and out of Sydney *(Australia)* with **two single tickets** or consider an **open-jaw ticket** if you're not sure what date you want to fly back on or if you're unsure how much of Australia you want to explore *(you may decide to do the laidback **west coast** after you've worn yourself out down the party mad **east coast**!)*. By having two single tickets or an open ticket you can may your way between the three countries at your own pace via regional flights

o **Looping itinerary:** Being made up of islands, this region doesn't really lend itself to simple looping itineraries but you can book a **standard return ticket** from either Sydney or Melbourne in Oz or from Christchurch or Auckland in New Zealand and use regional flights to explore the area and hop between the three countries

o **RTW ticket:** If you're lucky enough to be on a RTW ticket and want to include realistic and manageable 'surface sectors' across Australasia, consider flying into and out of Nadi *(Fiji)*, into Auckland *(North Island, New Zealand)* and out of Christchurch *(South Island, NZ)* and then into and out of Sydney *(Australia)* or Cairns *(North Australia)* or Melbourne *(South Australia)* to get the most out of your RTW ticket

There's no beating around the bush and whatever way you look at it Australia, Fiji and New Zealand are pricey destinations for any backpacker: the region is significantly more expensive than Asia and Central America and you'll find that it's similarly priced to most of Western Europe, albeit slightly cheaper. Of course there are regional variations: In terms of costs, Oz will disappoint and you'll find it the most expensive country by far with just about everything from accommodation and activities to food and alcohol being more expensive than elsewhere in the region. Consequently, most people who travel around Australia do so for a maximum of around six weeks, those who stay longer tend to have a Working-Holiday-Visa and look for employment. New Zealand's a fair bit cheaper than Oz and is much better value for money, although there's an absurd number of ways to spend you hard earned cash with so many adrenaline fuelled activities on offer! Fiji is the cheapest country out of the three and offers fantastic value for money with all-inclusive backpacker deals on tropical islands from as little as F$45 *(£15)* a night!

Daily budgets for first-time travellers range from **F$60 in Fiji** *(about £20)* to around **AUS$60 in Australia** *(roughly £30)*.

Below is a broad overview of your main expenses Down Under:

ACCOMMODATION... *Island retreats from as little as £18!*

Accommodation down under is very different from what you'll find in Asia and Central America. It's a better standard and more likely to be similar to what you'd expect to find in Europe and North America. Fiji's the only slight exception where you'll find beach-hut type accommodation on some island complexes, although again this'll usually be better quality, cleaner and more westernised than that in Asia.

Fiji: This tropical island nation offers the cheapest backpacker accommodation in the region with dorm accommodation starting from as little as **F$12** a night – that's around £4! Dorms on the more commercialised islands, such as the Yasawas, are significantly more expensive and tend to be larger catering for up to 14 or so guests. A few cater for even more – Beachcombers humongous dorm crams in a cosy 125 backpackers – making it interesting when you're trying to get some! Most guesthouses and island resorts offer a small number of double rooms albeit at slightly higher rates. Most backpacker digs offer internet and travel services, and nearly all have a fantastic schedule of evening entertainment that includes fire dancing, knife throwing, and traditional music with sociable kava sessions thrown in for good measure. Like SE Asia, communal kitchens are rare but the majority of accommodation *(with the exception of hostels in Nadi)* offer all-inclusive deals for a set number of days where the cost of up to three meals a day is included. These inclusive deals are common all over Fiji, especially in the Mamanucas and Yasawas Isles and typically cost anywhere from **F$45** a night upwards. The most popular Islands, such as Beachcomber, can set you back up to **F$100** a night.

NZ & Oz: Backpacker accommodation in Australia and New Zealand consists primarily of large scale multi-storey hostel chains which are completely tailored to meet the needs of budget-travellers. The main hostel Chain in Oz is **YHA** with **Base** and **Nomads** also offering a significant amount of decent accommodation. Perhaps surprisingly, hostels are generally larger in New Zealand than in Oz. **Base** and **Nomads** are the two biggest hostel chains in NZ with a smaller spread of **YHA** and **BBH** hostels. Of course you'll find independent hostels scattered around the major towns in both countries. Dorms are less crowded than those in Fiji and typically cater for 6 or so people. Hostels are competitively priced and offer everything from bars, restaurants and internet cafes to communal kitchens, TV rooms and laundrettes. Hostels will also assist you with visas, job applications and will organise day trips and activities from their travel desks. Prices typically range from **$20 to $35** in both Oz and New Zealand but you can arrange deals if you intend to stay any significant length of time. You can get great discounts with a range of backpacker cards – see discount card section page 206.

FOOD & DRINK... *Cook your own for a few dollars*

NZ & Oz: As in the UK, it's far too expensive to eat out in cafés and restaurants everyday so backpacker tucker in Australia and New Zealand is all about **cooking-it-yourself**. Ninety nine percent of hostels have fully kitted-out communal kitchens where you can utilise your culinary skills – or other peoples – to rustle up a satisfyingly cheap dish. Kitchens are bustling with backpackers so cook with others to get greater economy of scale and reduce your food bill further – providing you don't give them the shits you'll make new friends as well! Buy all of your ingredients at familiar western style superstores where you'll find the cost of food is similar to the UK – maybe even slightly cheaper in NZ. The cheapest supermarket chains in Oz are **Woolworths** and **Coles**. PAK'n'SAVE is by far the cheapest supermarket in New Zealand with the slightly more upmarket **New World** also offering reasonably priced grub. If you're lazy and just can't be arsed to cook everyday most hostels have a special daily discounted backpacker-meal that's usually served in their bar between certain hours – these are well advertised in the hostels. You can drink the tap water so refill your empty bottles and save the environment as well as your budget.

Fiji: Once again Fiji's a different story. You'll be catered for on most of the tourist-orientated islands where you'll often enjoy three feasts a day. The cost of these meals is usually included in the price of the accommodation – it's like five star backpacking. You won't find any Asian style street kitchens or food stalls, but away from the tourist islands and out of the backpacker areas you'll find heaps of very cheap **local cafés** and **'restaurants'** offering a range of food from traditional curries to more British style dishes. Some 'mainland' guesthouses have their own restaurants that serve western dishes and although they're popular, they're noticeably pricier than local eateries. If you manage to find the small scattering of accommodation with cooking facilities, you can get produce from local markets at very cheap prices – although still haggle! Tap water is usually ok on the Main Island although elsewhere it's advisable to buy bottled water.

ALCOHOL... *Save your pennies & knock back a goon!*

Oz: By backpacker standards alcohol in Australia is **very** expensive. You'll find that beer and spirits are similar to UK prices if not more expensive – a bottle of bud can set you back up to **AUS$6** even in backpacker bars and your standard UK pints are expensive, forget all that tiny scooner rubbish! While you can get jugs of beer for around **AUS$10**, most travellers reduce their alcohol expenditure by consuming boxes of wine *(goons/casks)* before they go out. These are great value for money and get you ruined before you even leave your dorm – when inflated the bag inside doubles up as a pillow for when you're too wasted and pass out on the floor! Despite the cost, you'll find a healthy party scene that's fuelled by lively bars and decent clubs.

NZ: Thankfully it's a better story in New Zealand where you get more beer for your buck and alcohol prices are significantly cheaper than Australia. You can enjoy reasonable prices in bars and clubs throughout the country – large party towns such as Queenstown have heaps of pubs and clubs with drinking promotions and special offers. Expect to pay around **NZ$5** for a pint of **Tui's** beer. You'll find that larger hostel chains, such as Base, hand out masses of **2-4-1 beer tokens** when you check in – these can be used in their energetic bars.

Fiji: Alcohol in Fiji is relatively inexpensive – it's cheaper than Oz and New Zealand but a little pricier than Asia and Latin America. You can pick up large bottles of **Fiji Bitter** and **Fiji Gold** – the country's most popular beers – from shops for little more than **F$2-3**. The price of alcohol is heavily inflated on the tourist island complexes – albeit still fairly cheap starting at around **F$6 a**

large bottle of Fiji Bitter – and bars do have happy hours so make the most of them! Bottles of spirits are expensive in Fiji compared to beer prices, so if you like your vodka or whisky buy a few bottles when you arrive at the airport where prices will please even the tightest of tight arses.

ACTIVITIES... *Skydive from only NZ$250!*

NZ & Oz: You're going to spend a stack of cash on activities down under from sailing the Whitsundays and diving over the Great Barrier Reef in Oz to bungy jumping and diving out of planes in New Zealand. If you're a true adrenaline junkie you'll probably spend a fair bit in New Zealand – but that's the whole point of going to the home of extreme sports! In terms of outdoor activities, New Zealand offers the best value for money and you can do anything from canyon swings and 192m tower jumps to street luge and jet boating. The general rule of thumb is that anything you can do in Oz, you can probably do in New Zealand a little cheaper – you'll be able to do more for your money. 12,000ft skydives start from **NZ$250** *(around £100)* while a full-days glacier hiking costs a mere **NZ$140** – and yes equipment is provided! You can jump off the world's first bungy jump – Kawarau Bridge – for **NZ$175** or test yourself with one of the world's highest jumps – Nevis – for **NZ$250**. Don't worry they're the more expensive activities and cheaper thrills can be found! Cheaper bungy jumps can be found outside of Queenstown – Taupo Bungy cost less than **NZ$100**. Five Luge runs in Rotorua will only set up back around **NZ$45** and a day's white-water-caving in Waitomo can be had for a little more than **NZ$80** *(Black Labyrinth Tour)*. **NZ$45** will get you some bruises from paintballing in Franz Josef – obviously you'll need a bit more if you're trigger happy! You can even swim with dolphins in Kaikoura for around **NZ$125** or splash around with seals for **NZ$55**.

Oz highlights include Frasier Island, the Whitsundays and Uluru. Prices for self-drive 3-day/2-night tours on Frasier will set you back around **AUS$250** (after all the extras have been added!) – not bad when you think that's two night's accommodation and vehicle hire. Sailing trips around the Whitsundays vary and cost from **AUS$125 for a day trip to AUS$250+** for multiple-day packages – competition is fierce so look around for the best deals! You can find 3-day trips to Uluru from **AUS$295** *(+Uluru park fee)*. You have to remember that, although most activities are pricey in Oz than NZ, they're still slightly cheaper than they would be at home and in a better climate! If you're a bit skint there are some fantastic things you can do in Oz for next to nothing: wine tasting tours in the Hunter Valley Region can be found for less than **AUS$10** while fantastic turtle tours in Mon Repos are very rewarding at less than **AUS$10**. Better still visits to the Koala Hospital *(Port Macquarie)*, tours around the Australian War Museum and Parliament in Canberra and the National Maritime Museum in Sydney are **free!**

Fiji: This island nation has its fair share of activities, albeit not as extreme at NZ, but most activities from diving and snorkelling to sand boarding and boat trips are cheaper here than in NZ or Oz but a little more expensive than SE Asia and Central America. While the tropical skydive is on par with skydiving in NZ in terms of price, costing around **F$348**, where else can you skydive without a jump suit and land barefoot on the beach in front of your resort!

Go balls out: Think of it this way; yes, you're going to spend a bit on activities but beaches aside, isn't this why you've come all this way to the other side of the world – when are you going to be here again?! This is the one place where even I don't hold back, I try and get involved as much as I can – and that's coming from a real tight arse! So don't be tight and miss out, go balls out and do it all! The activities in NZ really are great value for money.

TRANSPORT... *Backpacker busses*

Transport around Oz and NZ is similarly priced to Europe and North America. You'll find a number of convenient and reasonably priced **backpacker busses,** and 'boat-passes' in Fiji, that operate numerous routes around Fiji, New Zealand and Oz. Travelling around Australasia requires a bit more planning than Asia and Central America – not that it's more difficult, far from it, but it's popular so demand often out strips supply. Consequently, transport options, hostels and activities get booked up quickly. Therefore, you'll find a beefed up *'Your Transport Options'* section for **each** of the three countries to help you plan a little more.

$ THE BUDGET DIRECTORY $

This section covers countries from Australasia. The countries have been graded by **value for money** and **ease of travel** to help you create an affordable and realistic itinerary that's tailored to your budget, interests and travel experience;

- o **Value for money:** Perhaps overall, European and North American travellers will find it a little cheaper than home but generally speaking you're going to spend a pretty penny where ever you go in Australasia. You'll find that your money will go further in some countries and you'll be able to do more, see more and travel further with the same budget. This scale factors in the cost of food, accommodation, transport, communication and, perhaps more importantly, the <u>value</u> of those adrenaline fuelled activities!

- o **Ease of Travel** relates to how easy it is to get around a given country reflecting the general level of *(tourist)* infrastructure and also taking into consideration obstacles such as language barriers and culture shock. All three countries are heavily geared towards tourism and have fantastic tourist infrastructure but you'll find that some have more comfortable, economic and quicker options than others. This grading takes into consideration the quality of your available travel options, time and distance *(Australia has great, reliable transport but has scored lower because of the sheer distance and time between towns and areas of interest).*

The countries are graded from 1 to 10; 1 being very expensive and more challenging to travel and 10 being good value for money and more practical and easier to get around.

	Value for money	Ease of travel	Page
Fiji...	9	9	...142
New Zealand...	7	10	...156
Australia...	2	7	...168

FIJI

5-STAR BACKPACKING

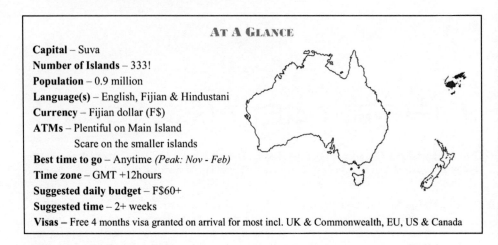
Palm fringed beaches, crystal clear seas, vibrant reefs, blue lagoons, lush tropical rainforests and the famous warmth of the 'Bula' spirit... Fiji's a truly unique tropical paradise. It's the colourful crossroads of the South Pacific where you'll wish you had longer. Islanders greet you on sun-kissed beaches singing and dancing with 'ear-to-ear smiles' – their adopting welcome is simply tireless, and without a doubt, they know how to look after a visitor or two! Rustic island resorts obligingly serve an endless dose of sunshine, stacks of culture and tasty traditional feasts with opportunities to swim, snorkel, kayak or simply chill-out! This is a country boasting a rich variety of traditions, and from Kava Sessions to fire dances, you're encouraged to join in. Whether you're a shoe-stringer or package-holidaymaker, get ready for some affordable five-star treatment...

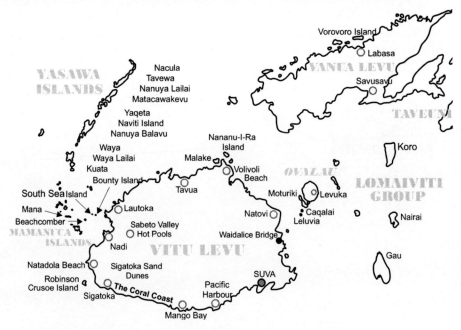

Unfortunately, most people tend to only spend a week or so on these beautiful Pacific Islands using it to break up the long-haul flight between the USA and New Zealand. It's nearly always included on RTWs so make the most out of this unique opportunity. Now, because there are so many islands and Fiji's very diverse, I've divided Fiji up into a number of distinct areas. Each area has something different to offer and has been allocated an advised 'time-span' so that you can explore them at a leisurely pace and help you plan your Fijian trip:

1. **The main island** *(Viti Levu): The heart of Fijian and Indo-Fijian Culture*

   1-2 weeks – easily merits heaps more time to admire the coral coast, boogie-board down sand-dunes, laze on scrumptious beaches, trek in rainforests, haggle in Suva's bustling markets and delve into a wealth of cultural and traditional towns

2. **The Yasawas and the Mamanucas:** *The main tourist trail*

   1-3 weeks max – just for your budgets sake! Dazzling beaches, rustic resorts and fantastic nightlife all blessed with glorious sunshine – you could hop between these magical islands for months but it's hard on the budget and they lack any *genuine* culture!

3. **Lomaiviti Group:** *Explore Fiji's colonial past, slightly off-the-beaten track*

   1-2 weeks – explore Ovalau and tuck into Fiji's colonial past before relaxing on the surrounding unspoilt tropical islands and enjoy simple island life away from the crowds

4. **Vanua Levu:** *Challenge yourself and venture off- the-beaten track*

   1+ week(s) – get really stuck into Fiji's second biggest island and lose yourself amongst the local villages and genuine culture well and truly off-the-beaten track

By no means stick religiously to these 'time allotments' – they're intended as a guide. **Mix 'n' Match** a bit. Got the 'classic' 2 weeks in Fiji..? Start off with 7 days exploring the **Yasawas** on the Bula Pass before heading off for 4 days on the FEEJEE Experience around **Viti Levu**. Use the odd 'leftover days' wisely and visit a few of the Mamanucas Islands on daytrips and 1 or 2-night all-inclusive 'stay-over's' using **Nadi** as a base. The possibilities are endless..!

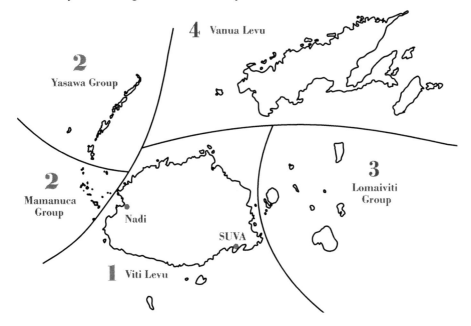

Despite the vast number of islands it's very simple and inexpensive to get around Fiji. Accessibility, price and transport options vary greatly depending on where you want to go. However, what you do, where you go and what transport you'll use will largely depend on how long you're going to spend in Fiji rather than your budget. If you've only got two weeks, you're best off just exploring the Yasawa Isles on the Bula Pass and possibly doing the FEEJEE Experience around the main island or a few Mamanucas Islands after. If you've got plenty of time you can get really stuck in and explore Fiji with some DIY options and get yourself off-the-beaten track once you've worn yourself out on the drunken mainstream route. To help you plan and utilise your time in Fiji, your transport options have been broken down by 'region':

THE MAIN ISLAND *(VITI LEVU)*...

With a choice of Do-It-Yourself options and backpacker busses, getting around the Viti Levu is very easy and relatively inexpensive. Here are your main options:

The FEEJEE Experience... *The backpacker bus*

Experience the 'real Fiji' on this backpacker bus – it's become the most popular way to explore Viti Levu. Similar to the Kiwi Experience and Oz Experience counterparts across the water, the FEEJEE Experience loops around the main island with overnight stops and a host of exciting activities along the way. There are a few add-on options that take you further afield to some of the other islands such as Beachcomber. It's perfect if you want to interact with other backpackers or you're short on time. You need at least 4 days to complete the shortest route but the more time you have the better. Check it out on www.feejeeexperience.com. You can book it through agents at home such as STA or through a guesthouse's travel desk once you arrive in Fiji – the latter is nearly always the cheapest option. Alternatively you can book it direct online where you won't pay any third-party a commission and you may find some promotional deals. Busses depart from Nadi five times a week.

Local bus... *Cheap & rewarding*

The main island is served by a good, punctual and reliable public transport system. Undoubtedly, this is the cheapest way to get around and even the tightest of backpackers will be shocked at the low fares! It's not all about saving money though, by using the open-window public busses you're sure to have some memorable experiences and great encounters with the locals. Arguably it's the most interesting way to explore the Viti Levu and a good option if you want to get away from the crowds of backpackers. You can do the same route as The FEEJEE Experience, pursue the same activities and stay at the same hostels for about half the price the DIY way with €public transport!

Car hire... *Convenient but unnecessary*

Cheap car hire coupled with low petrol prices makes this a viable option. It's more comfortable and convenient and a good option if you're short on time. However, even if there's a group of you it's a lot more expensive than the ludicrously inexpensive public transport. Of course a car will give you the freedom to venture at your own pace but there's not much scope to get off-the-beaten track and venture where the extensive public transport system can't already reach. If it's convenience you're after, the FEEJEE Experience is the better option. If you do hire a vehicle it's best to pick it up and drop it off at Nadi or Suva. For an idea of prices and vehicle options check out a few of these companies:

   o   **Aims Rent-A-Car:** www.aimsrentacar.com.fj

- o **Coastal Rental Cars:** www.coastalrentalcars.com.fj
- o **Europcar:** www.europcar.com.au
- o **PVV Rentals;** www.showmefiji.com
- o **Satellite Rent-A-Car:** www.satelliterentacar.com.fj

THE YASAWAS...

Despite the number of islands that make up the Yasawas and their distance from the main land, it's easy to navigate and explore these remote isles and they've become extremely popular thanks to a number of direct boats and infamous backpacker passes:

The Bula Pass... *The most popular backpacker pass*

The Bula Pass is a unique package operated by an experienced operator called **Awesome Adventures**. These passes offer a realistic and simple way for the average budget backpacker to explore these otherwise secluded and difficult to reach isles – perfect if you're a bit tight on time or can't be arsed 'doing-it-yourself'! Consequently, they've become **extremely popular** and are very sociable where you'll find a healthy night scene and plenty of hung over travellers nursing their sore heads on secluded beaches. Its 5-star backpacking in the Fiji that's depicted by the travel brochures – palm fringed beaches, crystal-clear waters, friendly islanders, tropical sun and lots of alcohol fuelled fun. You can choose between **7, 14 and 21-day passes** to suit your budget and time frame. If time allows, the 14-day pass is recommended.

Add ons: You can also combine your Bula Pass with an **accommodation pass** to save an extra few dollars – it's also convenient and hassle free as most island resorts don't except debit cards or travellers cheques! Other pre-set packages are available so check out all of the island hopping passes and 'island-stayputs' on www.awesomefiji.com. Passes and island trips can be arrange when you're in Fiji through guesthouses and island complexes. Boats depart from at Denarau *(near Nadi)*, transfers there are normally included. While you're taken to genuine Fijian villages and meet islanders, those looking for a quiet and more rustic Fijian experience away from the tourist crowds should consider other options, and in particular, other parts of Fiji!

Direct boats... *Quick & convenient*

If you're short on time or just want to explore one or two of the Yasawas Islands, it'll probably work out cheaper to take direct boats to your selected choices. Boats leave from the nearby Port and from Nadi beach. Daytrips, overnight stays and transfers to most of the islands can be arranged at the majority of hostels throughout Fiji.

THE MAMANUCAS...

Sometimes unfairly missed out in favour of the Yasawas, there's no excuse not to visit these beautiful tropical islands and getting to them couldn't be easier. Most islands in this group can be reached in under an hour from Denarau or Nadi beach and are actually a lot closer than the Yasawas:

Direct boats... *Quick & convenient*

Direct boats form the principle mode of transport to the Mamanucas Isles. Transfers by local speedboat grant access to most of the islands in the Mamanucas group – speedboats are usually owned and operated by the backpacker complexes and are usually included as part of a package deal along with the cost of accommodation, food and other benefits. Again, deals can be booked from most hostels and travel agencies in Nadi and elsewhere in Fiji. There are a few large-scale companies that provide more commercialised transfers to the most popular island resorts:

o **Awesome Adventures** – to South Sea, Bounty & Beachcomber *www.awesomefiji.com*

o **Beachcomber Cruises** – to Beachcomber & Treasure Islands *www.beachcomberfiji.com*

o **South Sea Cruises** – to most of them! www.ssc.com.fj

Sail boat... *Unique & relaxing*

Sail boats offer a truly relaxing and unique way to explore the Mamanucas and southern Yasawas Isles. While this option is often overlooked by backpackers who are blinded by the obvious draw of the Bula Pass, there are a number of companies that offer unforgettable experiences aboard some gorgeous sailboats. **Sailing Adventures Fiji** – www.sailingadventuresfiji.com – is a popular company that offers 1-day, 2-day/1-night and 3-day/2-night options aboard **Pelorus Jack**. You'll drop anchor in some peaceful secluded bays to enjoy freshly cooked food, stroll across pristine white sand beaches and visit some stunning uninhabited islands. Other onboard activities include snorkelling above vibrant coral reefs and deep sea fishing for Tuna and Walu. The finest Fijian hospitality and cuisine, coupled with low guest numbers, ensure that you'll have a memorable sailing trip. Tours depart from Denarau Marina and can be booked from travel desks and hostels across Fiji. Another great reputable sailboat company is **Captain Cook Cruises** www.captaincook.com.fj. Captain Cook Cruises also offer cruises that explore the beautiful Yasawas Isles.

'FIJI-TIME'... *Chill-out!*

Set your clock to 'Fiji-time'. Where-ever you're planning to go in Fiji, and however you're planning to get there, don't stress out about it – this is the 'isles of smiles' and it runs on 'Fiji Time'! If the boats running late or the staff seem to dawdle around at a leisurely pace they'll say they're on Fiji Time. Twenty minutes in Fiji roughly translates to about an hour! This laidback attitude can irritate some travellers but just chill-out, relax and slip into the carefree ambience and enjoy lethargic island life... Why rush around, travelling isn't a hurried experience! The exception are the Indian-Fijians who have a typically more 'businesslike' approach and are consequently more punctual, although you can haggle with them!

FIJIAN 'RESORTS'... *5-star backpacking*

Most visitors experience Fiji through the resorts and off-shore activities of the beautiful Mamanuca and Yasawa islands. Shoe-stringers and hardcore backpackers shouldn't despair and avoid them though. The word 'resort', in true Fijian style, is a loosely applied term in this laidback island nation. A backpacker resort may consist of little more than a handful of thatched huts with communal showers and a basic beachfront 'reception and dining area'. Rustic resorts and top-notch traditional grub coupled with the spectacular setting and the warmth of the locals makes Fiji the ultimate five star backpacking experience. The posh designer resorts tend to be concentrated well away from the backpacker hotspots, noticeably the family friendly Coral Coast, although flashpacker accommodation can still be found in these areas.

This mini guide has been split into the 'main areas' of Fiji as described in the earlier sections. The majority of backpackers enter Fiji via **Nadi** on the Main Island *(Viti Levu)* and, using Nadi as a base camp, head off to casually hop throughout the lively **Yasawas** and **Mamanucas Isles**:

(International flight➔) Nadi ➔ Yasawas ➔ Nadi ➔ Mamanucas ➔ Nadi *(➔ NZ / Oz)*

If you're staying longer than the 'typical two weeks' in Fiji, make sure you embark on the popular looping circuit around **Viti Levu** before making an effort to explore roads lees-travelled and soothe your hangover. The **Lomaiviti Group** provides the perfect rustic retreat boasting genuine culture, breezy picturesque towns and simple island life. **Vanua Levu** provides a challenge well off-the-beaten track where very few travellers venture.

VITI LEVU... *The main island*

It's fair to say that few people venture outside of **Nadi** during their time on Viti Levu. If you've got the time to spare, invest some of it exploring this interesting and varied main island and get away from the sometimes overcrowded commercial Yasawa Isles. There's more to do on this island than you think. You can do a great DIY looping itinerary along **Queens Road** and **Kings Road** or hop on the action-packed backpacker bus – the **FEEJEE Experience**:

Nadi ➔ Natadolo Beach ➔ Robinson Crusoe ➔ Coral Coast ➔ Suva ➔ Volivoli Beach ➔

Sabeto Valley *(Natural hot pools & mud pools)* ➔ Nadi

If you wanted to get off-the-beaten track, you can deviate to the **Lomaiviti Group** *(page)* and **Vanua Levu** *(page)* on your way between **Suva** and **Volivoli Beach**.

NADI... *Gateway to the Yasawas & Mamanucas*

Pronounced *N.A.N.D.I*, it's not the countries capital but the town where nearly every visitor enters the country and inevitably spends a few lazy days. The town's dark sandy beaches are pleasant enough but will disappoint anyone who's looking for an instant tropical paradise. However, it doesn't pretend to be an idyllic paradise and Nadi has a distinct character of its own with plenty of cheap accommodation and traditional food at local prices. It's a great destination to acclimatise, shake-off your jetlag, see what's-what and book up some tours,

> ### Tropical skydiving...
> This is the ultimate tropical adventure and you don't even need to wear jump suits or gloves! Transfers can be arranged from hostels in Nadi and the Coral Coast. You can even land on the beach in front of your resort!
> www.skydivefiji.com.fj

cruises and island hopping adventures. It's the tourist hub of Fiji, everyone's Fiji experience starts in Nadi and it should be utilised as a **'base camp'** – a place to go back to and recharge after each island hopping adventure. Ask the sunburnt faces of seasoned travellers for their recommendations! Enjoy Nadi for what it is and don't dwell on what it's not! Think of it as the Bangkok of Fiji, albeit cleaner and quieter and just a hop, skip and a jump away from tropical bliss!

On the plus side, Nadi offers some of the cheapest accommodation in Fiji and they usually throw in free airport transfers 24hrs-a-day. While some travel companies, such as STA, will try and persuade you to stay in hostels like Nomads SkyLodge that are located just outside the town *(albeit closer to the airport)*, backpackers swarm around **New Town Beach** where they're well catered for. **Mama's** guesthouse is a backpacker's favourite offering some of the cheapest dorm accommodation with air-con thrown in. A slick new complex called **Smugglers Cove** has quickly become the social hub of the New Town Beach area and operates an 'all are welcome policy' in its lively beachfront bar and restaurant. Boats and transfers to the main tourist islands of the Mamanucas and the Yasawas usually depart directly from the beach or from nearby **Port Denarau Marina**. Buses into the town centre cost less than a *(Fijian)* dollar each way where you find cheaper eateries. Taxi's are more expensive but still cheap.

Main backpacker area – New Town Beach

Highlights – Budget accommodation, cheap authentic food, markets & transfers. Skydiving!

NATADOLA BEACH... *Viti Levu's best beach*

Rivalling **Volivoli Beach** on the northern most tip of the Viti Levu, Natadola is one of the island's best beaches and it's easily accessible. Unlike the beaches along the Coral Coast further down the road, Natadola Beach isn't flanked by coral and provides good swimming and enough surf for body-surfing and general frolicking around! For those who prefer to stay dry, it's a great spot to relax, get into a good book, kick a ball around and soak up some rays. While you can stay here, it's a very pricey destination for shoe-stringers and most backpackers come here for a daytrip to the beach. The **FEEJEE Experience** stops here as part of its itinerary where you'll enjoy a BBQ lunch prepared by your friendly driver.

Getting there & away – Paradise Transport buses head to and from Sigatoka four times daily. The Coral Scenic Railway also runs tours to the beach

ROBINSON CRUSOE... *Backpacker's retreat*

A fantastic coral island located near Natadola Beach just off the main island's southwest coast. While daytrips are available, they're very commercial and cater for families. For the ultimate backpacker experience you want to stay here for a few days and you'll certainly notice the change in ambience when the hoards of day-trippers leave the island. It's what Fiji's all about – entertainment, kava sessions, relaxation and culture all captivated on beautiful quaint island. A long standing favourite amongst backpackers, this stunning coral island has a lot to offer and the enthusiastic and genuinely friendly entertainment team go out of their make to make you feel welcome. They work tirelessly around the clock to keep everyone happy and the party going! They're the heart and soul of Robinson Crusoe and unquestionably provide some of the best entertainment in the whole of Fiji – get into the island's *'I C U baby'* spirit!

> **Package deals...** *Great value*
>
> You can find great package deals that include a set amount of nights on RCI & Mana Island – typically 4-days Mana / 2-days RCI. This is perhaps the best package deal around in terms of value for money and rustic island experiences.

Although the main dorm is a bit of a crowded affair, the island offers a good range of accommodation from dorms to private bures. The showers are unique and innovative – refresh your hung-over-self in the 'back-to-basic bucket showers' – a true island experience! The buffet food is excellent with a satisfying hint of Fijian cuisine – Robinson Crusoe arguably offers the best Lovo of any resort. Backpackers are the bread and butter of this resort and Captain Paul will make you feel truly appreciated – even beer is cheaper once the day-trippers leave! www.robinsoncrusoeislandfiji.com

Getting there & away – Transfers by bus and boat *(RCI own vehicles)* are usually included in the price and depart from Nadi and a number of places along the Coral Coast

Highlights – Entertainment, food, daily activities *(volleyball, sea kayaking, snorkelling & more)*, the islanders & the nightlife

THE CORAL COAST... *Scenic coastline, inland adventure*

Stretching from Sigatoka to the Pacific Harbour, this scenic coastline is dominated by turquoise waters and flanked by a colourful coral reef. Hoards of package-holidaymakers – most about your parent's age – spend their entire time along the sun-soaked Coral Coast in an abundance of upmarket holiday complexes, but there's plenty for backpackers to do with a healthy sprinkling of budget accommodation and flash-packer digs – resorts like **The Beachouse** and **Mango Bay Resort** are very popular with shoe-stringers. This coastline is served by decent and punctual public transport so most places of interest can be easily reached with a few dollars regardless of where you stay. While few people stay in Sigatoka, its market is a great place to haggle and stock up on cheap food for your communal kitchens.

While the sea is shallow and impractical for swimming and most water sports, there's plenty to do 'inland'. If you're on the **FEEJEE Experience** you'll be busy along this coastline as activities include: **boogie-boarding** down the Sigatoka Sand Dunes, Jungle **trekking** through the Namosi Highlands and **tubing/rafting/longboat** down the Navua River. If you're 'D.I.Y-ing' it along the coast, you can still do most of these activities: Explore Fiji's first National Park – the **Sigatoka Sand Dunes** *(F$8 entrance fee)* – and explore other areas of interest including, the **Tavuni Hill Fort** and Fiji's only wildlife park, **Kula Eco-Park** – www.fijiwild.com. Other activities include **ZipFiji** *(Pacific Harbour)* where you can embark on an amazing rainforest canopy tour – www.zip-fiji.com – and **Sigatoka River Safari** *(Sigatoka)* where you'll spend the day jetting up the river into the cultural heart of Viti Levu visiting authentic Fijian villages – www.sigatokariver.com. **Diving** and **snorkelling** are also popular activities here with the best options available in **Pacific Harbour**.

Main backpacker resorts – Vakaviti, The Beachouse, Mango Bay Resort

Highlights – Sigatoka Sand Dunes, Tavuni Hill Fort, Kula Eco-Park, trekking, tubing, white-water rafting, jet-boat river safari, ZipFiji, snorkelling & diving

SUVA... *The capital*

This is the country's bustling multicultural capital and it oozes a mix of modern aspirations and colonial influences. It's the Pacific's largest city where you'll find plenty of modern shopping complexes for some extreme retail therapy. Suva also boasts some of the best bars in Fiji and an enjoyable nightlife – it's colourful, vibrant and not geared towards tourism, which gives you a real genuine experience and local perspective. Some of the best and safest bars for a good piss up are; **Bad Dog Café**, **Golden Dragon** and **O-Reiley's** – these are all within a few minute's walk of each other for a manageable bar-crawl no matter how wasted you get!

In complete contrast, and only 11kms from Suva, you'll find one of the areas highlights, **Coco-I-Suva Forest Park** – trek through lush forest following over 6kms of track, take a dip in natural pools, cool-off under waterfalls and make a splash from rope swings. Entrance to the park hovers around a mere F$5.There are a few cheap lodging options in town but most backpackers opt to get away from the busy downtown area and stay at **Raintree Lodge** – situated close to the Colo-I-Suva Forest Park and set around lush tropical rainforest and lakes, it's seemly light years away from the mass urban jungle of Suva.

Main backpacker hostels – Raintree Lodge. Sunset Apartments Motel is conveniently located in the heart of Suva and offers very basic but cheap dorm accommodation

Highlights – Fiji Museum, Colo-I-Suva Forest Park, shopping & nightlife

Beach lovers unite! Succumb to the sun and sea on postcard perfect isles – these gorgeous speckles of paradise are what you see in the glossy holiday brochures. This is Fiji's premier destination. Dotted across 90km of reef, these ancient and rugged volcanic islands are the perfect tropical escape boasting secluded bays and endless sunshine coupled with vivid snorkelling and diving. Here you'll discover the true meaning of **'Fiji-Time'** in low-key and locally owned island resorts. Most backpackers head straight from Nadi and spend their entire time in Fiji just hopping along this chain of isles basking on barren beaches. Thankfully, small-scale backpacker digs dominate these isles although fancier lodgings are beginning to emerge. There are simply too many magical islands and resorts to talk about, and most will be well advertised on your **Bula Pass** itineraries and info packs, so here's a brief selection of island resorts to whet your appetite – all can be reaches via Bula Pass and most have other **direct transfers to Nadi** as well:

WAYALAILAI RESORT... *Welcome to the Yasawas*

Slip into simple island life – situated on **Waya Sewa**, one of the closest of the Yasawa Islands, the Wayalailai Resort is a fantastic introduction to the gorgeous carefree Yasawa Isles. Cheerful Kava sessions, rustic Fijian cuisine and live Fijian entertainment ensure that you'll have a great cultural experience – village trips, traditional markets and Meke dances will complete your cultural education! Culture aside, this is a contrasting island of ultimate relaxation and exciting activities – laze the day away on idyllic beaches and top up the tan or take part in the wide range of land and marine activities from diving to volleyball. Either way, once the sun goes down gorge on delicious Lovo banquettes, attempt to get through the well stocked bar and get involved in the sociable drinking around the beach bonfire. This is the ultimate Yasawa introduction. The accommodation comprises of decent and spacious beachside bures, in traditional Fijian thatched style. Dorms, single and double rooms are available – there's even space available to pitch your own tent! For more info check out www.wayalailairesort.com

Highlights – Beach BBQ's, parties & bonfires. Kava ceremonies, guided treks, volleyball, fishing, village trips, diving & snorkelling

MANTA RAY ISLAND RESORT... *Snorkel with graceful manta rays*

Manta Ray Resort occupies its own tiny idyllic island – Nanuya Balavu. It's ideally nestled between two gorgeous white-sandy beaches so you get fantastic wide ocean views and you'll experience both sunset and sunrise! It's the perfect place to relax in a swinging hammock and doze the day away! However, as the name suggests, most people come here to catch a glimpse of the legendary **Pacific Manta Ray**. Each year between **May** and **October** the waters around the resort are blessed with the elegance of these Ray – as many as 13 have been recorded in front of the resort at one time. Daily **snorkelling trips** allow visitors to experience these magnificent creatures up close as they glide majestically through the turquoise waters. There's also top quality diving available to over 40 nearby sites. The elevated bar and dining area offers superb views to relax and chat about the days encounter with one of nature's most elegant creatures. For more info check out – www.mantarayisland.com.

Highlights – Swimming with manta rays *(seasonal)*, snorkelling & diving, kayaking, volleyball, game fishing & the bar!

OARSMANS BAY LODGE... *The furthermost tip of the Yasawas*

The hype about this resort is well founded. Located on one of the remotest Yasawa Islands, Nacula, beach devotees will be ecstatic to know that Nacula has spectacular swimming and snorkelling straight off of pristine beaches. This is a truly idyllic location where you can lounge around in beach hammocks, bathe and snorkel in spectacular crystal clear waters or enjoy an ice-cold beer in the open bar absorbing the scenic views across the bay. It's not as lively or as action packed as some of the other resorts but it's a great place to relax and recuperate after your lively journey up through the Yasawas. Good quality en-suite Bures complete this relaxing island experience.

Highlights – Pure relaxation, Fijian arts & craft, Sawailau Cave trip, diving & snorkelling, village trips, Blue Lagoon trip & fishing

POPULAR YASAWA RESORTS... *Island by island*

To illustrate just how many backpacker resorts there are on this sleepy chain of islands, here's a list showing the majority of resorts and approximate travel time from Nadi. All are accessible via the Bula Pass, and this perhaps gives you an indication of how long you could spend on these isles and suggests that the 14-day pass is a better idea, and better value, than the 7-day pass allowing you to call into the many bays and islands at an enjoyable and leisurely pace. This is why you need more than two weeks in Fiji! Don't stress out and try to plan what resorts to visit – you'll meet up with loads of travellers on the boat so 'go with the flow' and let the beer lead the way!

	Island	Resort	Travel time from Denarau
South	**Kuata:**	Kuata Natural Resort	2 hours
↓	**Waya LaiLai:**	Waya LaiLai Resort	2 hours
↓	**Waya:**	Naqakia Lodge	2hrs 15mins
↓		Sunset Waya	2hrs 15mins
↓		Bayside Resort	2hrs 15mins
↓		Adi's Place	2hrs 15mins
↓		Octopus Resort	2hrs 30mins
↓	**Nanuya Balavu:**	Manta Ray Island Resort	3hours
↓	**Naviti Island:**	Botaira Beach Resort	3hrs 15mins
↓		Coconut Bay Resort	3hrs 30mins
↓		Korovou Eco-Tour Resort	3hrs 30mins
↓		White Sandy Beach	3hrs 30mins
↓	**Yaqeta:**	Navutu Stars	4 hours
↓		Yaqeta Reef Resort	4 hours
↓	**Matacawakevu:**	Long Beach Resort	4 hours
↓		Bay of Plenty Resort	4hrs 15mins
↓	**Nanuya LaiLai:**	Nanuya Island Resort	5 hours
↓		Sunrise Lagoon Resort	5 hours
↓		Seaspray Resort	5 hours
↓		Gold Coast Resort	5 hours
↓		Kim's Place	5 hours
↓	**Tavewa:**	Coral View Resort	5 hours
↓		Kingfisher Resort	5 hours
↓		Otto & Fanny's	5 hours
North	**Nacula:**	Oarsmans Bay Lodge	4hrs 30mins
		Nalova Bay Resort	4hrs 30mins
		Nabua Lodge	4hrs 30mins
		Melbravo Resort	4hrs 30mins

THE MAMANUCAS... *The backpacker islands*

Perhaps due to the **Bula Pass**, fewer backpackers venture here than the ever popular Yasawas but these isles will not disappoint. You'll still find a healthy backpacker scene that's arguably more rustic, laidback and less commercialised than what you'll find in the Yasawas – with the exception of loud and proud Beachcomber! Boasting white-sand beaches, dazzling dry sunshine, friendly islanders, and world-class diving and snorkelling, the Mamanucas are a magnet for well-informed travellers and enthusiastic hammock dwellers.

Most island-resorts have an 'all-inclusive-price', typically 3-days/2-nights where food, accommodation and transfers from **Nadi** are included – you can usually extend your stay day-by-day once you're there. There's isn't really a popular itinerary with 99% of the islands having **direct transfers from Nadi** and several links to other islands. With 20 islands to choose from, you could spend weeks casually hopping around these gorgeous isles, so here's the pick of the bunch:

MANA... *The backpacker's island*

This charming but lively island is often referred to as **the** backpacker's island – it's the best of the bunch and offers something for everyone at any budget. It's probably the cheapest backpacker island you'll find in Fiji where you can find all-inclusive deals from around **F$45 a night**. You won't be disappointed by its white-powder sandy beaches, crystal clear turquoise seas and pristine reefs, perfect for snorkelling, diving and sun-worshipping! The soft hills are covered with luscious green vegetation and offer stunning views of the warm tropical waters and nearby islands that nestle idyllically on the horizon. But that's only the half of it – be entertained, pampered and spoilt rotten by some of the friendliest, hospitable and laidback islanders that you'll ever met. This island definitely runs on 'Fiji-Time'! Forget what you see in the travel brochures, this island is tropical bliss, in every way possible.

The accommodation on the island stretches from basic backpacker dorms to outrageously expensive luxury beachside complexes for the filthy rich. Backpackers sunbathe next to rich package holidaymakers and share beaches with newlyweds enjoying a romantic honeymoon. There are two main backpacker resorts, both similarly priced – popular with British and Irish backpackers there's always a lively drinking session every night of the week. Knock back a few cheap ice-cold beverages from the bar or simply BYO, they don't mind!

Main backpacker resorts – Ratu Kini Backpackers & Mana Lagoon Backpacker

Highlights – Deserted pristine beaches, the Fijian people, fishing, snorkelling & diving, social drinking & the fantastic night time entertainment

BEACHCOMBER... *THE party island*

This tiny dollop of tropical sand *(0.2 sq km!)* certainly packs a punch and boasts the best nightlife in the whole of Fiji. Join in the booze fuelled party mayhem and boogie the night away on the original party island! This is where the weekend never ends and the drinks keep on flowing! Loved by most and loathed by some, it is what it is – a must see, must do tropical island for any party animal. Essentially Fiji's answer to Spain's Ibiza, it's a credible rival to Koh Pha-Ngan in Thailand. Its nonstop party reputation ensures a constant stream of young energetic backpackers and sleepless nights! Highly recommended if you're single and want some loving!

All-inclusive daytrips are available but at the end of the day, it's the nightlife you want to come here for. Be warned though, this island is by no means cheap and will put a pretty hefty dent in any backpackers budget. Transfers, alcohol and accommodation are all very expensive – BYO is not appreciated and is forbidden – make the most of the islands happy hour! Spend no more than 2 or

3 nights here partying on the beach under the stars of the South Pacific or you'll break the bank – it's far too easy to get carried away! If you're not too hung-over during the day, and haven't blown all your cash, there's a comprehensive range of water sports on offer.

Getting there & away – The islands 'Fast Cats' will race you across to Beachcomber from Nadi in around 25 minutes

Highlights – Jet-skiing, water-skiing, parasailing, windsurfing, snorkelling, scuba diving, canoeing, mini-golf, non-stop drinking, the NIGHTLIFE & soothing your hangover on the beach!

SOUTH SEA ISLAND... *The smallest Mamanuca Island*

Although slightly pricier than other Mamanucas Islands, with the exception of Beachcomber, this tiny coral island is popular with backpackers. Good all-inclusive daytrips are available through **South Sea Cruises** *(and, yes, that includes unlimited free alcohol- O'Boy, O'Boy!)* but staying overnight is better value if you've got the time to spare – the island's 32 bed dorm offers great accommodation. Most people come here to **dive** and being the smallest island in the Mamanuca group, South Sea Island is surrounded by a beauty marine sanctuary – Fiji's best Staghorn Coral Garden and its incredibly diverse range of inhabitants – bat fish, turtles, octopuses and masses of reef fish – draw keen divers to this little gem. Introductory, certified dives and open-water courses are available through **Reef Safari** – www.reefsafari.com.fj.

When you're not diving, top-up your tan under the tropical sun on the large sundeck and sun loungers or if it gets too, hot have a splash around in the islands swimming pool with a few cold Fiji Bitters. If you want to get active, the resort has non-motorised water sports equipment available free of charge. The BBQ and salad buffet is also top-notch.

Getting there & away – Direct boats from other islands and Port Denarau Marina will take you here

Highlights – Swimming pool, kayaking, relaxing island life, snorkelling & diving

BOUNTY ISLAND... *Inspiring island wilderness*

Being cheaper than its surrounding rival coral islands, this idyllic island is a great option for budget backpackers. As well as the usual white sandy beaches and clear pristine waters that come as standard on these islands, you'll find 48 acres of wilderness, forest and gardens making it an ideal place to 'get back in touch with nature' – the islands forest is home to rare native birds and Hawksbill turtles nest on its white-sand beaches *(seasonal)*! The marine reserve also provides top-notch snorkelling and scores of tropical fish. You'll find the usual array of water sports if you're too sore for more sunbathing or too hung-over for another beer!

Getting there & away – Direct boats from other islands and Denarau Marina will take you here

Highlights – Kayaking, sailing, windsurfing, swimming pool, nature walks, snorkelling & diving

OTHER ISLANDS – Daytrips and overnight-stays are also available at a number of good resorts on the following islands:

Castaway Island – Treasure Island – Navini – Malolailai – Matamanoa – Malolo –

Tavarua Namotu – Tokoriki

You'll see loads of leaflets and flyers for these complexes so talk to other travellers and sunburnt faces for recommendations and see what deals the travel-agents are offering.

Fewer travellers venture over to these eastern islands meaning that you can enjoy authentic Fijian culture, hospitality and simple island life away from the crowds. Below are a few of the best hideaways – although I haven't written about it Caqalai's neighbouring island, **Leluvia**, is another fantastic island and having a similar set up, it's a good alternative to Caqalai:

LEVUKA *(Ovalau Island)... The old colonial capital*

This breezy seaside town is brimming with culture and character. Step back into the past and enjoy one of the most picturesque towns in the South Pacific where rustic wooden houses are set against a backdrop of lush green mountains. Little quaint Levuka is steeped in a rich colonial history with a distinct Fijian vibe – it was the first British settlement in Fiji and the country's first capital. It's a must-see for those of you who are interested in the historic background of the Pacific.

Today, Levuka is Ovalau's main town. There's a small 'cinema' and an amusing museum to check out, a number of tracks to explore and a few historic sites to visit, but in truth there's not too much to do in terms of activities. Levuka does however offer some of the finest and cheapest 'restaurant' cuisine in Fiji and is a welcome break from the tourist hubs. A wide range of eateries stretch the entire length of **Beach Street** where the killer menus are bursting with dishes from around the world from British fish 'n' chips and Italian pizza to exciting Chinese food and rustic Fijian delicacies. Use your time in Levuka to travel your taste buds – there are loads of places to sample but here's a few highly recommended places you should check out; Kim's *(Paak Kum Loongh)*, Café Levuka, Koro Makawa and The Whale's Tale.

Getting there & away – You can fly to Ovalau with **Air Fiji** but there are cheaper options:

a) **Patterson Brothers Shipping Company** run a bus/ferry/bus service from Levuka to Suva via Natovi

b) **Turtle Island Transport** offers a considerably cheaper service although it's more like truck/boat/truck and the trucks are crammed with everything from Kava to coconuts – a true budget backpacker's option and a great experience!

c) Both resorts on Caqalai and Leluvia will drop you off here after your stay on their islands

Main backpacker area – A number of backpacker hotels can be found along **Beach Street**, Mary's Holiday Lodge and The Royal Hotel are popular backpacker 'hotels'

Highlights – Bargain but brilliant traditional & international food, colonial architecture & the breezy laidback atmosphere

CAQALAI... *Island life off-the-beaten track*

Frustratingly pronounced *T.H.A.N.G - G.A.L - L.I.E...!* Those who are looking for ultimate relaxation and uninterrupted lazy days on a secluded, unspoilt tropical island will love Caqalai. A complete contrast to Beachcomber, this stunning coral island is the complete idyllic island retreat cloaked in coconut trees and mangroves, encircled by crystal clear tropical waters and completely fringed by unspoilt powder-white sand. From humble beginnings Caqalai has retained its rustic charm and unsophisticated style of island life. Only a handful of travellers venture to this island and it makes for a pleasant get away from the main stream tourist route where islanders often outnumber travellers. **Caqalai Resort** offers fantastic accommodation, ranging from a spacious dorm, to cute traditional private bures. The facilities are very basic and a fair bit of 'roughing it' makes for an authentic island experience.

Activities: The warm shallow waters teem with tropical marine life and Caqalai probably offers the best **snorkelling** in Fiji – catch glimpses of baby turtles, swim with reef sharks, scarper from sea snakes and glide through schools of tropical fish. If you're lucky enough you'll be able to spot dolphins on the way to the island. The dive shack offers superb **diving** at a number of locations around the island. Play **volleyball** with the friendly islanders as the sun goes down and take part in traditional **kava drinking sessions** next to a beach bonfire as the stars illuminate the night sky! If island life gets too slow – which it can – there are a number of daytrips to **Levuka, Leluvia** and **Honeymoon Island**.

Getting there & away – Contact the resort *(their latest contact details can be found on their flyers)* and arrange a time for their speed boat to pick you up. The pickup point is usually **Waidalice Bridge**, catch the Suva-Korovou bus and ask the driver to drop you off

Highlights – Simple island life, relaxation, sun worshipping, bonfire kava sessions, daytrips, spectacular diving & snorkelling

OTHER ISLANDS – Leluvia, Moturiki, Naigani & Yanuca Lailai

Off-the-beaten track... *Spice things up a bit!*

If times an issue and you can't stray too far off-the-beaten track, stick to exploring the **Lomaiviti Group** – you'll only find a handful of travellers there and plenty of authentic charm and a lethargic island pace of life. If you've a bit of spare time to invest, head over to Fiji's second biggest island and lose yourself amongst the local villages for the ultimate cultural education and authentic experience...

VANUA LEVU... *Challenge yourself on the 'mainland's' little sibling*

Fiji's second island exudes a true feeling of remoteness and has a personality of its own where you'll find spectacular snorkelling and diving, pristine forest, authentic villages and picturesque landscapes. Parts of this rustic island are currently experiencing a boom in development and tourism, but these are isolated pockets and the majority remains largely untouched.

A few 'Tip bits'...

I'm not going to tell you how to get around or what to do on this far-flung rustic island – the idea is for you to have your own authentic adventure off-the-beaten track, without the comfort of a guidebook and away from the crowds. I'll say this much though: The principle gateway is the town of **Savusavu** which is linked by ferry to **Suva**. From Savusavu it's logical to head east towards **Dakuniba** and **Rainbow Reef** where you'll find a small number of guesthouses. If you've got the time, pop over to neighbouring **Taveuni**. If you want to really challenge yourself, try and do a loop of Vanua Levu – most of the roads are unsealed and you'll meet few travellers.

The 'main-stream' alternative': If you're not after a challenge, either because you're a wimp or just short in time, but you still want to visit this intriguing island and enjoy some isolation, the FEEJEE Experience runs a unique 'tribal loop'. This experience flies you **Labasa** *(from Nadi)* and quickly whisks you away to the undeveloped island of **Vorovoro**. Here you'll be welcomed as a member of tribe wanted – you'll see posters for this and similar experiences in all the travel desks throughout Fiji – where you'll stay for seven days. This is a great 'responsible ecotourism' trip where you'll get the chance to live the Fijian way of live, embrace authentic Fijian culture and traditions on an spectacular island and play your part in sustainable tourism. A truly rewarding experience.

NEW ZEALAND

ADRENALINE JUNKIE

AT A GLANCE

Capital – Wellington
Population – 6 million
Language(s) – English & Māori
Currency – New Zealand dollar (NZ$)
ATMs – Plentiful
Best time to go – Anytime. Peak: Nov-April
Time zone – GMT +12hours
Suggested daily budget – NZ$60 excl. activities
Suggested time – 4-6 weeks; *2-3 wks each island*
　　　　　　　　　1-2 years with a working visa
Visas – 3-month visa granted on arrival for many nationalities
Useful websites – www.newzealand.com or www.visitnewzealand.com

New Zealand is captivating and inspirational. After all it's a contrasting and diverse country with a melting pot of cultures and where sheep outnumber the population 10 to 1! It's a country of sport fanatics, outdoor pursuits, adrenaline charged activities and immense natural beauty. Ancient

volcanic plateaus, mighty glaciers, and majestic fjords are just hours from ski resorts, sandy beaches and lush forest! Breathtaking landscapes and stunning natural assets are complemented by an unrivalled portfolio of gravity-defying activities and an epic nightlife. Don't be fooled by its compact sized. Everything's possible here and there's something for everyone. And when it comes to tourism, it's no new kid on the block. You'll find a well established and energetic backpacker scene boasting a network of well-known hostel chains and plenty of budget-orientated travel options. There's a lot to see and do here, so think about your priorities and allow plenty of time, above all, save enough energy to achieve them! More affordable than Oz, it's the well informed traveller's choice.

Come play with gravity! If you're a bit of a dare devil and need a fix, look no further. Despite its diminutive size compared to its big brother Australia, New Zealand has a formidable reputation for extreme sports boasting far more adventure than the land Down Under. This is the home of bungy jumping and the birth place of its founding father... the legendary AJ Hackett! Gravity-defying antics and adrenaline fuelled activities aren't just a past-time here; they're a lifestyle, a religious cult. No words can truly describe the incredible ground rush of a bungy jump as you take that leap of faith or the spectacular coast-to-coast views from under the ballooning canopy of a freshly deployed parachute. The cost of these activities is usually the biggest non-essential expense of most people's Kiwi adventure. You **can** eke out an existence on NZ$60 per day if you restrain your urge for those activities. If you want to give your adrenaline glands a thorough workout though, have extra cash on top of the suggested daily budget – it's all too easy to get carried away!

It's not all just bungy jumps and skydives though – New Zealand has a whole lot more to test what you're really made of! There are so many facilities and enthusiastic local operators to help you immerse yourself in almost

Top Adrenaline Rush
* New Zealand! *

every conceivable kind of activity it can be an expensive and time consuming affair to try them all. Consequently, I've listed the top extreme activity in each place so you can delve deep into a knee-wobbling world of adrenaline fuelled activities without spending a small fortune! Check out the 'Top Adrenaline Rush' to whet your appetite and see just how far you can push your limits. Don't be a pussy, make an effort to get involved – you've got to try everything once! And for all you tight arses, these activities are fantastic value – you won't be able to do the majority of these activities cheaper anywhere else in the world, especially when you consider the stunning backdrops – so don't be boring, get your wallet out! Bungyyyyyy...!

Non-thrill-seekers can still experience the country's famed wilderness and natural wonders without having to dangle from a bungy cord or take a leap of faith out of a plane. Guided walks, scenic flights, heli-hikes and cruises open up to great outdoors for the more conservative traveller. Other passive activities such as fishing, golf, mountain biking and even wine-tasting will give your adrenaline glands a rest while immersing you in spectacular surroundings.

GETTING AROUND... *Your transport options*

Travelling around New Zealand is an easy and comfortable affair where distances are smaller and more manageable compared to Australia. More compact and easy to handle, at 270,000 square kilometres, it's only slightly bigger than the UK and is pretty easy to get around. Your budget and time frame will be major factors that'll influence what type of transport you'll primarily be using!

Here are your main transport options:

1) Backpacker Busses...

A very popular option and they're definitely the cheapest and simplest option if you're on your own. Personally, this is how I'd recommend exploring New Zealand. All of the busses have a great friendly and sociable atmosphere where you'll met some fantastic people from every corner of the globe. These 'hop-on, hop-off' busses are very flexible and offer you a great way to explore New Zealand with heaps of routes and itineraries that are tailored to different budgets, interests and most importantly time limits. The laidback drivers are ace and are eager to show you everything New Zealand has to offer – they'll arrange for you to jump out of perfectly good planes, negotiate ferocious white-water rapids and plummet to earth on the end of bungy cords during the day and then encourage you to participate in an evening of sociable drinking and games! You'll get discounts on a range of activities from horse riding to bungy jumping and you'll get guaranteed accommodation reserved for you at every overnight stop – you don't have to stay at the hostels if you find cheaper alternatives! There are three main operators running backpacker busses. Check out all three as you'll find that one usually has a special promotion on and book online so you're not paying any third party commission!

- **The Kiwi Experience:** www.kiwiexperience.com

  This is a well established and popular company. Their big green busses are extremely popular with British and European backpackers. It's very competitively priced and offers flexible travel options so that you can see more and absorb all of NZ's best bits. You'll be spoilt for choice with around 25 varied routes to choose from and all of the passes are jam-packed with exciting itineraries that cover both islands with something for everybody. Your best bet is to fly into Auckland and fly out of Christchurch and take advantage of linear routes such as the **Zephyr** to maximise your time in NZ and minimise backtracking. You have 12 months to complete the route on your pass

- **The Magic Bus:** www.magicbus.co.nz

  Popular with Europeans, Aussies and Kiwis, The Magic Bus offers similar routes to The Kiwi Experience and is similarly priced. Make every day in New Zealand count and choose from a range of passes and itineraries that cover both islands with the flexibility that you need. There's no extra charge for the crazy and energetic drivers! Again all passes are valid for 12 months

- **Stray Bus:** www.straytravel.com

  Not as 'mainstream' as the other two, Stray Bus offers slightly different routes and itineraries and makes a conscious effort to go off-the-beaten track using smaller *(orange)* busses. Stray usually attracts a slightly more affluent and older age group, but whatever your age, don't let this put you off

2) Local Bus...

New Zealand has good infrastructure and offers some cheap public bus services. However, in reality, although cheap, it's hard to fully explore NZ using just local buses. They're practical to get between major towns and you can usually book busses through your hostel or direct at the bus station. Amongst the cheapest are;

- **Intercity Bus:** www.intercity.co.nz
- **The Naked Bus:** www.nakedbus.com

3) Campervan & Car...

Arguably, the only way to fully explore New Zealand! If there are two or more of you, hiring out a campervan or car **can be** a cheaper option – even after you've factored in the petrol costs. As good as public transport is, nothing quite matches the freedom of having your own vehicle to explore New Zealand's unique countryside at your own leisure and venture off-the-beaten track. Most people are shocked by the cost of renting a campervan but the longer you have one the more you'll benefit from it – in the long run a campervan will save you heaps on accommodation. The roads in NZ are good and well sign posted, traffic is light and distances are short. On the downside, it's not a very sociable option. You'll meet fewer backpackers if you're travelling around and sleeping in a campervan than you would if you stayed in hostel dorms and travelled by local busses or a backpacker bus.

Buying: Some people opt to buy a campervan or car but in reality it's not very economical if you're not planning to spend more than two months in New Zealand – it can also become a financial liability if you struggle to sell it before you leave. If you're staying longer than two months or just really want to buy one Auckland, Christchurch and Queenstown are the easiest cities to buy and sell. Otherwise look into a buy-back option where you buy a vehicle from a dealer who guarantees that they'll buy the vehicle back from you. The catch – you won't get a large percentage of the purchase price back but you're guaranteed to get rid of it at the end of your trip and you usually get breakdown cover included. Some actually allow you to sell it privately if you get a good offer so weigh up the benefits and costs: **peace of mind v financial costs**. If you're looking to buy or sell check out travellers car market; www.travellerscarmarket.com

Renting: More often than not, your best bet is to hire one. If you're planning on a more linear itinerary don't worry, most companies will be happy for you to drop it off at one of their depots in another location, although this attracts a fairly hefty 'one-way fee' usually around NZ$150. There are tons of companies to choose from, here are a few of the popular ones;

- o **Apollo:** www.apollocamper.co.nz
- o **Britz Campervan Hire:** www.britz.co.nz
- o **Backpacker Campervan & Car Hire:** www.backpackercampervans.com
- o **Escape Campervans:** www.escaperentals.co.nz
- o **Jucy Hire:** www.jucy.co.nz
- o **Spaceships:** www.spaceshipsrentals.co.nz
- o **Wicked Campers:** www.wicked-campers.co.nz – usually the cheapest company

4)   Domestic Flights...

While it's by no means necessary to fly around New Zealand, flying can be more comfortable, quicker and economical especially if you have to backtrack between the main islands or time is limited. It usually works out only a few bucks more expensive and a hell of a lot more convenient to fly between them meaning that you'll have more time to throw yourself off bridges and out of planes in places like Queenstown and Taupo! There are regular daily flights between Christchurch and Auckland. Here are some of the main operators;

- o **Air New Zealand:** www.airnewzealand.co.uk
- o **Jetstar:** www.jetstar.com
- o **Virgin Blue:** www.flypacificblue.com

Mini Guide

Small and compact, most travellers follow an action-packed and logical linear route down through both main islands from **Auckland** to **Christchurch**, crossing the Cook Straight via ferry, in a memorable **4-6 week** stint *(2-3 weeks each island)*. Those who have a return ticket from Auckland can create a looping itinerary back up, but most take a short and inexpensive domestic flight from Christchurch to Auckland to avoid tedious backtracking. Here are the most popular Kiwi destinations – strap on some balls and engage your adrenaline glands,'it's guna be one hell of ride'!

The North Island...

Welcome to New Zealand – the majority of travellers enter NZ via Auckland on the North Island. After straying north and spending a few sunny days in the Bay of Islands, there's a popular and diverse circuit that'll take you to the nation's capital and within touching distance of the South Island. Along this route you'll stew in hot springs, sizzle on beaches, hike scenic volcanic landscapes, navigate extensive caves, dabble with culture and enjoy sophisticated city life:

Auckland *(& Bay of Islands)* ➔ Taupo ➔ Rotorua ➔ Waitomo ➔ Wellington

AUCKLAND... *The big smoke*

Sprawling 50kms between two large harbours and home to 1.2 million people, Auckland is New Zealand's biggest

> **Top Adrenaline Rush**
> * The 192m Sky Tower *

city. Chances are you'll fly into Auckland when you arrive in NZ and its scenic setting and spirit often exceeds expectations. There's a fantastic array of budget hostels and an overload of useful traveller's info – Auckland's an ideal base to recuperate, get your bearings and plan your route through the 'land of the long-white-cloud'. This modern city boasts fantastic shopping, decent restaurants, great nightlife and a wealth of job opportunities. Many travellers extend their time in Auckland in pursuit of work to top up their funds while absorbing the city's enjoyable ambience. As far as cities go, Auckland's a good one!

Culture enthusiasts will enjoy the monumental-looking **Auckland Museum** where you can delve into Maori history, lifestyle and culture through various interactive exhibitions. The more adventurous will appreciate a surprising range of extreme urban activities where you can jump off **Sky Tower** or bungy from **Auckland Harbour Bridge**. Despite its urban environment, the great thing about Auckland is its close proximity to natural escapes: If you want to escape the hustle and bustle of city living and fancy some fresh air, hike up **Mt. Eden** for some enjoyable 360° views of the big smoke. Quiet beaches and rolling green fields are also only a short drive away. Dedicate a few days to explore inner-city Auckland and her charming harbours before heading off.

Main backpacker area – Central Auckland on and just off **Queen Street**. Two popular hostels, **Base** & **Fat Camel** can be found along **Fort Street**

Highlights – Job opportunities, shopping, bars & nightlife, sky tower activities, AJ Hackett Harbour Bridge bungy jump, Mt Eden, harbour cruise & Auckland Museum *(free!)*

BAY OF ISLANDS... *The winterless north*

North of Auckland, this area is famed for its stunning coastal scenery, unspoilt beaches and crystal clear waters.

> **Top Adrenaline Rush**
> * 1, 200ft parasailing! *

The region enjoys some of the sunniest and warmest weather in New Zealand. Visitors flock here envisioning lazy sun-filled days on sandy beaches and relaxing cruises exploring secluded bays. Despite being a popular tourist destination, the 150 or so islands have thankfully escaped development and backpackers congregate in the mainland town of **Paihia**. The town has a healthy backpacker scene where you'll find a host of familiar hostels, lively bars and swarms of tour operators. It's a competitive business and backpacker discounts are available on a range of tours.

Water-based activities are the name of the game here and you can't leave the Bay of Islands without pursuing some of them. The most popular activities are **scenic cruises** and **dolphin swimming**. Cruises through 'Hole in the Rock' feature high on the agenda where you can spot seals, dolphins and even whales. For the ultimate way to explore the Bay of Islands hop aboard the 22hr overnight backpacker cruise, '**The Rock**'. Onboard activities include, target shooting, kayaking, fishing, dolphin spotting and star gazing amid a truly breathtaking backdrop. It gets rave reviews and has been voted the best 'value for money' eco-tour by countless guides, check it out on www.rocktheboat.co.nz. **Dolphin swims** operate all year round and can be arranged through a number of operators. They have a high success rate and most offer a free second trip if the first is unsuccessful.

Adrenalin junkies can get there fix here as well. For the thrill of a lifetime sign up for New Zealand's highest parasailing experience – **Flying Kiwi Parasail** – and enjoy amazing views from 1,200ft. For coast to coast views, throw yourself out of a plane and experience New Zealand's warmest drop-zone through **NZ Skydive**. If you're after speed ride the '**Excitor Fast Boat**' where you'll hit speeds in excess of 85kmph along some blurry coastline!

Cape Reinga is a hugely popular daytrip from Paihia – travel along **Ninety Mile Beach**, dare to ride mighty sand dunes at Te Paki Stream and watch were the Pacific collides with the Tasman Sea at the country's northern most tip. Reasonably priced trips can be booked through awesome adventures: www.awesomeadventures.co.nz

Main backpacker area – Paihia

Highlights – Swimming with wild dolphins, Flying Kiwi Parasailing *(1,200ft!)*, NZ Skydive, boat trips *('Hole in the Rock' Cruises)*, sea kayaking, 'The Rock' *(backpackers)* overnight cruise/hostel, Cape Reinga daytrip, dune boarding, 'Excitor' fast boat ride, fishing & kayaking

TAUPO... *Adventure capital of the north!*

Taupo is a popular town nestled in the mountains, hugging a beautiful lake and overlooked by snow-capped peaks. But don't be fooled by the spectacular natural features of the area, Taupo is quickly emerging as the

> Top Adrenaline Rush
> * Skydiving *
> Don't be a wimp... jump from
> 15, 000ft!

Queenstown of the north boasting an impressive array of adrenaline fuelled activities. It's undoubtedly the **skydiving** capital of the world with unrivalled coast to coast views against the stunning backdrop of Lake Taupo and the volcanic plateau of the Tongariro National Park. The sheer number of skydive operators and the competitive market ensures that prices are consistently low. There isn't a better place to skydive! The town itself is lively and backpackers are well catered for with cheap hostels, energetic bars and lakeside cafés. The beautiful scenery can even help to take your mind off those insane activities you've signed up for!

Those looking for a physical challenge should venture into the Tongariro National Park and spend a day hiking the **Tongariro Crossing** with Tongariro Expeditions. It's worth the early start to soak up some of nature's most stunning volcanic landscapes – this walk is one of the top 10 one-day walks in the world! To cool down why not **bungy** into the Waikato River *(www.taupobungy.com)* or stew in the bubbling pools at **Wairakei Geothermal Park**! Attractions just outside of town include: **Huka Falls** and **Mt Ngauruhoe** aka Mount Doom from Lord of the Rings.

Highlights – Skydiving, Taupo bungy, Tongariro Crossing, breathtaking scenery, fishing, swimming and & bathing, Huka Falls, Wairakei Geothermal Park & nightlife

ROTORUA... *Sulphur city!*

This is New Zealand's most dynamic and intriguing thermal area and you can smell it in the air – erupting geysers, steaming hot springs and bubbling mud pools visibly vent plumes of sulphur to give the town a distinct rotten egg smell! Rotorua's a popular backpacker destination and you'll find the usually array of budget hostels and a mix of decent bars. A credible rival to Taupo's unofficial title as the North Island's adventure capital, you'll also find plenty of pulse racing activities on offer...

Activities: If it's exciting activities you're after check out **The Agrodome** where you can indulge yourself in a number of high octane and adrenaline fuelled activities from NZ's fastest **jet boat** *(AgroJet)* and **freefall simulators** to some innovative activities such as the **swoop** and **shweeb**. Wind down afterwards and enjoy the famous light-hearted **sheep show**. Check out these intriguing activities on www.agrodome.co.nz . Perhaps the most popular activity in Rotorua is **Luge** and the tracks here are arguably better than those in Queenstown. For a slice of culture, **Te Puia** *(www.tepuia.com)* is a worthwhile geothermal and Maori cultural centre and is home to Pohutu, a famous geyser that shoots hot water 30 metres into the air. While Te Puia incorporates the most active and popular thermal area, Whaka, if you're strapped for cash you can see plenty of smaller examples of thermal activity in the parks throughout the centre of town for free!

Highlights – Agrodome *(bungy, sheep show, shweeb, the swoop, freefall xtreme, Zorb)*, street luge, white-water sledging, river boarding, thermal activity, Polynesian spa, Te Puia & nightlife

WAITOMO... *Home of the legendary caving*

Breathe in, slip into a snug wetsuit and get out your abseiling gear – there's only one reason to come to this town and that's to explore nature's mysterious and ancient underground labyrinth of caves, rivers and rock formations. Abseil into the seemingly bottomless depths of caves, take leaps of faith from cascading underground waterfalls and drift through spectacular glow-worm studded caves on rubber inner-tubes before clambering up crevices and emerging into the warm sunlight. It's an amazing underground tubing experience that's talked about around the world. It's a must-do kiwi activity. Most of the cheaper lodgings can be found scattered along the road approaching Waitomo. **Juno Hall Backpackers** is the cheapest option while **Kiwi Paka** is a popular alpine style hostel.

Tours can be arranged by a number of companies who cater for all levels of fitness and ability. Wetsuits and other equipment is provided. **The Black Water Rafting Company** *(www.waitomo.com)* was New Zealand's first and remains the biggest black water operator. They're the only operator who'll take you through the incredible Ruakuri Cave and run the ultimate caving adventure – **The Black Abyss**. If you're a bit strapped for cash the **Black Labyrinth** tour is an equally rewarding but significantly cheaper alternative. Another good reputable company is **Rap, Raft 'n' Rock**, who advertise themselves are Waitomo's best value blackwater rafting tour. They also offer decent **BBH** backpacker accommodation. www.caveraft.com

Main backpacker hostels – Kiwi Paka YHA, Juno Hall Backpackers & Buds B&B *(BBH)*

Highlights – Caving!

WELLINGTON... *The capital*

Wellington's a scenic city set on steep hillsides and bound by a magnificent harbour. Compact and walk-able, it's only the third-largest city in the country. It's a slick, fashionable city blessed with an abundance of open spaces, parks and spectacular views. Home of the Government, Wellington is also the undisputed capital of culture and the arts – the fun interactive **Te Papa Museum** is here and it's free! Tours of the parliament buildings are also complimentary. The city's energetic nightlife, fine dining and thriving café culture is world class – apparently the city has more cafés per head than New York! Cinemas, theatres, absorbing art galleries and designer shops make Wellington an enjoyable place to dose up on some modern comforts and give your adrenaline glands a rest. It's a major travel crossroads between the North and South Islands and the city's sheer vibrancy and colourful character warrant at least a few days – but that's only if you've got the time. There's a good spread of backpacker hostels including, YHA, Base and Nomads.

By Kiwi standards, Wellington's a bit tame for all you adrenaline junkies – there's no I'm guna make you shit yourself and squeal like a girl types sports here! However, there are a few outdoor activities to get your pulse racing. **Mountain-bikers** will love the trails around Makara Peak: www.makarapeak.org.nz. The Hutt Valley and Porirua also offer a variety of challenging tracks – the locals rave about them. Bikes can be rented through **Mud Cycles** who offer free pick-up and drop-off and they'll also design guided tours based on your ability: www.mudcycles.co.nz. If you're skint and just want some exercise stroll up to **Mt Victoria** for the best views of the city, harbour and surrounding area. For sun-worshippers and lethargic beach floppers, buses depart from **Oriental Parade** to nearby sandy strips.

Main backpacker area – Familiar budget hostels can be found along Cambridge Terrace & Wakefield Street

Highlights – Shopping, Te Papa Museum *(free!)*, Cable Car & Zoological Gardens, parliament tour, mountain-biking, Mt Victoria, café culture & nightlife

THE SOUTH ISLAND...

The mountainous, cooler and unhurried pace of the South Island offers a well-trodden, action packed and scenic route where you'll hike majestic glaciers, cruise scenic fjord lands, dangle from bungy cords and party in NZ's premier adventure town, **Queenstown**. During the winter months you can also find some top-notch affordable skiing. This is the popular linear route:

Nelson ➔ West Coast ➔ Queenstown ➔ Christchurch *(➔ Kaikoura ➔ Nelson)*

Those who have a bit of spare time could consider straying-off this route to explore the deep south where **Dunedin** and **Stuart Island** standout as popular less-travelled destinations. For those who need to get back up to the North Island, **Kaikoura** breaks up the trip from Queenstown to Nelson creating a looping circuit.

NELSON... *Outdoor adventure*

Tucked away in a secluded corner of the country, Nelson's often overlooked by travellers who rush past on

Top Adrenaline Rush
* Skydiving / kayak tours *

their way to the obvious attractions of the west coast and the far south. Nelson's a laidback coastal town perfectly situated for the adventurous traveller. Nelson's not only the centre of NZ but it's the gateway to the beautiful **Abel Tasman National Park**. Envied nationwide for its milder climate, it enjoys more sunshine than any other part of NZ and boasts sheltered bays, golden beaches, lush native forest and tranquil coastal paths. Seals and dolphins are regularly sighted in the crystal-clear waters. If time permits, this region is well worth a few days. Most travellers base themselves in Nelson where there are plenty of tour operators and high quality hostels. While most of the activities take place way out of the city, operators usually offer return transport from Nelson. Some travellers base themselves in the nearby smaller and quieter town of **Motueka**.

You can explore Abel Tasman National Park by foot, bike or kayak! There are plenty of trails close to Nelson that are ideal for mountain biking and bikes can be rented through a number of outfits in town. An alternative and popular way to explore the National Park is through **Kaiteriteri Kayaks** – www.seakayak.co.nz. They have a number of options to suit different budgets and time limits with hiking, kayaking and 'Aqua Taxi' tours on offer. By far the most rewarding is the **Big Tonga Overnighter** – you'll delve deep into the park by Aqua Taxi before discovering the Tonga Island Seal Colony, Shag Harbour, Falls River Lagoon and other hidden gems by kayak. The next day you'll get to explore the park at a leisurely pace on foot. If you don't have time to explore the National Park over ground, view it all from a dizzy 15,000ft as you launch yourself out of a perfectly good plane – www.skydive.co.nz. If you're strapped for cash stroll up to the centre of NZ, tramp along some coastal tracks or top up your tan on numerous golden sandy beaches that lie within easy reach of the city.

Highlights – The centre of NZ! Abel Tasman National Park, walking, hiking, mountain biking, beaches, skydiving & Kaiteriteri trips.

THE WEST COAST... *Hike a glacier*

Lace up your hiking boots, clip on your crampons and discover an incredible world of ice as you travel through

Top Adrenaline Rush
* Ice-climbing *

the Westland Tai Poutini NP. This coastline displays some greediness by having not one, but two frozen gems grinding relentlessly down its valleys towards the sea. Descending from their origins deep in the lush rainforest, the **Franz Josef** and **Fox Glaciers** are some of New Zealand's most amazing natural assets and the ultimate adventure tour. The popular Franz Josef Glacier is easily accessible and offers novice visitors the opportunity to explore the most spectacular glacial environment anywhere in the world! Fantastic guided half-day and full-day tours are excellent value and cater for all levels of fitness and ability – all equipment is provided and trips are led by experienced guides. The full-day tour is better value for money as you'll get more 'ice-time' and venture further up the glacier. If you want to take your ice-experience to the next level, try some **ice-climbing** – it's like Cliff Hanger but on a glacier and with harnesses, and don't worry, you get to practice on an indoor ice-wall first! If you've got money to burn and want to show off, you can go crazy and splash out on a helihike up the glacier – it takes the hard work out of it! Check out all the hiking options available through **Franz Josef Glacier Guides** at www.franzjosefglacier.com

Fox Glacier is another equally thrilling glacier 25kms up the road. **Fox-Glacier-Guiding** (*www.foxguides.co.nz*) offers a fantastic range of glacier hikes similar to those at Franz Josef. Some argue that the Franz Josef Glacier is the superior ice experience, although the walk to Fox's face terminal is shorter, meaning that you get more ice-time, and the village is quieter and arguably more picturesque. Both are equally thrilling and whatever ice-experience you opt for you'll find a scattering of backpacker hostels in both of these sleepy villages.

Main backpacker area – Franz Josef & Fox Glacier villages

Highlights – Glacier hikes, ice-climbing, helicopter hikes & skydiving. Jungle paintball!?

QUEENSTOWN... *The adrenaline capital!*

> Top Adrenaline Rush
> * Nevis Highwire Bungy *

Don't be fooled by its size and magnificent natural setting. Adventure crazy by day and party town by night, Queenstown steals the show and is usually the highlight of anyone's Kiwi adventure. Set in the awe-inspiring landscape of the Southern Alps, its majestic beauty is combined with an unrivalled portfolio of extreme activities and it's developed a formidable reputation as a premier four-season adventure destination. Queenstown is the world's favourite adrenaline destination where the brave come to challenge themselves and get a thrill–seeking overdose. Only a complete idiot would neglect to have this exciting town on their itinerary! Be warned though, you'll need a wedge of money if you want to give your adrenaline glands a thorough workout! For some, Queenstown represents an exciting opportunity to put down some roots and find some employment.

Activities: Home of the first bungy jump, it would be rude not to play with gravity while you're here. The insane throw themselves off the **Nevis Highwire** – at a knee wobbling 134m over Doolan's Creek, it's the highest jump in the country and one of the highest in the world. For those of you who are true adrenaline junkies, you should entertain the idea of completing the **'Thrillogy'** – all three AJ Hackett jumps in Queenstown for a heart racing experience at a discounted price! Heights aren't everyone's cup of tea and if you want to indulge in some other activities there's plenty to keep you entertained from white-water rafting, river boarding and kayaking to street luge, mountain biking and indoor mini-golf. You'll spend half your time wandering around nervously thinking about the next shit-scary activity and the rest on a natural high – you definitely won't forget your time in Queenstown! During the winter, Queenstown transforms into an **alpine playground** where you can find some of the cheapest skiing & snowboarding deals around – Queenstown itself usually sits below the snow line but the two closest ski fields are **Coronet Peak** and **The Remarkables** although others, such as Cardrona and Treble Cone are within reach.

Nightlife: Queenstown's buzzing nightlife is another huge draw and this town really comes to life at sundown. You're going to inflict some serious damaged to your liver during your time here! Blessed with an abundance of bars and restaurants, it's a lively night out that attracts an energetic young crowd. Organised pub crawls, promotions and themed-nights spur on the drunken mayhem every night of the week. From sports bars and traditional pubs to cocktail bars and nightclubs, Queenstown's nightlife is exceptionally varied. In fact, it's rated amongst the best in the country, so make sure that despite an action-packed day, you save some energy for a legless night out and some loving! Pull or not, round-off the evening with a gigantic gourmet burger from the NZ Famous **Fergburger** – a great drunken feast after drinking teapots of cocktails in **World Bar**!

Daytrips: If the hype of this restless town gets too much, or you just need to sooth your hangover, head over to the awe-inspiring **Milford Sound**, or the quieter but equally breathtaking **Doubtful Sound**, on a daytrip and explore these stunning fjord lands. Return transport and cruises can be arrange through many operators in Queenstown but for an idea of its sheer beauty and the cruise options check out www.realjourneys.co.nz

Highlights – Where do I start!? Nevis Bungy, Nevis Arc, Kawarau Bridge Bungy, the platform bungy, *(The Trilogy)*, NZ Sky-Dive, Shotover Canyon Swing, Jet Boating, street luge, rafting, Mad Dog River Boarding, Lake Wakatipu & kayaking, indoor mini-golf, skiing & snowboarding *(seasonal)*, tandem hang gliding and paragliding, mountain biking, hiking, job opportunities, bars & great nightlife *(World Bar)*. Fergburger! Milford Sound & Doubtful Sound daytrips

CHRISTCHURCH... *NZ's slice of England!*

The 'Garden City' is often described as the most English of all New Zealand cities and you can see why – trams glide down streets bearing familiar British names, the aptly named Avon River runs through the heart of the city and the grand Anglican cathedral all give Christchurch a quintessential English feel. However, if you look closer Christchurch has a very distinct Kiwi charm with modern art galleries, bustling cafés and fashionable bars and restaurants. Market stalls, sculptures and human street art fill the lively Cathedral Square. The city has a comprehensive range of backpacker lodgings and a lot of these hostels are conveniently located within a few streets of **Cathedral Square** – Base has the prime location right on the square.

Boasting a busy international airport, Christchurch is often overlooked by travellers who are pursuing a linear itinerary using the city as merely an exit/entry point. Some find Christchurch a bit of a bore and perhaps, in part, this is because Christchurch is a conservative girl and her charm isn't as obvious as the average Kiwi town and there's a severe absence of adrenaline kicks, but it's worth a few days to chill-out and soak up the cities enjoyable atmosphere.

Main backpacker area – Hostels are scattered on the streets close Cathedral Square

Highlights – Cathedral Square, shopping & moderate nightlife

KAIKOURA... *The ultimate aquatic experience*

Kaikoura is New Zealand's eco-tourism hotspot and boasts one of the country's most rewarding aquatic

> Top Adrenaline Rush
> * Cage-diving with sharks *

encounters. A once sleepy seaside town, and the South Island's best kept secret, Kaikoura is now booming thanks to the numerous species of whale and dolphin that swim along its coast. Kaikoura offers richly rewarding interactions with whales, dolphins and the under-rated seals. The dolphins here aren't fed or enticed in anyway and you can swim with them entirely in their natural habitat. The area also has a wealth of bird species including the legendary Albatross.

Tours: Most travellers come here for the dolphin encounters. **Dolphin swims** can be arranged by a number of operators in town and offer an unforgettable experience with acrobatic hectors, dusky and bottlenose dolphins. Pods of 300+ aren't uncommon. **Dolphin Encounters** is a popular tour operator – www.dolphin.co.nz. Another popular activity is **whale watching** where you'll spot several of Kaikoura's semi resident sperm whales surface for air *(www.whalewatch.co.nz)*. Several seal colonies bask on the rocks here and you can dive, snorkel and kayak with these blubbery beasts or simply take a stroll and watch them sunbathing. For the ultimate aquatic encounter jump in at the deep end and sign up for some **cage-diving** with the oceans most ferocious predator – the shark. Keen birdwatchers will enjoy tours with **Ocean Wings Albatross Encounters** – www.oceanwings.co.nz.

In Maori, Kaikoura means 'to eat crayfish' so be sure to devour some of the local delicacy which can be brought from roadside stalls. Apart from the town's famous crayfish, local specialities include grouper, cod and green mussels. Considering the town's size, it has a stack of high quality accommodation. The weather can be somewhat unpredictable so try and allow a few days leeway for your dolphin swims and whale watching tours.

Main backpacker area – Some decent affordable hostels can be found along **Beach Road**

Highlights – Freshly caught local seafood, dolphin & seal swims, whale watching & shark dives

Off-the-beaten track... *Spice things up a bit!*

Most of New Zealand is well-trodden, but some places are less popular with tourists than others – this doesn't mean that they don't offer as much, usually it's because they're out of the way and are an 'inconvenient detour' from the conventional 'Auckland to Christchurch' linear routes. If time and money permit, here are a few places slightly off the popular route to check out:

The North Island:

MERCURY BAY & AROUND... Ok, so if you're on one of the backpacker busses, you'll more than likely come here as part of their pre-set itinerary but if you decided to DIY-it around NZ try and dedicate a few days to this scenic coastline. As well as Mercury Bay itself, highlights include the nearby **Cathedral Cove** where you can flop on fine sandy beaches and stroll along some spectacular coastal walks. **Hot Water Beach** is a must-do, where thanks to a geothermal outlet, you can dig your own personal hot pool in the sand to stew in – bring a spade and try not to burn your arse! Head towards **East Cape** and follow soak in the picturesque views along the less-trodden **Pacific Coast Highway**.

The South Island(s):

DUNEDIN... NZs most famous student town is also the most Scottish city outside the land of tartan. Fewer backpacker busses venture here but the city boats an excitable dedication to rugby, beer *(Speight's)* and after dark activities! There's also beautiful beaches and decent surf to keep you occupied during the day. Other highlights include **the worlds steepest street** *(Baldwin Street)*, **Launch's Castle, Speight's Brewery** and **Cadbury World**.

STEWART ISLAND *(Just off the South Island)*... This southern outpost is the smallest of New Zealand's three main Islands where only a handful of backpackers venture. Blessed with a wealth of wildlife, sandy coves, scenic walks, and welcoming local folk, you can kick back, relax and get back in touch with nature on this chilled-out friendly island. It's also one of the few places where you can spot NZ's iconic bird, the shy Kiwi, in the wild.

CHATHAM ISLANDS... Lying 850kms east of NZ's main islands, the Chatham Islands offer the ultimate off-the-beaten track Kiwi destination where you'll be rewarded with a diverse lush landscape, an abundance of endemic birdlife and the unique ancient Moriori culture. This family of 'extended islands' can be reached by air from Auckland, Christchurch and Wellington. However, once you're there getting around and hoping to the outer islands isn't easy but this is half of the adventure, otherwise they'd be on the well-trodden-route!

AUSTRALIA

BEACH BUM!

Beach bums unite! For many, Australia's 'surfy' eastern seaboard with its sun-kissed realm of beaches, waft of sizzling BBQs, laidback beach towns, buzzing cities, expanse wilderness and bubbling nightlife is the complete backpacking experience. It's also the scene for some of the best road-trips where the rolling highways will whisk away from magical and diverse cities to golden sands and countryside retreats. When you're not flopping on the beaches, knocking back schooners of VB and drifting between the towns in proper campervan fashion, you can spot surfacing whales, feed wild dolphins, cuddle koalas, sail majestic islands and sample top-notch wine. Boasting some unique indigenous wildlife and natural wonders that include the Great Barrier Reef and Ayers Rock, Australia's got a lot to shout about. Understandably, it's been a long standing favourite with backpackers. However, in terms of costs, Oz will disappoint. It's undeniably an expensive destination for budget travellers but this is offset by plenty of employment options. Get a Working Holiday Visa or have a big budget – you don't miss out, do you?

Like its little brother New Zealand, travelling around Australia is a simple and comfortable affair. However, distances are great and journeys are long – don't be surprised if you find yourself driving for hours on end with little else but sand in between towns!. Generally, roads are in good condition and destinations are well sign posted. Here are the best ways to see this sunburnt country.

You'll have similar transport options to New Zealand:

1) Campervan & Car...

Getting a campervan and embarking on the great Aussie pilgrimage up the eastern seaboard in true beach-bum style is the ultimate dream for many backpackers. This is what it's all about and the only credible way to see a country blessed with such an epic sundrenched coastline. Consequently, hiring campervans and buying cars has become

Blues & twos...

The police are out in force along Australia's roads eager to catch abusers of speed and drink drivers – I met heaps of travellers who'd been hit with speeding fines and parking tickets so watch your speed or keep your eyes peeled!

extremely popular. As you want have the knowledge and wisdom of the hostels, check out the **Tourist Information Offices** as you roll into each town to check out what to do.

There are a number of pros and cons to consider:

The Pros: Not necessarily the cheapest way to explore the mass expanse of Australia but it's definitely the coolest way to get around and makes you feel part of the surfer's crowd! It gives you the freedom to truly explore this continent. Be brave and adventurous and remember that the best thing about getting lost is what you find on the way! Due to the sheer size of Australia, some of the country's best places tend to be out the way off-the-beaten track and there's nothing more exciting than discovering your own deserted beach, lagoon, camping ground or swimming hole. Remember travelling is about the journey, and whether you want a saucy romp or a cosy night's sleep, a campervan gives you more freedom to explore Oz whilst reducing your accommodation costs! Again, hiring or buying a camper van can be a cheaper way to travel especially for groups of 2 or 3 – there's a lot of miles to cover but petrol is fairly cheap – that's if you're from the UK or Europe!

The Cons: It's somewhat surprising, but Australia isn't as campervan friendly as you may think. You'll find it very hard to just pull up along an esplanade and sleep there for the night – parking restrictions are plentiful in towns and along beachfronts and they're heavily enforced spoiling the fun and restricting your freedom. Rest areas are free to stay in but these are located well outside of towns in remote areas. Therefore, many travellers often opt to stay in campsites – while this takes the point out of having a campervan, it also dramatically increases your costs. Campers are a pain in major cities, such as Sydney and Melbourne, where parking is either sparse or expensive. Even hostels charge you to use their car parks! Ideally do a bit of planning and spend a few days in Sydney/Melbourne/Cairns before you pick up your van and arrange to drop it off the first day you arrive at your final destination.

While campers are a great way to get about, they're somewhat unsociable – you'll meet fewer travellers because you won't be staying in as many hostels and while rest areas are abundant, they tend to be quiet and sleeping in them can be a lonely affair. It's good if you can find some other travellers with a van and form a sociable convoy!

Getting a vehicle: While those flush with cash may wish to buy a vehicle, as with New Zealand, it only really pays to purchase one if you're planning to stay longer than **two months**. Again, to avoid any financial liability, your best bet is to rent one and you'll find arrange of familiar companies to those in New Zealand:

- **Apollo Campervans:** www.apollocamper.com
- **Backpacker Campervan & Car Hire:** www.backpackercampervans.com
- **Britz Campervan Hire:** www.britz.com.au
- **Escape Campervans:** www.escapecampervans.com.au
- **Jucy Hire:** www.jucy.co.nz
- **Spaceships:** www.spaceshipsrentals.com.au
- **Wicked Campers:** www.wicked-campers.com.au – usually the cheapest company – although you'll see many on the back of recovery vehicles. The engine of our **wicked camper** seized up after a just a week!

If you really want to buy a campervan check out www.travellerscarmarket.com. If time is short and you want some financial peace of mind check out **TRAVELLERS Auto-Barn.** They offer a guaranteed buy back option with most sales including 24hr roadside assistance and various warrantees. Again, just be warned that this service comes at a price and you won't get anywhere near the value that you originally paid for it. On the positive side you do get some financial peace of mind knowing that you'll definitely get rid of it before you leave and the additional benefits, such as breakdown cover, are certainly useful! Check them out on www.travellers-autobarn.com

2) Backpacker Busses & Local Busses... *Fun, cheap and practical*

By far the cheapest option if you're planning to explore Australia's vast continent by yourself and you'll meet lots of fellow minded travellers too. These companies are commonly used by budget backpackers;

- **Greyhound** *Australia*: www.greyhound.com.au

   A very practical and affordable option. Greyhound *Australia* has an extensive and reliable network across Australia and is extremely popular with shoe-stringers. They offer special backpacker passes with preset routes around the country where you can hop-on hop-off as you like. Among the most popular options are: **Kilometre Pass** *(totally flexible, travel wherever, whenever)*, **Explorer Pass** *(explore pre-set routes, hop on & off as you travel)* and **Micro Passes** *(travel between two chosen destinations and enjoy a limited number of stops in between)*

- **Premier Motor Service:** www.premierms.com.au

   Similar to Greyhound *Australia*, Premier Motor Service has good network coverage along Australia's East Coast – from Cairns to Melbourne. Premier Motor Service doesn't offer the same level of flexibility or the same range of backpacker options but it's a lot cheaper than Greyhound *Australia*. The busses tend to operate on some very unsociable hours but the whole fleet is well equipped to make your journey comfortable and easier on your wallet!

- **The OZ Experience:** www.ozexperience.com

   This is the 'the backpackers bus'. Similar to The Fiji Experience and The Kiwi Experience, it offers a number of routes and itineraries at reasonable prices. A good option if you want to meet likeminded travellers and mix wacky activities with a rich nightlife. A good choice if you don't feel like, or aren't, confident planning activities yourself – The OZ Experience really is effortless backpacking!

3) **Domestic flights...** *Quick, convenient & sometimes necessary!*

Australia is one big arse country and just about everyone underestimates the sheer size of it before they go! Realistically if you're short on time you'll need to take a few internal flights, especially if you want to get deep inland and check out places like Ayres Rock and Alice Springs. Qantas, Jetstar, Virgin Blue, and Tiger Airways are the main airlines in Australia. The latter three no-frills airlines are popular amongst backpackers. Generally the sooner you book, the cheaper the tickets will be:

- o **Jetstar:** www.jetstar.com
- o **Quantas:** www.qantas.com.au
- o **Virgin Blue:** www.flypacificblue.com

MINI GUIDE

Most travellers pursue the infamous and logical linear route across the two sun-drenched states of **New South Wales** and **Queensland** from **Sydney** to **Cairns**. Those who have more time often add-on a looping itinerary that sees them venture from **Sydney** to **Canberra** *(via Blue Mountains)*, then through the state of Victoria over to **Melbourne** before heading back around the corner to Sydney via **Lakes Entrance** and a few other places in between! If you've got the time and some money to burn, consider some of the lesser-travelled but equally popular destinations such as **Ayers Rock** and **Cape Tribulation** or take some time out to absorb the scenic views along the **Great Ocean Road** from **Melbourne** to **Warrnambool**:

NEW SOUTH WALES...

Sydney is Australia's principle gateway, and for the majority of travellers, the first-taste of life Down Under. Most backpackers begin their epic road trip by heading northbound through NSW along this well-trodden path:

Sydney *(Blue Mountains)* ➔ Newcastle *(Hunter Valley)* ➔ Seal Rocks / Port Macquarie ➔
Byron Bay ➔ Nimbin *(➔ Queensland)*

SYDNEY... *The ultimate Aussie introduction or farewell*

Unofficially Australia's capital city, Sydney is the ultimate traveller's destination – it's pretty unlikely that it won't feature on your Aussie itinerary, and for good reason. This sassy city's got it all boasting unrivalled architecture and iconic buildings, fantastic year-round weather, beautiful urban beaches, awesome shopping, a bustling entertainment scene and, to top it all off, an energetic nightlife coupled with a healthy backpacker scene. This vibrant city is the best introduction to the land Down Under and the perfect place to start or even bid farewell to your Aussie experience – it offers almost everything you could ask for in a travel destination. Catering extremely well for backpackers and you'll find no shortage of hostels and bars, particularly around **Kings Cross**, offering everything from discounted admission to attractions and free internet to meal deals and drinking promotions. There's plenty to keep you occupied here for a good few days and many, charmed by the cities style and multicultural energy, end up staying indefinitely.

This list of what to do and what to see in Sydney is endless. From strolling around her charming harbours and checking out the world-famous landmarks to soaking up the sun on legendary beaches and staying up late in the lively bars, Sydney won't disappoint. Popular touristy attractions include the brilliant **Tarango Zoo, Sydney Aquarium** and the **Royal Botanical Garden** while the more lethargic types and hung-over party animals tend to spend their time snacking on fish 'n' chips and burning on the beaches. While **Manly** and **Bondi** are the two most famous beaches in Sydney, the entire metropolitan area boasts no fewer than 30 beaches! **Coogee** is a more laidback, smaller beach where you'll find fewer footprints. If you're in Oz for the New Year festivities, make sure that you're in Sydney for one of the best NYE experiences you'll ever have. Just make sure that you book accommodation months in advance – this can't be stressed enough!

Main backpacker area – Kings Cross *(by the Coca-Cola sign!)* where there's plenty of boozers, cafes, restaurants and backpacker hostels

Highlights – Bondi Beach, Manley Beach, Sydney Opera House, Harbour Bridge, Darling Harbour, Sydney Tower, Taronga Zoo, Sydney Aquarium, colonial architecture, National Maritime Museum *(free basic tour)*, Kings Cross area, shopping, job opportunities, restaurants & nightlife. Daytrips incl. Blue Mountains & Hunter Valley

If you're a wine connoisseur, fancy a tipple or just want to get pissed, Hunter Valley is NSW's tranquil wine country! If you've got a campervan, this region's a great detour from the main east coast route where you can sample a variety of wines from heaps of quality vineyards. It's fair to say that some of the wineries are a bit snobby and unwelcoming to 'young & scruffy' backpackers. This may make you feel awkward, as it did me, but don't let this put you off. There are loads to choose from so hunt around and you'll find some great vineyards with decent tours that are run by down-to-earth guides who have a sense of humour. Tours end with everyone's favourite bit – the testing, and no, you don't have to spit it out! Some of the wineries have fantastic staff that enthusiastically run through their wine lists, and more often than not you, you'll stagger away fairly pissed and usually with a bottle or two that you've bought. Unfortunately, you can't buy goons of the stuff! If you hunt around a bit, tours should cost no more than AUS$10. A very entertaining, down-to-earth and cheap tour *(AUS$5 in 2010)* is run by **Tyrrell's Wines.**

In between Vineyards and the 'fine wine sampling' you can savour some great gourmet cuisine – you'll find numerous factory outlets and shops scattered throughout this region from cheese and olive shops to chocolate and sweet stores! **The Hunter Valley Gardens Village** is a popular complex with plenty to keep you occupied! If you haven't got a camper to get your head down for the night, the popular YHA hostel is a good base offering a variety of tours and day-excursions.

Getting there & away – Campervan & Car: Most people drive here so they can hunt around, absorb the vast 'vineyard-landscape' and perhaps pass out in the back of the van after tasting sessions! This is by far the best option. Daytrips can be arranged in towns along the east coast although these can be fairly expensive and don't tend to attract shoestring travellers!

Useful website – www.winecountry.com.au

Backpacker's hostel – Hunter Valley YHA *(100, Wine Country Drive, Nulkaba)*

Highlights – Vineyards, wine-sampling & getting a bit tipsy!

PORT MACQUARIE... *The underrated beach-bums retreat*

This pleasant beach town remains largely off the backpacker's radar but it's a great respite from the flock as they herd their way up the highway! It also breaks up the long trip, and stops your campervan from overheating, from Newcastle to Byron Bay. If you can, on your way to Port escape the lethargic trance of the Pacific highway and embark on a scenic detour through **Lakes Way** and **Seal Rocks** for some refreshing coastal views and a dip in the sea.

Undeniably the nightlife's better up the coast in energetic Surfers Paradise and Byron, but if you just want to escape the crowds of flash-packers and relax on the beach, Port wins hands down. Boasting no fewer than 15 beaches in the Greater Port Macquarie region, there's always plenty of space to spread your towel! Practically anything you can do in the water you can do here from surfing, swimming and wallowing to jet-skiing, kayaking and dolphin watching. You can even trash around a 4x4 on a couple of the beaches – you just need to get a permit from The TIC on Gordon Street. Back in the water, you can hit the waves and learn to surf with **Port Macquarie Surf School:** www.portmacquariesurfschool.com.au.

A visit to the **Koala Hospital** is a must – run purely through donations, it treats more than 200 injured koalas a year and it has a few permanent residents who are too unwell to be released back into the wild. The best time to visit is during feeding time when the koalas will sleepily make their way down from the enclosed tree tops *(about 3pm)*. The **Billabong Koala Park**, just outside of town, is another great koala encounter. Other little spots of interest, like the Observatory, historic sites and numerous museums draw in a mixed and interesting crowd and ensure that there's something to keep everyone here a little longer. If you've got time head over to **Lake Cathie** where you can splash about in the saltwater lake, stroll along the beach, laze around, fish and fire up a barbie! There are some good wineries around as well if you want to sample some local Aussie wine – a good opportunity if you don't intend to explore the larger Hunter Valley region down south.

Great overnight spot – Nobbys Point makes a great place to park up in your campervan and get your head down for the night – it's slightly off the road and comes with sea views either side and toilet facilities and public BBQ around the corner just up the road.

Highlights – Beaches, Lake Cathie, local vineyards, Kooloonbung Creek Nature Park, Koala Hospital & Billabong Koala Park

BYRON BAY... *The backpacker's beach town*

Boasting more beaches, a more relaxed pace of life, genuinely friendly locals and a great climate, Byron Bay is the shoe-stringer's alternative to over-packaged and over-priced Surfers Paradise. This really is a surfer's haven and the energetic nightlife tops it all off ensuring a constant stream of young laidback travellers. Here surfer dudes outnumber package-holidaymakers and the whole place feels like what you expected from Surfers Paradise. More importantly, it's got what Surfers Paradise lost a long time ago, an authentic chilled-out and genuine 'surfy' atmosphere that's dominated by carefree shoe-stringers and friendly locals. You'll find a large concentration of surf shacks, beachfront bars, cheap hostels and affordable eateries scattered throughout this seaside town – perfect for socialising with the new friends you've just met in the waves!

These fantastic characteristics do pose a problem – they can pull in a few too many travellers, and at times, Byron can be overcrowded. You just have to remember that, at its heart, this desirable beach town is a low-key town that's set up to cater for only a few thousand permanent residents! If development attempted to alleviate any peak-season overcrowding by erecting vast shopping malls, widening the roads and brining in foreign investment, this quaint beach town would inevitably lose its distinctive charm! Just book your accommodation in advance during peak times.

Surfing: Start your surfing career here – this is the best place to learn to surf in Australia boasting heaps of top-notch surf schools, experience instructors, beautiful sandy beaches and the best waves. **Mojosurf** is a unique 'mobile surf school' – since the surf conditions constantly change, this school innovatively searches for the best waves in the area everyday! They offer a decent range of 'Learn to Surf Adventure' packages from ½-day 'surf adventures' and 2-day 'surf & stays' for those with limited funds to the complete 5-day 'Byron to Sydney' pilgrimage which includes transfer, accommodation, equipment and tuition. **Waves** is another highly recommended surf school that offers similar 'learn to surf' camps and boarders road trips. This company also offers a 'Byron to Sydney' adventure *(or vice-versa)* over a seven day period with a self-drive option.

Besides surfing and partying there's plenty more to make you prolong your stay in Byron Bay. Sea kayaking and a chance to play with wild dolphins is always a popular activity. For more info, check out; www.goseakayakbyronbay.com.au. You can also explore the magical underwater world through the **Byron Bay Dive Centre** www.byronbaydivecentre.com.au. As always in NZ and Oz, why not chuck yourself out of a perfectly good plane and grab yourself some great views over the Bay, for prices and details check out; www.skydivebyronbay.com. For a bit of exercise, some fresh air and stunning coastal views stroll up to Cape Byron – if you've got a camper and can't be arsed, you can drive!

Surf schools: MojoSurf – www.mojosurf.com

   Waves Surf School – www.wavessurfschool.com.au

Highlights – Beach-life, surfing schools, dolphin kayak tours, diving, bars, nightlife & skydiving

From the glitz of the **Gold Coast** and the natural splendour of the **Great Barrier Reef** to the thrills of **Frasier Island** and wonders of the **Whitsundays**, Queensland boasts some of Australia's most desirable destinations that'll satisfy hardcore party animals, carefree beach-bums and outdoor enthusiasts alike. Reclusive types maybe prefer to chill-out on the quieter sands of **Mission Beach** *(and the nearby Dunk Island)* where you'll find a hand-full of travellers, a low-key chilled-out backpacker scene and fewer footprints on the beach. Flash-packers will enjoy the energetic seaside town of **Noosa**. However, away from these tourist traps you'll also find plenty of less-travelled towns and secluded beaches – this is why you need a campervan so you can really get into the guts of this sunburnt coastline to find the well-hidden gems that'll really make your trip. Here's the most popular route that hugs the golden coastline through Queensland...

Surfers Paradise ➜ Brisbane ➜ Noosa / Tin Can Bay ➜Fraser Island ➜ Bundaberg *(Mon Repos)* ➜ Airlie Beach *(Whitsundays)* ➜ Magnetic Island ➜ Mission Beach ➜ Cairns

SURFERS PARADISE... *For the urban beach-bum*

At the heart of the Gold Coast you'll find the bright lights of Surfers Paradise. For some it's the pinnacle of this coastline but, believe it or not, this epic town isn't as backpacker friendly as you may think and shoe-stringers maybe bitterly disappointed. Essentially, it clearly caters largely for package-holidaymakers who have fatter wallets! It's not all bad news though and it still has some of the magic that made it so popular. If you've got some money to burn you won't leave too disheartened. There's no denying that the half-decent beaches and popular surf schools are a major draw but it's the emphatic nightlife that's perhaps Surfers' biggest attraction these days – dozens of shops, restaurants, bars and clubs dominated the main strip. While it's generally overpriced for backpackers, a few cheap hostels remain and you'll find the usual budget supermarkets *(Coles)* allowing you to sleep cheap, whip up a few bargain culinary delights and enjoying one of Australia's iconic party hubs. If your low on funds, save your cash for Byron Bay.

Backpacker digs – Cheers Backpackers, Surf 'n' Sun Backpackers & SP Backpackers Resort

Highlights – Beaches, surfing schools, shopping, restaurants & nightlife

BRISBANE... *Top up your travel funds*

The sunshine state's capital has all the trappings of a big city, plus the laidback style which epitomises this captivating state. In terms of prestige and sheer intensity, it's light years away from Sydney and Melbourne but Australia's third largest city is worth a good few days. Warm to hot summers and very mild winters coupled with a carefree lifestyle and a vibrant cosmopolitan café scene have made Brissie a year-round destination. Culture vultures will appreciate the dozens of theatres, art-house-cinemas, concert halls, galleries and museums while beach-bums will enjoy the cities close proximity to the Gold and Sunshine Coasts. Moreover, the surrounding area is arguably the best region to find work – this is the place to stop travelling and start working to boost your dwindling bank balance! If you're just in Brissie for a flying visit, there are a few activities to keep you busy. Get your bearings and hop on the **Brisbane Night Tour** *(www.goannaadventures.com.au)* or climb the **Story Bridge** *(www.sbac.net.au)*. At the very least, make sure you hug a koala at the **Lone Pine Koala Sanctuary** *(www.koala.net)*.

Moreton Bay, to the east of the Brisbane, provides a great escape from the city boasting around 360 secluded islands where pods of friendly dolphins *(that you can feed)* and whales frolic. **Moreton Island** is a large rugged sand island that's great for wilderness lovers where you can go bushwalking, chill on beaches and cool-off in freshwater lakes. **Langalooma**, which has been put on the tourist map by friendly dolphins, and **North Stradbroke Island** are also popular retreats.

Highlights – Employment, Lone Pine Koala Sanctuary, culture & Moreton Bay

FRASIER ISLAND... *Sandy 4x4 thrills!*

Three days exploring the world's largest sand island complete with two ice-boxes full of grog and a 4x4 full of new friends whose name you can't quite recall by morning – Frasier Island is one of Australia's most incredible experiences and a magnet for backpackers. It's a place of exceptional beauty, with its long uninterrupted white-sand beaches flanked by strikingly coloured sand cliffs and dunes. It also boasts a number of stunning freshwater lakes that are ringed by white sandy beaches and ancient rainforests that line the banks of fast-flowing creeks. This fantastic island is popular with thrill-seekers, water-babies, hikers and nature enthusiasts.

Thrill-seeking backpackers travel in Convoys of 4x4s attempting to negotiate potential deposit-damaging wash-outs on the beach, conquer steep dunes and frantically dig themselves out of sandy tracks while lethargic types laze on the hot sands and cool-off in refreshing creeks and picturesque lakes. As darkness fall's the underinflated chunky tyres grind to a halt and the convoys set up camp behind the dunes for a night of sociable drinking and BBQs – just look out for the wild dingoes, they're shy and aren't much of a danger but they'll steal your lunch given half a chance!

Booking a tour: You can get to Frasier Island and book tours from **Rainbow Beach** and **Hervey Bay**. If you're planning to stay at Hervey Bay, don't be fooled by the size of the town – there really isn't much to do so just spend a few days either side of your Frasier Island adventure! **Self-drive 3-day/2-night 4x4 tours** are the best way to experience this fantastic island and can be booked through a number of outfits. Two very popular hostels in Hervey Bay – **Fraser Roving** *(www.fraserroving.com.au)* and **Koala Beach Resort** *(www.koala-backpackers.com)* – have their own fleet of distinctive 4x4's and offer very good self-drive tours and decent itineraries – tours here are very popular so you'll no doubt be in a very sociable convoy of up to four 4x4's!

Main sleeping area – Suggested camping areas will be listed on your itinerary

Getting there & away – Tours are usually booked from the nearby mainland towns of Rainbow Beach and Hervey Bay where travellers spend a few days before and after their sand adventure

Highlights – 4x4 action, drunken camping, Eli Creek, Maheno Wreck, Lake Wabbi, Lake McKenzie, Indian Head, Champagne Pools, wildlife & beaches!

BUNDABERG & MON REPOS... *Rum & turtle tots!*

Bundaberg is the home of Queensland's favourite spirit and the world famous Bundaberg Rum! It's a popular place for 'working travellers' who flock here to pick fruit and get brown in the surrounding fields under the baking sun. **Bundaberg Backpackers & Travellers Lodge** is a good place to get your head down for the night and get clued-up on your employment options. For those not looking for work, Bundaberg is the gateway to numerous natural attractions along the Fraser Coast including **Lady Musgrave** and **Lady Elliot Islands**. Moreover, it's a stone's throw away from one of nature's incredible nurseries... Mon Repos.

Mon Repos offers one of the cheapest and most rewarding experiences in Australia where you can get up close and personal with logger head, green back and flat back turtles....

Turtle season(s)...

- o **NESTING... Nov - Early Feb:** Watch huge turtles emerge from the white-wash of the ocean and drag themselves up the beach. Settle down nearby on the moonlit beach and experience these wonderful ancient creatures painstakingly dig a perfect egg chamber and lay a cluster of around 130 eggs before returning into the sea. You may even be lucky enough and get the opportunity to relocate a nest!

- o **HATCHING... Jan - Mid March:** Witness a volcano of small turtle tots emerge from their sandy nesting chamber and scramble to the sea guided by the moonlight. You'll be asked to help guide them to the sea as a group by forming a 'tunnel of light' where a hundred plus cute turtle tots will scurry between your legs down to the great ocean

Try and time your visit around **Jan** where, if you're lucky, you can witness nesting & hatching!

Tours: Fantastic ranger guided tours are run through the **Mon Repos Conservation Park**. The information centre opens at 19:00 and tours run from Nov-late March *(exc. 24th, 25th & 31st Dec)*. Bookings are essential – access to the centre and beach is by ticket only and don't forget you camera! Tours to the beach are conducted in groups but you're welcome to stay on late into the night with the rangers after the families have gone – this is by far the best way to see them and with fewer people. The small tour fee assists with conservation, monitoring and research. Book direct through Mon Repos Conservation Park Info Centre:

Contact info – www.bookbundabergregion.com.au Tel: 07 4153 8888

Highlights – Rum distillery, employment opportunities & turtle tours

NIMBIN... *Relive the 60's!*

If you're fed-up picking sand out of your arse, Nimbin's a great little detour from the coast! This humble little town is a real throw back to the 60's where the laidback hippie atmosphere rubs-off on everyone. There's a mix of colourful retro-shops bearing amusing names, 'Bring-a-bong' being my personal favourite, selling an array of legal highs and funky souvenirs. You may even encounter a few weary locals wandering round offering tourists hash cakes and joints – all quite openly! If you think you missed out of the flamboyant 60s, this is the best chance you've got to relive that carefree decade with friendly weed smoking hippies and carefree longhaired travellers! To really slip into the hippie vibe, make sure you stay overnight in this tranquil town and ask some inquisitive questions! Set in lush gardens, **Nimbin Rox YHA** is a great affordable hostel to base yourself where you can relax in their 'tropical-pool' or mong-out in a hammock.

Highlights – Retro shops, unique souvenirs & the hippie atmosphere

AIRLIE BEACH... *Gateway to the Whitsundays*

Tigermoth Acrobatics... *Pure adrenaline!*

View the Whitsundays from a dizzy height as you twist and turn in this open bi-cockpit plane! Prices start from **AUS$195**. It's a bit pricey for the average backpacker, but it's a must do for hardcore thrill seekers! www.tigermothadventures.com.au

This town has a formidable reputation for its epic nightlife and established backpacker scene. It attracts swarms of keen divers, sailing enthusiasts and nocturnal party-animals in their droves. A typical 'Airlie Beach day' involves lazing around the manmade lagoon to cool-off during the hottest part of the day and recuperate before gorging on delicious seafood in one of the top-notch restaurants and hitting the lively pubs and clubs in the evening. If you want to get your heart pumping and want to do something a bit different – bungy jumps and skydives can become monotonous and too ordinary after your umpteen jump, check out the **Tigermoth Acrobatics Plane** for a unique and exhilarating aerial experience. You'll see and hear the plane twisting and turning above the bay from the lagoon *(see text box)*. As far as accommodation is concerned, budget backpackers are spoilt for choice. **Magnum Backpackers** *(www.magnums.co.au)* and **Beaches Backpackers** are popular 'social-hubs' boasting great bars and cheap accommodation that's conveniently located in the heart of town. Essentially, Airlie Beach is the mainland base for famous **Whitsundays** where you can book an endless list of tours and courses.

Whitsundays: The Whitsundays are a paradise of protected waters boasting no fewer than 74 stunning islands each covered in sub-tropical rainforest and surrounded by white-sandy beaches and fringing coral reef. Most shoe-string travellers opt for the relatively affordable **sailing tours** which are typically 3-days/2-nights. I've met heaps of travellers with complaints ranging from irritable bed bugs to annoyingly unorganised operators, so when you're flicking through the glossy brochures in the countless tour agencies that line Airlie Beach's streets, look for the WCBIA tick, or better still, follow up recommendations from other travellers. You can often hunt around and pick up good value 'Whitsunday & Fraser Island' packages, although they **can** limit your options to prolong your stay in lively Airlie Beach. **Whale watching** tours are also available between July and September.

Crewing and **bareboat-charters** are great if you're a keen boatman or wannabe sailor. Opportunities to join a crew are usually advertised on the notice boards in hostels. For flash-packers with a bit of cash to burn, a number of companies offer bareboat-charters – you don't have to get naked onboard, the name refers to the fact that you essentially get a boat without a skipper or a crew! This is a unique and exciting opportunity to get all hands on deck and sail a yacht – you don't need any formal qualifications but you'll need to demonstrate that you're capable of operating the vessel. Briefings and 'lessons' will be given before you set off and where you'll have to show that you're capable!

Highlights – Whitsundays, whale watching, Tigermoth Acrobatics Plane, the lagoon, restaurants, bars & nightlife

CAIRNS... *Gateway to the Great Barrier Reef*

This is one of Australia's major transport hubs and whether it's the beginning or end of your Aussie adventure, Cairns will not disappoint! It's not as lively or as captivating as other Australian cities, but what it lacks in spirit, it certainly makes up for in services – Cairns boasts a concentration of backpacker orientated digs, an array of shops and affordable restaurants coupled with comprehensive budget travel services, an armada of tour operators and fantastic transport links. Since it's where the majority of travellers start or end their Australian odyssey, you'll also find a happening night scene with plenty of enthusiastic party-goers – **Gilligan's** and **Shenanigans** have emerged as the major social hubs of carefree drinking! If you're a bit strapped for cash and need a few extra dollars to continue travelling, there are some worthwhile employment options in and around Cairns. While anything is possible here, from **bungy jumping** above the forest canopy to **white-water rafting** on the popular **Tully River** *(www.raft.com.au)*, Cairns is essentially the gateway to the **Great Barrier Reef**...

Great Barrier Reef: As iconically Aussie as the Sydney Opera House and Ayers Rock, this is one of Australia's most remarkable natural assets. Boasting a mesmerising abundance of marine life, hundreds of post-card perfect tropical islands and spectacular sun drenched beaches, it's the world's largest living coral reef. There's a mind boggling array of sailing tours, snorkelling trips and diving options. Competition is fierce meaning prices are competitive so be sure to shop around in the masses of tour agencies that line the streets in town. Prices generally vary according to the inclusive itineraries – you'll pay more to get to the outer reefs but this is where you'll find the better diving and more secluded beaches.

Recommended hostels – **Gilligan's** has emerged as one of the most popular hostels where you'll find an energetic bar smack bang in the middle of where you want to be! Check it out on www.gilligans.com.au. **Nomads Beach House** is probably the cheapest hostel in Oz! It's located a bit away from the lagoon but it boasts a decent bar and pool and offers free pick-ups/drop offs into town. Book via **hostelworld** to get the best deals. More info www.cairnsbeachhouse.com.au

Highlights – Great Barrier Reef, the lagoon, snorkelling & diving trips, bungy jump, job opportunities & nightlife

In Victoria the scenery gets greener, the air gets comfortably cooler and you'll find one of Australia's most enchanting and loveable cities – **Melbourne**. From this captivating city, there's a well-trodden and scenic coastal route that heads east taking you 'around the corner' and up to Sydney *(or vice-versa)*. Here are the popular stop-off points along the way:

Melbourne ➔ Philip Island ➔ Wilsons Promontory NP ➔ Lakes District ➔ Bega ➔ Sydney

If time permits, venture west and travel along the scenic **Great Ocean Road** towards **Warrnambool** through the famous and picturesque **Port Campbell NP.** Along the way stop-off at a few gems like **Otway NP**, before embarking on the usual route back towards Sydney.

If you've just trekked from Sydney along this common-path, but still need to get back there and don't fancy backtracking, consider heading north into the arid desert-like landscape and hit the federal capital of Canberra before setting off towards Sydney via the Blue Mountains to form a looping circuit:

Melbourne ➔ Canberra ➔ Blue Mountains ➔ Sydney

MELBOURNE... *Australia's most liveable city*

Melbourne is a magnet for beach dwellers, coffee connoisseurs, urbanites and party animals alike boasting everything from golden beaches, modern shopping complexes and a happening nightlife to sophisticated cafés, museums and galleries. For many, it's Australia's most loveable and liveable city where you'll find tree-lined avenues, generous open spaces, character filled neighbourhoods and grand colonial architecture. Dozens of festivals fill the city's calendar to celebrate everything from film and art to food and sport. In fact, Melbourne has become a cult destination for **sport fanatics** where 'Melbournians' seem religiously devoted to celebrate every sport they possibly can from F1, motor GP and horse racing to football, tennis and cricket! This is an extraordinary city that you'd be crazy to neglect from your Aussie hit-list.

Unsurprisingly, this vibrant cosmopolitan city draws in hoards of backpackers from every corner of the globe and many base themselves here with the hope of employment. Affordable accommodation is spread throughout the city and inner-suburbs – the majority of backpackers tend to stay in the **city centre**, where you'll find a concentration of hostels, or the beachside suburb of **St Kilda** where the cheaper hostels can be found. To the north in **Fitzroy**, you'll find the colossal **YHA** that's very popular and thoroughly kitted out. It's worth booking in advance during the summer months and expect to pay a bit more during peak season.

If you're not going to prolong your stay to earn a few bucks, there's plenty to keep you here for a few days. To get your bearings, check out the sights from the 55th floor of the **Rialto Towers** for some 360° city views or hop on the free *(!)* city circle tram *(the burgundy & gold coloured one)* and explore the cities charming neighbour, numerous attractions and bustling city centre. When you're done for the day, just park yourself at one of Melbourne's many outdoor cafés to sample the city's enjoyable coffee culture and recuperate for a night on the grog bar hopping! Then there are all the stadiums and sporting events to be savoured all year round. For all of you Neighbours fans, no visit to Melbourne would be complete without a trip to Ramsay Street and the studios – www.neighbourstour.com.au.

Main backpacker area – City centre *(convenient but pricey)* & Kilda *(grungy but cheap)*

Highlights – Markets *(check out Queen Victoria Market)*, festivals & colonial architecture. Beaches, café culture & nightlife. Job opportunities, the fanatic sports culture & attractions incl. The Neighbours tour, Rialto Towers & Melbourne Aquarium

WILSONS PROMONTORY... *The great outdoors*

Easily accessible from Melbourne, this is one of Australia's most famous and adored national parks. Covering the southernmost tip of Australia's mainland, Wilsons Promontory or Prom as it's affectionately known by locals, is flanked by 130kms of scenic coastline boasting native mammals, an abundance of birdlife, lush forest and wide sandy beaches. Hiking is the major activity here, where avid walkers will find a comprehensive range of rewarding walks to suit all levels of fitness. The beaches at **Norman Bay** and **Squeaky Beach** are popular with sun-worshippers, active swimmers and equally lethargic types.

Tours and overnight hikes are available through a number of outfits, but can be fairly pricey for the average backpacker. DIY options are **much** cheaper and very manageable. **Tidal River**, 30km inside the park boundary, is the focus for tourism and recreation where you'll find the useful **Parks Victoria Information Office**. There are no affordable hostels within the park itself but the popular **Prom Coast Backpackers** *(YHA)* hostel, situated 25km away in **Foster**, is an ideal and popular budget base camp. Regular busses link Foster with Tidal River. Alternatively, if you want to get in touch with nature, you can **camp** in Tidal River where you'll find all the basic facilities – book in advance as campsites are in great demand!

Useful websites: www.promcoast.com.au & www.parkweb.vic.gov.au

Main backpacker options – Foster & camping @ Tidal River

Highlights – Walks, native wildlife, scenic coastline, beaches, snorkelling & the great outdoors

LAKES DISTRICT... *Scenic coastal views*

The Lakes District is Australia's largest inland water-system providing a haven for a staggering variety of wildlife – black swans, pelicans, dolphins, koalas, kangaroos, possums and even wombats are a common sight. Combined with the amazing stretch of the **Ninety Mile Beach** – a strip of golden sand backed by dunes, swamplands and lagoons – this region's a great spot to linger for a few days breaking up the trip from Philip Island to Sydney.

Sale is the Gateway to the Lakes District boasting a number of backpacker-orientated digs amid lively bars and slightly upmarket restaurants. By far the best, and cheapest place to stay, is throughout the **Sale wetlands area** and along the road towards **Loch Sport** where you'll find a stretch of near beachfront 'camping enclaves' and a healthy sociable scene. To get the most out of this laidback coastal gathering you need two things – a campervan and an ice-box full of refreshing beer! While the beaches aren't great for swimming, they're ideal for some lethargic sunbathing and a spot of relaxing shore-fishing. Around Loch Sport, you can even spot kangaroos grazing on lush grass against the backdrop of sandy beaches! At **Lakes Entrance** you'll find a number of look-out points that offer some spectacular views over this scenic water-system.

Main backpacker area – Sale town & free camping areas

Highlights – Scenic views, wildlife, sociable camping, Ninety Mile Beach & Lakes Entrance

CANBERRA... *The purpose built capital*

Canberra, a name that's fittingly derived from the aboriginal term for 'meeting-place', is diplomatically located between rivals Sydney and Melbourne – the two cities that fought for capital status – and is Australia's purpose built capital. Consequently, it's a completely planned city that's totally different to any other Aussie settlement. You'll notice an abundance of green open spaces, wide tree-lined avenues and an orderly layout that's arranged around Lake Burley cumulating into a spacious modern city that's bizarrely set in a barren desert-like wilderness.

While Canberra may not be bursting with activities and buzzing with nightlight, it's a true **cultural heartland** celebrating Australia's past and present and it warrants a couple of days. Culture vultures will unearth a wealth of interactive museums, galleries and national buildings set amongst some of the best examples of modern Australian architecture. There's also some reasonable **shopping** and a hint of **nightlife** if you're all cultured-out! Being set in a national park, there's an abundance of **bush walks** should you feel the need for a bit of exercise and wilderness exploration! For more information visit www.visitcanberra.com.au

Getting there & away: Canberra is set a fair bit inland. You <u>can</u> take a short flight here from Melbourne or Sydney. Alternatively, if you've got your own transport, consider coming through ACT on your way between Melbourne and Sydney as an alternative to the well-trodden coastal route.

Main backpacker area – There isn't a strong backpacker scene here but you'll find some of the big hostel names dotted around the centre such as YHA

Highlights – Parliament House *(free tour!)*, Old Parliament House, Australian War Memorial *(free entry and tours!)*, National Zoo & Aquarium, shopping & bushwalking

Popular add-ons...

The energetic east coast is by far Australia's biggest attraction and it makes for a simple, beach blessed and logical route, however, if time and money allow try and peel yourself away from this alcohol induced route and check out a few other worthwhile places. Here are some of the most popular 'add-ons' to the classic east coast pilgrimage:

ULURU... *The spiritual heart of Oz & one bloody big rock!*

If your budget permits, no trip to Oz would be complete without a visit to Uluru. In the past getting here has always be problematic for hurried travellers who are short on cash, however a number of companies now offer reasonably priced package-trips to Uluru and budget flights are available from most major cities across Australia – don't fret at the term 'package-trip' – groups tend to be small and cater well for *(budget)* backpackers, just be sure to shop around as competition is fierce. Your friendly agent will help you book your tour and flights and will no doubt give you a full rundown of the included itinerary so be sure to check, and compare, what you're getting for your buck. Most tours have a similar 3-day/2-night format where **Alice Springs**, **Kings Canyon** and the **Lost City** amongst other highlights will be crammed into your itinerary. Nearly every tour ends at least one day with an amazing sunset over **Uluru** and starts the next day with an equally spectacular sunrise over the imposing big red rock.

Useful websites & companies: There are heaps of companies and tour operators eager to get you 'inland' but for an idea of price and itineraries check out a popular company on www.therocktour.com.au

Highlights – Uluru *(that big red rock!)* and incredible sunsets, Alice Springs, Kings Canyon, & the Lost City

CAPE TRIBULATION & BEYOND... *Isolation where the 'rainforest meets the reef'*

Many backpackers who are looking to extend their stay beyond Cairns should head north to Cape Tribulation and beyond. This place is a fantastic setting for a few days relaxation. With pristine rainforests and sandy beaches, it's gob-smackingly beautiful! While a number of tours operate from Cairns, backpacker accommodation is available on the beach or in the forest. This area offers you a great opportunity to get back in touch with nature. Around Cape Tribulation you can find a tempting array of activities including, zip-line canopy tours, horseback treks, bushwalks, sailing and kayaking. A cruise along the **Daintree River** *(through the Daintree Nation Park just west of Cape Tribulation Nation Park)* is one of the best places for some croc spotting and bird watching in some stunning rainforest settings.

Further north, it's pretty much dirt roads towards **Cooktown**. Beyond here there are only a few small rural communities all the up to the remote **Cape York Peninsula** – the northernmost tip of Oz. Very few travellers venture past the popular Cape Tribulation, and while the conditions can be harsh, the rewards are huge. It's a great opportunity to get off-the-beaten track and the challenge to get around will make it both authentic and memorable.

Mini itinerary: Cairns ➔ Cape Tribulation ➔ Cook Town ➔ Cape York Peninsula

Useful websites & companies: Again, like Uluru, there are tonnes of companies offering different tours and itineraries. For an idea of price and activities check out this popular tour operator, Jungle Tours www.jungletours.com.au

Highlights – Rainforest treks, natural beauty, wildlife, beaches, Daintree River Cruise, Mossman Gorge & off-the-beaten track adventures

It's almost as if Australia was formed with road trips in mind – with such a scarce population, dreamy landscapes and sundrenched coastline, no placed quite lends itself to an epic road trip like this barren sun-baked continent does. Picture this; just you and a couple of close mates, an iPod full of top tunes and a cool box stacked with refreshing beer and enormous steaks with the enticing tarmac of the great open road stretching endlessly before you. Golden beaches, secluded lagoons and tranquil rest stops await – the freedom of the great open road is yours!

Away from the East Coast... *Adelaide, the Red Centre & Darwin*

There are so many potential road trips and fantastic itineraries that you could create. Here are a few ideas to get you thinking: Crossing the **Nullarbor Pain** – the vast stretch between **Adelaide** and **Perth** – will earn you some credit for a sense of adventure while any drive through the middle of the continent brings the rewards of all the amazing rock formations in the **Red Centre** – the corridor between **Adelaide** and **Darwin** is a good route. I met two Swiss guys who started their Aussie odyssey in Darwin, bought a campervan and headed towards Adelaide before hitting Melbourne and embarking along the well-trodden east coast finishing in Cairns to create a 'horse shoe' itinerary.

Western Australia... *Broome to Perth*

The West Coast is a great coastal alternative to the alcohol fuelled mayhem of the eastern seaboard. One of Western Australia's biggest wonders is the lack of tourists! From the sunset camel rides of Broome in the north to Margarets River's surf region to the south, diving with immense whale sharks on the **Ningaloo Reef** or just whale watching off Eyre Highway, this less-travelled coastline has plenty to offer. **Perth**, the isolated state capital, is a laidback city boasting more sunshine than any other Australian city and a fair share of beaches, it's the ultimate place to stop travelling and start relaxing! What's more, the WA economy has weathered the global economic meltdown and is still booming meaning there's plenty of work for hard up travellers!

The 'Full Monty'... *The complete experience!*

Ultimately, the very best way to experience everything this vast country has to offer is to buy a campervan and do the complete circuit off your own steam – just give yourself a few months for it mind! For the complete trip, you could even create a kind of loose figure-of-eight itinerary by cutting through the arid centre:

Cairns ➔ Sydney ➔ Melbourne ➔ Red Centre ➔ Darwin ➔ Broome ➔ Perth ➔ Adelaide

Or you could 'cut this in half' and to create do two more manageable looping itineraries:

1) Sydney ➔ Cairns ➔ Darwin ➔ Red Centre ➔ Melbourne ➔ Sydney

2) Darwin ➔ Red Centre ➔ Adelaide ➔ Perth ➔ Broome ➔ Darwin

Grab yourself a map and take a look, the potential routes are endless! Just keep your eyes on the road, your beer fridge well-stocked and watch out for erratic Kangaroos while monitoring your fuel closely – petrol stations can be very sparsely distributed. Be safe, get a jerry can! **Hema maps** are brilliant – you can find them for individual states or less detailed countrywide ones. The only cost a few bucks and they've got useful info on petrol stations and rest areas so you can plan your fuel stops and overnight spots for a smoother road trip!

Round-the-World

Sheer Diversity ◊ Grand Adventure ◊ Natural Wonders

ROUND-THE-WORLD TICKETS...

... THE *FULL MONTY!*

Round the World Tickets *(RTW)* have become extremely popular and are one of the cheapest ways to explore the globe. They're essentially a series of *(discounted)* **pre-booked single flights** and are **valid for 12 months.** Most tickets are **fully flexible** where you can alter your departure dates en-route. They're usually advertised, priced and based on a certain number of stops. Tickets average around £1,200 after taxes. For more information on RTW tickets check out **Section 6...** *Booking your trip (page 243).*

WHY CHOOSE A RTW TICKET...?

If you're thinking about a RTW ticket, have a quick peek at the advantages and disadvantages outlined below. A RTW ticket may not be entirely suitable for nervous first-time backpackers but it may be just the challenge that more confident and adventurous backpackers would relish:

Advantages:

- o **See a lot of the world** – this is the number one reason for embarking on a RTW trip. It gives you the opportunity to explore a range of **diverse countries** and **cultures** in a single trip

- o Generally **good value** for money – **Oneworld** and **Star Alliance** both offer a wide range of competitively priced routes

- o **Reassuring** – anxious backpackers *(and their families!)* will feel reassured to have a set time frame and itinerary of countries to follow

- o **Help & Security** – if you choose to book your RTW ticket through an agent, such as STA, you'll have professional help and support throughout the planning and duration of your trip and a point of contact should anything go wrong

Disadvantages:

- o **Can be time consuming** and **difficult to plan** – it can be a daunting task for a first-time backpacker *(although agents will assist you).* You'll have to think about these questions:

  - **a)** What countries you want to see and plan a logical route

  - **b)** Work out the dates and locations for **all** of your flights

  - **c)** Plan the seasons correctly – easier said than done!

  - **d)** Time in each place – how do you know that say, a month will be long enough in Thailand and 3 months in Australia won't be too long!?

- o **Cost** – while the tickets themselves are good value, they're still a big expense and a large initial outlay. RTW trips tend to be long adventures, often well in excess of 6 months, so you'll need a fair wedge of money to support yourself during this time frame if you don't intend to work at any point during your trip

- o **Budgeting** – budgeting will be harder. You'll have to 'ration' your money for each region/country and be well disciplined and avoid the temptation to spend, spend, spend at the beginning of your trip!

- o **Time** – a 'round-the-world trip' requires a lot of time to get the most out of it and make it worthwhile and financially sensible. Some people simply can't take 6-12 months out of the career or current lifestyle! It's also a long time to be away for a first- trip. If you become too homesick you won't appreciate where you are and what you're actually doing

- Limits your ability to be **spontaneous** and follow fellow travellers that you've met *(which is half the fun!)* – flight dates and destinations are flexible to a degree, but changes can be subject to fees and admin charges. Changing any aspect of your itinerary will have a knock on effect on the rest of your pre-planned route and will consequently cause a lot of rearranging and further planning

SUGGESTED GLOBAL ITINERARY... *The winterless trip!*

There's an endless combination of destinations but for an idea, this here's one of the most popular routes that'll ensure you have an epic and varied adventure:

USA *(New York, Vegas, LA)* ➔ **FIJI** ➔ **NEW ZEALAND** ➔ **AUSTRALIA** *(East Coast - Sydney to Cairns)* ➔ **SE ASIA** *(Singapore, Malaysia, Thailand, Cambodia & Vietnam)* ➔ **HONG KONG**

Suggested time:	8+ months
Suggested budget:	£6,000+
Best time to leave:	September / October...

This way you'll hit LA at the end of their summer. Fiji's good at pretty much any time of year but this will ensure that you hit Fiji during the more bearable 'dry season'. While you'll enter NZ at late spring/early summer you'll move on to Australia at the perfect time and be able to celebrate Christmas/NYE on the beach! It also means that you won't be hitting Asia too late and you'll be able to enjoy the best of the Asian weather during late Jan/early Feb, March, April and early May.

```
━━━━━  Popular flight path
·······  Trans Mongolian Railway
```

Escape another cold winter and enjoy endless sun on this manageable, diverse and exciting global itinerary. It's not only logical but it's packed with every just about everything from cultural extremes and tropical getaways to bustling cities and infamous road trips with heaps of inane activities thrown in for good measure. Start your trip by loosing yourself in some of Americas fascinating cities before soaking up the sun on gorgeous Fijian Islands. Dose up on some stunning scenery and extreme activities in New Zealand before heading up Australia's sun-drenched east coast in true beach bum style. Round up your trip and spend the last of your dwindling cash reserves on an epic overland sector through the diverse countries of colourful SE Asia.

Be imaginative & flexible: While this may illustrate the 'classic' RTW route, be as adventurous as you like. It's fairly common for travellers to substitute the USA with Latin America or head to Africa instead of SE Asia after their stint in Oz, New Zealand and the Pacific. You can add bits on as well: during your time in SE Asia you may have more money left over than you though you would have near the end of your trip so you could decide get some cheap regional flights and explore the Philippines or Indonesia – have an open mind and be spontaneous!

Planning an itinerary for a RTW **can** be a difficult task with so many *(peak)* seasons to juggle but it can be exciting and tonnes of carefree adventurers create their own tailored routes. Jot down your desired exotic locations and grab yourself a map – this will help you visualise your journey and piece together a logical route. Once you've got a rough itinerary, go to a travel agency or check out a few sites that offer RTW tickets to see if your route is achievable and tweak it if necessary – RTW tickets have a number of limitations and restrictions relating to the number of stops, total distance and coverage of airline alliances.

Here are a few basic pointers to help ensure that your trip goes as smoothly as possible:

- o Try and include the **more expensive countries** at the start of your itinerary – it's easier to budget for and it's better to be low on cash at the end of your trip in the poorer countries where your precious remaining funds will go further!

> **Useful websites...**
> STA Travel – www.statravel.com
> Gapyear – www.gapyear.com

- o Be aware of **'prices from'** when you're looking to book your trip. Most RTW tickets are advertised with a basic number of stops during the quietest and coldest months! Ensure that you have the price of your specified route <u>with</u> taxes included

- o Involve as many interesting **surface sectors** as you can *(see next subsection)* to get the most out of your trip and the best value from your ticket

- o By heading **westerly** around the globe – towards America from Europe – the affects of jetlag will be easier to cope with and culture shock will be more gradual

Which way around the globe... *Clockwise or anti-clockwise?*

- a) **Anti-clockwise** – via the USA and Pacific Islands first, then into Australia and New Zealand before heading back home through SE Asia

- b) **Clockwise** – via SE Asia first, over to Oz and New Zealand, then the Pacific Islands before heading home via the States

It doesn't matter which route you decide to pursue although heading anti-clockwise does have a few benefits. First of all, if you're a bit nervous it's better to head anti-clockwise as you'll be hitting the less challenging countries of the USA, the Pacific Islands, New Zealand and Australia before the more demanding countries of Southeast Asia. Secondly, and perhaps more importantly, it also means that you'll be doing the more expensive countries first, leaving the cheapest towards the end of your trip when you're skint and where your remaining funds will go further!

SURFRACE SECTORS... *Getting the most out of your RTW ticket*

To make the most out of your RTW and get the best value from it, include as many surface sectors as you can. Surface sectors require you to make your own way, usually across a number of countries, by land, sea or shorter *(regional)* flights that are separate from your RTW. You wouldn't want to get a RTW ticket and just fly to six different cities around the world – what would be the point! You want to delve deep into each country and explore it in depth. You can be as conservative or ambitious as you like with your surface sectors. A cautious overland sector could be as simple as flying into LA and out of San Francisco. A more adventurous overland sector could involve a flight into New York and out of LA leaving you the get from coast to coast and travel through the entire USA – by bus, train and/or short domestic flights! A very common surface sector, involves flying into Fiji *(Nadi)* and out of Sydney *(Oz)*, leaving travellers to make their own way through each country and hop between them via short regional flights. Surface sectors also reduce the amount of stops you have on your RTW ticket further reducing its cost and your initial outlay.

Here's a sample of the most common surface sectors:

SE Asia...

Most people follow a series of mini looping itineraries that start and end in Bangkok. However, it's perfectly logical to follow a linear surface sector and still include the majority of SE Asia's higlights on your itinerary to create a great surface sector:

- o **Start / finish:** Singapore *(Singapore)* / Kuala Lumpur *(Malaysia)* / Bangkok *(Thailand)*
- o **Start / finish:** Hanoi *(Vietnam)* / Hong Kong *(Hong Kong)*

Central America...

Due to her slender figure, linear routes are the most practical option through Central America and allow for a fantastically action-packed and culture rich surface sector:

- o **Start/finish:** Cancún *(Mexico)*
- o **Start/finish:** San José *(Costa Rica)* / Panamá City *(Panamá)*

Australasia...

This collection of islands makes it impossible to pursue complete over land sectors. You'll have to fly between the three countries – these can be, but don't have to be, separate flights that aren't part of your RTW ticket – but there are several overland surface sectors that are common in each country:

a) **Oz:** **Start / finish:** Cairns / Brisbane

 Start / finish: Sydney / Melbourne

You'll find that some international flights won't fly direct to Cairns and a lot of travellers are forced to fly to either Brisbane or Sydney first and get a connecting flight to Cairns before they embark on the pilgrimage down the eastern seaboard. Even start in Sydney and work your way up the coast, you'll probably have to get a connecting flight from Cairns to Brisbane – Where you start will largely depend on the timing of your trip and the seasons.

b) **Nz:** **Start / finish:** Auckland

 Start / finish: Christchurch

Most people fly into Auckland *(North Island)* or Christchurch *(South Island)* and out of the other following a linear surface sector that covers both islands – you can get between the islands via a ferry across the Cook Straight. Few people do a looping itinerary that backtracks through many of the same towns.

c) **Fiji:** **Start / finish:** Nadi

There's no need for a linear surface sector to explore Fiji. Nadi is the international transport hub and where most of the tours, backpacker passes and boats depart from and return to. Even if you want to explore the Main Island, a looping overland itinerary is your most practical option.

Trans-Siberian/Mongolian Railway... *The Vodka Train!*

Obviously this will largely depend on your time and already squeezed budget but if you can afford it, definitely DO IT! It's a great finish to a RTW trip after SE Asia. The Trans-Siberian/Mongolian spans eight time zones and takes you across three vast and very diverse countries – China, Mongolia and Russia – to take you within touching distance of Europe. At 9,216kms *(Moscow - Vladivostok)* it's <u>longer</u> than **Route 66** in the US and is the longest direct rail route in the world!

Essential info...	
Min. Budget:	£1, 500+
Min. Time:	3+ weeks
Countries:	Russia
	China
	Mongolia
Length:	9, 216kms

You'll share a 4-berth cabin with strangers and have basic washing facilities onboard fascinating carriages. You'll inevitably meet other backpackers, especially during the summer months and in the second class cabins! You'll also meet and have some memorable encounters with monks, students, traders, and regular vodka drinking locals – you may even share your cabin with them at some stage during your trip. During the winter you'll have to huddle together for warmth and battle against sub zero temperatures while you admire the snowy landscape – it's half the appeal!

There's no denying that it's a fairly pricey trip but don't forget you won't need an airline ticket from SE Asia, just a shorter one from Moscow or St. Petersburg, so that'll save you a few quid. While the train only takes around a week to complete the journey nonstop, it's wise to leave yourself at least three weeks so that you have the time to hop-off and explore as many intriguing cities along the way as your budget will allow! Even if you get on a pre-paid tour, you'll want some extra time at the beginning and end of it to explore the start/finish stops.

Essentially there are **2 main routes** that travellers embark on:

1) **Trans-Siberian line...** *9,216kms across Russia*

   Moscow ➔ Ekaterinburg ➔ Irkutsk ➔ Lake Baikal ➔ *Vladivostok*

2) **Trans-Mongolian line...** *9,001kms through Russia, Mongolia & China*

   Moscow ➔ Irkutsk ➔ Lake Baikal ➔ Ulaanbaatar ➔ Hohhot ➔ *Beijing*

Personally, I think the Trans-Mongolian line offers a more varied route and will get you more stamps in your passport! The destinations listed in the above routes are a guideline and only illustrate the most popular stops – they are many more interesting and diverse towns to explore along the way. It's very common for travellers to carry on towards ST. Petersburg after Moscow. Both routes can be travelled in either direction allowing you to head home towards Europe from SE Asia. If you're feeling really adventurous and your funds allow it, you can extend the Trans-Mongolian journey with additional popular routes that include **Beijing** to **Shanghai**, **Hong Kong** or **Hanoi** *(Vietnam)*. Hardcore backpackers can even take the **Reunification Express** the entire length of Vietnam from Hanoi to HCMC!

Booking your Siberian adventure... *Visas & tickets*

Visa restrictions in China, Mongolia and Russia are very strict. Whatever route you embark on, it's advisable to book all of your tickets, visas and accommodation at known stops through a specialist agency well in advance. This will ensure that you'll have all of your paperwork in order and help guarantee a smoother hassle-free trip. Most companies with have a range of pre-paid set itineraries that are tailored to different time restrictions and budgets. These 'tour groups' are usually headed by a series of local guides known as **'Honchos'**. They provide priceless local info about the stops along the way and help you get the most out of your journey. Most tours include family stays and day excursions but also allow you to do your own thing in the major cities and steer clear of restrictive sightseeing schedules and enforced meal times. Trips typically cost from £1,300 and generally take 2-3 weeks to complete. For more information check these out:

Recommended guidebook:	Trans-Siberian Handbook *(Trailblazer)* by Bryn Thomas
Recommended websites(s):	www.trans-siberia.com
	www.siberianrail.com
	www.seat61.com/Trans-Siberian.htm
Recommended agencies:	STA: www.statravel.co.uk

3) BUDGETING...

... *See more, do more, travel further*

CONTENTS

WHY BUDGET..? *BIG plans, small funds!*

It's all too easy to get carried away and 'spend, spend, spend' when you're out travelling. There's so much to see and do, so many new environments to explore, diverse foods to devour, extreme activities to pursue and, of course, a rich social life to savour. During a 12 month trip you can spend as little as £6,000 **backpacking** or you can blow anything up to £20,000 **flash-packing** around the world. However, it's amazing just how little you can actually spend when you're travelling without having to sacrifice any activities or miss out on anything – so spend a little and do a lot!

This section has been designed to:

A) Illustrate what you need to budget for – before you go and while you're away

B) Help you manage and organise your funds before you go and create a realistic budget

C) Help you budget and make your funds go further whilst you're away so that you can cram in as much as possible on your trip of a lifetime!

How you organise and manage your budget is entirely up to you. Some people have such large budgets that they can afford to do whatever they want to do without much thought about budgeting! Realistically, backpackers tend have large amounts of time and not so much cash, so ideally you want to make your money go as far as you possibly can! You'll only have a set amount of money to spend so it makes sense to do as much with it as you can. If you budget carefully you <u>can</u> **see more, do more** and **travel further**. There's no right or wrong way to budget, it's not an exact science, so don't get too stressed. This section breaks down and discusses some of the most common and practical ways to manage your travelling funds – the suggestions are guidelines so don't be afraid to modify them to suit your needs or methodology.

CREATING A BUDGET... *Working out how much you'll need*

This is the biggie and how much money you'll need for your entire trip depends on a number of things:

1) **Where you're going** – some regions / countries are more expensive than others

2) **How long you're going to be away for** – to state the obvious, the longer the trip, the more money you'll need!

3) **What you intend to do** – you'll need additional money on top of your daily budget *(general living expenses)* if you want to pursue some expensive activities such as scuba diving, skydiving or plan to rent/buy a campervan or car

Once you know where you want to go and roughly how long you're planning to be away for, you can begin to create a realistic budget. You'll need to factor in any costs before you go away as well as your spending money for when you're actually away. It also helps to plan a little for when you come home and budget for unexpected emergencies that you may have to fork-out for when you're away. All of these costs are explained in detail in the subsections throughout this chapter.

A very rough guideline...

Generally speaking, when you're out there you'll need at least **£500 a month** for regions such as Central America and SE Asia and no less than **£800 a month** for countries such as Oz and NZ.

A SIMPLE FORMULA!

If you're starting to save for your trip and want a fairly accurate idea of how much you'll need, here's a basic formula to work it out:

Initial costs – expenses before you go *(See page 196)*

+

Daily budget(s) **x** number of days you're away *(See page 198)*

+

Any planned expensive activities

+

Emergency funds & a 'coming home' fund *(optional. See page 199)*

Save towards this but the more money you have the better – especially as a novice backpacker – you'll always find other things that you want to do and haven't budgeted for when you're away. It's worth pointing out that generally speaking the longer you're away, the better value for money your trip will be. This is because getting there is your single biggest expense. Living costs in the majority of backpacker destinations are minimal – it's hard to justify a £600+ airline ticket to the Philippines for a three week trip. Surely with daily expenses so low once you're there, it would make sense to stay out there for longer as you can and make the most of out of this expensive airfare by effectively 'spreading its cost over more days'. You can see this when you look at the **overall daily cost** of your trip. This is illustrated in the **simplified** example below *(using a daily budget of £15 and a £600 return flight)*:

o   **Trip A:**   3 weeks in the Philippines would cost approximately:

21 days x £15 = £315 living costs + £600 flight = **£915** giving you an overall daily cost of **£43.57**

o   **Trip B:**   10 weeks in the Philippines would cost roughly:

70 days x £15 = £1,050 living costs + £600 flight = **£1,650** giving you an overall daily cost of **£23.57**

Of course you can't afford to stay away forever and there's no doubting that you need more money for a longer trip even if it is better value for money – it's just to illustrate the way that you should be thinking and the type of costs involved with your trip. You'll find than once you've factored the other initial costs into the simplified example above, such as equipment and travel insurance, Trip B works out even better value for money! Most backpackers aim for a **3-6 month trip** to make the most of their airfare while creating a realistic and achievable budget to save for.

The rest of this chapter is broken down into **3 logical steps** *(illustrated below)* that explore all of the costs involved in the formula. You'll also notice a few additional sections that help you deal with your money on the road.

1. INITIAL COSTS   **2. BUDGETING BEFORE YOU GO**   **3. BUDGETING ON THE ROAD**

There are a few essential things that you need to purchase before you begin to save your spending money. These initial costs are *(highest ➔ lowest)*;

A) Airline ticket (s)... **£400 - £800**   For a standard return ticket

£1, 000 - £2, 200   For a RTW ticket

Book your ticket first. It should be your priority purchase and will be your largest single expense! When you're booking any airline tickets, be sure to leave yourself enough time before your departure date to organise everything and save enough money – be realistic! See Section 6... *Booking Your Trip (page 243)* for information about airline tickets, how to beat the travel agent and find out what type of airline ticket(s) suits your needs.

B) Equipment...   **£150+**

You won't need as much equipment as you may think. Your backpack will probably be your biggest expense but thereafter there's not much expensive 'specialist' equipment that you'll need to buy. To be honest you'll be surprise how little you actually need. Refer to Section 4... *Equipment (page 215)* for lists of suggested inventory. The more luxury items that you decide to pack from the optional list *(the second 'luxury' list of inventory)*, the more you'll have to pay out. Ideally you should buy your backpack first. After that buy a few bits and bobs every now and then, say a guide book once a month, and ask for practical gifts, such as a first-aid kit for a leaving present or an MP3 player for a birthday present, to spread out the cost of your equipment.

C) Insurance...   **£80+**   Annual backpacker insurance

Don't risk backpacking without any travel insurance just to save a few quid – you never know what'll happen! Refer to Section 6... *Booking Your Trip (page 243)* for information about choosing the right travel insurance and advice on how to reduce your premiums.

D) Immunizations...   **£0+**   For the average 'armful of jabs'

There's a range of nasty diseases that you're going to expose yourself to so you'll need to have a few jabs before you go – you'll feel pretty stupid dying in agony from something that you could have prevent with a simple injection! If you live in the UK, you'll be able to get the majority of them on the NHS for free – Yey! However, Anti-Malarial drugs and shots against Yellow Fever and Rabies will set you back a fair few quid – that's if you decide that you want them. Refer to Section 5... *Health (page 231)* for advice on the arm full of jabs that'll you'll need and which ones are 'destination specific'.

Some of the biggest savings you'll be able to make are those before you go... see Section 6... *Booking Your Trip (page 243)*, for advice on trimming down these expenses. After forking-out for your initial costs you can begin to think about your 'spending money'. You should manage and organise your travelling funds from the very start and try to think in terms of:

o   **Regional Budgets & Daily Budgets** – the bulk of your spending money

o   **Emergency Funds** – for the unexpected

o   **A 'Coming Home Fund'** – to soften the blow of coming home!

GETTING IN THE RIGHT FRAME OF MIND... *Think about your spending habits*

I'm not going to preach about how you should save your money – but as a tight arse I will say this: When you're saving up for your trip just think how far your money will go in some of the countries that are on your itinerary. For instance, you could blow £50 on a night out down your local pub – that's the equivalent of around 5-day's budget in Vietnam – so is that average drunken night really that essential?! If you start to think like this and cut back a bit, you'll have no problem saving up for your trip. Sounds like a bore but all of your skimping and saving before you go will be worth it when you're away having the time of your life and your mates are all back at home working 9 till 5 and going down the same old local for another ordinary Friday night!

Some useful websites... *To help you save that bit more!*

If saving just isn't your strong point and you struggle keeping your cash in your pocket, check out these sites; www.moneysavingexpert.com and www.moneysupermarket.com. They offer tips on everything from the highest paying saving accounts and ISAs to the best deals on travel insurance. They'll also help you save money on your day-to-day living expenses so you've got more money left over at the end of each month to put aside for your trip.

PLAN YOUR SPENDING MONEY... *Regional budgets*

Generalizations are dangerous...

No two countries are the same so it makes sense to have a budget for each country/region. On a round the world trip the variations between regions are very extreme – Australasia is significantly more expensive than Africa, so you wouldn't have the same daily budgets for each region! Saying that, there are also great regional differences –Thailand and Malaysia are certainly more expensive than Cambodia and Vietnam in SE Asia and Mexico and Costa Rica are noticeably pricier than Guatemala and Nicaragua in Central America. So mentally divide your travelling fund up into a realistic budget for each country or region. For example, if you have £5,000 and are planning to disappear around the world for 6 months to the USA *(1 month)*, Australia *(1 month)*, New Zealand *(1 month)* and then finish your trip in SE Asia *(3 months)*, you could divide you money up like this;

- o **USA:**   £900
- o **Australia:**   £1, 200
- o **New Zealand:**   £1, 100
- o **SE Asia:**   £1, 800 *(saving a bigger chunk for Thailand & Malaysia)*

It's also worth bearing in mind that no matter how cheap a country **can be** or **is perceived to be**, you always have the potential of **making it** an expensive destination if you don't plan your budgets and keep an eye on your spending. It's a boring and sobering fact but you can't do EVERYTHING everywhere you go!

Physically dividing your funds...

It's a good idea to keep the budget for the country that you're currently exploring, in your current account, and the rest of your travel fund in an instant access savings account that's linked to your current account. So in the above example; when you're in the USA, have £900 in your current account and £4,100 in your savings account. When you get to Australia have £1,200 in your current account and the rest of your budget *(£2,900)* in your savings account *(as you've spent £900 in the USA)* and so on. This will help you stay within your budgets as you will be frequently reminded how much cash you've got left for that country every time you visit the ATM! This will also help you mentally create daily budgets...

DAILY BUDGETS... *Keeping track of your spending!*

Ideally you should also begin to think in terms of daily budgets – they're a simple and practical way of mentally managing your money and keeping track of your expenditure when you're out travelling. It's important to calculate these budgets before you go and they can also help you plan an overall budget for your trip *(see next sub-section)*. Obviously your daily budget will depend on what country you're visiting. Your daily budget should take into account;

- o **Accommodation** *(usually your largest compulsory expenditure)*
- o **Food & *(soft)* drink**
- o **Transport** *(not your flights!)*
- o **Internet usage** *(in moderation)*
- o **A few beers & day excursions** *(these are the 'luxury / unnecessary' expenditures that can significantly increase or blow your daily budget)*

Daily budgets aren't exact; you're not going to go on a daytrip every day, use the internet every day and hopefully not binge drink everyday – they should be used as a general budget, a mental guideline to help you stay within your overall budget for that country or region. So sticking with the earlier example you would have the following daily budgets;

	Region	Allocated Budget		Time		Daily Budget
o	**USA**	£900	÷	31 *(days)*	=	£29.03
o	**Australia**	£1, 200	÷	31 *(days)*	=	£38.71
o	**New Zealand**	£1, 100	÷	31 *(days)*	=	£35.48
o	**SE Asia**	£1, 800	÷	93 *(days)*	=	£19.35

It's important to realise these aren't target amounts to spend every day! Bear in mind that your daily budget should take into account transport costs. Try not to spend your entire daily budget everyday and in theory these small leftover amounts will add up over time and cover the cost of your transport and day trips that would otherwise appear to blow your daily budget; for example, a bus ticket that costs AUS$100 from Cairns to Brisbane, or a snorkelling trip in Thailand that costs 600BHT. If you're planning to do any activities, such as diving, skiing or bungy jumping, you should take this into consideration and have extra money on top of your daily budget to accommodate these more expensive activities. The majority of travellers work in terms of daily budgets although some people prefer to work with weekly or even monthly budgets – just adopt a method that suits you.

Using daily budgets to create overall budget for your trip...

Don't worry, as a first time traveller you're not expect to be familiar with these costs *(food, accommodation & transport)* in unfamiliar countries and be able to factor them into daily budgets and create a realistic overall budget for your trip – **minimum daily budgets** have been provided for each country in this book. For accuracy, all the daily budgets are given in local currency *(because currencies constantly fluctuate against each other on a daily basis)*. You can convert these daily budgets into a familiar currency using a site, such as www.xe.com or apps on your phone, for accurate and up to date currency conversions.

You can use these daily budgets to create an overall budget for your trip – simply multiple the daily budget(s) by the number of days you're planning to spend away. For example, if you want to go to Thailand for 2 months, you could work out your overall budget like this;

- o **Daily budget for Thailand:**   800 BHT
- o **Converted into your currency:**   £13.63 *(£1 = 55BHT)*
- o **Overall budget for trip =**   Daily budget x Number of days

---

Total minimum needed: £13.63 x 62 = approx. **£845**

Work towards saving **at least** these amounts, but it's advisable to have more and don't forget to include your initial costs; ticket, insurance and equipment! Have extra money if you intend to pursue those more expense activities.

A Quick Note: The daily budgets provided in this book have been designed for the 'average *(first-time)* budget backpacker' sharing a double/triple room in guesthouses or staying in dormitories. If you're a beer monster and like to party or you're an adrenaline junkie and want to pursue heaps of extreme activities you could easily spend more. Alternatively, if you're good at budgeting, a bit of a tight arse or want to be a beach bum you could easily spend less. Think of them as a happy medium. Don't think that you have to withdraw your daily budget from an ATM everyday! Be practical and sensible – withdraw small amounts regularly, say 4 to 7-days budget at a time, and try to make it last that long!

EMERGENCY FUNDS... *Be prepared!*

It's a good idea to have a stash of money hidden away somewhere that's totally separate from your travelling fund, perhaps in another bank account or accessible funds in the form of a credit card. In reality it's a challenge to stay within your budget. It always comes down to an all so familiar scenario: 'It's a once in a life time trip, I should do it when I'm here' – and perhaps rightly so! Impulse buying, adrenaline fuelled activities and binge drinking always puts a dent in your travelling funds and be prepared for the unexpected! You may find yourself needing to book new flights, replace a broken camera, pay for hospital bills in advance *(as many travel insurers require you to do)*, or you may be unfortunate and have some cash stolen or even lose your backpack!

It's hard enough to save up a reasonable wedge of money for travelling so asking already hard-up backpackers to put some money aside for emergencies is beyond them – and fair enough. A **credit card** is usually the preferred choice for access to money in emergencies. Just make sure you don't get stung with large interest charges, so shop around and try to get one with 0% interest for 6 months or so! **Overdrafts** are another great option and they usually attract lower interest payments than credit cards. Failing that, if you have rich, stupid or kind **parents** they can be your emergency fund – just talk it through with them first, they'll probably agree just to get rid of you! Personally, I've find that an arranged overdraft is the most practical and affordable source of emergency funds.

A COMING HOME FUND... *Soften the blow!*

Don't feel as though you have to have a 'coming home fund' but you should try and plan a little for when you do eventually come home! Despite the emotional ups and downs, the arguments with friends over petty incidents and the occasional homesickness when you're away, it can be very stressful and depressing coming back from your travels. Generally speaking, the longer your trip's been, the harder it is to come back and the more skint you'll be! **Returning to reality is a shock**: You'll probably have **no** home, **no** job or **no** car to come back to. You'll no doubt be skint when you get back – you're likely to have exhausted all of your travelling funds and you'll probably have dipped into your emergency funds, so it's a good idea to soften the blow of returning home with a bit of money to come back to. Whether you use the money to go down the pub and catch up with mates, use it to actively seek work or pay rent in advance, it'll help you more than you think. Ideally, if you're organised and the options are available, it's great if you can arrange a career break or have a job in place for when you come back – before you go! Some people know themselves too well and give this money to mum and dad to look after while they're away! To be honest I've never had a coming home fund but I always regret it as soon as I get back and end up using what's left of my vast overdraft and frantically looking for work – learn from my mistakes!

BEAT THE BANK... *Choosing an account*

It's all very well budgeting but you'll also need a good flexible bank account to complement your hard work. Your present account may not be suitable for your travel needs and where lots of travellers could save a stack of money is simply through their choice of bank account. It's important to make sure that every pound you've saved is working as hard as it can for you! There are a few simple things to look out for that'll utilise your travel funds and make the chore of managing your funds not only cheaper but less painful and time consuming:

A) **Basic Current Account...** Select a basic current account that has little or no monthly charge. Choose an account that offers a well known debit card, such as **Cirrus**, **Maestro** or **Visa**, so you can use it worldwide. If you can, try and find an account that comes with a low interest prearranged overdraft – an ideal form of emergency funds!

B) **Withdrawal Charges...** Sneaky banks will often charge you absurd amounts to withdraw your own money abroad. This will either be a percentage of what you draw out, or more commonly, a set charge. Think about it, if you're away for three months you're likely to withdraw money say, twice a week, so you'll be charged 24 times! Even if you avoid the ATM some banks charge you a commission percentage for all Visa transactions! These charges vary enormously from bank to bank ranging from £1 to £5 for each individual withdrawal. So, in this example you could save yourself up to £120 – clearly that money is better in your pocket! The lesson here is to shop around for a bank with no or little withdrawal charges. **Nationwide's Flex Account** *(UK)* is one of the best bank accounts for travellers with minimal fees for using your debit card and ATM withdrawals worldwide – it's a good idea to link an e-savings account to it.

C) **Internet Banking...** Make sure you account has internet banking and set it up before you go. It'll give you flexibility, instant access to your money and will allow you to efficiently manage your funds between accounts anywhere in the world. Internet banking will also allow you to communicate directly with your bank – very handy when you want to beg and plead for an overdraft extension!

D) **Savings Account...** Watch your savings $_{GR}OWW$ and attach an **e-savings account** to your current account – they're simple to open and require minimum effort! Keep the majority of your money in the e-savings account and keep your budget for the particular country you're in, available in your current account. Not only will this help you budget by physically dividing your funds, you'll also earn a higher rate of interest on your travel savings – every little helps! In the event of your card being lost or stolen, it'll also protect the bulk of your travel money *(as it will be in your e-savings that's only accessible <u>online</u>).*

Make sure that you notify your bank and the issuer of your card *(not always the same as your bank – check the back of your card)* of the countries you're intending to visit. This is important. In an age of global fraud banking activity is closely monitored. If your account's showing unusual activity and your card's being used internationally, banks will block it to protect your money. It can be frustrating when you try to get some cash from the hole in the wall and the ATM rejects your card leaving you stranded in a country with little or no local cash! This exact thing happened to Frida and me just after Central America when we were on the last stint of our trip in Italy!

STICKING TO YOUR BUDGET... *Self-discipline & compromise!*

Unfortunately, it's unlikely that you'll be able to do and see everything in one trip – you'll simply not have the time, money or energy. Easier said than done, but be strong and try to avoid getting over excited and immersing yourself into everything you possibly can at the beginning of your trip! Backpacking is different from a normal holiday – you're away for a long time so you'll have to compromise and make your money go as far as possible! As with saving before your trip, you should have the same mentality when you're out and about. Be a bit thrifty, shop around and haggle for that extra few pennies off – it all adds up and those few pennies could be a day's food! You'll also have to remember that you can't have all of the luxuries that you enjoy at home. If you want to be away for a long time on a tight budget you'll need to have a lot of self-discipline! Remember travelling is about testing yourself, experiencing a new way of life, immersing yourself in new cultures and activities, and enjoying a new lease of freedom. You'll have to sacrifice those home comforts and the first few weeks may be hard – you'll crave a few things now and then – but you'll soon get into the travel mode, adapt and enjoy your new *(less hygienic!)* lifestyle.

Every first-time backpacker is in the same boat, just make the most of your new found freedom and enjoy the experience! Remember your daily budgets and make use of your on-line banking facilities and check your finances regularly to help keep track of your expenditure. You may find it easier to keep on budget by withdrawing a certain amount of cash out at a time from the ATM, say a week's budget – it's easier to budget when you can physically see how much you have to spend in a given amount of time!

Remember your planned itinerary... *But allow for spontaneous moments!*

With so many temptations it's hard, but try and stick to your planned itinerary – the more expensive activities that you've planned to do should already be factored into your overall budget and additional to your daily budget. Prioritise the extra things you want to do and see. Do what you can with your time and available funds. Try and stay within your daily budget and don't be tempted to dip into your next countries/regions budget – you'll just find yourself in fantastic places with little or no money for the last few weeks of your trip, a depressing situation for anyone!

However, just to confuse the situation and sound completely contradictory, don't rule out everything and don't be too rigid! Travelling is **spontaneous**. You may stumble across those 'once in a life-time opportunities' – like the chance to join a crew and sail around the Caribbean or you may discover extra activities that you hadn't known about and budgeted for – just use your judgement and common sense and re-organise your finances and itinerary accordingly! It'll probably mean sacrificing other planned activities on your original itinerary. It's all about finding the right balance – you have to weigh everything up and think to yourself what you really want to do! You still won't be able to do everything so it goes back to prioritising what you want to do!

HOPELESS AT BUDGETING... *Pay before you go!*

If you're absolutely hopeless at budgeting, it often helps to pay for as much of the **major expenses** as you can before you go, instead of just putting the money aside. This way you won't have the opportunity or temptation to dip into that cash and spontaneously spend that money on other things when you're out globetrotting! These larger expenses may include the Kiwi Experience in New Zealand, the Amtrak national rail pass in the USA, a PADI dive course in Thailand or campervan hire in Australia. Try and book these direct with the relevant companies via the internet and cut out the middleman to get the best deals. Some travellers ask their parents to help them manage their money and get them to transfer a set amount into their bank account each week or month – again just find a method that suits you.

If you decide to book things from home don't go over the top and try not to book **everything** in advance, especially activities towards the end of your trip. The more stuff that you pre-arrange before you go, the less flexible you can be if you want to change your route, pursue different activities or explore other places – half-the-fun of travelling is having the freedom to be spontaneous and most travellers end up altering their plans... often several times! You'll always find new things to do when you're there – no matter how many guidebooks you've thumbed your way through or seasoned travellers you've spoken to!

You'll be sick and tired of watching the pennies but where ever you decide to go there are a few simple things that you can do to trim down your daily expenditure so that you'll have more cash for those exciting activities you can't do at home. It's all about doing more, seeing more and travelling further with the same budget – being efficient with the precious funds that you've got! It's not always the big things that you have to cut back on – it's usually the small things that you don't notice that add up and really make a huge difference to your daily expenditure.

When you think how far your money will go in some countries you'll begin to think twice about all of your 'unnecessary' purchases. It may only be a fiver *(£5)* here and a few quid *(£s)* there but when you consider that you can get by in Guatemala for little less than a tenner *(£10)* it puts things into perspective and that couple of quid could be a night's accommodation or a day's worth of food! Remember this even when you're haggling – it may only be over a few quid or even a few pennies but that may buy your meal latter that evening! You have to get things into context and get to grips with the value of money in the country you're in – it may be only a few pence to us, but it goes a lot further in poorer regions! Obsessed with being a tight arse, I've taken this too far at times. I've often met up with my mates out travelling and we've had competitions to see just how little we can get by on! It's got down to less than £2 or £3-a-day in some countries! Be tight with caution though – keeping your wallet firmly shut can be pointless at times as you'll find yourself missing out on lots on stuff! It's important that you get the balance right and spend money on the things that you couldn't do at home! Don't cheat yourself out of experiences just to save a few pounds – the whole idea is to immerse yourself in different things and try new stuff!

Below is a very broad overview of ways to significantly reduce your daily budget and make your money go further. You can make savings on everything from accommodation and food to transport and communication without missing out on anything. Most of this advice will become second nature soon after your arrival and you won't even notice yourself doing it:

ACCOMMODATION... *Hostels, guesthouses & camping!*

Generally you'll find that accommodation is your largest daily expense. You can reduce the cost of your accommodation in a number of ways depending on the region you're in:

Asia & Central America: You'll find it hard pressed to find dorm accommodation in hostels around Asia but **beach huts** and double/triple rooms in **guesthouses** are cheap as chips anyway. Budget accommodation in Central America amounts to **hostels** and a scattering of **guesthouses.** **Hostels** provide lots of dorm accommodation which is a great way to reduce your costs if you're on a real tight budget and travelling on your own. Double/triple private rooms generally work out cheaper if you there's a group of you. To save money in guesthouses stay in rooms with shared communal bathrooms that are located away from the room – not only are these cheaper, they don't smell in the humid climates and tend to be cleaned on a more regular basis. Fans rooms are always cheaper than air-con rooms and you usually pay for the room and not the number of people sharing it. So if you pay for a triple room make sure that you fill it with 2 of your friends or newly acquired travel buddies and split the cost – I've shared a single bed with two of my mates to skimp on accommodation costs and have more for beer! You'll find numerous opportunities to get back to nature and camp in Latin America and this provides a great way to reduce your accommodation costs. Generally speaking camping options in SE Asia are nonexistent or somewhat unsafe!

Australasia *(& wealthier countries)*: **Dorms** in **hostels** are always the preferred choice amongst backpackers – they're a lot cheaper and allow you to mingle with fellow travellers. Check out sites such as www.hostelworld.com – booking in advance with these sites will usually save you a few dollars a night compared to the hostels standard check-in rates and ensure you have a place to stay. If you use these sites regularly it pays to create an account with them and for a small one-off fee, usually around US$10, so you won't be charged for every single future reservation.

If you know you'll be staying somewhere for a fair while – say a week or more – haggle for a discount. Hostels often have a weekly rate that works out significantly lower than their daily rates. It's always worth checking out www.couchsurfing.com where fellow travel minded individuals offer their couch for a few nights free of charge – you'll make lots of new friends while travelling across a country for next to nothing!

EATING... *Eat local & cook your own*

This is potentially another large daily expense. Again it's possible to reduce the cost of your food bill in a number of ways depending on the region you're in:

Asia & Central America: The golden rule to trim down your food bill in less developed regions is to eat the local food. It'll be a challenge to find any facilities to cook your own food but it's cheap enough to eat out every day! Although to the average westerner food prices may seem cheap everywhere, prices are always inflated in tourist areas *(even backpacker areas)* and in guesthouses so do some exploring and **eat where the locals eat!** A good tip is to look for small plastic chairs and tables next to **street kitchens** – they're the sign of bargain food! You'll find great food in the most unlikely of places! Western food is usually the more expensive option and the least appetising. **Street food** is perhaps the best way to reduce your

> ### STREET FOOD... *Cheap & delicious*
>
> Be adventurous and tuck into the street food to discover a mind blowing world of delicious and ludicrously cheap delicacies from fried rice and spring rolls to barbequed giant spiders and fried seasoned insects. Watch them whip up a fresh Pad-Thai from a street cart in Bangkok or fire up your taste buds with some tasty tacos from a market stall in Guatemala and feed yourself for less than 60p! Don't believe the horror stories you hear!

food bill and feed yourself for next to nothing while enjoying some fantastic and interesting grub. **Local markets** are buzzing with tantalising smells, **food stalls** and local produce – they're a great place to eat cheap and offer a fantastic way to experience new exciting dishes. In Central America you'll find an increasing amount of accommodation *(hostels)* that have communal kitchens making it viable to cook your own food – buy your ingredients from local markets and cook in groups.

Australasia *(& wealthier countries)*: In more developed countries restaurants and cafés are nearly always too expensive for the average backpacker to eat in everyday so **cooking your own food** is the way forward. With dorm accommodation you usually have access to a fully kitted-out communal kitchen. Buy your food from supermarkets and go back to living like a student – pasta, noodles, soup, and beans on toast feature regularly on the menu and form a staple part of a backpacker's diet! It's always more economical to cook for more than one person, so if you're travelling in a group take it in turns to buy and cook meals or just split the cost of the ingredients. The exception here is Fiji where local cafés, markets and restaurants are very reasonably priced even by Asian standards. In addition, you'll find

> ### THE FREE SHELF... *Eat for free!!!*
>
> Most hostels *(in Oz & NZ)* have a **'free-shelf'** in their fridges and cupboards. It's a collection of bits and bobs that other backpackers have left behind so have a rummage around and see what interesting meals you can rustle up for free! You can find anything from half full bags of pasta and spaghetti to chunks of cheese and loose eggs. The free shelf is always a good place to stock up on salt & pepper, spices, herbs, butter, oils, sauces and ketchup – the extra little things that add up and make your shopping bill expensive!

that on the majority of Fijian islands, your food, accommodation and transport is included in a 'package deal'. Refill your water bottle from the tap/faucet *(where it's safe)* – it's good for the environment and your budget!

This can easily become your biggest expense – it's usually mine! Drinking's a very popular past-time when you're out travelling and it pains me to say it but try and cut back on the booze, or at the very least drink the cheapest stuff like local rum! There's no denying it's very sociable and a great way to meet people – all the best plans start with 'let's get drunk and then...' – but you can get pissed anytime back home. I know it sounds boring but regular nights out can more than double your budget – especially over a long trip and in destinations like Oz where alcohol is notoriously expensive. Rationing your nights out is the best way to dramatically reduce your daily expenditure so that you'll have more cash for activities and trips that you couldn't necessarily do at home. However, there are a few things that can help get you stumbling around a bit cheaper:

Down Under: Unfortunately, Australia and New Zealand are notoriously expensive for alcohol. The best way to make your night cheaper is to buy alcohol from local shops where prices are more reasonable. 'Goons' *(boxes of wine)* are a cheap favourite in Australia and you'll find lots of travellers drinking these back in their dorms! Generally speaking you'll find Australia more expensive to drink in than the UK while beer in NZ is slightly cheaper than at home. Both countries are heavily geared to backpackers so drink in hostel bars where prices will be easier on your wallet! Most bars in backpacker areas have heaps of drink promotions and extended happy hours so make the most of them and get a taste for discounted drinks! Beer in Fiji is fairly cheap for westerners and a lot cheaper than Oz & NZ. Prices are obviously inflated on the main tourist islands but all bars have happy hours while beer in local shops is fantastically cheap. Buy spirits at the airport though as prices of vodka, whisky and rum tend to be inflated compared to beer prices.

Central America & SE Asia: Thankfully, it's a better story in Central America and SE Asia where it's very cheap to get drunk and you'll find monster 1.25litre bottles of beer! Even in the tourist areas alcohol in bars and restaurants is still cheap compared to the UK. Again, as at home, it's cheaper to buy beer from shops and laws on public drinking throughout most Asia and Latin America are very relaxed – you can happily wander up Khao San Road in Bangkok with a cheap bottle of Chang from a shop and not get any hassle from the authorities. You'll more than likely get a taste for local rum during your travels – probably because rum's always one of the cheapest options across these regions! You'll find people drinking buckets of Samsung Rum & Red Bull on beaches in Thailand and Flor de Caňa rum with coke out of plastic bags on busses across Central America! Basically, buy beer from shops and drink on the beach or outside your beach hut before you hit the 'bars' and clubs – you'll meet loads of people as well and saving a pretty penny!

TRANSPORT... *Use local transport*

Get amongst it and use **public transport** wherever possible – it's usually the cheapest and most interesting form of transport and it'll get you mingling with the locals and fellow shoe-string travellers. If you're travelling with a group of people, it can work out cheaper and more convenient to **hire a car** splitting the cost 3 or 4 ways – just don't forget to factor in the cost of fuel! If you want to travel any significant distance, consider taking **night busses, sleeper trains** and **overnight ferries** – they're nearly always cheaper and it'll also save you forking out for a night's accommodation in a hostel! Look out for long distance budget bus services such as **Greyhound** that operates in Australia, Canada and the USA – they usually offer the cheapest transport links between major cities. Backpacker busses, such as the Kiwi Experience in New Zealand, although tourist-orientated, offer a fairly cheap and very convenient transport option.

COMMUNICATION... *Talk for longer, on-line*

International phone calls: Speaking to loved ones back home can be an expensive affair and will become a major drain on your limited funds. **Phone cards <u>can</u>** be good value, just be sure to scrutinise the small print – they're often plagued with tons of hidden charges in the form of connection fees, activation fees and even daily charges! Global Gossip cards *(Australasia)* provide very cheap international calls and don't have any nasty charges.

Internet: You'll find internet services on even the most remote islands these days so keep in touch for less and try to use free internet based services, such as **Facebook, e-mail** and **MSN** which are easy on your wallet! Make sure that you take advantage of **Skype** *(see box)*. As with restaurants and cafés, internet tends to be more expensive in hostels and tourist areas, so hunt around for local internet cafés and enjoy cheaper internet *(especially in the wealthier countries)*. **Global Gossip** cards across Australia and the Pacific are quite good value but again local internet cafés can be cheaper. If you're planning to take a laptop, some hostels offer free or discounted wireless. Local cafés and large franchises, such as Star Bucks, often provide free wireless access for customers, so nurse a coffee for an entire afternoon and enjoy free wireless until you drain your battery!

SKYPE... *Talk for free!*

Skype has been a revolution for travellers providing good quality video conversation to friends and family around the globe and best of all... it's free! If you're a Skype virgin check it out on www.skype.com and set up an account. Encourage your friends and family to do the same before you go and take advantage of a great free service. If your parents aren't very computer literate, set up an account anyway because you can use your Skype account to make regular phone calls to landlines and mobiles at unbelievably cheap rates. You simply top up your credit on-line and use your account as a pay-as-you-go service. Rates for international calls are extremely cheap and are much more competitive than phone cards.

Mobile *(cell)* **phone:** Check with your service provider before you go, **Texting** *(SMS)* provides a convenient and instant form of contact that doesn't cost an arm and a leg. If you're staying in a particular country for a while, it's worth purchasing a **local SIM card** so that you won't be charged to receive calls and you'll be able to make cheaper international calls and texts.

TRAVEL DISCOUNT CARDS... *Why pay full price?*

There's always a bargain to be had! You can save a stack of money with travel discount cards allowing you to do more and see more with your budget. Travel agencies, such as STA and Kilroy *(Scandinavia)*, will often apply for discount cards for you. If they don't, keep an eye out for useful discount cards such as *(in alphabetical order)*;

o **B.B.H...** The Budget Backpacker Hostel card offers discounted rates in participating hostels around Australia and New Zealand. Check out all the discounts and other offers on their website and order a card www.bbh.co.nz

o **International Student Identity Card *(ISIC)*...** If you're a full-time student or on a gap year then this card is for you. It opens up a world of great discounts and offers on much more than just accommodation. Better still it can be used worldwide and even in the UK! www.ISICcard.com

o **International Youth Travel Card *(IYTC)*...** If you're not a student but 25 or under you can still save some cash with one of these! Benefits include discounts on a range of things from accommodation and transport to attractions and activities

o **NOMADS Adventure Card...** NOMADS members receive cheaper rates at 600 hostels in no less than 23 countries. You'll also be eligible to cheap international phone calls, discounted internet and tonnes more. The Adventure Card is particularly useful in Australia and New Zealand. Check out what nomads can offer and order an Adventure Card on www.nomadsworld.com

- o **V.I.P Backpackers...** Get discounts in over 1,200 participating hostels worldwide. This bright yellow card also gets you discounts on transport, activities, and international phone calls, attractions, restaurants and much more. It's valid in <u>Australia</u>, <u>New Zealand</u>, <u>South Africa</u>, <u>Europe</u> and <u>North America</u>. Check it out <u>www.vipbackpackers.com</u>

- o **Y.H.A...** This card gives you discount in over 4,000 hostels in over 80 countries. You are also eligible for the usual discounts on selected activities, attractions and trips. <u>www.yha.org.uk</u>

For more information and comparisons check out <u>www.gapyear.com/cards</u>. Don't feel as though you have to buy a load of them – public transport and major attractions often have a special 'backpacker price' which you're entitled to when show any form of traveller's discount card.

HAGGLING... *Get it for less!*

Why pay full price when you can haggle! To a lot of westerners it can be an alien concept but it's an everyday way of life in many countries and a custom that could save you a small fortune – some people take to it like a duck to water and others will always feel embarrassed and awkward by the whole saga. Just embrace it and enjoy it! Personally, I love haggling and find it a really fun way to interact with the locals – I'm also a bit of a tight arse so I feel really satisfied when I get a bargain! The art of haggling is acquired through practice so don't be shy and get amongst it. Haggle for everything you can!

Asia and Latin America are prime haggling destinations – you can always get it for less than the advertised price and almost everything is open to negotiation! It's not all about saving a few pennies though, haggling offers you a fun and easy way to interact with the locals – just smile, laugh and joke when you're haggling and don't feel pressured into buying – you can always walk away. Just make sure that you have small denominations to pay for the item(s) otherwise they won't be impressed when you hand over a large note after haggling over pennies! From Thailand and Vietnam to Nicaragua and Guatemala you can barter for anything from souvenirs and gifts on market stalls to accommodation rates and snorkelling trips!

Getting the best deal... *The art of haggling*

1. **Know when to bargain...**

   Most things in Asia and Latin America are open to negotiation unless you see a fixed price. You'll get the best deals in the morning where vendors believe that it's lucky to seal an early deal and are therefore willing to go that little bit lower. Prices are always inflated in the main tourist areas so hunt around and source out more local-orientated markets a few streets away! See how much other travellers pay, and more importantly, take not how much locals pay before you start to haggle.

2. **Start low & use the calculator...**

   They're always going to start way over the top so play the game and start low – very low! Begin with no more than **25%** of what they say and aim to get it for around **30-50%** of their original asking price – just don't take the piss and try to pay less than what you see locals paying for goods! In fact, expect to pay slightly more than locals – that's just the way it is. Play the calculator game; type in how much you want to pay and pass it to them to counter your offer – increase your offer in very small increments and keep handing the calculator back to them! If the country uses two currencies, use this to your advantage and keep converting between the two making it sound like you're willing to pay more – if anything it'll make them laugh!

3. Smile, laugh & stay cool...

Haggling is an everyday way of life in many countries. It's a fun and interactive affair so don't get angry if it's not going your way! Be patient and don't underestimate the important of a smile. Use phrases like, 'what's your best price', 'I want happy hour, special price' and 'good for you, good for me' in a bid to get them to laugh and play along. I always try 'okay, if I have no bag can I have it for..!' Haggling should be fun!

4. Start a bidding war, be persistent & bulk buy...

Bargaining with more than one seller at a time always leads to lower prices! Be persistent and play the vendors against each other to drive the price down! Just say "He'll sell it for x amount, what's your best price" and keep going back and forth! Again remain cool, smile and have fun! No matter how stubborn they appear to be about the price, persistence is a great weapon to wear them down to your price! Simon and I have sat on the floor in the middle of a Thai shop just repeating and singing what we wanted to pay for some legendary Spiderman suits – all in good humour of course – and she got so fed up with us in the end she gave in. So we gave her a nice big hug and a smile! If you intend to buy more than one item, negotiate a price for one, and then ask 'how much for two' and try to get a further reduction for 'bulk buying'! If you're haggling for bus tickets and tours booking in numbers always increases your bargaining power.

5. Act skint...

Don't go into a pocket and pull out a wedge full of notes! Work out how much you want to pay for an item and place that amount in one pocket. Strategically distribute small amounts of money in your other pockets before you begin to haggle. If the vendor is refusing to go as low as you're prepared to pay, empty your pocket in front of them and say 'this is all I've got'. Tap your other pockets and act skint, beg and plead! If they still won't budge, root around in another pocket and act surprised to find a little more!

6. Know when to turn away...

It's bad practice to haggle for an item, agree on a price and then don't buy it! However, turning away and walking off slowly is a powerful way to get an item for the price you want. If you feel they won't go any lower, state the price you want to pay smile and turn away, you'll often find that as you're **slowly** walking away they'll come chasing after you as they realise they've lost a sale and agree on your price or very close!

GUIDEBOOKS... *Exchange them*

You don't need to buy a guidebook for every country that you're planning to visit before you set off. Not only would that be expensive, it'd also be impractical. Buy a few guidebooks before you go and trade them with fellow travellers. You'll find that you can buy the well-known guidebooks – new, second-hand and often photocopied versions – from local entrepreneurs along the well-trodden routes, usually at much cheaper prices. You'll also find that the majority of hostels and guesthouse have book exchanges brimming with used travel guides where you can exchange them as you go! It'll save you a small fortune as well as your back!

WASHING *(Laundry)... Do it yourself!*

Even in wealthier countries laundrettes and laundry services in hostels are relatively cheap, however if things are really tight and you desperately want to cut back, simply wash your own clothes! Bars of soap are readily available from most supermarkets and are fantastically cheap – just don't forget to pack your universal sink plug *(string & dental floss make good clothes lines!)*.

Working can be a great way to boost your budget and inject some extra cash into your travelling funds. It doesn't take much more effort to get a working visa either – contact the relevant embassy to check out the latest regulations and visa requirements. If you think you may want to work but are unsure, get a working visa before you start your trip anyway. This way you'll always have the option to work even if it turns out that you don't need to in the end. Working while you're away is great for a number of reasons;

1) Financially it can mean two things – you can leave for your travels earlier as you won't need to save as much money before you go OR it'll mean that you can stay longer than you originally planned!

2) It's not all about the money though – working will also allow you to have a truly authentic cultural experience away from the tourist gaze. You'll begin to see and feel places from a 'local' perspective

3) Working will create a wealth of opportunities that aren't necessarily available to you as a regular backpacker as you build up some local knowledge and develop 'local contacts'. In some cases it'll give you an opportunity to learn new languages and skills.

While this book doesn't go into any depth – there's just too much to talk about – here's a brief 'bare-bones section' to give you a taste on what's on offer:

DOWN UNDER... *A wealth of opportunities*

Perhaps the best place to look for work and top up your funds when you're out travelling. If you're between 18 and 30 you should qualify for a **Working Holiday Visa** *(WHV)* and there's a wealth of employment opportunities down under. Check out www.immi.gov.au for visa options. Working in Australia and New Zealand has become extremely popular – you really can work your way around these countries! The bad news is that wages on the whole aren't that impressive and the majority of it involves hard manual work, but a few months slogging it out can give your finances just the boost you need to keep travelling! Having said that, there are some very well paid jobs out there, especially if you've got a trade or boast some sought after qualifications.

There's lots of work out there from slogging it out in the searing heat of the outback breaking your back picking fruit, to more conventional work in air-conditioned hostels dealing with fellow backpackers and cleaning duties. You don't have to secure work before you leave – most hostels will help you find work once you're there and the vast majority of them have notice boards bristling with job vacancies and employment agencies. If you're an outdoors person there are plenty of activity based job opportunities in New Zealand from glacier hiking tour guides to bungy jump operators. It does help to do some research before you leave your home country. Here are some useful websites:

Australia:
www.goharvest.com
www.goworkabout.com
www.gowrecruitment.com
www.jobmap.com
www.jobsearch.gov.au/harvesttrail
www.visitoz.org

A Tax File Number *(TFN)* is essential if you plan to work in Australia, if you don't get one the government will take a staggering 47% of you hard earn wages in tax – the good news is, getting one couldn't be easier and you only need to do it once. You must provide this to your employer within 28 days once you've commenced work. Most Working Holiday Maker *(WHM)* visa holders can apply online at www.ato.gov.au. If you end up getting caught out and robbed by the greedy Ozzie government you can get support and claim it back through the **travellersxpress team**. Register online at www.travellersxpress.com

New Zealand: www.nzherald.co.nz/employment
www.seasonalwork.co.nz
www.seek.co.nz
www.traveljobs.co.nz

You'll need a **working visa** to legally work in any of the three countries and you'll have to get this before you arrive in Australasia. Contact the relevant embassies to apply for working visas *(see Section 5... Booking your trip.)*

CENTRAL AMERICA... *Work your way around!*

Sometimes it can pay to do a little work in countries such as Costa Rica, Guatemala, Mexico, Nicaragua and Panama. According to law you must have a working permit to work anywhere in Central America. However, in practice you may get paid under the table or through some bureaucratic loophole in hostels, restaurants and bars! Consequently, a few backpackers work in the recreation business *(diving and hiking type jobs)* but most backpackers will stay and work in backpacker hostels for 'survival wages':

Survival wages: The majority of hostels offer travellers small term contracts, often a month, where you're offered 'survival wages' and benefits such as accommodation and food in return for a few hours work a day – great if you're on a very tight budget and have stacks of time to spare. Typical duties include; cleaning, food preparation, reception work, bar work and general kitchen chores. This is very common in Central America and opportunities are usually advertised in hostel receptions. It provides a great opportunity to explore Central America from a different perspective *(and with very little funds!)* and offers a superb chance to really get stuck to into and truly grasp the Spanish language.

SOUTHEAST ASIA... *Not financially viable!*

Strictly speaking it's not really worth working in most of SE Asia because it's so cheap anyway and the wages won't go far – you'll work a lot for very little by our standards and then there's the red tape and paperwork! Working in some areas can be beneficial though. If you're a keen diver and want the opportunity to become a dive master, many of the dive resorts *(especially Thailand's Southern Islands)* offer to pay or subsidise you in the form of food, accommodation and your course(s) in return for a short term contract, typically 2-3 months. Essentially, you'll increase your number of dives and become a dive master by working as a kind of apprentice – an on the job training scheme where everyone's a winner! You'll come across many Europeans who have stayed in Thailand after completing their courses to work and enjoy the 'diving lifestyle'.

If you've got a teaching qualification, such as TEFLA or CELTA, it can open up many doors. Teaching English is a popular option all over Asia and in some cases it's very well paid *(for example in Hong Kong).*

HOW TO TAKE YOUR MONEY... *Cash, card or traveller's cheques?*

A simple question but you'd be surprised how many people worry about how to take and access their money when they're out and about in foreign countries. Despite heaps of different currencies, it's not as difficult and confusing as you may think. Ideally you want flexibility, convenience and easy access to your money coupled with security and back up should things go wrong. Below are the most common options for a backpacker. It's common for travellers to have/use a mix of these options to suit your needs and suppress your apprehensions:

Cash... *Flexible & practical*

Perhaps, obviously, cash is the most common, flexible and practical way to use your funds and pay for goods and services where ever you are in the world. As opposed to paying with plastic, cash is also a good **budgeting mechanism** – if you've got 1,000BHT in your pocket you can keep track of what you've spent! Local currency can be withdrawn from ATMs and it's a good idea to withdraw a few day's budget at a time. You'll also find currency exchange services everywhere from airports, train stations and bus depots to guesthouses, travel agents and border crossings. Security is the main disadvantage with cash as stolen notes cannot be traced. Lost or stolen cash is usually always excluded from travel insurance policies – which is fair enough really! The moral of the story here – don't carry wads of cash around with you and make use of your money belt.

Different currencies: Another major inconvenience with cash is varying local currencies. If you're travelling between a lot of countries in a short space of time that all use different currencies – like in SE Asia – it's useful to have a small wedge of a common currency, for example US-dollars, in case you get caught short and run out of local currency. In some countries, such as Cambodia and Vietnam, you'll often find yourself paying for meals, accommodation and other stuff in a combination of US-dollars and local currency.

$ THE US-DOLLAR $

Forget being patriotic about your own mighty currency, unfortunately you'll find that the **US-dollar** is the hard currency of choice across the globe. It's the most practical and widely accepted currency which makes it ideal for travelling. Many countries across Asia, Latin America and the Pacific happily accept it alongside local currency – in some cases US-dollars are actually preferred to local currency! However, it's important to make sure that the notes are **clean, new issue, unmarked** and **free from holes, tears** and **severe creases**. If they're not in near pristine condition they're unlikely to be accepted. This goes both ways – check your change and refuse unusable notes otherwise you'll be stuck with them! As with local currency, make sure that you have **small denomination notes** – $1, $5 & $10 notes. Not only are small businesses unlikely to have the cash reserves to offer you change, it's harder to haggle and justify your negotiated price when you whip out and try and pay with a $50 note!

ATMs, debit & credit cards... *Practical & economical*

Debit cards are a very economical and practical way to access your funds and manage your money. It's probably the most convenient way to access your funds. **Debit cards** that are part of the **Visa, Maestro** and **Cirrus** networks are accepted in shops, restaurants and other establishments worldwide and can be used to withdraw local currency from ATMs in towns and cities across the globe. The majority of travellers, including myself, use debit cards to pay for the larger expenses, campervan hire for example, and withdraw sensible amounts – maybe 4-day's or a week's budget – from a cash point *(ATM)* for general day-to-day living costs and activities. Most cards are issued with the 'chip and pin' feature to reduce fraud should you lose your card(s).

Credit cards can also be used worldwide in shops and at ATMs but they're usually utilised by budget backpackers as a source of emergency funds – just use them with caution as they usually attract hefty interest rates.

The Gap Year Card... *The prepaid traveller's card*

The Gap Year Card is a pre-paid MasterCard designed by backpackers for backpackers. It's great for anxious backpackers – not only is it one of the safest ways to carry your money abroad, it also doubles up as a travel discount card where you can make savings on tours and hostels worldwide.

The service allows you to manage your money online and comes with generous ATM withdrawal limits. You can top-up your account in a variety of ways including regular standing orders or at over 14,000 UK locations including Post Offices and e-pay locations. Friends and family can also transfer money into your account. However, if you've got on-line banking with your current bank account and manage your money between your e-saving accounts and your regular account, there's little need for this card.

For more info check out www.gapyearcard.com

Traveller's cheques... *Old school but secure*

Some people swear by traveller's cheques but in reality they're a bit old school and more practical for your conventional 'package-holiday' in Greece. You can't deny that traveller's cheques are great for security and peace of mind but they do have a number of major disadvantages and impracticalities that make them unsuitable for budget backpacking;

o   Traveller's cheques are always subject commission when you purchase them – usually at 1-1.5%

o   You'll more than likely be stung again and have to pay further commission and sometimes extra fees, such as a stamp duty charge (!?), when you cash them in

o   They require careful handling and management – all cheque numbers must be recorded as you cash each one in, mismanagement **can** result in them being irreplaceable, hence useless, should they get stolen!

o   If you lose your passport your travellers' cheques are pretty much useless!

o   They're not always exchangeable in remote areas 'off-the-beaten track' and poorer countries

If you decide to use them, be careful whose cheques you carry – **American Express** is arguably the most widely accepted brand worldwide. They're issued in a number of currencies and again US-dollar cheques are the preferred choice, especially if you're planning to go off-the-beaten track. Keep the receipt from the original purchase and take it every time you want to cash cheques in – some banks required it as a security measure to reduce fraud. Despite their disadvantages, it may be worth having a small amount of traveller's cheques hidden away safely for use in emergencies albeit they're not essential.

CARRYING YOUR MONEY & CARDS... *Money belts*

As far as carrying cash in concerned, don't carry loads around with you! Store the bulk of your cash in your **money belt** and have the smaller denomination notes and coins in your pockets. Nowhere in the world is entirely safe but exercise particular caution in poorer regions, such as SE Asia and Central America, where you'll be seen as very rich and wealthy. Always store your bank cards in separate places and carry them with you or with your other valuables in a safe deposit box should your accommodation have one.

Look, getting mugged isn't part and parcel of your trip but unfortunately there are some despicable human beings scraping around out there and it's a sad fact that you **may** find yourself at the hands of a petty criminal. As well as your cash, they'll be interested in your phone, camera and anything else of value! Whether you're travelling on your own, with a friend or in a group, you're potentially a target. One of my travelling buddies had his bag snatched from his hands by a mounted mugger on a motorbike and another mate woke up to find 'a local' climbing out of his beach hut window with his money belt and shorts(!), so isolated cases do happen.

Thankfully, there are a number of simple and practical ways to reduce your chances of becoming a victim – most of its just common sense:

Conceal your valuables...

Use your money belt as much as possible to keep all of your valuables safely concealed. If your hostel has a safe deposit box, use it and keep all of your valuables safe and sound back at your hostel.

Be sensible...

Most incidents are opportunist crimes, so don't be a twat and tempt them by flashing your camera or i-Pod around! If you need to take pictures make sure you have the strap around your wrist and keep any bags over your shoulder to reduce the chances of them being snatch off you by a mounted moped mugger!

Decoy wallet...

If you're feeling particularly vulnerable consider carrying a spare wallet containing some small denomination notes and coins with you *(the bulk of your main money being in your money belt or hidden else on your person)*. The despicable human trying to rip you off will get what they're looking for and you won't lose as much! It'll also reduce the chances of violent and prolonged confrontation.

Discretion...

Getting lost in a city can be a great way of discovering it, but exercise caution if you require the services of a map. Try not to whip it out in the middle of a city – you may as well have a flashing neon light saying 'tourist' aka 'easy target' above your head! If there are some undesirable looking characters loitering around the place, pop into the nearest café and study the map instead.

IF THE WORST DOES HAPPEN... *Lost or stolen cards & insufficient funds!*

If it all goes tits up don't panic! Whether you've lost your cards, had money stolen or have simply over spent and can't get any more money from the hole in the wall *(ATM)* there's always a solution! Here are the most common scenarios and practical solutions:

Lost / stolen cards...

Cancel your cards immediately and contact your bank for replacement ones – most banks and building societies will send new cards direct to your relevant embassy. It's always a good idea to store your cards in separate places; 'don't put all of your eggs in one basket' so if the worst does happen, at least you'll have access to other cards whilst you're waiting for the replacements – keep one with you at all times *(in your money belt)* and one hidden inside your main backpack at your hostel or in a safe deposit box.

Insufficient funds...

Run out of money – woken up with a bad head to find that you've blown all your money on Mr Chang, gone on a mega shopping spree or got carried away pursing tonnes of adrenaline fuelled activities and need some cash quickly? It's possible to have money 'wired' to you for a small charge. **Western Union** *(www.westernunion.com)* and **MoneyGram** *(www.moneygram.com)* both offer a great service to transfer money to you from a willing donor – cue mum & dad!

No cash or ATMs...

Sometimes you'll get caught short and end up in places where cashpoints are very sparse finding yourself somewhere with no local currency. This can be particularly problematic in the less-developed countries such as Laos, El Salvador and less tourist orientated towns in Vietnam. Don't panic – many hotels and travel agencies offer a service known as a **cash advance.** This service is like cash-back but you don't buy anything! It usually attracts a small percentage charge, often around 2-5%.

HOW I ACCESS & CARRY MY FUNDS... *Learn from my mistakes!*

I didn't really have a clue when I embarked on my first backpacking trip – I just went armed with a debit card without much thought about local currency and the availability of ATMs! Luckily it turned out that there are loads of ATMs across SE Asia! I've turned up in towns like Vinh *(Vietnam)* with no local currency and had to frantically traipse around the city for hours in search of a compatible ATM. I've also ran out of cash in towns like Luang Probang in Laos where there are no ATMs and had to borrow money of generous and trusting travellers or get cash advances!

Over my numerous trips and learning from my many mistakes, I've developed my own techniques to access and carry my money:

Debit cards:	I use these to access my funds and get local currency via ATMs. I always have two cards for two different accounts. I always have one card on me and the other either hidden in my backpack or in a safe deposit box
Cash:	I never get any local currency before I go – I get it when I land at the airport at the start of my trip via an ATM. I tend to withdraw and carry less than a week's budget at a time and try to get the smallest denomination notes as possible. If I get large denomination notes from the ATM I just go into local shops and try to exchange it for smaller notes or buy something small to break into it. Small notes are great for haggling! I pay for nearly everything in cash because it's convenient and it makes it easier to budget and keep track of my expenditure
Overdraft:	I always use an overdraft as a source of emergency funds and prearrange this with my bank before I go
US-dollars:	If I'm travelling in SE Asia or Central America I always have a small stash of US-dollars on me, say $50 in 5, 10, and 20 note denominations, in case I get short of local currency
Money belt:	I've seen my mate being pick-pocketed in plain view and in broad daylight outside a café in Manila *(Philippines)* so I always use my money belt in poorer regions. I hide the bulk of my money, my debit card and passport in it. I have a small amount of low denomination notes and coins in my pocket so I can pay for food and busses without having to fumble around in my money belt all of the time and make it obvious I'm carrying valuable stuff!
Planning:	If I'm heading off-the-beaten track for a few days or heading through towns that I know won't have any cash points, I'll plan ahead and withdraw extra money before leaving. Sounds simple, but lots of people get caught out!

4) EQUIPMENT...

...*What to cram in your backpack*

CONTENTS

Guidebooks are bursting with varying lists of itinerary and advice, but at the end of the day, it's down to personal preference and your chosen destination. A word of caution though, theft occurs everywhere – even in paradise – and we all lose the odd camera or phone on a binge drinking session, so whatever you take be prepared to come home without it!

Use common sense and don't pack too much, if you're not sure whether you'll need something, the chances are you won't, so don't pack it! Don't panic and don't be scared to pack light, **less really is better**! Be economical and don't assume that you have to take everything with you from home. A lot of your equipment you'll be able to get hold of, usually at cheaper prices, along the way. Travelling isn't a fashion show so if you want to travel light, don't be scared to leave those hairdryers and straighteners at home! **You can't take everything** and the stuff you do pack should be as **light** and **compact** as possible. Above all, make sure that you pack a sense of adventure!

Use the following **2 lists** of suggested inventory as a guideline:

1) **The essential *(budget)* list:** An inventory of the basic items and documents that you'll need on an 'average backpacking trip' whether it'll be a month or a year, in Australia, Costa Rica or Thailand

2) **The optional list:** This second list includes *(optional)* items that you don't necessarily need, but bits and pieces that will make you trip a little easier and more comfortable – although not necessarily more enjoyable!

THE ESSENTIALS... *'Budget' list*

Backpack *(+ daypack)*

Backpack Vs wheelie case? Some people argue that you can travel adequately with a suitcase, wheelie case *(basically a suitcase with wheels)* or something similar. If you're planning a small trip and you don't intend to go far off-the-beaten track, a wheelie case will **probably** be <u>ok</u>. However, it's fair to say that if you're planning to travel for longer than a month a backpack wins whatever way you look at it – especially if you're going to go on roads less-travelled. Realistically it's the most practical way of travelling. After all, it's called **backpacking** for a reason! Here are just a few reasons to choose a backpack over a suitcase or wheelie case:

o Suitcases are awkward to carry over long distances and even wheelie bags are a pain in the arse to drag along bumpy roads, lug up flights of stairs, board boats with and hop on a motorbike taxi with!

o Some wheelie bags do have straps, essentially transforming them into a backpack, but they're size and shape means they're not as comfortable or practical as a proper ergonomically designed backpack

o Unlike a backpack, wheelie bags tie your hands up and make simple tasks like reading your guidebook or a map very awkward

o Wheelie bags are not securely attached to you and can be easily snatched from you

o A backpack will make you look like a hardcore seasoned traveller and a suitcase make you look a stupid package-holidaymaker!

Backpacks are hard wearing and are far more versatile boasting practical features that are specifically designed for travelling and other activities involved with backpacking. See page 227 for advice on your backpack and daypack.

Passport!

· Make sure you do those final checks for your passport before you leave for the airport! A **passport holder** is a good idea – after many months on the road stuffed in your money belt your passport takes a lot of punishment! Border officials in foreign countries can get bullish when they're presented with dog-eared and creased passports – believe me it's just not worth the hassle!

Driving licence

Your driving licence is an ideal form of additional ID. It saves you carrying your passport around with you and risk losing it, especially when you're out knocking back a cold beer or two! Your driving licence will give you more freedom and flexibility opening up a whole range of exciting adventures – go off-the-beaten track on a hired motorbike and find secluded beaches on tropical islands in Thailand, hire out a 'Wicked' campervan and make the great Aussie pilgrimage up the eastern seaboard of Australia, or rent a yellow school bus and embark on a wild road trip across the USA along the famous Route 66! While you'll rarely be asked for a driving licence in countries such as Thailand and El Salvador it's a good idea to apply for an **international driving licence** to avoid disappointment in other countries where the driving laws are likely to be enforced – they're available from most Post Offices *(in the UK)* and don't cost much. Have a quick check and make sure that your licence won't expire while you're away!

Travel insurance

Travel insurance will provide cover for a range of incidents ranging from theft and lost luggage to cancelled flights and even hostage situations! Most importantly, a good travel insurance policy will cover you for any medical treatment. Don't gamble and be stung by huge medical bills. Hospital charges, particularly in the USA, can quickly rack up so be prepared and make sure you are covered for any unfortunate incidents. Refer to Section 6... *Booking your trip,* for the low-down on travel insurance and tips to reduce your premiums *(page 259).*

Photocopies

In case you lose the original items, it's a good idea to photocopy all of your important documents, such as:

- o   Insurance policies
- o   The main passport pages and any pre-arranged visas
- o   E-tickets for your flights & any hostel bookings

It's also a good idea to scan these photocopies and e-mail them to yourself for added security. Whilst these copies can't be used as replacements for the original items, they can make things a little easier if the worst does happen.

Money belt

Absolutely essential! Remember that you'll most probably be visiting some very poor countries where you'll be seen as extremely rich and wealthy – and there's no question that you're comparatively rich when you consider that the daily minimum wage in Thailand hovers around 175BHT – that's only just enough for 2 large bottles of shop bought Chang *(beer)*!

Some people travel with bum-bags *(fanny-packs)* – not only will you look like a twat, they're a security nightmare since they're easily removed from you in a matter of seconds without you even knowing! Don't become an unfortunate victim of mugging or theft, money belts provide the easiest and safest way to carry your money, cash cards, passport and driving licence with you at all times. They're worn around the waist and under your shorts or trousers *(pants)*, or around your neck and under your t-shirt, to conceal your valuables – they're designed to be slim-line and almost invisible so don't over pack them. The most important things to guard are your passport, tickets, money and cards. Don't put items in there that you'll need access to every 10 minutes! Fabric money belts are better than their leather or plastic counter parts as they don't get as sweaty and uncomfortable. Monet belts are available at most outdoor shops, travel shops and airport stores.

First-aid kit

Obviously you're not planning on hurting yourself, but be prepared for anything from headaches and mosquito bites to those unavoidable scraps and bangs. In hot humid climates open wounds take a lot longer to heal and infections set in very quickly. Armed with a first-aid kit your can treat wounds immediately and reduce the chances of infection and relieve your discomfort. See Section 4 for advice on constructing a basic first-aid kit. Plasters are great to repair holes in mosquito nets while painkillers and rehydration salts are perfect for soothing those murky heads – although we found that prolonging hangovers through sustained drinking *(4-day benders)* was just as effective!

Sarong *(instead of a towel)*

Shake of that girlie image of the sarong and make sure you have one. It's amazing what you can do with this versatile piece of flamboyant: you can use it as a bath and beach towel, a lightweight blanket, a bag for your dirty washing and even wear it! They're cheap, lightweight and quick drying making them an ideal alternative to a conventional bath towel *(even travel towels)* that can be heavy and slow drying. Sarongs are readily available everywhere from Thailand to Costa Rica.

Digital camera

Pictures are a must have souvenir! Prove where you've been, what you've been up to and capture your adventures for others to enjoy in envy and for you to look back on in years to come. You can pick up a half decent digital camera almost anywhere at a reasonable price. It's worth buying a few large size memory cards so you don't run out of space when you get snap happy – and don't forget to back your photos up every few weeks onto a CD or data-stick in case the unfortunate does happen and you lose your camera along with all of your treasured pictures!

Slim line camera or digital SLR?

There's always the debate whether it's worth forking out and lugging around an SLR. There's no doubt that you'll get far superior photos with an SLR but they're not entirely suitable for backpacking – they're heavy, take up a lot of space and are expensive. Most travellers find that a slim line digital camera is more than adequate with appropriate features that make them ideal for travelling – they're cheaper, smaller, lighter and more durable than an SLR. If you really can't decide consider getting a **bridge camera** – a SLR-slim line hybrid. They're a great comprise between an SLR and a slim line camera.

If you go for a slim line camera, you'll definitely benefit from having a one with a good optical *(not digital)* zoom. If you can afford it, get your hands on a waterproof digital camera – you won't regret the extra few quid that you spend when you capture some awesome images of life beneath the waves when you go snorkelling or diving. They're also great for mucking about on the beach.

Mosquito repellent

A cheap and simple form of mosquito-bite protection, mosquito repellent is an effective way to reduce the risk of being bitten and it won't cost you the earth. Buy a little before you go and stock up on the road.

Sun glasses, suntan lotion & moisturiser

Protect yourself from the punishing sun. As well as the health risks, there's nothing more uncomfortable than sunburn when you're travelling – the combination of red raw flesh and a sandy bed doesn't make for the best night's sleep, so be sensible and slap on that cream! Moisturiser will also preserve your tan for longer! For further advice, flick through to page 234 in Section 5.

Travel guide(s)

Keep in the know. Packed with highlights and recommendations on everything from food and accommodation to activities and volunteer opportunities, travel guides are a very valuable resource. They offer firsthand experience and allow you to make the most out of your time in each destination. Saying that, check out their recommendations, but don't stick too rigidly to them. You simply will not have the time to do everything that is written in them, and many of the top recommended hostels will be crammed with travellers clutching the same guidebook as you! Be adventurous – going off-the-beaten track adds excitement and authenticity to a trip making it more challenging and rewarding. This is where you'll meet some of the most interesting people and have the wackiest adventures!

Choosing a guidebook...

Choosing a guidebook is completely down to personal preference, you may prefer one series because they have clearer maps or better activity recommendations. Take your time and have a good look through the guides before you buy. It's often a good idea to borrow some from the library to compare and test drive a few before you part with your hard earned cash. There are many good travel guides to choose from, but you can't go wrong with any guidebooks from these titles – **Lonely Planet**, **Rough Guide** and **Footprint**.

Notebook / diary (journal) & pen(s)

Internet blogs and e-mail are probably the most practical way of recording your trip and keeping in touch with folks back home, but it's always nice to have somewhere to jot down fellow traveller's contact details should you find yourself away from the modern comforts trekking in the middle of a tropical jungle or enjoying the delights of a remote tranquil island.

Be a travel Guru: Keep a record of the hostels you stayed in and your wacky activities so that you can pass on your own advice to people who are looking to venture where you've already been. Jot down your day-to-day activities, observations and emotions – you'll appreciate it in years to come – it's amazing just how much you forget and it'll make a great souvenir. My friend and I have a great diary of our drunken rampages through Asia and it makes for some interesting reading now a few years later! Keep track of your budget and note down the cost of hostels, transport and your daily expenditure.

Contraceptives, tampons & sanitary towels

Oral contraceptives, such as the pill, can be hard to get hold of, and may not be as reliable as the brand prescribed by your GP. Condoms are a must if you're hoping to get lucky and are looking for some love with fellow travellers or the local folk – lads you don't want it to fall off or get an unexpected and expensive knock on the door 9 months later, so make sure you bag up! Buy only recognizable brands of contraceptive when you're out travelling and it's advisable to buy them from air-conditioned shops so the rubber hasn't perished in the heat. Sanitary items, such as tampons, can be hard to find in some regions such as SE Asia and out of main urban areas, so make sure you bring a decent supply with you.

Toiletries

Think simple and just take essentials. Here's a basic list, although many of these toiletries can be bought while you're on the road:

- **Toothpaste & Toothbrush** – everyone hates bad breath and everyone dreads dentist bills!
- **Razor & shaving foam / gel** – errrr for shaving!
- **Shampoo** – if you must have conditioner, consider a 2-in-1 to save space & weight!
- **Shower gel** – bars of soap are impractical – they don't last long, get dirty very quickly and are awkward to store. If you're on a real tight budget and short of space in your bag, shower gel makes a great alternative to soap, shampoo and shaving gel!
- **Deodorant** – dry-sticks & roll-ons are better. Fragrant body-sprays attract insects and mosquitoes. Sprays can also pierce/burst in transit and take up more space than a dry-stick

Be sensible and use a bit of common sense; buy small bottles of toiletries to conserve space and weight in your backpack – you can stock up when you're out travelling. Don't forget that your backpack will take a bit of a beating, so think ahead and buy practical. Hard tubes of toothpaste and plastic packaged toiletries *(as opposed to glass bottles)* can help avoid unnecessary spillages in your backpack. You can take a travel wash bag if you like but a simple carrier bag is all you really need to put your tooth brush in! Place shampoo and shower gels in a plastic bag to help contain spillages if they do occur.

Padlock *(ideally coded & keyless ones)*

Although they <u>can</u> scream 'I've got something to steal', a set of small sturdy padlocks will provide a visual deterrent for opportunity thieves at airports, bus terminals and train stations. If you're planning to stay in dorms or plan to rough it camping, a sturdy padlock is an essential security measure. Dormitories often provide generously sized lockers, but no padlocks, so make sure you pack a decent one before you go. In addition, many guesthouses have features that allow you to use your own padlocks on their room doors as well as the standard lock for additional security. It's a good idea to have more than one key, and keep them in separate places. Ideally, as my best mate now knows, get **coded padlocks** so you can't lose the keys and end up with compartments of your bag permanently locked up!

Torch *(flashlight)*, preferably a head-torch

It's hard to believe but not all parts of the world have electricity! Forget fumbling around in remote beach huts or rummaging through your daypack on busses in the middle of the night – make sure you pack a torch! If you're planning to camp regularly, a torch and spare batteries are essential. Maglites are good but they're heavy and abuse batteries like there's no tomorrow *(even the mini-Maglites)*. Generally, LED head-torches are the preferred choice – they're smaller, lighter and more efficient, and are therefore more practical for travelling. You can find some decent and efficient 'wind up' torches from outdoor shops that don't require any batteries – ideal!

Pocketknife

It always pays to carry something like a Swiss Army Knife with you on your travels. Whether you use it to spread cream cheese on some bread for a quick snack on a bus or to open beer bottles down on the beach, you'll soon realise how handy they are. Keep it close to hand or in your daypack but just don't forget to put it in your backpack at the airport or security and customs will confiscate it!

Clothes...!

Packing light is the name of the game. Remember that in most places you can always buy additional clothing, usually at cheaper prices! Whether you're planning to go away for 3 months or 12 months, you won't necessarily need to pack different amounts of clothing – you can wash your clothes so pack as little as possible! See later sub-section for advice on what to pack. No matter where you're travelling it's a god idea to bring a warm jacket, preferable a breathable and waterproof one.

Travel adaptors

You'll no doubt be taking some kind of electrical equipment like a camera, mobile phone or mp3 player so you'll need an international travel adaptor to charge all of these wherever you are. To save you carrying more than one, you can get durable light weight all-in-one adaptors that fit into any socket worldwide. You can pick them up at most major high street chains, travel shops and outdoor stores. You'll also find them at airports, albeit at an inflated price!

MP3 player & portable speakers *(Personally I'd say essential!)*

Relieve the boredom of those long tedious bus journeys or chill-out on the beach with your favourite tunes. Swing in a hammock on the veranda of your beach hut to the music bellowing from your MP3 player and mini speakers. Chuck in a few cold beers, even a few Samsung buckets, and you'll appreciate the social benefits of having an MP3 player. Be the centre of the party! It's a great way mix with other backpackers and make travel buddies.

Playing cards *(Personally I'd say essential!)*

A simple pack of playing cards can provide hours of *(free!)* entertainment. Play, teach and learn card games with strangers on busses, fellow travellers in your hostel and even locals in the street – it's a great way to 'break the ice' and meet new people almost anywhere and they'll fit neatly into your daypack. Shit Head is a popular traveller's game!

Mobile *(cell)* phone

Check with your service provider before you go, texting *(SMS)* can provide a very quick and economical way of keeping in touch with friends and family back home. If you're planning to spend a long time in a particular country it's often very economical and convenient to buy a local SIM card. Make sure you're awake for those early morning busses and make the most of the happy hour down at the pub – a mobile is ideal for wake up alarms and general timekeeping.

Mosquito net *(& hanging kit!)*

Mosquitoes don't rank high on anyone's list of favourite animals! The bites of Mosquitoes are not only uncomfortable and itchy, they carry a very real risk of several potentially life-threatening diseases – see page 235 in Section 5. Prevention is better than cure and a mosquito net can provide the first line of defence against these little pests. Some people argue they're essential but I lugged one around Asia for 6 months and didn't use it once – I've never taken one with me travelling since. Where mosquitoes are a pain hostels usually provide nets anyway. However, it's fair to say that the ones in beach huts are usually riddled with holes big enough to fit your head through – use plasters to patch up any holes! If you are going to buy one, make sure that your net has a hanging kit *(to hang up your net)*, if not buy one separately.

Guitar

At times it'll be a pain in the arse to carry around with you but they're fantastically sociable. There's nothing better than someone playing the guitar to relieve the boredom on a tedious boat journey or strumming a few songs on the beach relaxing with a few cold beers. With the annoying surplus charges imposed by most airlines to take musical instruments onboard, it's probably more economical to buy a cheap one when you're there – you can pick them up pretty cheap in countries such as Thailand and Mexico. If you can't play and want to learn there's no better time when you're away! If you're a bit skint you could even play for a few beers!

Digital cam-recorder

Sometimes a camera just can't capture it all. You'll look like a Japanese tourist but you'll be able to record all of you exciting activities, crazy adventures and capture all of the cultural diversity and stunning landscapes of fascinating 'alien places'.

Laptop

The advantages of taking a laptop are endless – you can organise and store all of your photos, save precious time and money in internet cafés by using Wireless facilities, entertain yourself and others anywhere at any time with music, games and DVDs! However, with the very real possibility of theft and accidental damage in transit, coupled with the additional space and weight a laptop can take up, it's not always practical to take one. If you want to take one pack a **Netbook**. These small, lightweight laptops are more practical for travelling being reasonably priced and only weighing around a kilo – and don't worry, the keys are still big enough for even the chunkiest of fingers! In general, the longer your trip is the more you'll benefit from taking a laptop. Personally, I've always taken a laptop and would recommend it – although I have been fortunate and haven't had it stolen or damaged. Always keep it in your daypack so that you can take it with you on busses etc..

Neck pillow

A 24-hour bus journey isn't great at the best of times, but on some of the bumpiest and run down roads in the world you'll be screaming out for a neck pillow. Inflatable, lightweight and cheap, this little life saver will give you that extra comfort and will slip neatly into your day-pack without taking up valuable space. Just make sure you get an inflatable one.

Sleeping bag liner *(my best mate would say essential!)*

Even if you're not planning on camping, a sleeping bag liner can be extremely handy and provide a little extra comfort for minimal space and weight. It'll provide a practical barrier against irritable hazards such as bed bugs, dirty bedding and poor cleaning standards that can be found in many hostels. During a bus journey in the cold of night, or tossing-and-turning in a chilly dorm it can provide a little extra warmth without making you sweaty and uncomfortable. My best mate took one during our six month trip around SE Asia and he got so attached to it he even used it when we got home! Sleeping bag liners can be found at the majority of camping and outdoor stores and are reasonably priced.

Pocket calculator / calculator watch

Not too good with numbers? It can be a nightmare to get to grips with the value of money in some regions when you're travelling through many countries that all use different currencies. With some absurd exchange rates like 30,000 Vietnamese Dong to just one British Pound, coupled with low denomination notes, you'll literally be a millionaire in some countries and have a stack of unrecognisable notes to fumble through. It's easy to get confused so carry a pocket calculator. It'll save you a lot of time, frustration and money. In some instances you'll be see products priced in a local currency, haggle in the local currency and then be charged in US-dollars and at the end you'll most probably try and compare that to your own currency! Alternatively, if want to get retro, take a classic calculator watch – they're very practical, cheap and a great haggling tool! They're also great for money exchange – particularly at border crossings where people will try and take advantage of weary travellers who are eager to get some local currency and are unfamiliar with the exchange rates.

Universal sink plug

Simple, light and very handy, a universal sink plug can save hours of frustration and will slip easily into your backpack. You'll find that a lot of hostels and guesthouses do not have plugs so they're very useful if you plan to wash your clothes yourself *(to save money!)*, for general day-to-day hygiene and wet shaving.

Tent *(especially for Central America & Australasia)*

Carrying a tent and camping is a great way to save huge amounts of money on accommodation. The only big down side is the weight of the dam thing! Whether you decided to take one should largely depend on where you're planning to travel to – they're pretty useless in SE Asia but are great in Central America. Make sure that you can strap it securely to your main backpack as most airports and airlines won't let you take it onboard as hand luggage *(for security reasons)*. Don't feel that you have to buy a tent before you go and lug it around with you for your entire trip. It's often cheaper and more practical to buy one when you're out and about. You can always buy a tent from other cash-strapped travellers who are heading elsewhere. Do the same once you've finished with yours and sell it – it'll give you some extra beer money and save you the hassle of carrying it with you.

Lightweight sleeping bag

Camping? Even in hot climates you'll need something to sleep in. The temperature can plummet during the night and a sleeping bag will provide an extra barrier against mosquitoes and other insects that you accidentally zip in! Obviously, the smaller and lighter, the better.

Outdoor clothing & equipment

If you plan to do any specialist outdoor activities, such as hiking, bring appropriate clothing and equipment. For example, you'll need warmer clothing and appropriate footwear if you intend to do any activities such as volcano hikes or trekking. For activities such as snorkelling, diving and skiing equipment is nearly always provided. After you've finished your specialised activities, send your equipment home and save yourself lugging it around!

Essentials	Optional
Backpack & daypack	MP3 player
Passport	Playing cards
Driving licence	Mobile *(cell)* phone
Travel insurance	Mosquito net *(& hanging kit)*
Money belt	Guitar
Photocopies of documents	Digital cam-recorder
First-aid kit	Laptop
Sarong	Neck pillow
Digital camera	Sleeping bag liner
Mosquito repellent	Pocket calculator / calculator watch
Sunglasses, suntan lotion & moisturiser	Universal sink plug
Travel guide(s)	Tent
Diary *(journal)* / notebook & pen	Lightweight sleeping bag
Condoms, tampons & sanitary towels	Outdoor clothing; waterproofs & footwear
Toiletries	
Padlocks	
Torch *(flashlight)*	
Pocketknife	
Clothes!	

Once again... *Less is better!*

This really can't be stressed enough. Nearly everyone 'over-packs' on their first trip and of course you would if you've only been on the typical two week package-trip. The essential list may look fairly long, but if you take a close look, most of its just paperwork, toiletries and medical stuff – nothing really that bulky or weighty. I arrived in Bangkok at the start of my first trip with a near empty backpack – probably because my best mate and I woke up late and hung-over the day we were due to fly and we hadn't packed the night before – filled with little more than a couple of shorts, a few t-shirts, a first-aid kit and a guidebook! And to be honest, I didn't really buy much along the way expect a few cheap tops from Khao San Road, sun cream and bottles of Samsung *(the legendary Thai whisky)* for the bus!

CLOTHING... *Packing for different climates*

Packing for hotter tropical climates... *Light & loose*

As you'll most probably be venturing into hotter climates you can leave the thick tops, jeans and jackets at home! For these hotter tropical climates you'll need clothes that are loose and lightweight. You'll be in boardies and flip flops most of the time so you want need much underwear! Bear in mind that waist lines usually shrink so if you're boardies are a bit loose now they'll be hanging down exhibiting your arse crack and more within a matter of weeks! As a guideline you should be looking to take no more than;

- o 2 or 3 pairs of Shorts, preferably boardies *(for both swimming and general wear!)*
- o A couple of Bikinis – obviously for the ladies, unless it's a man-kini!
- o A pair of lightweight long trousers *(pants)* – preferably not jeans
- o 1-2 pairs of ¾ length trousers / light skirts / dresses *(ideal for evenings)*
- o Underwear *(a minimal amount – none required for boardies! More for cooler climates where you need to wear trousers e.g. New Zealand!)*
- o 2 lightweight long sleeve tops *(for the odd chilly night and to keep mosquitoes at bay)*
- o 5+ t-shirts/tops/vests
- o 1 lightweight waterproof jacket *(preferably)* or a hoody / fleece like top
- o Flip-flops *(Jandals / Thongs)* – you'll live in these!

If you're planning to venture around SE Asia or Central America it's wise not to take your favourite clothes – their washing techniques take their toll on your clothes and they won't last long, so avoid spoiling the best of your wardrobe and take a set of clothes that you don't mind ruining. Your best bet is to take a few tops and buy the bulk of your travel wear when you're there – you can pick up most stuff from shorts and t-shirts to flip-flops and sunglasses dirt cheap at markets and street stalls!

Packing for cooler climates... *The layers technique*

Obviously be sensible and pack suitable warmer clothing if you're planning to go to cooler climates and substitute items such as shorts for jeans and flip flops for trainers! If your trip only includes a few weeks in a colder climate, say New Zealand or the mountainous regions of Guatemala and Nicaragua, go for the layers technique – this makes the most out of your 'tropical clothing' and allows you to pack lighter. Just remember that even in Thailand and Laos the high altitude regions are significantly cooler so pack according. You may also like to pack a few additional items, such as a winter jacket, a few more pairs of trousers, trainers, a hat, gloves and scarf and some thicker socks. Bear in mind that you can always send the heavier 'cooler climate clothing' home once you've reached the 'tropical sector' of your trip.

Specialist equipment... *Send it home after you've finished with it!*

If you're planning to take part in any extreme sport check if the equipment is supplied. With the majority of sports, such as skiing, diving, snorkelling and even glacier and volcano hiking, equipment is nearly always provided. However, it's advisable to bring your own boots and decent socks if you're a keen hiker. It may also pay to take other equipment such as a compass, thermos flask, thermals and quality waterproofs with you if you're really serious about the outdoors. Just don't forget that you don't have to lug any of this specialist equipment around with you for your entire trip. Be practical and send it home once you've finished with it!

CHOOSING A BACKPACK... *Try before you buy!*

Your backpack is the most important piece of equipment. Boring as it may seem, it's worth investing a considerable amount of **time** and **money** in a decent backpack, it needs to be tough, durable and comfortable – you'll be living out of it for your entire trip! You won't regret the time and effort you put into choosing the right backpack. It's the one piece of equipment you shouldn't skimp on so be prepared to pay anywhere between £80 and £200. It's worth buying a reputable brand, such as, **Berghaus, Everest, Haglöfs, Karrimor, Lowe Alpine** or **The NorthFace.** You really do get what you pay for and the better makes will have sturdier zips, better quality synthetic fabrics, more comfortable padded straps and will boast more practical features. A good quality backpack will last you for many trips to come.

The golden rule – make sure your backpack is comfortable. **'Try Before You Buy'** is the best advice when looking for a one – you don't want to get half way around the world to find that your backpack rubs, digs in and gives you a sore back. Comfort and practicality should come before looks! Shop around – you can find great deals on the internet but don't order blind. If you find a bargain backpack on the net, see if you can find the same model in a shop and try it on to see if it's comfortable and practical!

What features to look for...?

o   **Detachable daypack:** These zip off of the main backpack and are usually about 10-15 litres in size. They're perfect for trips to the beach, day excursions and bus journeys *(see page 229).* If your backpack doesn't have a detachable daypack, be sure to you buy a small ordinary rucksack *(like the ones you use for school)* – they really are priceless!

o   **Adjustable frame:** Not everyone's the same height! A backpack with an adjustable frame will allow you to adjust the straps in relation to the frame, and hence, it'll be a lot more comfortable. This feature is particularly important if you're not 'average' size or build *(tall, short, stocky etc..!)*

o   **Side loading:** This basically means that your bag will have zips down either side so your backpack will open up more like a suitcase. It'll allow you to pack easier, quicker and more organised than a conventional top loading backpack

o   **Internal compression system:** Put simply, a set of adjustable straps inside your backpack that clip together. These are very useful to hold the contents of your bag in place and allow you to cram more stuff in and pack in a more organised fashion

o   **Zip-away straps:** Protect your straps and prolong the life of your bag. Airports can get fussy when your bag has straps hanging off everywhere, often you'll need to lug your bag off to the oversized luggage section, so zip away your straps and keep them happy!

o   **Rain cover:** Pretty obvious – protects your backpack from the rain, very useful in tropical downpours! When you're wearing your backpack or storing it in the luggage compartment of a bus, use the rain cover – it'll make it trickier for opportunist thieves to unzip your bag for a rummage and deprive your of your hard earned goods and dirty clothes!

o   **Waist & chest straps:** These are pretty standard features, even on cheaper backpacks. These adjustable straps distribute the weight of your backpack and take pressure off of your back and shoulders distributing it down your back and onto your hips and legs – the strongest and sturdiest part of your body. Better quality packs tend to have thicker padded hip-belts. Your bag should 'sit' on your hips and not sag around your bum!

The 'thinner' the backpack the better – an ideal backpack shouldn't be much wider than your shoulders. Huge side pockets, although handy, won't make you any friends on busses where you'll find yourself smacking everyone on the head as you walk up the aisle!

What size...? *As small as possible*

You need to compromise here. Sure you need a bag big enough to fit everything in, however the usual scenario is – the bigger the bag, the more stuff you will cram in that you don't need! As a general rule, a **55 litre** backpack is more than adequate, even for longer trips. I tend to travel with a 55 litre bag and find that it's only half full most of the time, so don't be afraid to use a 45 or even 35 litre backpack. If you've a smaller bag you may be able to take it on as hand luggage saving you time *(and possibly money)* at the airport – although, thanks to idiots who think it's fun to fly planes into buildings, strict restrictions on certain items in your hand luggage has somewhat spoilt and restricted this option.

PACKING YOUR BACKPACK... *Making life on the road a little easier*

It sounds like a simple task but you'd be surprised how some people just randomly chuck their stuff into their backpack. Now believe me when I say this – if you pack your bag properly it'll make your life on the road a lot easier and less frustrating. It only takes a bit of common sense but here are some pointers;

- o Pack light and try to distribute the weight around the rucksack – if you pack all of the weight at the bottom or cram the heaviest things in the top pocket of your bag it'll be very uncomfortable and you'll find it hard to keep your balance! Ideally try and keep the heavier things as close to your body as possible and distribute the weight evenly from top to bottom

- o Make use of your bags features. Compression systems and compartments will help you to pack more and will give your bag more support and help prevent sagging and random weight distribution in your backpack

- o Try to pack in a structured and organised fashion – place things that you don't need regularly at the bottom of your bag *(like dirty washing, your sleeping bag etc...)*. Take a few plastic carrier bags with you to separate your dirty washing and keep your clean clothes smelling fresh!

- o Keep anything you need regularly or in an emergency near the top of your bag, in your side pockets or in the top compartment of your bag *(such as your first aid kit)* – just don't keep valuables in them as it's easier to steal from your side pockets

- o Place your toiletries either in a toiletry bag or simply in a plastic carrier bag to keep them together and to contain any spillages or leaks. It's a good idea to pack these near the top of your backpack so they aren't squashed between everything else!

- o Think about the electrical items you're taking – try to reduced the amount of plug adaptors and chargers you need to take with you as they take up space and will add considerable weight

- o Make your bag easily identifiable at airports and bus stations and tie your sarong or a brightly colour string to your bag! Alternatively, sow on flags to your bag as you visit each country – you'll easily be able to recognise your bag and it'll make a cool souvenir while making you look like a seasoned traveller!

- o Most importantly, make use of your **daypack** *(see next page)*

You should be able to pack and unpack your backpack quickly. Sounds stupid but practice packing and unpacking – you'll soon find a routine and find specific practical places for certain items. Sometimes you'll be in a rush for a bus and you'll not regret the time you spent practising!

Weigh it! Pack **all** of your equipment and jump onto some regular household scales with your pack on and note the weight. Do the same without your pack – the difference in weight will be the weight of your backpack. Check it against the weight allowances for **all of your flights** before you get to the airport! Bear in mind that your backpack tends to get heavier as you travel – as you pick up souvenirs, stock up on water, books and so on – so don't pack it near the weight limit. REMEMBER PACK AS LIGHT AS POSSIBLE!

Adjust your backpack so it's set up for **you**. Make sure the frame is adjusted and the straps are correctly adjusted so your backpack is comfortable from day one. Pack your backpack and put it on – you should be able to carry it around for a good amount of time before it gets too uncomfortable. If it gets uncomfortable quickly, repack, redistributed the weight and adjust the straps and try again.

Think ahead, your backpack with take a bit of a beating on the road so ensure that anything breakable is packed in between clothing. It's a good idea to place liquids in a plastic bag to try and contain any spillages that do occur. Once your bag is packed, pick it up and throw it around a bit, sit on it and even walked over it! Even if you're careful, when you're out travelling other people will toss it around and trample on it! If something does break, reassess and repack – it's better that it happens at home than when you're out travelling.

MAKING THE MOST OUT OF YOUR DAYPACK... *How to utilise it*

Whether it's your zip-off daypack or a regular rucksack, your daypack can make your life on the road a lot more comfortable. They're an ideal size to chuck in the essentials for a lazy day on a scrumptious white sand beach, or throw in a guidebook, map and camera for a day of sightseeing. A daypack is also great for security and added comfort. When you're taking public transport, a daypack allows you to keep all of your important and valuable items with you and to have anything you may need close to hand – keep food, drink, and warmer clothes in your day pack to make journeys more comfortable. Bear in mind that baggage is often put on top of busses where there may well be other passengers riding alongside it or sitting on it! Delicate and valuable items may be damaged or stolen if left in your main backpack during transit. When you're walking around with your main backpack on, wear your daypack on your front – not only will this help you balance but it'll ensure that nobody can rummage through it undetected and help themselves to your stuff!

What to pack in your daypack...

Pack anything that is fragile, valuable or items that you think you'll need regularly to make your journeys more comfortable. Consider packing the following items *(alphabetical list)*;

- o   Electrical items: camera, video camera, mobile phone, laptop etc...
- o   Food & water
- o   Guidebook(s) & books
- o   Sun cream, sunglasses & neck pillow
- o   MP3 player / playing cards
- o   Pen – you'll be forever filling out immigration cards etc...
- o   Torch *(flashlight)* & pocketknife
- o   Sanitary items

5) HEALTH...

... *Staying healthy*

CONTENTS

VACCINATIONS... *Prevention is better than cure!*

There always seems to be a cloud of confusion amongst travellers when it comes to vaccinations. The best advice is to **talk to your GP** – vaccinations for travelling have become a daily routine for most doctors. I didn't have a clue when I was planning for my first trip and it's not as complicated as some people will have you believe The most important thing is to leave yourself enough time to have them all – for instance, the combined Hepatitis A&B vaccination involves a course of 3 injections that have to be given over a certain period of time to ensure effective protection. The name of the game is to seek advice as early as possible. Also be aware that vaccinations don't offer lifelong immunity so it's important to check with your GP and review your inoculation record to see if you require any boosters. Personally, I'm a bit of a pussy when it comes to injections so I grin and bear them while dosed up on copious amounts of Diazepam! Here are the most common and recommended armful of jabs that the 'average backpacker' will have... ouch!

Suggested vaccinations...

These are generally considered the 'routine vaccinations' for travellers whether you're travelling to Australia, Mexico or Thailand – these aren't destination specific:

o **Hepatitis A:** A course of **2** injections given a few months apart offering 10 years protection

o **Hepatitis B:** The vaccine is given as a course of **3** injections over 6 months offering long term protection. For increased convenience, especially if you're needle phobic, a combined vaccine for Hep A&B is usually offered

o **Polio, Diphtheria & TB:** A single combined injection. Most people will have been inoculated against these during childhood. These diseases are rare in the western world but are still common in some poorer regions of the world. Boosters are required every 10 years. Mild side effects include a sore arm and very mild fever

o **Tetanus:** A routine vaccination is the western world – most people will have had the inoculation. Check with your GP the date of your last booster, you'll require one every 10 years

o **Typhoid:** A single injection providing 2-3 years of protection. Tablets are also available but the single shot is the preferred choice with GPs – it has fewer side effects and usually costs less!

Optional vaccinations/medications...

The optional vaccinations generally depend on where you're planning to go, and personal choice. You'll more than likely find that these aren't free on the NHS *(UK)*;

o **Anti-Malarial Tablets:** A high level of protection can be obtained orally via a range of anti-malarial drugs and O'Boy is there a big debate about these – see later sub section 'Mosquitoes... *More than just bites*' for further advice *(page 235)*

o **Japanese B Encephalitis:** Inoculation involves a course of 3 injections given over month. Unfortunately, the vaccination provides only partial protection and you'll find that most travellers, including myself, don't bother with this injection

o **Rabies:** The vaccine is a course of 3 injections <u>before</u> departure, and then a booster shot is required – the first shot between 6 and 12 months after the initial course and then a booster every 2-3 years. Vaccination before departure doesn't give full protection.

Should you get bitten by a suspect animal, seek immediate medical attention and you'll require further vaccinations – although your treatment will be a more straight forward affair! Most travellers don't bother with this jab. I never have!

o **Yellow Fever:** Vaccination comes in the form of one simple jab. Usually required for regions such as Africa and South America where yellow fever is endemic. You're likely to be asked for documents if you're travelling to/from these regions so it's worth getting a copy of your medical card to prove what vaccinations you've had – in some countries it's an entry requirement and scams are not unknown!

Further information...

Your GP should be your primary source but check out the **World Health Organization** *(WHO)* website – www.who.int – for the latest information on health scares, vaccination requirements and recommendations for particular countries and regions.

YOUR FIRST-AID KIT... *Be prepared!*

A first-aid kit is essential for those minor scrapes, bumps and bruises. Despite a nasty mix of painful diseases, on your travels you'll encounter lots of bacteria that are foreign to your body and you're bound to have a spout of traveller's tummy! Open cuts take longer to heal and will become quickly infected in humid climates. A basic first-aid kit will reduce and relive the discomfort of these minor injuries and symptoms and will prevent trivial injuries progressing into more serious conditions that could potential ruin your tropical bliss.

Constructing a basic first-aid kit...

Compact and light weight medical kits are available from most outdoor shops and are generally good value. Expect to pay between £5.00 *(€6)* and £25.00 *(€30)* – obviously the more expensive kits have more equipment in them. However, whichever first-aid kit you buy it's always a good idea to 'personalise' your medical kit and tailor it to your individual medical requirements by adding additional items.

Alternatively, you can construct your own first-aid kit entirely from scratch and store the items in a heavy duty plastic container – a plastic Chinese take-away box is perfect! This usually works out the cheaper option and allows you build a first-aid kit that meets your specific medical needs.

This is a list of recommended items for your personal medical kit:

Oral rehydration salts & diarrhoea relief tablets – ORS are also great for hangovers!

Pain killers – a mix of Paracetamol & Ibuprofen *(for anti-inflammatory)*

Antiseptic cream – for example Germoline

Antiseptic wipes or Spray – cleans wounds and also ideal to clean hands before eating!

Magnesium Sulphate paste – to draw out infections

Malaria Tablets *(if needed & felt necessary)*

Tiger Balm – to relieve itchy mosquito bites, aches and pains

Vaseline – to prevent and soothe chaffing and blisters

Scissors & tweezers

Plasters *(a must)*, bandages & gauze

Thermometer *(not mercury)*

Safety pins – good for in case your zips break!

Plus: Any personal medication if you're prone to illnesses/infections such as, urinary-tract infections, thrush, boils or migraines. If you take any regular medication bring more than you need in case of loss or theft. Some of the newer drugs can be hard to find in regions such as Latin America and Asia.

Avoid getting the third degree!

Ninety-nine percent of the time you'll be fine but to avoid any difficult questions at customs and over-land border crossings, a little bit of preparation goes a long way. Pack medication in their original, clearly labelled boxes/containers. For newer drugs or rare conditions, a signed and dated letter from your physician describing your medical condition and medication, may be a good idea. A few travellers like to carry their own supply of sterile needles and syringes – a good idea in theory but it can lead to some awkward questioning and accusations – personally I'd advise against taking them. If you do decide to take some, be sure to have a physician's letter explaining their medical necessity/intended use – it's better to be safe than sorry!

STAYING HEALTHY... *Hazards on the road!*

It's easy to underestimate the dangers of otherwise wonderful climates and surroundings. From 'dribbly bums' to deadly diseases, this section has been designed to 'clue you up' with some basic tips to reduce and relieve all of those unpleasant health related interruptions that may crop up during your adventure.

PROTECTING YOURSELF FROM THE SUN... *Slip, Slop, Slap!*

In reality most backpackers head for the tropics or Australasia in search of hotter climates and a great tan – this is where the sun is very intense. It's important to protect yourself from the sun and learn how to cope with the heat – **dehydration**, **sunburn** and **heatstroke** are a constant underestimated threat in hot climates.

Bear in mind what they say Down Under; ***Slip, Slop, Slap!***

- o **SLIP** on a T-Shirt...

- o **SLOP** on the Sun cream...

- o **SLAP** on a Hat...

Sunglasses

Take care of your eyes – after all you've only got one pair! Sunbathing is one of the most common causes of cataracts. Sunglasses filter out the harmful UV-rays so it's worth investing in a decent pair – you could be doing more harm than good if you wear cheaper glasses that have insufficient or no UV protection. Avoid snow-blindness and burning your eyeballs and make sure you're sporting a pair of sunglasses if you pursue any snow based activities such as skiing, snowboarding and glacier hiking – I speak from experience when I say this – I didn't wear any sunglasses when I was hiking the Franz Josef Glacier in New Zealand. Consequently, I burnt my eyes, couldn't see for two days and then contracted conjunctivitis! Be sure to wear sunglasses on the beach – not just to protect your eyes but so you can spot the half naked fitties without being busted!

Sun cream

You can practically smell the burning flesh of westerners on tropical beaches all over the world so protect your skin from the sun and apply sun cream to exposed areas of skin – especially your face.

It's a good idea to take two bottles of sun cream – a high sun protection factor *(SPF)*, for when you first arrive and for your face and forearms, and a medium SPF for when you've built up a tan. Be liberal and slap on sun cream regularly. Remember that in Oz and New Zealand the suns UV-rays are very intense and the ozone layer is severely depleted. Skin cancer rates down under are the highest in the world. In New Zealand, the burn-time is so short that your skin will begin to frazzle in as little as 5 minutes so protect yourself against Australasia's punishing sun! Aloe Vera is great for soothing your sunburn for when you do inevitably get burnt. Your skin will be dry after hours of intense UV-rays, salty air and seawater, so make sure you pack after-sun and moisturise regularly – it'll also preserve your tan!

Stay hydrated

It's important to keep your body fluids topped up throughout the day to avoid heatstroke and heat exhaustion. Humidity is a real danger – you'll soon realise just how quickly you become an uncomfortable sweaty mess! It's important that you replace that lost fluid. Here are some tips to keep yourself hydrated:

- o   For tropical climates **2-3litres of water a day** is the rule of thumb and sorry coke and beer don't help at all!! If you're suffering from diarrhoea you should be drinking a lot more

- o   Make sure you have some sachets of **oral rehydration salts** *(ORS)* with you. Mixed with fresh cold water they taste like flavoured water and replace the vital minerals that you lose when you perspire. ORS are also a great **hang over cure** – take one before you go to bed and a few when you wake up to feel fresh as a daisy and ready for another night on the beer!

- o   **Wear a hat** – this keeps your head cooler and therefore you sweat less. Exposed skin actually increases your body heat

- o   **Increase your salt intake** – sounds a bit contradictory to what we're told by the dieticians at home but many travellers add a pinch of salt to their food to help replace what they've lost through sweating – obviously just don't go over the top! It's commonly acknowledged that regular cramps are an indication of low salt levels in your body

Practical measures!

Avoid *(excessive)* sunbathing and be extra careful between 11am and 3pm, especially in Australia and New Zealand. Expose yourself slowly to the sun, even 20 minutes on the beach on your first day is an awful lot for a pasty white westerner – a fact that my ginger friend very quickly found out in Thailand! There's no escape and even in the shade the burning rays will get you through the reflection of the sea! Be sensible, hydrate and remember to slip, slop and slap! Avoid a sore blistered back and wear a t-shirt when you're snorkelling. Remember that when you're showing off in the pool or wallowing in the sea, the sun's rays are being reflected back at you increasing your UV exposure, so add cream more frequently or even wear a rash vest or t-shirt.

MOSQUITOES... *More than just bites!*

Mosquitoes love sucking you dry and are a constant pain in the arse. You should try to prevent mosquito bites at all times not only for your own comfort but to reduce the risk of life threatening diseases, such as **Malaria, Dengue Fever** and **Japanese Encephalitis**. Malaria is one of the nastiest and most common tropical diseases worldwide. When you do inevitably get bitten, try not to scratch the bites or they'll become infected. Use **Tiger Balm** to reduce irritation, just avoid sensitive areas like your eyes or groin – that's worse than a bite!

The best advice to protect yourself against such diseases:

1) Mosquito-bite prevention... *Practical measures*

- o Wear long trousers and long-sleeved tops at night times and at times of low light intensity

- o Avoid using scented perfumes, aftershaves, body sprays and hair products as they attract mosquitoes

- o Perhaps the simplest and easiest prevention – use Mosquito repellents that contain the compound **DEET** on exposed skin *(Sample on a small area of skin first to check for irritation and discomfort)*

- o Where they're a pain use a **mosquito net** whilst sleeping – use plasters *(band aids)* to patch up any holes!

- o **Mosquito coils** are an effective and cheap way to ward off these little pests – once lit each coil should smoulder for about 8hrs and are great if you're spending the evening drinking outside on your veranda

- o **Lights off, fan on** – mosquitoes hate the wind so keep your fan on. Lights attract the little buggers so keep room lights and outside lights off when they're not necessary and the door shut when you've got them on!

- o If you're a regular feature on the mosquito's menu try taking **garlic capsules, vitamin B1 tablets** and drinking **tonic water** in a bid to ward off these pests. Sounds like something from Buffy the Vampire slayer but belief amongst many locals and travellers suggests that these make your blood less desirable – it's worth a try!

Unfortunately, there's **no vaccine** available to offer protection against **Dengue Fever** – it can only be prevented by avoiding mosquito bites in risk areas! In addition, the vaccination for **Japanese Encephalitis** provides only partial protection!

2) Anti-Malarial tablets... *Last line of defence!*

Malaria tablets can be prescribed by your local GP. Talk your trip through with your GP – they can make the best informed decision on the most suitable type **if** you need them and you feel that **you want** to take them. As resistance to medication varies from country to country, different types are suitable for different regions. There's a variety of medication available, offering varying levels of protection and possible side effects, all at different costs. Here are some of the most common:

- o **Malarone** – one of the newest and well known drugs available. Malarone is probably the most effect and safest option. Side effects are uncommon and mild. Although Malarone is the most expensive option, it's the preferred choice of anti-malarial tablet amongst travellers. Malarone only needs to be taken for one week after leaving the risk area in addition to your time spent there

- o **Doxycycline** – a daily tablet offering a good level of protection. It can also help prevent a range of other tropical diseases such as, Leptospirosis and typhus. However, it does have a number of irritating side effects including, a tendency to sunburn *(photosensitivity)*, thrush and interference with the contraceptive pill *(in women!)* and nausea. Doxycycline should be taken with meals as stomach ulcers are another *(more serious)* side effect. These tablets must be taken 4 weeks after leaving the risk area

- o **Lariam** *(Mefloquine)* – a weekly tablet that's ideal for forgetful people! Serious side effects include anxiety and depression. These side effects are rare but anyone with a history of depression or other psychological disorder should not take Lariam. Resistance to the drug is growing in some parts of northern Thailand, Laos and Vietnam but generally provides an effective protection. Annoyingly it must also be taken for 4 weeks after leaving the risk area

Anti-Malarial tablets, to take or not to take... *A personal decision*

Whether to take anti-malarial drugs is a hotly debated topic amongst travellers. Many backpackers feel that the costs of taking antimalarial drugs outweigh their benefits – and in all honesty you're likely to come across a great deal of travellers who don't take them. Personally, I've never taken any form of anti-malarial tablets during my numerous trips, and perhaps luck has been on my side, but I haven't contracted Malaria! Although, when I haven't fallen asleep outside in an alcoholic state, I've always tried to prevent mosquito bites. Cleary the number one reason to take them is to prevent Malaria but here are some of the most common arguments <u>against</u> taking anti-malarial drugs:

- o **The financial cost** – probably the number one reason against them for most shoe-stringers and there's no denying that these drugs do have a considerable financial cost – especially if you're going to be away for a long period of time – but some argue, can you really put a price on your health?

- o **The side-effects** – the drugs often have severe side-effects including nausea, restless nights, bad dreams, and in extreme cases, hallucinations. Medication isn't suitable for everyone and it's advisable not to take some types if you have a family history of mental illnesses or depression. This is probably this biggest and justifiable argument against taking them

- o **The actual real risk** – some people feel that the actual real risk of contracting Malaria is small, especially in urban and resort areas and doesn't justify taking the tablets and suffering the associated side-effects. It's a personal decision, and one that should be taken seriously. Check out the W.$H.O website for up-to-date 'risk regions' and discuss it with your GP

- o **More than one disease** – mosquitoes have a lot to answer for when you consider the amount of diseases they carry and some people argue that because the tablets only offer protection for one disease – Malaria – you should therefore practice mosquito bite prevention to your best ability at all times anyway!

If you decide to take them, don't rely solely on antimalarial drugs – **they are not 100% effective.** Follow the above advice and avoid getting bitten, **tablets do not guarantee that you will not develop Malaria**.

DIARRHOEA & SICKNESS... *Traveller's tummy!*

Diarrhoea is extremely common when you're travelling – the state of your stomach and the consistency and colour of your stools becomes a popular topic of discussion amongst backpackers! There are numerous causes for having a spout of 'traveller's tummy' from a straightforward reaction to a change of water and diet, to more unpleasant bacteria and viruses. Don't be alarmed but diarrhoea and sickness strikes the majority of backpackers, even the well seasoned ones, at some time during their travels – usually near the start of their trip as your body's adjusting. It'll only be a matter of time until you're discussing and laughing about *'the time you shit the bed in Mexico'* or *'the time you couldn't get off the toilet for three days in Laos'* with other travellers! Most travellers come back a lot skinnier!

Preventing diarrhoea & sickness...

If you're particularly vulnerable to diarrhoea, there are a few simple things you can do to reduce your chances of this annoying illness striking you down!

- o Perhaps obvious but **don't drink the local tap water** – drink only bottled water in regions such as Asia and Latin America
- o Use a **straw** when drinking from cans & bottles

- o **Avoid ice cubes** in your soft drinks and alcoholic drinks – they're often made from local tap water despite what they say!
- o Ease yourself into the local food – it's good, tasty and cheap, but you've got to get used some of it and allow your body to adapt to your new diet. However, it is widely acknowledged that chillies and spicy foods, **once your body has got used to them**, will reduce your chances of diarrhoea

Dealing with diarrhoea & sickness...

Apart from embarrassment and shitty pants, the main danger you'll face with diarrhoea is dehydration so it's important to focus on rehydrating as soon as stomach ache/cramps occur.

Follow the usual hydration steps:

- o Drink more than **3 litres** of clean water a day – even if you're vomiting, it's important to take regular sips of water to try and replace as much lost fluid as possible
- o Take **oral rehydration salts** regularly – to replace vital lost minerals
- o Use anti-diarrhoea tablets **extremely sparingly** – diarrhoea ejects toxins from your body. Tablets aim to halt your digestive movements and hence retain these harmful toxins inside your body, which in turn can make you feel a lot worse. Although it's literally a pain in the arse, try and let it run its course. On the other hand, anti-diarrhoea tablets are essential if you absolutely have to travel – there's nothing worse than having to stop a packed bus in a cold sweat so that you can squat down for a runny shit at the side of the road with everyone watching through the window. Just make sure to get some pictures if it happens to your mate! And believe me, it happens! you'll often be scared to fart in fear of shitting yourself!

In most cases a spout of 'traveller's tummy' should run its course in two or three days. If you've been drinking *(water!)* regularly you should be OK and will be able to start eating again. Begin with bland foods in small quantities, such as boiled rice, and build the size *(and intensity)* of your portions up over the next few days. Don't push your luck and delve straight into a spicy kick-arse curry or some greasy fish 'n' chips or you'll quickly see it again!

As long as you keep yourself hydrated, diarrhoea isn't that dangerous, just more of an inconvenience and annoyance – although it does make for some interesting and humorous stories to laugh about further into your travels! I've been sharing a bed with my best mate – obviously to save money – and woke up to find that he had shit the bed! Luckily, still incapacitated with buckets of rum, I slipped back into my alcoholic coma but awoke horrified a few hours later with trickles of dried up shit down my leg and crusty bed sheets! If your diarrhoea is particularly severe, accompanied by traces of blood/mucus in your faeces or persists for longer than 3-days without signs of easing, it's probably cause by some nasty bacteria/virus so seek medical treatment.

JETLAG... z z Z Z Z

Falling asleep at the dinner table and wide awake at 4am with hunger pains? Welcome to jetlag! Flying can play havoc with your body clock. Symptoms to look forward include; hunger pains at unusual times, disturbed sleep patterns, fatigue, lethargy and looking like shit! Everyone suffers from jetlag, some more than others, and it's caused by flying across several time zones – basically, since we no longer get around by horse & cart, we travel too far and too fast for our body to adjust! The longer the flight and the more times zones you cross, the more severe your jetlag will be and the longer it'll take for your body to adjust.

It's commonly acknowledged that eastbound flights are worse than westbound flights – logic being it's harder to force yourself to sleep earlier than stay awake for longer! The majority of advice suggests that it takes a day to recover for every hour in time difference. So if you fly from London to Thailand, where there's a 7 hour time difference, you should feel fully adjusted after one week.

You can reduce the effects of jetlag and adjust quicker by:

- o   Drinking plenty of fluids and avoiding alcohol and caffeine drinks *(I find this hard on flights where the alcohol is free!)*
- o   Upon arrival, seek exposure to **natural sunlight** and set your watch/mobile to **local time**
- o   **Adopt the daily routine** *(meal times, sleeping patterns etc)* of your destination as soon as you arrive. Eat *(light)* meals at the appropriate times, breakfast at breakfast time and lunch at lunch time – even if you're not feeling hungry!

DEEP VEIN THROMBOSIS... *A hidden danger*

Deep Vein Thrombosis *(DVT)* is a hidden but very real danger that has been highly documented in recent years. It's widely associated with long periods of immobility coupled with dehydration which makes the blood flow in your legs slow to a level where clotting can occur. Usually these disperse causing nothing more than discomfort and pain in your tights. However, DVT can become life-threatening if a clot fails to fully disperse and travels to other parts of your body – if it reaches your lungs it can cause a lethal pulmonary embolism. Frequent and long haul flights exacerbates the risk of DVT. While the chances of DVT are relatively low, it's wise to do what you can to reduce it. Current advice suggests that you can minimise the risk of DVT by:

- o   **Avoid sitting with your legs crossed** – helps maintain a healthy blood flow
- o   **Wear loose clothing** – tighter clothing can restrict blood flow
- o   **Move around** – avoid prolonged periods of inactivity and get up and walk around as often as possible to reduce the chances of blood pooling in your legs
- o   **Simple exercises** – sounds stupid but exercises, such as rotating your feet and simple stretches, can help maintain blood flow without you having to move from your seat! You'll probably find suggested exercise routines on the plane's information sheet once aboard
- o   **Keep hydrated** – it's hard, especially when it's free, but avoid excessive alcohol and caffeine products pre-departure and whilst onboard

Establish a basic knowledge of the potential diseases and take advantage of this *A-Z Diseases & Definitions* directory. Below is a brief description of the **most common** diseases that you might be exposed to during your travels. Refer to previous subsections for suggested vaccinations and precautions and be sure to discuss your proposed trip with your GP. Unfortunately, you'll notice that many of the major symptoms are common between numerous diseases, so in most cases medical assistance should be sought ASAP!

Cholera...

An intestinal disease that's caused by bacteria in contaminated food. Rehydration is the most important treatment, if left untreated Cholera can be lethal within hours so seek urgent medical attention. Treatment usually involves a course of antibiotics

Symptoms: Muscle cramps, vomiting, diarrhoea & dehydration

Dengue Fever...

This nasty viral disease will have you as close to deaths door as you'll ever come. You'll require immediate medical attention and hospitalisation. It's usually spread by *(Aedes)* mosquitoes that bite during the day. There is no vaccination and the disease is currently on the increase worldwide, and is becoming particularly problematic in SE Asia. Follow the mosquito bite prevention advice!

Symptoms: Initial symptoms include severe fever, headaches, joint & muscle pain. Many patients also suffer from nausea, vomiting & a pink rash

Hepatitis...

There are a number of strains of this delightful disease including, Hep A, B, C, D & E! In all cases the virus attacks the liver. There are effective vaccinations against Hep A & Hep B, although there's no vaccine against C, D & E strains of the virus. Hepatitis A is the most common strain and is transmitted via contaminated food, water and saliva. Hepatitis B is more serious and is spread by sexual contact and through contaminated blood, needles and syringes

Symptoms: Yellowing of the skin & eyes *(jaundice)*, exhaustion, fever, joint pains, severe loss of weight & diarrhoea

HIV / AIDS...

A high profile virus commonly passed via bodily fluids though sexual intercourse and infected needles. There's no known prevention or effective cure. Practice safe sex **at all times** – and not just in developing regions. No glove, no love! It'll reduce your chances of contracting other STDs as well

Symptoms: No initial symptoms

Japanese B Encephalitis...

This is a **very** serious and nasty disease that's spread via mosquitoes. Japanese Encephalitis is a viral infection targeting and resulting in inflammation of the brain. The disease has a very high death rate and unfortunately survivors are usually subject to some degree of brain damage. It's commonly restricted to rural areas and again it is widespread spread throughout Asia and in poorer, developing countries. Vaccinations are available pre-departure but inoculation only provides partial protection

Leptospirosis...

A bacterial disease that is contracted by exposure to contaminated fresh water or soil. It's fairly common in tropical climates. If left untreated it can lead to liver failure and meningitis. Unfortunately there is no vaccine, seek medical treatment as soon as possible

Symptoms: High fever, chills, nausea & vomiting

Malaria...

A nasty tropical disease that is difficult to treat and often reoccurs. Malaria is probably the most common disease that travellers are exposed to. The risk of contracting malaria in urban areas is generally low risk but greatly increases in rural locations. There are several strains of malaria; all are serious and potentially fatal. Immediate medical advice should be sought after. Keep any suffer as hydrated as possible. The parasites that cause Malaria are carried by night biting *(Anopheles)* mosquitoes and unfortunately the incubation period varies anywhere between 10 days and 4 weeks. Anyone considering travelling to malaria risk areas should *consider* taking preventive anti-malarial drugs although the risk of side effects can outweigh their benefits – see earlier subsection 'Mosquitoes... *More than just bites*'

Symptoms: Most important symptom is fever, although headaches, diarrhoea, cough & severe shivering can occur. Diagnosis is made via a blood sample

Measles...

This disease remains a problem throughout many developing regions. It's a highly contagious bacterial infection that's spread via coughing & sneezing. While there's no specific treatment, most travellers from Europe and North America will have been vaccinated against measles during childhood – in the UK this is part of your MMR jab

Symptoms: Starts with a high fever & a rash.

Rabies...

Another nasty, widespread and often fatal disease. Rabies is spread via the bite of infected animal, usually a dog or monkey. It's a prevalent disease in India, Southeast Asia, and most developing countries. Avoid mangy looking dogs especially if they're foaming at the mouth! If you get bitten by a suspect animal wash the area thoroughly with clean water and seek immediate medical attention. There's a 3 course vaccine given over a 21-day period available before departure. While you'll still need post-exposure treatment should you get bitten, post bite treatment is greatly simplified. If you haven't had the pre-vaccination you will need to receive rabies immunoglobulin ASAP

Typhoid Fever...

Spread by contaminated food and water. This is a nasty bacterial infection and suffers must seek immediate medical attention. While it can be treated with antibiotics, vaccines are available pre-departure and offer a high level of protection. Be especially careful what you drink

Symptoms: Extremely high and slowly progressive fever & headache. Suffers may also have abdominal pains, a dry cough & red spots on the patient's chest and abdomen.

6) BOOKING YOUR TRIP...

... *The big adventure!*

CONTENTS

Before you begin to book your trip you'll have 3 important considerations to mull over:

1) **Whether you want to travel with someone...**

2) **Do-It-Yourself or go on an organised tour...**

3) **How long you want be away for...**

These considerations are explored in detail below...

1) TRAVEL COMPANIONS... *Take a buddy or go it alone?*

Perhaps you've already been planning your trip with your partner or a mate, if you haven't you should seriously consider whether you want to go solo or ask someone to come along with you. There's pro's and con's associated with travelling solo and backpacking with company, and it depends what you want to get out of your trip. I've travelled with my best friends, my girlfriend and both at the same time – believe me there are ups and downs with any combination! I prefer to travel with company where as my best mate has, in the past, preferred to travel on his own.

TRAVELLING SOLO... *Sad or a great idea!*

There's no better way to experience the extremes of backpacking than doing it on your lonesome. You'll be throwing yourself in at the deep end and fending for yourself. It's probably the biggest scope for self development that you're ever likely to get. It's raw travelling at its most intense!

Below is a rundown of the ups and downs of travelling alone:

The ups...

Rewarding – travelling on your own is potentially more rewarding as you're not relying on anyone to do anything for you. You can take satisfaction from achieving your goals without input from anyone else.

Independence – you can do what you like, when you like! Travelling is a great way to enhance your independence, develop your decision making skills and boost your confidence.

Maturity – when you're on your own you're forced to fend for yourself, grow as a person and 'mature'. You see things and do things that you wouldn't necessarily have to do at home and everyday you'll have to overcome different challenges by yourself. You'll experience new cultures face on and consequently you'll come back with a different outlook to the world.

Approachable – it can be easier to talk to other people if you don't already appear to be 'in a group'. If you're travelling on your own, you're more likely to stay in dorms where you'll meet lots of other independent and like-minded travellers.

The downs...

Loneliness – there will be times where you'll spend days on your own and it can be depressing sleeping on your own in a double room! If you're out for a few months you'll long for familiar company – only a handful of travellers will be pursuing the same itinerary as you!

Less security & safety – unfortunately you're more likely to be a target of petty crime if you're roaming around on your own. You'll feel vulnerable in some situations if you're on your own and they'll be no-one to 'watch your back'.

Little bargaining power – you'll find it harder to get discounted rates if you're not going to purchase multiple items, tickets or rooms.

More expensive – while you're going to have little bargaining power, if you're not planning to stay in dorms, and some regions don't have dorms, your accommodation will be significantly more expensive and you won't have anyone to share the cost of food or additional equipment with.

Tips for the single traveller...

If you're about to set off on your travels on your lonesome you'll probably be feeling a bit daunted by the whole prospect. Check out these tips to make you feel at ease and make that trip on your own a little less lonely:

Go on organised tours/daytrips

Book yourself onto tours and day excursions and you're usually forced to mingle and talk to other travellers! If you're a bit shy, don't worry, the initial questions that you'll hear so often; 'so where have you been', 'how long have you been out travelling' and 'what do you do at home' usually break the ice! You'll quickly find yourself forming small travel groups and make travel buddies that are following similar itineraries to you.

Go out, drink & be happy!

There's no denying that even the most timid people are more sociable once a few glasses of cheap beer or wine are consumed! Get yourself down to the hostel bars, show your face and get involved – you'll meet people in no time. If you're uncomfortable going alone to the bar potentially looking like a loner, see if there's any organised pub crawls going on for a night of sociable drunken frolics! Just try to remember everyone's name in the morning – easier said than done!

Stay in hostel dorms

Hostels have many plus points. Granted, one of them is they're cheaper than the Hilton, but another one is the amount of communal space. Use it! Take advantage of common rooms, communal kitchens, TV rooms and exploit this fantastic opportunity to meet new people. Although slightly more expensive, stay in smaller dorms – it makes it far easier to get to know your roommates. Talk about anything – the person snoring in the top bunk, the girl with the nice arse, ask what they recommend to do or laugh about how pissed you were last night – just anything to get the conversation going!

Open up to fellow travellers

Don't sit there on the bus with your head buried in a book, nodding along to your i-Pod or snoring away fast asleep on the back seat – be sociable, make eye contact with other travellers and speak! Don't shy away in private rooms and don't avoid communal areas, try and get amongst it wherever you are. It's amazing how far a simple 'Hi' will get you! The more you put in, the more you'll get out of it and the more travel buddies you'll make – you'll be amazed just how much your confidence will grow.

Rustle up a storm in communal kitchens

Do lots of cooking in hostel kitchens and you'll reap the rewards! Rustle up a storm in the kitchen and somebody is bound to comment "Oooooh that smells good"! Offer to share your culinary delights and cook for groups of people – it'll make you a lot of grateful friends *(and reduce your food bill!)*. Equally, by hogging the gas hob or kitchen utensils you're bound to get talking to someone and make a friend!

Research, plan & even pre-book

Arriving in a strange destination on your own for the first time can be a little intimidating, make sure you do a bit of research before you arrive. Find out what is the best way to get to your hostel from the airport, bus or train station. Be sure to jot down the address of any pre-booked hostels or source out the main backpacker areas before you get there. If you're arriving in a new country and you're a bit apprehensive, pre-book the first few initial nights so you're not spending hours helplessly roaming around a strange town feeling vulnerable trying to find some accommodation.

Keep in touch with those back home

As you jet-off to lands far away, your folks back home are bound to be concerned about you, so do them a favour and keep in touch with them regularly. You'll also find it comforting to hear stories of events back home and hear the voice of loved ones, especially when you're feeling a little down.

TRAVELLING WITH A FRIEND / PARTNER... *Company or quarrels!*

As a first time-traveller it's a very good idea to explore strange parts of the world with the support of a close friend. Just bear in mind that while there are many plus points to travelling with a friend or partner, choose your travel buddy carefully – remember that you're going to spend 24 hours-a-day with this person for the next few months. Avoid travelling with more than one of your friends as the larger the group the more split decisions and disagreements you'll have. Invest a lot of time and evaluate the ups and downs that are highlighted below before you ask any of your friends!

The ups...

Company & support – probably the number one reason to travel with someone. It's nice to share experiences and create great memories with your friends or partner. It's always reassuring and comforting to have a friend there to pick up the baton of enthusiasm and support you through the rough times when you're feeling rundown and home sick! You'll definitely appreciate the moral support, motivation and enthusiasm of having someone you know with you throughout your adventure. Above all it's fun with your best mates!

Security – safety in numbers. You're less likely to be a victim of a mugging or assault if you're travelling with company. Lone female travellers in particular can often feel intimated and vulnerable in other cultures, travelling with a friend can ease this discomfort.

Cheaper – travelling with a friend will dramatically reduce your main daily expenses. You can split the cost of food if you're cooking in hostel kitchens but more importantly half your accommodation costs if you're not staying in dorms.

More bargaining power – it's always easier to get a discount if there's more than one of you! You'll get reduce rates on tours, bus tickets and souvenirs if you 'buy in bulk'.

The downs...

Arguments & fall outs – you may not know your mates as well as you think you do. Spending 24 hours-a-day with even your best friend puts considerable strain on your friendship! It's common for friends to part company and go their separate ways after only a few months of intense backpacking. Even couples can break up while on their 'trip of a lifetime'!

Two's company & three's a crowd – the old saying is definitely true and the bigger your group the more divisions and cracks will appear in your tight knit group of 'best mates'. If you're travelling with an odd number of people you'll also find it harder to get triple rooms and someone will always end up on their own and have to pay more!

Unapproachable – it can be harder to meet people if you're travelling as a couple or in a group as people feel uneasy trying to 'get into' a crowd where it appears that everyone already knows each other! You may meet fewer people than if you were on your own.

2) ORGANISED TOURS... *Taking the leg work out of your trip*

When you've chosen your region and have got a rough itinerary, you should consider whether an organised tour would be suitable. For a first-time traveller they can take some of the leg work out of your trip and make it more manageable to organise and budget for. It's also a lot more reassuring to have someone to guide you around strange and intimidating countries! Alternatively, you may be seeking the freedom to go where ever you want at your own pace and relish the challenges of unfamiliar countries, cultures and languages – then an organised tour is definitely not the best choice.

Organised tours do exactly what they say on the tin – they take you to your chosen country/region with a pre-set, pre-paid itinerary that's all organised and conducted by the company or associated third parties. They essentially do all the leg work for you and ensure a smooth trip so you can stay focused on having fun unhindered by any worries or planning nightmares. Tours operators and booking agents will usually assisted you in visa applications and flights to the region will often be booked for you as part of the tour albeit usually at an extra cost. Essentially, the majority of your trip is organised for you! This is a great option if you are truly overwhelmed by the prospect of booking and organising your own trip. Some travellers begin their trip with an organised tour and stay on in the region or move to another area after the tour has concluded and they've gained enough confidence and knowledge to continue their adventure on their tod. On the other hand seasoned travellers only really opt for organised tours in potentially volatile and dangerous regions for added safety and security.

TO GO OR NOT TO GO *(on a tour)... That is the question!*

Organised tours are often the subject of scrutiny by the 'hardcore backpacker', but they may be suitable depending on your circumstances, confidence and what you want to get out of your trip. If you're feeling a little overwhelmed by the thought of planning your own itinerary, then perhaps you should consider going on an organised tour. Personally, I think organised tours are expensive, far too commercialised and very restrictive. However, in some regions where there's political insecurity and areas that are notoriously dangerous, such as parts of Africa, I think they're very practical and worthwhile offering you a unique chance to explore areas that are otherwise inaccessible. Despite my personal views, below is a brief and balanced rundown of the pro's and con's of organised tours;

Advantages:

A few reasons why people prefer to go on an organised tour rather than venture into the unknown on their own:

- o Tours are **effortless** with a **fixed itinerary** – great if you're a bit apprehensive about creating your own itinerary and venturing into the unknown in lands far from home. Tours often have local guides who are experts on your chosen region meaning you'll have to do less research!

- o Very **practical** if you have a **strict time limit** for your trip – probably one of the main reasons for embarking on an organised tour

- o **Peace of mind & security** – both financially and personal safety, particularly in areas of political instability, such as Africa, where it's undeniably more challenging and dangerous to travel

- o **Lone-travellers** – organised tours are great if you're planning to go travel on your lonesome ensuring that there'll be fewer lonely nights and intimidating encounters!

- o Often **more comfortable** – tours use better *(and perhaps safer)* modes of transport and higher quality accommodation *(although this adds to the cost as DIY options are usually cheaper)*

- o **Budgeting practicalities** – tours are great for people who are useless at budgeting! With just a single one-off payment you'll pay for most of the transport, accommodation and tours up front before you go, meaning that you only need to budget for food, drink and souvenirs while you're out exploring!

- o **Home stays** – the vast majority of organised tours in Africa, Asia and Latin America involve home stays allowing you to get up close and with the locals and their lifestyle!

Disadvantages:

Granted there are a few advantages to going on an organised tour, however, it's fair to say that the majority of backpackers have an unfavourable view of these tours for a number of reasons:

- o **Backpacker friendly** – Probably the chief reason against organised tours. Regions such as SE Asia and Latin America are very backpacker friendly and many feel that there's little need to be dragged around by a tour guide like a herd of sheep

- o **Very restricted** – they eliminate the real joy of backpacking restricting your freedom and providing little room for spontaneity

- o **Uninspiring** – little scope for self-development and an organised tour takes away the excitement of 'what shall we do next' – you always know what to expect on an organised tour!

- o **Less rewarding** – everything's done for you and you can easily get bored and feel like you're spending hours on a bus with little perspective of where you actually are!

- o **Short** – organised tours typically only last a few weeks to a month or so. If you want to be away for months, organise tours will fall short of your expectations

- o **Very commercial** – sure, some tours make a distinct effort to get off-the-beaten track but you can only truly get off-the-beaten track and have an authentic experience on your own away from the crowds and influence of foreign investment

- o You only have contact with a **limited number of people** – little room to add to your international network of friends

- o Generally **more expensive** – whether charges are transparent or not you'll be paying the tour company a fee for their expertise, organisation and associated guides. The price of accommodation and transport is usually built into the price meaning that as they generally use higher standard amenities the overall price of your trip will be significantly higher than DIY alternatives. Roughing it in dirty guesthouses and travelling by rickety local transport is what travelling is all about – and it's cheaper!

Booking a tour... *Do your research & shop around*

If you decide that a tour is the best option for you, look around and do your homework as there are a number of operators that provide organised tours around Africa, Asia, Europe, Latin America, the USA and Canada. Tours can be booked direct or through agents such as STA. Among the best and well established tour operators are *(in alphabetical order)*:

- o **Dragoman...** *Unique & rustic overland adventures*

  Starting with one truck between London and Nairobi, Dragoman has been offering trips for nearly 30 years and now operates epic overland adventures throughout Africa, Asia and Latin America. Be it a three week holiday or a 12 month break, Dragoman's range of exciting overland adventures caters for anyone looking for something a little bit different during their time off. Escape, discover and encounter... Dragoman's trips use local guides and make a huge effort to get off-the-beaten track. www.dragoman.com

o **Intrepid...** *Experiences off-the-beaten track*

Started by a two friends in 1989, Intrepid has a passion to get traveller's off-the-beaten track. With a huge variety of travel styles, a commitment to small groups and the use of local guides, Intrepid traveller's have the freedom and flexibility to explore the world's most amazing places – 'discovering real people, real cultures and having incredible real life experiences along the way'. www.intrepidtravel.com

o **Real Gap...** *Inspirational travel ideas & volunteer opportunities*

Real Gap experiences provide hundreds of gap year opportunities and travelling ideas in over 45 countries round the world from paid work, learning new skills and teaching English to extreme sports & adventure travel. Along with expert advice and support, Real Gap also offers some of the best volunteer opportunities out there. www.realgap.co.uk

3) HOW LONG YOU WANT TO BE AWAY FOR... *3-6 months is ideal*

It sounds a very obvious question but how long you want to be away for is a very important question to mull over. It's all very well having a departure date but if you want book return flights you need to have a date in mind to come back! If you intend to purchase an open-jaw ticket you can be a bit more vague about your return date. You've probably got a good idea of how long you want to be away for already but the length of your trip is largely dependent on:

o **Where you're going** – you don't want to spend months in a small country where time will drag or only a few weeks or even days in a vast country and feel rushed. It's important to think carefully how long you want to spend in each country and structure your time frame accordingly. But it's always better to have too much time than too little!

o **Your budget** – unless you intend to work whilst you're out globetrotting, the size of your budget will be the major constraint on the length of your trip. There's no point getting a 12-month career break if you've only got a few thousand quid saved up and don't intend to seek employment in countries such as Australia and New Zealand!

o **You current job** – can you get a career break? Most companies offer career breaks between three and six months. Otherwise can you afford to leave you current job and seek other employment when you return? Maybe you can secure work for when you come back before you go

Refer to **section one** and look at suggested time frames for each country in the **'At a glance'** sections

A general guideline...

As a guideline, a backpacker's trip can last anywhere between a few weeks to a few years! A reasonable trip length for a first-time traveller would be **3 to 6 months** – this gives you plenty of time to explore even a large region and experience the freedom and spontaneity that backpacking gives you but it's not too long that you really begin to miss home, lose your inspiration and don't appreciate your beautiful surroundings! When you have an idea how long you want to be away in your chosen region you can begin to think about *(return)* airline tickets, budgets and a more detailed itinerary.

BOOKING YOUR TRIP... *Step by step*

After all of your planning, deciding where you want to go, drawing up an exciting itinerary, checking out the inventory lists, familiarising yourself with the health issues, getting to grips with budgeting and started saving, it's finally time to book your trip and make it all become a reality!

So how do you go about booking your trip? Where should you start? Do you book your tickets first? When should you apply for visas and arrange some travel insurance? At what point should you schedule your inoculations? The process can seem quite confusing!

As always, don't panic. There's no right or wrong way to book your trip, but there are a few things that you should prioritise and try to get done first. Here's a basic 'logical order' that I usually follow to book your adventure:

○ STEP *1... Your airline ticket* (page 250)

As your biggest expense your airline ticket should be your priority purchase. Have a quick check at the visa requirements before you buy a ticket just to ensure that you meet the requirements to gain access to the countries on your itinerary! By booking your ticket first you'll have a set date to work towards – just be sure to leave yourself enough time before your departure date to organise everything and save enough money, and **be realistic**!

○ STEP *2... Visas & travel insurance* (page 255 & 259)

Once you're flights are booked, it's time to apply for visas should you need any in advance – for instance if you're planning to go to Australia where you can only get visas in advance. With your itinerary planned and dates set you want to start looking into the right travel insurance to cover yourself for any unfortunate incidents!

○ STEP *3... Equipment & vaccinations*

Tickets booked, visas pending and insurance purchased, it's time to kit yourself out with everything you need from toiletries and clothes to a cameras and adaptors. As soon as you've sorted out the red tape *(tickets, visas & insurance)* and have pencilled in a leaving date, pop down to your GP to discuss and arrange a vaccination schedule.

The following sections run through everything discussed in the above steps from visas and airline tickets to reducing your insurance premium and what you need to book in advance.

YOUR AIRLINE TICKET... *Getting there & away*

If you're going to go it alone and avoid organised tours it'll be up to you to organise your airline ticket and it should be the first thing you book. If you're going on an organised tour the agency that you book through will usually offer you assistance with your flights and source out a good deal for you. However, even if you're going on an organised tour it's worth doing some research yourself to make sure you're getting the best deal. You're tour may only make up a small proportion of your trip and you may wish to leave earlier than you organised tour starts or travel elsewhere after its finished. Your airfares are your biggest expense and where you can make the biggest savings of you trip so do some serious research. Take a peek at your ticket options and how to get the best deal:

Your type of ticket will usually depend on where you're going and the nature of your trip. Here are the most popular types of airline tickets:

Return tickets... *The 'bog standard' airline ticket*

They do exactly what they say, getting you from **A to B** and back again. These are great for regions that allow looping itineraries such as SE Asia where everyone flies in and out of Bangkok *(see sub-section 'Reducing the price of your airfare')*. Some backpackers will modify this and arrange **2 single tickets** – A to B and then from C to A to pursue a more linear itinerary. Why do this? Although two tickets usually works out slightly more expensive than a standard return ticket, it can reduce the amount of 'backtracking' in a particular region. For example, if you're planning to go to Central America, the geography of the region doesn't give you much freedom to create a looping itinerary, so rather than flying in and out of San Jose *(Costa Rica),* and risk backtracking through at least 3 countries if you venture up to Mexico, it would make more sense to book **2** single tickets – one into Costa Rica and one out of Mexico and pursue a more linear itinerary! You have the option to do this in SE Asia too by flying into Singapore and out of Hanoi *(Vietnam).* Alternatively, you may find a cheaper or more practical option if you look into an **open jaw ticket**...

Open jaw *(ended)* tickets... *For the undecided*

In a nut shell these are standard return tickets but with a **flexible return date** and **departure location**. These tend to be slightly more expensive than a standard return ticket but cheaper than two single tickets. They give you more flexibility when you're planning your itinerary and when you're away by allowing you to choose different airports for your arrival and departure and even have an 'open-ended' date for your return. Some airlines allow you to fly into one country *(say, Mexico or Thailand)* and fly out of another *(say Costa Rica or Hong Kong)*. This can minimise the backtracking you'll have to do and give you a lengthy **'surface sector'** of your trip to enjoy where you can explore more countries and get more out of your trip.

Round-the-World *(RTW)* tickets... *For the adventurous*

While they appear to be a fairly large initial expense, RTW tickets are great value for money and allow you to have a very diverse trip. RTW tickets will cost you anything between £1,000 and £2,200 depending on how imaginative your route around the globe is – they're usually priced by **'number of stops over a certain distance'** and can be arranged through specialist agents such as **STA** *(www.statravel.com)*, **The Flight Centre** *(www.theflightcentre.co.uk)* and **Kilroy Travels** *(www.kilroytravels.com)* as well as **local travel-agents**. RTW tickets aren't so sensitive to the factors that can inflate the cost of a return ticket.

The best value RTW tickets are those composed by the main airline alliance groups. The two most popular alliance groups are:

o **Oneworld:** www.oneworldalliance.com Consists of Aer Lingus, American Airlines, British Airways, Cathay, Quantas and their associated partners

o **Star Alliance:** www.staralliance.com Includes Air Canada, Air New Zealand, bmi, Lufthansa, Singapore Airlines, Thai Airlines and their affiliates

Both alliances offer competitive prices and similar routes. Prices in travel agents windows are often advertised <u>without</u> taxes included and with a very basic number of stops during low seasons and will therefore appear significantly cheaper than the actual final price, so don't be disappointed or disillusioned!

Overland / surface sectors: To make the most out of your RTW and get the best value from it, include as many surface sectors as you can. Surface sectors require you to make your own way by land, sea or shorter flights that are separate from your RTW. It's common for travellers to fly into Bangkok *(Thailand)* and out of Hong Kong or Hanoi *(Vietnam)* on their Asia sector of their trip, and into Cairns and out of Sydney during their time in Australia. See Section 1... *'Where to go'* for suggested RTW itineraries and further information.

REDUCING THE PRICE OF YOUR AIRFARE... *Be flexible*

You can make the biggest savings of your trip before you go and you could save hundreds of pounds on your airfare simply with a bit of research! Prices vary greatly from region to region but the cost of your ticket will not only depend on your destination but a number of other factors. The key to reducing your airfare is **research** and **flexibility**;

o **Do some serious shopping around:** Great deals can always be found in this hugely competitive business. Do some serious research and make use of all of your resources and compare quotes from internet companies, travel agents and different airline companies – all regions tend to have at least one budget airline like Ryan Air for cheap regional flights and some are now doing long-haul international flights. For example, Air Asia now flies from London Stansted to Kuala Lumpur in Malaysia for attractive prices

o **Time of year:** During peak seasons the price of airline tickets are heavily inflated. If time isn't an issue, and you have bundles of it to spare, try and arrange your trip so that you fly in and out just before and just after peak season(s) – a couple of weeks could save you a small fortune and the savings you make will often cover the cost for you to stay longer!

o **Major regional hubs:** Fly to and from major international/regional hubs, such as Bangkok *(Thailand)* in SE Asia, San José *(Costa Rica)* in Central America and Sydney *(Australia)* in Australasia – generally they offer more routes and more flights per day at lower prices than smaller airports and are served by far superior infrastructure

o **Be creative:** Sometimes direct flights can be more expensive than two single tickets. The best example here is Central America where direct flights to San José from Europe **can be** more expensive than a flight London to New York, and then New York to San José! So be imaginative and play around with flights – it'll inevitably mean waiting around in airports for a few hours between flights but the savings are potentially huge

o **Unsociable hours:** You'll find that if you're willing to fly at unsociable hours *(usually between 22.00 and 08.00)* you can reduce the cost of your ticket even further. Try and avoid flying at the weekends *(especially Sundays)* and even the weekend buffer days of Friday and Monday as ticket prices tend to be slightly higher

o **Non-refundable flights:** These flights are always cheaper and are great if you're certain you're not going to alter your plans! It's best to buy these tickets for shorter impulsive flights, say from Vietnam to the Philippines, or domestic flights, say Cairns to Sydney, where they're not so much of a financial commitment. In essence, the flight is cheaper because you don't get any money back should you cancel or wish to change you flight, hence it's better for impulsive decisions where you book and go within a few days and don't commit yourself to a flight that's in two months time or so!

o **Go direct:** Although you can sometimes sniff out a great deal with them, don't forget that travel agents are a middleman and get commission – go to them first for a few quotes and use these as a guideline because it usually pays to shop around on the internet and book your tickets yourself direct with the airline. However, in some cases, for example with RTW tickets, travel agents do give you some added security though if things should go wrong!

You can book your tickets yourself direct with the airlines or you can book your flights through an agent. There are advantages and disadvantages with both options and it largely depends on what type of ticket you want to buy:

Booking it yourself... *Cheap & exciting*

Be confident and don't be scared to plan your own trip and book your own flights – by cutting out the middle man it **can** be cheaper. So beat the travel agent and book direct. Booking your own tickets and planning your own itinerary is an exciting experience. Make use of all the resources available to you. Go to the travel agents to get quotes and use these prices as a guideline. The internet is perhaps your best resource where you can compare airfares of numerous airlines through dozens of search engines. Go to the websites of major airlines and get quotes – quite often any special deals are only advertised on a company's own website. Booking your flights yourself is ideal for standard international return tickets, one-way fares and domestic/regional flights. If you want some added financial security when you're booking your own flight, pay with a credit card *(see text box)*.

Through an agent... *Added security & expertise*

Perhaps the safer approach. If you book through a regular travel agent or a specialist backpacker agency you'll probably pay slightly over the odds but you'll receive expert advice and have the added peace of mind that you'll have someone to contact if anything should go wrong. If you're looking into a RTW ticket, booking it through an agency can be very beneficial, and for first-time backpackers, strongly advised. They can offer you useful information on climate, peak seasons, logical routes and exciting itineraries that could otherwise be complicated to compile. They'll help ensure that your trip runs as smoothly as possible through sound planning and experience.

If you want to get an open-jaw ticket it's a good to go through an agent to make sure you understand the conditions, restrictions and options related to your ticket. You'll also find that the larger travel companies have access to special deals and promotions that aren't available to the general public. Among the best and well known specialist backpacker agents are:

- o **STA:**   www.statravel.com *(UK, Ireland, Oz, NZ and many more)*
- o **Kilroy Travels:** www.kilroytravels.com *(Scandinavia and Netherlands)*

Saving the last few quid: However you book your ticket, make sure you exhaust all of your discount options – if you're a student ask for student discount, if you've got any airline loyalty cards, use them. If you don't ask, you don't get. A simple 'do I get student discount' could save you hundreds of pounds on a RTW ticket, all they can say is no! If you've got two quotes from two different agencies see if they'll compete and 'out price' each other, they'll usually knock off a few quid just to beat their rivals quote!

Book your flight with a credit card... *Added security*

As I've constantly banged on about budgeting and saving money it may come as a shock when I say 'try to book your flights with a credit card', but there's logic to my madness. By paying for your airline ticket with a credit card you have **purchase protection** – now the boring stuff; under section 75 of the 1974 Consumer Credit Act card issuers and retailers take joint responsibility for any purchases between £100 and £30,000. If an incident occurs that affects your flight, for example the company goes bust, you can claim a refund from the card provider! You're also protected against fraud. Just make sure that you pay the balance of the card in full by the date shown on your statement to avoid those rip-off interest charges.

Useful websites... *Finding the cheapest flights*

Here's a list of websites for some major airlines, widely used search engines and recognised budget airlines that you may find useful to scan for flights and more importantly, source out cheaper airfares:

Flight search engines... *Find it cheaper*

Worldwide flights: www.worldwideflights.com

Expedia: www.expedia.com

Kayak: www.kayak.com

Skyscanner:www.skyscanner.co.uk

Travel Buddy: www.travelbuddy.co.uk

The Flight Centre: www.theflightcentre.co.uk

Major Airlines... *Long-haul flights*

American Airlines: www.aa.com

British Airways: www.ba.com

Emirates: www.emirates.com

Singapore Airlines: www.singaporeair.com

Quantas: www.qantas.com.au

Virgin: www.virgin-atlantic.com

RTW tickets... *Main alliances*

Oneworld: www.oneworldalliance.com

Star Alliance: www.staralliance.com

Round-the-World Experts: www.roundtheworldexperts.co.uk

Europe... *Main budget airlines*

Easy Jet: www.easyjet.com

Ryan Air: www.ryaniar.com

Asia... *Main budget airlines*

Air Asia: www.airasia.com

Tiger Airways: www.tigerairways.com

Américas... *Main budget airlines*

Jet Blue: www.jetblue.com

Australasia & Pacific... *Main budget airline*

Virgin Blue: www.virginblue.com.au

Changing your flights... *Things change!*

Don't be scared to change your flights. Whether you're homesick and want to come home early, have no choice because you've spent all of your money or you've changed your itinerary you always have the option to amend or cancel your flights and many backpackers do. It's a simple affair and takes no more than a phone call – contact the relevant airline direct and see what they can do and what fees you'll incur. The earlier you contact them the better. Generally most major airlines won't charge you to change the date of your flight but they'll almost certainly charge you to re-route your flight – i.e. alter your departure or arrival location – regardless of whether the new route would have cheaper than the original. Charges vary between airlines but fees typically hover between £25 and £75. Some airlines will allow you a certain number of changes free of charge. You will find, however, that smaller airlines and budget airlines nearly always charge you to amend any aspect of your flight and it often works out cheaper to cut your losses and just book a new flight!

RTW tickets are usually more flexible than standard return tickets and airlines almost expect backpackers on a RTW ticket to alter their flight dates and even re-route some of their itinerary! Again, you are more than likely to still be charged if you wish to re-route your itinerary on a RTW ticket but you'll probably have the luxury of free unlimited date changes – although they don't like to advertise this fact!

WHAT ARE THEY...? *Let's get back to basics!*

The idea of visas can be very daunting – especially for first-time travellers – but they're very simple and there's really not much to worry about. Basically, everybody needs a visa for whenever they go outside of their own country *(movement between EU countries as an EU citizen is an exception)* and they're just a stamp/sticker in your passport that grants you access into a certain country for a specified amount of time. Different nationalities have different entitlements in certain countries – so it's nothing personal! Entitlements and requirements for visas are constantly changing – particularly in politically corrupt countries – so keep up-to-date via the website of the relevant countries embassy. Your visa will have your entitlement or a date of departure clearly marked on it. Most visas entitle you to stay for a period of 3 weeks, 30 days, 60 days, 3 months or even 6 months at a time. The majority of countries grant visas at their borders while a few require that you apply for them in advance – see later subsection. The most important thing is to make sure that your passport is up-to-date and valid for at least **6 months** after your intended date to return home. In the end you'll look forward to getting your visas and find yourself trying to fill your passport up with as many different ones as possible – they're a great souvenir!

TYPES OF VISAS... *Work or play!*

Essentially there are **2 types** of visas that you'll be interested in – **holiday visas** and **working** *(holiday)* **visas:**

1) **Holiday visas:** These are the bog standard visa that you need to enter a country for non-business holiday purposes. They allow you to stay and roam freely in a country for a specified amount of time. Generally speaking holiday visas are much easier to get and most can be obtained on arrival at the border or airport *(see next section)*. They **do not** permit you to seek employment or live in a country. In some cases holiday visas can be extended at a relevant embassy.

2) **Working** *(holiday)* **visas:** If you want to live and work in a particular country you'll need to obtain a working visa. Working visas entitle you to work in a given country for a specific amount of time and usually come with a number of employment conditions – for example restrictions on what industries and sectors of the economy you can work in. Working visas are more difficult to obtain than standard 'holiday visas' and are often subject to the applicant meeting strict criteria. Australia is notorious for its point system where you have to be between 18 and 30, have a certain amount of savings and are more desirable if you have certain qualifications or trades. Embassies are the best place to source information about applicant criteria. It's best to apply for working visas well in advance in your home country, some embassies may want to interview if you don't completely satisfy their criteria.

APPLYING FOR VISAS... *When, where & how*

If you turn up at the border of a country without a visa you can be refused entry! Luckily getting a visa is a very simple and straight forward affair. For most of your travels you'll be getting visas on arrival and using travel agencies/guesthouses in neighbouring countries to get any visas in advance that you may require:

Visas on arrival... *Be nice to men with guns & rubber stamps!*

Travelling around SE Asia and Central America is an easy affair in terms of visas – these poorer regions are crying out for tourists to come and boost their economies. Consequently, the vast majority of countries grant visas on their borders – usually for free – and don't require you to get one in advance. This means that you can fly to SE Asia or Central America and not have to worry about visas at all. Even Fiji and New Zealand grant generous visas for free on arrival. Just remember, be nice to people with rubber stamps and plan your route to make the most of your free visa entitlements! Vietnam is the notable exception in SE Asia where they're very strict on visas and do not grant them at its borders for the majority of nationalities. In some cases you can only get visas on arrival at certain land border crossings – Cambodia is a good example here – but you'll have little problems if you stick to well-trodden-routes and you'll be well informed at guesthouses and travel desks when you're booking busses over the border. There are a few things that you should be aware of, although these won't cause you much of a problem:

a) **Onward tickets** – a few countries require that you have proof of onward travel – either ticket to another country or a flight home already booked. However, in reality immigration officials rarely check and seldom seem concerned if you arrive without proof. In all my years of frequent travel I haven't been asked a single time! If you've got an onward ticket it's always a good idea to have a photocopy as confirmation just in case

b) **Varying entitlements** – in a few a cases you'll be granted a longer visa if you enter the country via an international airport – most visitors can expect to get a 60-day visa if you enter Malaysia via an international airport but only a 30-day visa overland. Thailand grants most nationalities a 30-day visa on arrival at airports but only a 14-day visa at all overland border crossings. This is can be real pain and has been introduced to try and reduce visa/border runs and stop you staying 'indefinitely' by abusing and exploiting the free visa entitlements!

c) **Open/free borders** – in some regions you'll be surprised have relaxed they are about visas and border crossings to the point where you'll be paranoid and wondering if you do actually need a visa! Open borders are fairly common in Central America where the borders of El Salvador and Honduras are 'open' borders if you have visas for their neighbouring countries. The borders are there physically but you'll receive no stamp – a bit of a disappointment if you're trying to fill your passport with exotic ink marks! Just double check with the border officials. You won't find any open borders in SE Asia

Getting visas in other countries... *Simpler than you think*

For the minority of countries where you need to get a visa in advance, for example Vietnam, don't panic and feel that you have to get them in your home country before you leave – unless you're starting your trip there of course! Nearly all travellers armed with a few passport photos apply for them in other countries throughout the region, such as Thailand. Most guesthouses and travel agencies offer **visa services** where you can get visas to almost any country. It's a very popular and well advertised service. At first, it feels uncomfortable handing your passport to a complete stranger in a travel agency, but it'll quickly become common practice for you, especially in Asia. These visa services usually take around 4 days and typically costs between £10 and £20. If you pay more you can usually speed up the process! It'll all become clear once you get there, honestly!

Applying well in advance... *Sometimes you have to*

It's a pain in the arse but some countries require that you apply for any type of visa in advance. Australia is perhaps the most widely known example here. You can apply direct to the relevant embassy in your country or, more commonly, through the embassy's website. You'll probably find that it's not as complicated as you think and many countries are now offering **Electronic Visas** that are linked to your passport so there's no need to send your passport off – when you scan your passport at immigration the officer will be notified via his terminal and his stamp the appropriate visa there and then. If you intend to work in any country you nearly always have to get a prearranged visa and have to pass stricter controls and meet particular criteria. It's best to arrange these visas before your trip when you're at home.

Visas-as-you-go

Here's an example of a typical trip around SE Asia and how you could go about getting your visas 'as-you-go' based on a return flight to Bangkok:

HOME – no prearranged visas

Fly into **Thailand:** 30-day visa granted on arrival *(free)* – travel around Thailand. Apply for a *Vietnam* 30-day visa in a travel agency in Bangkok costing 1,400 BHT taking 4 days

Overland into **Laos:** 15-day visa granted on arrival *(free)*

Overland into **Vietnam** with your prearranged visa from Thailand – travel south down Vietnam and apply for 30-day *Cambodia* visa in a guesthouse in HCMC costing US$25 taking 3 days

Overland into **Cambodia** with your prearranged visa from Vietnam

Overland into **Thailand:** 14-day* visa granted on arrival *(free)*

Overland into **Malaysia:** 30-day visa granted on arrival *(free)*

Overland into **Thailand:** 14-day* visa granted on arrival *(free)*

Fly HOME from Bangkok

*see 'varying entitlements' in the 'applying for visas' section *(page 256)*

If you intended to go to Australia straight after SE Asia, you should've sorted your Oz Visa out at home before you left.

Expiring visas... *Extending your stay*

It's not a good idea to over run your visa entitlement – if you do you'll usually be fined for everyday that you've overstayed your welcome and could possibly be subject to criminal convictions and deportation! If your visa's running out don't panic, there are a number of things you can do:

1) **Visa/border runs:** This is a very popular and great option in compact regions such as SE Asia and Central America. It's not illegal but it's frowned upon in some countries! Basically as your current visa nears its expiration date you hop across to a neighbouring country, get stamped in, spend five or so minutes loitering around before going through the same border control and back into the country you just came from with a fresh new visa – job done! It's a great way to abuse your free visa entitlements!

Visa-runs are advertised and can be arranged in lots of guesthouses and travel agencies throughout SE Asia and Latin America and it's a very popular way to increase your stay in a country, especially Thailand. Some include daytrips to places close to the border and some just blatantly drive you to the border help you get across and bring you straight back!

2) **Go to the relevant embassy:** Most countries allow you to extend your visa if you go direct to their embassy and see what your options are. Expect to pay a fair bit and don't expect loads of additional days! Embassies can be found in most major cities. Again guesthouse and hostels will offer you advice and assistance.

3) **Plan/re-plan you route:** From the very start you should try to plan your route so you make the most out of your *(free)* visa entitlements and a bit of research can avoid you overstaying your welcome or rushing through a country. However, sometimes this isn't possible and itineraries change. If you can't extend your visa your only option will be to re-plan your route and move on into a different country where new opportunities await.

The visa situation is continuously changing so it's always best to check with the relevant embassy before you go. Below is a very broad indication to your visa entitlements for the regions covered in this book. At the time of writing, all of the visa info was correct but things change so double check:

	Length of visa	Issued *(approx. cost)*	Entitled nationalities
SE Asia...			
Cambodia:	30-days	On arrival *(US$25+)*	Most incl. UK, EU, USA, Canada, Oz & NZ
Indonesia:	30-days	On arrival *(US$25)*	Most incl. UK, EU, USA, Canada, Oz & NZ
Laos:	15-days	On arrival *(US$20+)*	Most incl. UK, EU, USA, Canada, Oz & NZ
	30-days	**In advance** *(US$20+)*	Most incl. UK, EU, USA, Canada, Oz & NZ
Malaysia:	30-90 days	On arrival *(free)*	Most incl. UK, EU, USA, Canada, Oz & NZ
Philippines:	21-days	On arrival *(free)*	Most incl. UK, EU, USA, Canada, Oz & NZ
Singapore:	30-days*	On arrival *(free)*	Most incl. UK & Commonwealth, EU & USA
Thailand:	30-days*	On arrival *(free)*	39 countries incl. UK, EU, USA, Oz & NZ
Vietnam:	30-days	**In advance** *(US$25+)*	Majority of countries must apply in advance
C. America...			
Belize:	30-days	On arrival *(free)*	Many incl. UK, EU, N.America, Oz & NZ
El Salvador:	30-days	On arrival *(free for some)*	Free - UK & some EU. US$10+ for US & Can
	30-days	**In advance** *(US$30)*	Oz & NZ citizens must apply in advance
Guatemala:	90-days	On arrival *(free)*	Most incl. UK, EU, US, Can, Oz and NZ
Honduras:	90-days	On arrival *(a few US$s)*	Most UK, EU, Can, Oz & NZ. US get 30-days
Mexico:	<180-days	On arrival *(free)*	UK, EU, US, Canada, Oz, NZ, Japan & more
Nicaragua:	90-days	On arrival *(free)*	Most UK, EU&US. Can, Oz & NZ get 30-days
Panamá:	30-day+	On arrival *(free for some)*	Free - UK, EU. US$10+ for US, Can, Oz & NZ
Down Under...			
Australia:	3+ months	**In advance** *(varies)*	Most. Check out: www.immi.gov.au
Fiji:	4 months	On arrival *(free)*	Most incl. UK & Commonwealth EU, US, Can
New Zealand:	3 months	On arrival *(free)*	Most incl. EU, US & Can. UK get 6 months

* 30-day visa are issued at international airports. 14-day are issued at overland borders

Note: Where EU is listed, it refers to the majority of EU states – a few may have different entitlements

Don't underestimate the importance of a good travel insurance policy. Your policy should cover you for a range of incidents including **theft**, **loss** but most importantly <u>**medical assistance**</u>. You really don't want to sacrifice travel insurance just to save a few quid – even in poor regions hospital bills can escalate very quickly into thousands of pounds and you may even be refused treatment without adequate insurance – while I've never had to make a claim, Frida's claimed every trip *(see box below)*! This section runs through the basics of travel insurance to make sure that you're confident to select the right policy at the right price and claim if things do go wrong.

Our hospital visit in El Salvador... *The US$1,000 B&B!*

During our trip through Central America, my girlfriend had to stay overnight in hospital for some fairly minor treatment in El Salvador. As soon as we arrived we had our pants well and truly pulled down. They were quick to basically conduct every scan they could – of course, we were paying for them to be extra thorough after all! They even 'checked us into a room' after the treatment. We questioned it and wanted to leave but they actually said it's like a hotel and if you check out now you'll still be charged! We couldn't do much as they had our debit cards behind reception and armed guards were outside the hospital gates!? In the morning we were presented with a bill for over US$1,000. Now that's an expensive B&B! Luckily we were able to claim it back once we got home through our travel insurance. The lesson here, make sure you're insured!

TRAVEL INSURANCE... *The basics*

Travel insurance for backpacking is slightly different from a policy for a typical one or two week holiday. Regular holiday insurance usually only covers you for a limited period – typically 30 or 60 days – not good for a six month trip. If they do extend their standard policies to meet the length of your trip it usually works out very expensive. However, most companies now cater for travellers with specialist backpacker insurance and it's become a highly competitive market – so there are lots of bargains to be found!

There's no 'one-size-fits-all' with travel insurance and there's plenty of packages out there so it's important that you select the right one, at the right price. Most policies will cover you for the exact amount of days you'll be away for – usually up to 24 months – and offer varying levels of cover. These levels of cover are often labelled as Bronze, Silver and Gold or Budget, Standard and Premium policies. It's up to you what 'package' you select for your trip – just make sure it has these key elements of cover included:

- o **Medical expenses** – unfortunately there's no NHS out there so make sure your insurance covers you for at least £5million as medical bills can very quickly add up overseas

- o **Baggage cover** – it can be a costly exercise replacing a decent backpack and all of your belongings on the road so for peace of mind it can be worth getting a decent level of cover for your belongings. Just don't over insure your stuff. If you've got £500 worth of stuff, there's no point paying more for a policy that covers you for £2k worth of stuff!

- o **Cancellation cover** – again for peace of mind. Although, there's not much point having it for just a return ticket. It's a better idea for RTW tickets where you have multiple flights. If you've paid for your ticket with a credit card this will be covered anyway

- o **Passport cover** – getting emergency passports are costly, so this is a handy benefit to look out for in a travel insurance policy

To be honest, more often than not, the cheaper 'basic-packages' are more than adequate providing decent levels of medical cover and a range of other benefits including reimbursements for flight cancellations and lost luggage. The only exception is extreme activities – these are rarely covered by the basic budget/bronze policies:

Extreme activities

If you intend to pursue any outdoor activity check if your policy will cover it. Some policies will cover you for certain sports while excluding some of the more 'dangerous' activities. You'll usually find a list detailing all of the activities that your policy will cover you for. It's important to cover yourself for activities such as skiing and snowboarding where accidents are common!

The 'single-item limit'

> ### Mopeds... *An insurance nightmare!*
>
> Nearly all policies refuse to cover you for anything to do with motorbike usage. Roads are often poor, riders frequently don't need to have a licence to hire one and drink-drive laws are relaxed in some countries hence accidents are very common. The insurance companies know this! Just be aware that if you have an accident you'll probably be on your own – well financially at least!

You need to be aware that insurance companies usually have a 'single item limit' between £200 and £500 which means you can't claim for more than this on any one item you have with you. So you may want to consider leaving that £1,000 laptop at home! If want to take your netbook, don't fret, some policies will cover you for laptops – just read the small print.

REDUCING YOUR INSURANCE PREMIUM... *Don't pay more than you should*

Sometimes it does feel like an unnecessary expense and money that's better spent on beer but travel insurance is an important policy to have. Fortunately, there are a few things that you can do to reduce the price of your policy without compromising your level of cover:

Shop around... *Do I really need to say this?!*

You'd be surprised how competitive the insurance industry is. It really is time well spent and a quick shop around on the internet could save you a small fortune – well at least a few days budget in Thailand or Costa Rica! There are many companies that specialise in backpacker insurance and will offer very competitive quotes.

Get rid of the US & Canada... *They're expensive!*

Medical treatment in the US and Canada costs an arm and a leg and insurers know this! You'll find that policies will often have two levels of cover:

- o   Worldwide *(including USA & Canada)*
- o   Worldwide excluding USA & Canada

The latter option is always cheaper so if you're not going to the US opt for this policy and enjoy cheaper premiums *(quite often the World wide incl. USA & Canada is pre selected or pre-ticked so make sure you unselect it!)*.

Don't over-insure yourself... *Be sensible!*

This is an easy way to reduce your premium. It's worth bearing in mind that the more cover you have, the higher the travel insurance premium will be. Are you really going to have £3,000 worth of stuff with you? Are your airline tickets worth £2,000? Don't over insure yourself! You can't claim for more than your baggage or airline tickets are worth so keep costs down by finding sensible insurance cover that meets all your needs!

Increase your excess... *An effective but sometimes risky strategy!*

By increasing the amount you have to pay should an incident occur, you can reduce your initial premium quite substantially. Excess typical ranges anywhere between £50 and £500. It's a good idea to select a level of excess that reduces your premium enough to warrant the risk. Just make sure that your excess isn't so excessive that it'd ruin your trip should anything go wrong! If you're accident prone or have a habit of losing stuff – especially when your half-cut – this can be a risky strategy to reduce your premium!

Opt out of extreme sports... *Are you actually going to jump out of planes?!*

If extreme adrenaline fuelled activities aren't your cup of tea, make sure that you're not paying for an insurance policy that covers them. Carefully read what the policy covers you for. Don't opt for a policy that covers you for a hat-full of extreme sports that you don't intend on pursing – you'll just be paying a higher premium to cover you for stuff that you don't want to do. Some sports are automatically covered, even with the most basic policies, but some will have other activities included and these can sometimes be 'unselected' resulting in a slightly cheaper premium – every penny counts! Saying this some policies will outright refuse to cover you for any extreme sports so you can't get any discount *(or cover should you wish to get your adrenaline fix)*.

Use your bank... *No need for an additional policy!*

While I've preached about ditching your premium account if it attracts a monthly charge in favour for basic accounts with little or no fees, there are some benefits to keeping such accounts. Extra accounts, premium accounts or whatever your bank dresses them up as will come with a range of benefits. The benefit you're looking for is free travel insurance – this can mean that you won't need to purchase an additional policy or you'll need a shorter policy. The banks insurance will probably only cover you for a period of 30-60 days but that's ideal for shorter trips. If your trip is longer, start your additional policy from the date that the bank's insurance cover would end! Just make sure you look into what it covers you for and where it covers you – some only cover you in Europe. Some home insurance will cover you as well, so get mum and dad to check theirs!

CLAIMING ON YOUR INSURANCE... *Be organised*

As soon as an incident occurs contact your insurer via e-mail or by telephone to explain the situation and discus your options. Annoyingly a lot of insurance companies only reimburse you once you get home meaning that you still have to find the money from somewhere when you're out there – queue mum and dad! You'll usually be expected to file a claim once you return home from your travels where you'll need to organise your evidence carefully to validate and speed up your claim. Consequently, should the worst happen and you need to claim keep everything you can relating to the incident including; any **receipts, police incident reports** *(for thefts)* and copy of any **medical files** to back up your claim. As well as the date of the incident itself, it's worth jotting down any follow up dates that relate to ongoing treatment, checkups or purchases of related medication.

Typically it's not worth claiming for cameras, i-Pods and clothes as your excess will probably cost nearly as much anyway and then there's the hassle of police reports, but travel insurance is **essential for medical assistance**. If it is worth claiming for stolen goods make sure you get a **police report** relating to the incident to back up the claim. Above all read the small print and make sure you satisfy all of their validation requirements and have all the necessary evidence so they can't wriggle out of and drag their heels reimbursing a valid claim!

As your trip draws nearer, your first few days can seem daunting as you become more and more anxious and excited. So what kind of attitude should you have? Is it right to just have a relaxed and laidback attitude about the whole thing and just think 'it'll be ok' or should you plan your first few even weeks in detail? To be honest it's entirely up to you. Obviously you should do some homework and get an idea of what to expect and have a rough itinerary for your trip. Your best bet is to get a balance between the two – be relaxed and open minded but at the same time *(roughly)* plan your first few days and maybe book your first few days accommodation. You really don't want to book too much up – after just a few days of you'll have found a ton of stuff that you want to do and places you want to visit that you didn't even know about! I relish the excitement of just turning up in a region with absolutely nothing booked up at all! However, you do need to do some planning in some of the popular countries – just because demand outstrips supply!

BOOKING YOUR ACCOMMODATION & ACTIVITIES... *Where, when & how?*

To be honest, you need to book very little in advance and this will add to the excitement of your whole trip. The more stuff that you book up, the less room you have to change your planned itinerary and be spontaneous – believe me your plans will change in terms of time scales, destinations and activities!

Accommodation... *Just turn up!*

All of the regions covered in this book boast an abundance of backpacker digs from beach huts and guesthouses to hostels and budget hotels. It may be a good idea to book somewhere for the first few nights of your trip to give yourself a stress free introduction – especially if your flight lands at 3am!

However, and this cannot be stressed enough, **you don't have to book any lodgings in advance throughout the remainder of your trip.** A quick look in your guidebook to work out the general backpacker area while you're on the bus is all you need to do. Prices and

> **Don't be a wonderer...** *Business cards*
>
> Don't make the ultimate school boy error and leave your hostel without getting the name of it first – you'll be surprised how many people can't make their way back or remember the name of their hostel, especially after a few beers! Best bet is to carry one of their business cards around with you – not only will you not have to remember a weird foreign name that contains several strange characters, but it eliminates all language barriers – just whip it out and point at it to a tuk-tuk, cyclo or taxi driver!

standards are constantly changing meaning guidebooks become outdated and inaccurate quickly after publishing, so just look around once you get there compare and haggle – it's half the fun of travelling! Often you'll meet other backpackers on busses and arrange to find somewhere to stay with them – a good way to meet people and reduce your accommodation costs. The biggest advantage of travelling like this is that you're not committing yourself to anywhere, and therefore, you have the freedom to spontaneously change your plans on a daily basis. In the majority of towns you can just rock-up and find some cheap accommodation no problem.

Touts & scams: In many cases throughout Asia and Latin America you'll be greeted by a host of eager touts hassling you and pre-selling rooms as soon as you step off the bus – even before you get off your seat you'll see random arms poke through open windows waving flyers and ranting on about prices etc! Just be aware of the usual scams, their favourite being; 'everywhere else is full' and outright declaring that any other guesthouse you've got in mind has closed down! They'll often have pictures of rooms but don't hand over any money until you've checked out your room!

Peak seasons: Bear in mind that during peak season(s) accommodation can become scarce and prices are heavily inflated. It's not uncommon to see travellers hunched over their backpacks fast asleep on the beach – Koh Pha-Ngan *(Thailand)* is a prime example here – so make sure you check out festival dates and either arrive a few days earlier or pre-book it! Sydney is perhaps the worst case scenario where bookings for New Years need to be well in advance!

Check it out: Whatever country you're in, it's a good idea to check the room and its facilities before you pay. Don't agree blindly to rent a room/beach hut even if the touts are showing you good photos of 'their' accommodation, the camera lies – another good reason **not** to pre-book your accommodation! This cannot be stressed enough in regions such as SE Asia and Latin America!

In regions such as Australasia, Europe and North America – where demand often outstrips supply and where hostel staff are less reluctant to cram a fourth person of your group into a double room – it's more practical to pre-book your accommodation about a week in advance as you move from town to town, especially during peak season(s). This way you still have a great deal of freedom to move around as you wish coupled with the security of guaranteed accommodation. A great website to check out accommodation is **Hostelworld** – www.hostelworld.com. In some cases, if you're on a backpacker bus such as the Kiwi Experience in New Zealand, recommended accommodation is reserved for you at every stop along the way.

Activities... *When you feel like it*

You don't need to pre-book many activities before you arrive. As with accommodation, booking well in advance only limits you're ability to be flexible and change your plans. Half the time you only vaguely know what there is to do in a given town anyway, so you don't actually know all of your options before you get there! You can book 99% of your activities completely spontaneously. Even extreme activities like bungy jumping and skydiving can be booked on the same day that you decide you need an adrenaline fix. Generally speaking, daytrips are arranged a day or so in advance once you get to a destination and checked out what there is to do – even scuba diving courses can be booked the night before. Activities can be booked through most guesthouses, hostels and travel agencies. In New Zealand and Oz, activities can be booked through backpacker busses a few days or even hours in advance. If you're planning a bit of a road trip, it's worth booking a campervan or car as early as possible in order to secure the best deals and ensure availability – pilgrimages up Australia's eastern seaboard are very popular and vans get booked up weeks, even months, in advance.

Transport... *As and when!*

Same story, you don't need to book anything well in advance – just book it as and when you want to move on. Transport varies dramatically from region to region:

Down Under: You'll only need to book a few types of transport well in advance. These include backpacker busses, such as Magic Bus in New Zealand and the Oz Experience in Australia, primarily because demand often outstrips supply. Here, travellers follow a preset itinerary and don't have to worry about booking further transport. Otherwise travelling Down Under is the same as it is at home with the familiar options of busses, car hire and flights. Bus tickets can be bought from bus stations, guesthouses and on-line. As in Europe, it's probably best to book flights as early as possible – if anything just to secure the best deals. Conveniently, most airline tickets can be booked on-line where you'll be issued e-tickets which are linked to your passport and a booking number.

SE Asia & C. America: Transport in these regions is far more versatile and random! To get around town you can use anything from cyclos and tuk-tuks to jeepneys and regular taxis. There's no need to book these forms of transport in advance. Between towns, minivans and boats form the principle mode of transport – with many tourist orientated options. These usually have set departure times – even in Cambodia and Vietnam – and you'll need to buy tickets at least a few hours in advance. Guesthouses and travel agencies will give you info on routes, timetables and sell you tickets. A lot of the time – particular in less tourist orientated countries such as the Philippines – you'll have to take several busses or a combination of busses and ferries to travel any significant distance making your way town by town as direct busses are rare.

Inter-regional flights, for example from Vietnam to the Philippines, can all be booked when you're out travelling if you decide you want to venture over there – this gives you a lot of freedom to alter your itinerary and be as spontaneous as you like. Transport in Philippines and Indonesia is less-tourist orientated with jeepneys and bemos operating like western busses linking towns – they run on a *(loose)* schedule and drivers are paid as you get in and say where you want to go. Hundreds of boats link the thousands of isles in these two island nations and tickets can be purchased at the relevant ferry terminals – just get a trike or bemo to take you to them.

WHAT TO EXPECT... *Culture shock*

Travelling is fun, exhilarating and rewarding but at the same time it's frustrating, tiring, demanding and testing. Dealing with different cultures that appear so extreme to our own can be daunting at first and will become wearing after a while. At times, even the most seasoned travellers need to dig deep, be patient and understanding. There'll be times that you'll crave a taste of home or you'll do anything for your own bed! The irony is that as soon as you get home you'll be wondering what you were moaning about and wishing that you were back there again! After a few weeks of travelling you'll settle into the 'travel mode' where you'll be used to sleeping in grubby guesthouses, acquired a taste for the local cuisine, got to grips with some basic lingo and grown used to the apparent lack of health and safety standards! The level of culture shock will depend on what regions you're going to be exploring. For more in depth info refer to the **'Costs, money & what to expect'** sections for each region in **Chapter 1**.

Asia & Latin America... *Big culture shock!*

The degree of culture shock is more extreme in poorer, less-developed regions such as SE Asia and Latin America. Being transplanted from a familiar modern western city to a bustling choked up Asian city or a poverty stricken Central American suburb is one hell of a shock! Everything from food and drink to accommodation and transport is very different from what you'll be used to. Just to make you feel that little bit more out of your depth, you'll have to cope with a baffling array of tonal languages throughout Asia and variations of Spanish with a few minority languages thrown in for good measure across Central America! These daunting characteristics will be the making of your trip and are why travellers go to these regions in the first place. If you want a luxurious and comfortable break in the sun, go to Spain or consider Oz!

Australasia... *Home-Sweet-Home, well almost!*

For the not so brave and hygienically conscious, don't despair, there's **Very Little Culture Shock** in New Zealand and Oz where health and safety standards coupled with familiar style western living will settle your nerves! Even the beach huts and island complexes on Fiji, although still rustic, are well above Asian standards. Food and drink is very similar to what you're used to and accommodation and transport is of similar standard to Europe and North America. All three are also English speaking countries. Generally, any cultural differences you'll find in Fiji are pleasing rather than shocking!

Dealing with culture shock & homesickness...

Culture shock: There's not a lot you can do to prevent culture shock. You can only prepare for what you're about to experience by doing some research but you're still going to be in for quite a shock. No amount of research can truly prepare you for the often shocking poor living conditions, lack of health & safety standards and extreme poverty of some regions. Just the change in diet can be extreme and come as a shock. Eventually, you'll learn to embrace the extremes of different cultures and discover what travelling is all about. If it all gets too much take the opportunity to book yourself into a posh upmarket hotel with all the trimmings – although you're on a tight budget you'll have a unique chance to indulge yourself in some luxury that is still very affordable by western standards and that you'd never be able to afford back home!

Homesickness: However limited the culture shock, at some point you will be homesick, fed up and annoyed living out-of-a-bag. On our first trip my friend and I spent days locked away in our room in Malaysia just watching Sky, eating pot noodles, living in our expanding rubbish heap, depressed and wanting to go home – it did eventually pass and we snapped out of it! This is true even in places like Australia where there's little culture shock for the average westerner but the sheer distance from home plays on everyone's mind at some point. There are few things that you can do and the best way to deal with homesickness is to keep in regular contact with loved ones and your mates back home. Make use of social websites, such as **Facebook** and **Twitter**, and utilise other free online services such as **MSN messenger, e-mail** and **Skype** – all are easy on the wallet and internet is available even in the most remote places across the globe. You'll make yourself feel better in the knowledge that they're jealous of where you are and what you're doing! You'll also realise that you're not missing out on anything back home and all of your mates are leading their usual 9 till 5 jobs and getting wasted in the same old pubs with the usual crowd!

Getting the most out of your trip... *Don't be boring, get amongst it!*

The cultural differences will come as a shock but don't shy away from them. Culture shock is, by large, a good thing. Immerse yourself in everything that's different and embrace these new cultures and your new environment – that's the whole point of venturing away from home. I've met quite a few 'travellers' who just stay in air-conditioned hotels, refuse to try street food, eat in upmarket western style restaurants and only travel by plane and taxi – I think what's the point of travelling then, you might as well be on holiday in your own country or take a short luxury break in Spain! Use local transport, sleep in hostels and guesthouses, sample the local cuisine, and snack from local food shacks, street kitchens and restaurants. Surely you want an authentic experience rather than a 'fake packaged' trip. After a while you'll relish the dodgy hostel standards, unpunctual forms of rickety transport, delicious cuisine and these characteristics will be the making of your trip! At the end of the day, you only get out of travelling what you put in. If you sit on a bus dozing away listening to your i-Pod, or your head buried in a book, you'll miss out on what's going out of the window and the many interactions with fellow travellers and local folk on the bus. A good example here is the argument between cheap airfares and more rustic local transport:

Local transport Vs flying

You'll find that a minority of travellers preach the benefits of cheap airfares around regions. While some of their points may make sense, flying is undoubtedly quicker, more comfortable and often not that much more expensive, but choosing local transport over flying has some real benefits – if you've got enough time. You get to see the real country, go through rural villages, experience some innovative types of rural transport, see firsthand the living standards and everyday activities of the 'average citizen' – you'll miss all this by flying where you'll not doubt meet the upper-class citizens who have secured the higher paid jobs at the airports and tourist infrastructure. So try and take advantage of what the local transport offers. Of course there'll be times when you want some luxury, but it's all part of the experience and you'll get a lot more out of it – believe it or not, the most uncomfortable bus trips and horrendous boat journeys will become your most memorable experiences and the funny stories that you'll be eager to share with everyone back home. These trips will be the making of your adventure. On the flip side you can't argue against flying when it saves you backtracking over 100's sometimes 1,000's of miles and you're short on time!

Guidebooks... *They are what they say, 'a guide'*

Look, guidebooks are a very important tool for planning your trip and while you're away, but as I've mentioned before, don't stick religiously to them. They're a **guide,** usually illustrating the well-trodden paths – even the less-trodden paths become popular shortly after being listed in a guidebook. So, be a bit different and don't be scared to venture to less-known places that either, have sketchy information, or aren't covered by a guidebook – these are the places where you'll have the most authentic experiences away from the crowds travelling on your own wit!

It's also worth pointing out that guidebooks become out-of-date very quickly – including this one – prices generally increase, websites shutdown and hostels either close or change name! The information in this book was accurate at the time of writing and I've tried to steer clear of over-doing it on the pricing side and have opted for 'general price guidelines' for this very reason.

LOCAL CURRENCY... *Do I need some before I go?*

And finally, a question that stresses a lot of people out as they trip draws near, do you need some local currency before you set-off? Don't feel as though you have to change a huge chunk of money into any local currency before you go. If you're a little nervous and apprehensive it may be reassuring to have a **small** amount of local cash in **small denomination notes**. Just bear in mind that money exchanges make a stack of money by effectively giving you a poor exchange rate, so only get enough currency to last you a few days. There are always ATMs at airports where you can withdraw local currency and not get stung by charges and fees imposed by companies such as **Travelex**! If it'll ease your mind to have a bit of local currency burning a hole in your pocket, take advantage of no commission offers – there are always offers in banks and post offices.

Sometimes it's impossible to acquire foreign currency before you touch down – currencies such as the Indian rupee and Vietnamese dong are not available outside of the country. Some other currencies are also partially restricted resulting in limited availability. Just get some from an ATM when you land.

I haven't bothered creating an index for this book for two reasons. Firstly, I've tried to design this book to be as user-friendly as possible – you'll find a contents page at the start of every chapter as well as a detailed contents page at the start. Second of all, and most importantly, I've done all that I can to keep the print cost down. Bearing in mind that I'm not a huge international company, every little helps, and I've made every effort to keep the costs down so that I can pass this saving onto you and other shoe-string backpackers by making the retail price as cheap as possible – that's also why I haven't included any colour pictures, as much as I would like to have. My vision isn't to make millions from this, breaking-even would be nice, I just want everyone to experience backpacking while we still can.

Thanks...

I'd like to take this opportunity to say a quick thank you for buying this book... I'm a 'one-man-band' and all of the information in this book has been completely researched by myself and Frida and we've actually been to 98% of the places! Like most good ideas, a lot of the concepts of this book were fined-tuned over a beer or two so I apologise for any errors and spelling mistakes. I've thoroughly read and reread it, but there are bound to be a few blindingly obvious ones – I hope these just add to the charm of the book and my rustic approach!

I've tried to include as many maps and useful information boxes as possible but I've written and designed this book with limited resources using my own very limited expertise – I've painstakingly drawn each map myself, dam copyright laws! Any profits will go into writing and publishing further guidebooks so keep your eye out! I hope you find this book very useful and I hope you have a great time skimping your way around the globe. Safe travelling...

I'd be glad to receive any feedback. Feel free to drop me an email...

info@backpackerguides.co.uk

or check out...

www.backpackerguides.co.uk

A final few words before you go...

...whatever happens on your travels, the uncomfortable scenarios you may find yourself in and all of the ups and downs you're going to have to tackle, this trip you're about to embark on will make you the envy of all stay-at-homes! The most horrific days you're going to endure will become fond memories that you'll laugh about when you safe and sound back at home. Don't be embarrassed if you shit the bed or throw up on a bus with a stinking hangover, it happens to the best of us! Now embrace and enjoy! I wish you all the best...

NOTES... *Space for your scribbles!*

Lightning Source UK Ltd.
Milton Keynes UK
05 September 2010

159438UK00001B/24/P